Beijing Maps

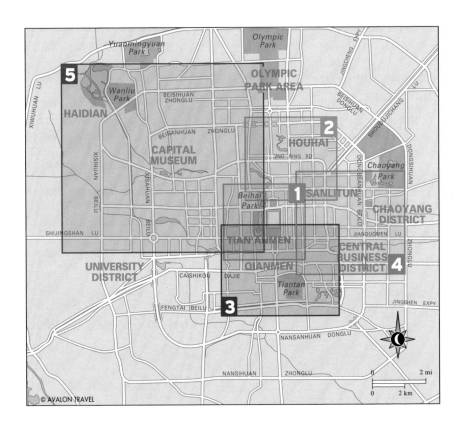

Shanghai Maps

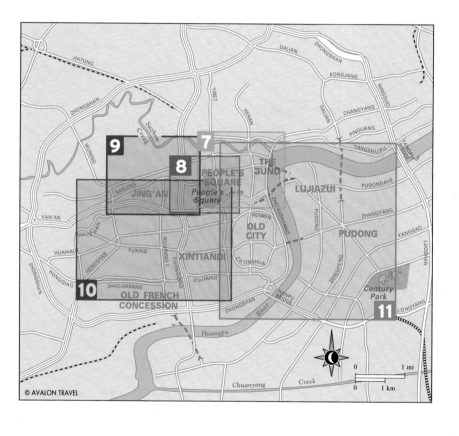

SEE MAP 2

🔵 SIGHTS
- 8 FORBIDDEN CITY
- 28 WORKERS' CULTURAL PALACE
- 34 GREAT HALL OF THE PEOPLE
- 35 TIAN'ANMEN SQUARE
- 37 MAUSOLEUM OF MAO ZEDONG

🔴 RESTAURANTS
- 3 BIG TREE CAFÉ
- 6 SHI
- 10 COURTYARD
- 12 DONGYANGE
- 16 SHUN YI FU
- 22 QUAN JU DE
- 27 GRANDMA'S KITCHEN
- 29 DOMUS
- 30 TIANDI YIJIA
- 31 ZOE'S CAFÉ AND BISTRO
- 38 RISTORANTE SADLER

🟣 NIGHTLIFE
- 11 RED YARD
- 21 EARL BAR
- 24 WHAT? BAR
- 32 REDMOON

🟢 ARTS AND LEISURE
- 1 BEIHAI PARK
- 2 JINGSHAN PARK
- 4 BICYCLE KINGDOM
- 5 NATIONAL ART MUSEUM OF CHINA
- 23 BEIJING CONCERT HALL
- 25 ZHONGSHAN PARK
- 26 FORBIDDEN CITY CONCERT HALL
- 36 NATIONAL MUSEUM OF CHINA
- 39 BEIJING POLICE MUSEUM

🟠 SHOPS
- 13 DRAGONFLY RETREAT
- 17 BEIJING FOREIGN LANGUAGES BOOKSTORE
- 18 WANGFUJING AVENUE
- 33 THE MALLS AT ORIENTAL PLAZA

🟤 HOTELS
- 7 THE EMPEROR
- 9 PEKING INTERNATIONAL YOUTH HOSTEL
- 14 TANGYUE
- 15 HOTEL KAPOK
- 19 HILTON BEIJING
- 20 THE PENINSULA BEIJING

Beihai Lake

Ping'anli

Xishiku Cathedral

Beihai Park

XISI

White Pagoda

Xisi

Zhongshan Lake

SEE MAP 5

LINGJING HUTONG

Lingjinghutong

YUETAN DAJIE

XICHENG

PIKU HUTONG

XIDAN

Xidan

Nanhai Lake

FUXINGMENNEI DAJIE

XICHANG'AN JIE

Xidan

Tiananmenxi

23

XIRONGXIAN HUTONG

XIJILILIANZI HUTONG

GAO BEIHUTONG

XIJIAOMIN XIANG

FUXINGMEN

Nantang Cathedral

XUANWUMEN DONGDAJIE

QIANMEN XID

Changchunjie

XUANWUMEN XIDAJIE

Xuanwumen

Hepingmen

DI'ANMEN

Huangchenggen
Relic Park

Children's
Palace

Jingshan
Park

National
Art Museum
5 A

SHIJINHUAYUAN HUTONG

YUQUN HUTONG

QIANLIANG HUTONG

LONGFU SIJIE

SHATAN HOUJIE

JINGSHANQIAN JIE

A 2

3 R

WUSI DAJIE

DONGSIXI DAJIE

Dongsi

Moat

North
Gate

Imperial
Garden

Palace of
Earthly Tranquility

Hall of Union

Palace of
Heavenly Purity

Gallery of
Clocks And
Watches

Imperial
Treasure
Gallery

BAOFANG HUTONG

SEE MAP 4

6 7

QIHELOU DAJIE

4

Huangchenggen
Relic Park

DENGSHIKOU DAJIE

Hall of Preserving
Harmony

Hall of Central
Harmony

Hall of Complete
Harmony

Forbidden
City

Gate of Supreme
Harmony

West
Gate

8

East
Gate

DENGSHIKOU DAJIE

BAISHU HUTONG

XITANGZI HUTONG

GANYU HUTONG

16 R

Dengshikou

9

10 R

DONGHUAMEN

Donghuamen
Night Market

JINYU HUTONG

Meridian
Gate

Moat

11 12 13 14 15

DONG ANMEN DAJIE

17

19

20

21

DAJIE

Pudu
Temple

NANHEYAN

CHANGCHANG JIE

22 R

DATIANSHUIJING HUTONG

26

25

Zhongshan
Park

Zhongshan
Park

27 R

DONGLAN

18

Grand Hyatt
Beijing at
Oriental Plaza

31

32 N

33

Oriental
Plaza

Tian'anmen
Gate

Workers'
Cultural
Palace

28

30 R

29

DONGCHANG'AN JIE

Wangfujing

Dongdan

Tiananmendong

34

Great Hall
of the People

35

Tian'anme
Square

36

China
National
Museum

CHONGWENMEN

37

Mausoleum
of Mao Zedong

39

DONGJAOMIN HUTONG

NEIDAJIE

38

QIANMEN DONGDAJIE

0   500 yds

0   500 m

SEE MAP 3

Qianmen

QIANMEN

Chongwenmen

DISTANCE ACROSS MAP
Approximate: 2.8 mi or 4.6 km

© AVALON TRAVEL

SIGHTS

5	LAMA TEMPLE	21	HOUHAI	25	DRUM AND BELL TOWERS
7	CONFUCIUS TEMPLE				

RESTAURANTS

6 THE VINEYARD
12 CAFÉ DE LA POSTE
14 TRAKTIRR PUSHKIN
17 SOUTH SILK ROAD
18 CAFÉ DE SOFA

19 NO NAME RESTAURANT
20 HUTONG PIZZA
24 CAFÉ SAMBAL
28 LAO HANZI HAKKA
33 DALI COURTYARD

35 CAFÉ ZARAH
36 ALBA
40 SAVEURS DE CORÉE
45 DRUM AND GONG
50 HOT BEAN COOPERATIVE

NIGHTLIFE

2 VA BAR & CAFÉ (VANGUARD)
3 SCHOOL
8 EL NIDO
9 HOT CAT CLUB
16 TAO YAO

23 BED BAR
27 NO NAME
29 EAST SHORE LIVE JAZZ CAFÉ
34 MAO LIVEHOUSE
37 AMILAL

38 GREAT LEAP BREWERY
44 SALUD
48 MAO MAO CHONG
49 JIANGHU BAR
51 YUGONG YISHAN

ARTS AND LEISURE

11 BEIJING LDTX MODERN DANCE COMPANY

46 PENGHAO THEATER

SHOPS

4 PIG BALANCE
10 OLD-TOXIN TIN TOYS
26 XING MU'S HANDICRAFTS

30 MEGA MEGA VINTAGE
31 TRIPLE MAJOR
32 GOOD GOODS COMMUNE

39 PLASTERED T-SHIRTS
41 BEIJING POSTCARD
43 NANLUOGUXIANG

HOTELS

1 IMPERIAL COURTYARD
13 LAMA TEMPLE INTERNATIONAL YOUTH HOSTEL

15 RED LANTERN HOUSE
22 BAMBOO GARDEN
42 DOWNTOWN BACKPACKERS

47 LUSONGYUAN

HEPINGLI

DAJIE

Liuyin Park

Qingnianhu Park

ANDINGMEN

ANDE LU

Andingmen

JIAODAOKOU

ANDE LU

Xihai Lake

GUOWANG HUTONG

ZHANGWANG HUTONG

CHENIANDIAN HUTONG

WANGZUO HUTONG

Houhai Lake

DOUFUCHI HUTONG

ZHONG-LOUWAN HUTONG

XIAOJINGCHANG HUTONG

Drum and Bell Towers

GULOU DONGDAJIE

ZHENGJUE HUTONG

XINJIEKOU

NANYAN

BEIGUANFANG HUTONG

FANG-ZHUAN-CHANG HUTONG

JU'ER HUTONG

HOUYUAN'ENSI HUTONG

SEE MAP 5

NANGUANFANG HUTONG

Qianhai Lake

YU'ER HUTONG

SHA JING HUTONG

QUIN HUTONG

BEIBING MASI HUTONG

BANCHANG HUTONG

CHAO DOU HUTONG

DONGMIANHUA HUTONG

Houhai

DI'ANMEN DONGDAJIE

DI'ANMEN XIDAJIE

Beihai Park

DI'ANMEN

Beihai Lake

SEE MAP 1

Guangximen

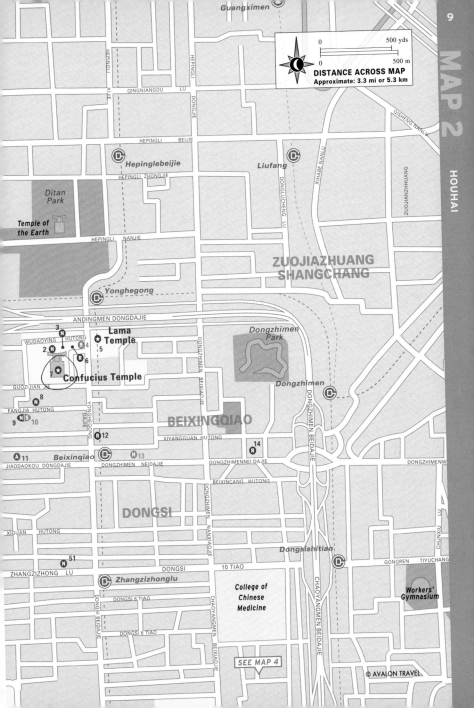

DISTANCE ACROSS MAP
Approximate: 3.3 mi or 5.3 km

0   500 yds
0   500 m

HEPINGLI   XIJIE

QINGNIANGOU

HEPINGLI   DONGJIE

HEPINGLI   LU

HEPINGLI   BEIJIE

Hepinglebeijie

Liufang

QISHENG NANLU

XIHABE NANLU

ZUOJIAZHUANGNANLU

HEPINGLI   ZHONGJIE

Ditan
Park

DONGLUCHENG   LU

Temple of
the Earth

HEPINGLI   NANJIE

ZUOJIAZHUANG
SHANGCHANG

Yonghegong

ANDINGMEN DONGDAJIE

Dongzhimen
Park

WUDAOYING   HUTONG   3

Lama
Temple

2 N   4
   R   6
7   5

DONGZHIMEN BEIXIAO JIE

Confucius Temple

Dongzhimen

GUOZIJIAN JIE

8
FANGJIA HUTONG

YONGHEGONG DAJIE

9 N   10

BEIXINGQIAO

DONGZHIMEN BEIDAJIE

R 12

XIYANGGUAN HUTONG

A 11   Beixinqiao

14
R

DONGZHIMENW

JIAODAOKOU DONGDAJIE

DONGZHIMEN NEIDAJIE

H 13

DONGZHIMENNEI DAJIE

BEIXINCANG HUTONG

DONGZHIMEN NANXIAOJIE

DONGSI

XIGUAN   HUTONG

Dongsishitiao

DONGZHIMENW

GONGREN TIYUCHANG

51
N

CHUNXIU LU

ZHANGZIZHONG   LU

DONGSI

10 TIAO

Zhangzizhonglu

College of
Chinese
Medicine

CHAOYANGMEN BEIDAJIE

Workers'
Gymnasium

DONGSI 8 TIAO

DONGSI BEIDAJIE

CHAOYANGMEN BEIXIAOJIE

DONGSI 6 TIAO

SEE MAP 4

© AVALON TRAVEL

✪ SIGHTS

2	SOUTH CHURCH	10	QIANMEN
5	LEGATION QUARTER	16	OX STREET MOSQUE
7	MING CITY WALL RUINS PARK	17	FAYUAN TEMPLE
8	SOUTHEAST WATCHTOWER	33	TEMPLE OF HEAVEN

ℝ RESTAURANTS

3	MAISON BOULUD	26	GOUBULI BAOZI
11	CAPITAL M	30	XINCHENG NOODLE HOUSE
12	LI QUN	31	DUYICHU
15	LITTLE SHEEP	32	GONGDELIN
20	TAN FISH HEAD HOT POT		

Ⓐ ARTS AND LEISURE

4	BEIJING CENTER FOR THE ARTS	23	TIANQIAO ACROBATICS THEATER
9	RED GATE GALLERY	27	DAGUANLOU CINEMA
13	URBAN PLANNING EXHIBITION HALL	34	BEIJING EBIKE TOURS
19	HUGUANG GUILD HALL	36	RED THEATER
22	TAORANTING PARK	37	LONGTAN PARK

Ⓢ SHOPS

1	BANYAN HOUSE BODY & MIND	25	MADE IN PARADISE
14	LIULICHANG CULTURAL STREET	29	DAZHALAN
24	QIANMEN PEDESTRIAN STREET	35	HONGQIAO MARKET

Ⓗ HOTELS

6	CAPITAL HOTEL	21	RAINBOW HOTEL
18	FAR EAST INTERNATIONAL YOUTH HOSTEL	28	LEO'S HOSTEL

DONGDAN

SEE MAP 4

JIANGUOMENNEI   DAJIE

Jianguomen

DONGCHANG'AN JIE

Tiananmendong   Wangfujing   Dongdan

Beijing zhan
Railway Station

Dongdan
Park

Beijing zhan
Railway Station

4   5   Legation
        Quarter   6

Ming City Wall Ruins Park and
Southeast Watchtower

7,8   9

QIANMEN   DONGDAJIE

CHONGWENMEN
XIDAJIE

CHONGWENMEN   DONGDAJIE

2   13

Chongwenmen

XIXINGLONG JIE   DONGXINGLONG JIE

QIANMEN

CIQIKOU

DONGDAJIE

ZHUSHIKOU

CHONGWENMENWAI DAJIE

A 34

Ciqikou

ZHUSMIKOU

TIANTAN LU

North
Heavenly
Gate

Hall of Prayer
for Good Harvest

XINGFU DAJIE

S   35

36   Red
      Theater

Longevity
Pavilion

33   Temple of
      Heaven

Tiantandongmen

Tiantan
(Temple of Heaven)
Park

TIYUGUAN   LU

LONGTAN   LU

West
Heavenly
Gate

East
Heavenly
Gate

Tiantan
Stadium

Longtan
Velodrome

A 37
Longtan
Park

Yuandushi
Temple

Longtan
Lake

TIANTAN

DONGLU

Beijing
Amusement Park

South
Heavenly
Gate

Puhuangyu

YONGDINGMEN   DONGJIE

YONGDINGMEN DONGBIHE LU

JINGTAI

JINGTAI

LU

YONGDINGMEN
QIAO

0   400 yds

0   400 m

DISTANCE ACROSS MAP
Approximate: 4.3 mi or 7.0 km

© AVALON TRAVEL

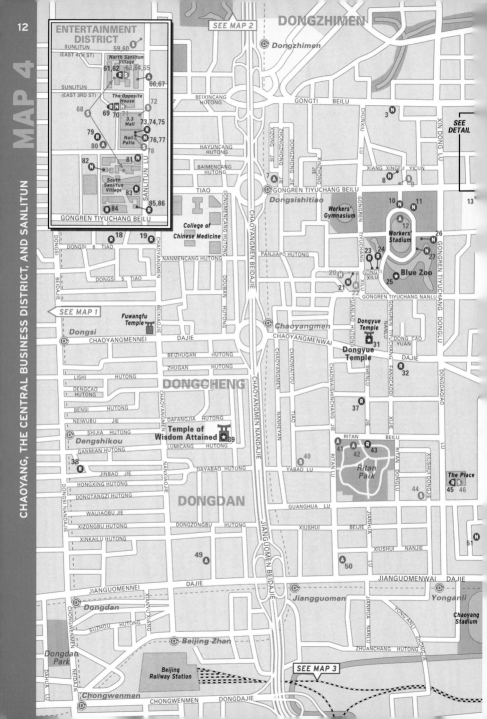

SIGHTS

- 25 BLUE ZOO AQUARIUM
- 31 DONGYUE TEMPLE
- 39 TEMPLE OF WISDOM ATTAINED
- 48 NEW CCTV TOWER

RESTAURANTS

- 2 CHEF TOO
- 4 BRASSERIE FLO
- 18 CRESCENT MOON
- 19 PURPLE HAZE COURTYARD
- 23 BELLAGIO
- 24 THREE GUIZHOU MEN
- 29 HAI DI LAO
- 32 HAITANGHUA PYONGYANG COLD NOODLE RESTAURANT
- 37 ANNIE'S
- 38 DA DONG
- 43 XIAO WANG FU
- 45 TRENDS LOUNGE
- 55 HERBAL CAFÉ
- 58 FAT DUCK
- 61 COLIBRI
- 62 LET'S BURGER
- 69 BEI
- 73 MOSTO
- 74 THE SADDLE CANTINA
- 75 MUSE BRASSERIE
- 79 NEARBY THE TREE
- 83 HATSUNE
- 84 KIOSK
- 85 KARAIYA SPICE HOUSE
- 86 MODO
- 52 LAN CLUB
- 53 XIU
- 70 MESH
- 76 APOTHECARY
- 77 ENOTERRA
- 81 LUGA'S
- 82 THE STUMBLE INN

NIGHTLIFE

- 1 CD BLUES LIVE MUSIC
- 3 PADDY O'SHEA'S
- 5 WORLD OF SUZIE WONG
- 8 ALFA
- 10 Q BAR
- 11 THE HOUSE
- 13 THE DEN
- 21 DESTINATION
- 26 FUBAR
- 27 GEORGE'S
- 28 D LOUNGE
- 30 GLEN
- 33 ALANTING LIVE BAR AND CAFÉ
- 35 ICHIKURA
- 36 LAGOON
- 51 ATMOSPHERE

ARTS AND LEISURE

- 6 CHAOYANG PARK
- 7 POLY THEATRE
- 12 WORKERS' STADIUM
- 16 PACIFIC CENTURY CLUB
- 34 TUANJIEHU PARK
- 41 CREATION ART GALLERY
- 42 RITAN PARK
- 49 CHANG'AN GRAND THEATER
- 50 HIAS GOURMET
- 54 EM-ART
- 56 89 PROMENADE DES ARTS GALLERY
- 66 BABU SPACE
- 67 WANDA INTERNATIONAL CINEPLEX
- 80 C5ART CENTER

SHOPS

- 9 BODHI
- 14 ROUGE
- 17 THE BOOKWORM
- 40 ALIEN STREET MARKET
- 44 SILK STREET MARKET
- 46 THE PLACE
- 57 CANDY&CAVIAR
- 59 BELITA JEWELRY
- 60 ERIC PARIS SALON
- 63 SHANGHAI TRIO
- 64 BRAND NEW CHINA
- 65 ELDI
- 68 SANLITUN VILLAGERED
- 72 PHOENIX CLOTHING STUDIO
- 78 PALOMA SANCHEZ

HOTELS

- 15 FRIENDSHIP YOUTH HOSTEL
- 20 HOTEL G
- 22 ZHAOLONG INTERNATIONAL YOUTH HOSTEL
- 47 KERRY CENTRE HOTEL
- 71 THE OPPOSITE HOUSE

DISTANCE ACROSS MAP
Approximate: 4.0 mi or 6.5 km

0   500 yds

0   500 m

© AVALON TRAVEL

DISTANCE ACROSS MAP
Approximate: 7.4 mi or 12.0 km

0   600 yds
0   600 m

SEE MAP 2

★ SIGHTS

1 ◉ SUMMER PALACE
3   OLD SUMMER PALACE
13 GREAT BELL TEMPLE
17 ◉ FIVE PAGODAS TEMPLE
19 BEIJING PLANETARIUM
21 TEMPLE OF ANCIENT MONARCHS
22 TEMPLE OF GREAT CHARITY
29 FINANCIAL STREET
37 WHITE DAGOBA TEMPLE

Ⓡ RESTAURANTS

6 ◉ GANGES
8   HOLY FRIES
9   BRIDGE CAFÉ
10 FALAHFEL
11 MIDDLE 8TH
14 BAI FAMILY MANSION
16 GOLDEN PEACOCK
24 JINYANG
25 OH! MARCO
26 CEPE
30 THE WHAMPOA CLUB

Ⓝ NIGHTLIFE

5   D-22
7   LUSH

Ⓐ ARTS AND LEISURE

4   ARTHUR M. SACKLER MUSEUM OF ART & ARCHAEOLOGY
18 ◉ BEIJING ZOO
20 LU XUN MUSEUM
33 YUYUANTAN PARK
34 BEIJING WORLD ART MUSEUM
35 MILITARY MUSEUM
36 BEIJING CAPITAL MUSEUM

Ⓢ SHOPS

12 ◉ FENGGUO BOX STORE
28 ORIENTAL TAIPAN MASSAGE
32 JOY CITY

Ⓗ HOTELS

2 ◉ AMAN AT THE SUMMER PALACE
15 ALOFT BEIJING
23 KELLY'S COURTYARD
27 ◉ RITZ CARLTON FINANCIAL STREET
31 THE WESTIN BEIJING FINANCIAL STREET

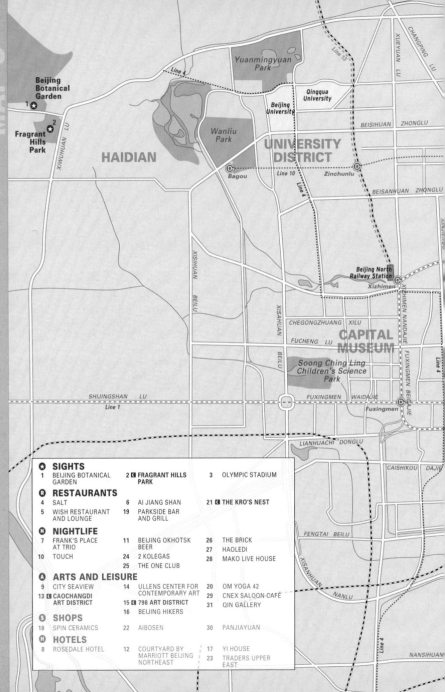

Beijing Botanical
Garden

1 ★

Fragrant
Hills
Park

2

HAIDIAN

Yuanmingyuan
Park

Line 4

Qingqua
University

Beijing
University

Beijing North
Railway Station

Xizhimen

CHANGPING LU

XUEYUAN LU

Line 13

BEISIHUAN   ZHONGLU

Line 10

Zinchunlu

Bagou

UNIVERSITY
DISTRICT

Wanliu
Park

XISHUAN BEILU

XISAHUAN BEILU

BEISANHUAN   ZHONGLU

CHEGONGZHUANG   XILU

FUCHENG   LU

CAPITAL
MUSEUM

Soong Ching Ling
Children's Science
Park

SHIJINGSHAN   LU

Line 1

LIANHUACHI   DONGLU

FUXINGMEN   WAIDAJIE

Fuxingmen

CAISHIKOU   DAJIE

FENGTAI   BEILU

XISANHUAN

NANLU

NANSIHUAN

XIWUHUAN LU

XIZHIMEN NANDAJIE

FUXINGMEN BEILU

Line 4

To Shunyi Villas Area

SHOUDU JICHANG HWY

To Beijing Capital Airport,
Ⓐ 9 City Seaview, Ⓝ 10 Touch, and
Ⓝ 11 Beijing Okhotsk Beer

XIWUHUAN LU

Forest Park

Forest Park

DATUN LU

Line 8

ANLI LU

Line 5

ANDING LU

HUIZHONG BEILU

HUIXING XIJIE

Line 13

JINGCHENG EXPY

OLYMPIC
PARK AREA

Olympic Ⓒ 3
Stadium

Olympic
Stadium

eitucheng-
donglu

Huixinxijie

4 Ⓡ   5 Ⓡ

6 Ⓡ   Ⓝ 7

8 Ⓗ

CHAOYANG

12 Ⓝ

JIUXIANQIAO
BEILU

13 Ⓐ

DONG WUHUAN LU

BEISIHUAN DONGLU

Sanyuanqiao

Ⓝ 21

Line 10

SHOUDUJICHANG LU

JIUXIANQIAO LU

20 Ⓡ
18 Ⓢ
20

17
Ⓐ Ⓡ
14,15,16

Ⓢ 22

23 Ⓗ

24 Ⓝ

LIANGMAQIAO LU

DONGSISHUAN ZHONG LU

Line 2

DESHENGMEN DONGDAJIE

Line 5

ANDINGMENWAI DAJIE

DONGSSANHUAN BEILU

Dongzhimen

Chaoyang
Park

HOUHAI

Zhangzizhonglu

hai
Park

Forbidden
City

TIANANMEN

Dongsishitiao

Dongsi

Chaoyangmen

Tuanjiehu

Hijialou

CENTRAL
BUSINESS
DISTRICT

25 Ⓝ

JING TONG HWY

Dendshikou

Ritan
Park

Jintaixizhao

Dawangqiao

Line 1

Dongdan

Dongchang'an Jie

Yonganli

Tiananmen
Square

Line 2

Chongwenmen

Beijing Zhen

Jianguomen

Guomao

JIANGUOMEN RD

Beijing
Railway Station

Ⓝ 26

Beijing East
Railway Station

29 Ⓐ

ZHUSHI KOU

QIANMEN

GUANGQUMEN

DONGSSANHUAN NANLU

Ⓝ 27   Ⓝ 28

JINSONG LU

DONGSIHUAN NAN LU

Tiantan
Park

Temple of
Heaven

Jinsong

Ⓢ 30

31 Ⓐ

JINGSHEN EXPY

ijing South
way Station

NANSANHUAN   DONGLU

BEIJING-TIANJIN-TANGGU HWY

Songjizhuang

ZHONGLU

0   1 mi

0   1 km

DISTANCE ACROSS MAP
Approximate: 18 mi or 29 km

© AVALON TRAVEL

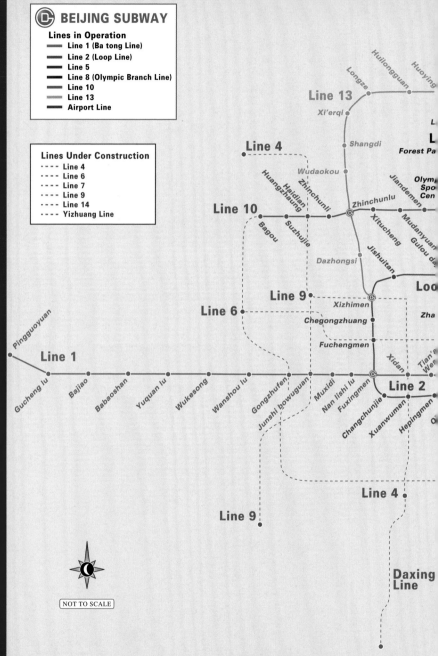

BEIJING SUBWAY

Lines in Operation
- Line 1 (Ba tong Line)
- Line 2 (Loop Line)
- Line 5
- Line 8 (Olympic Branch Line)
- Line 13
- Airport Line

Lines Under Construction
- - - - Line 4
- - - - Line 6
- - - - Line 7
- - - - Line 9
- - - - Line 14
- - - - Yizhuang Line

Line 13

Longze   Huilongguan   Huoying

Xi'erqi

Shangdi

Forest Pa

Line 4

Wudaokou   Jiandemen   Olym Spo Cen

Huangzhuang   Haidian   Zhinchunli

Line 10   Zhinchunlu   Xitucheng   Mudanyuan

Bagou   Suzhujie   Gulou da

Dazhongsi   Jishuitan

Line 9   Loo

Line 6   Xizhimen   Zha

Chegongzhuang

Fuchengmen

Line 1   Xidan   Tian'a Wes

Gucheng lu   Bajiao   Babaoshan   Yuquan lu   Wukesong   Wanshou lu   Gongzhufen   Muxidi   Nan lishi lu   Fuxingmen   Line 2

Junshi bowuguan   Changchunjie   Xuanwumen   Hepingmen

Line 4

Line 9

Daxing Line

NOT TO SCALE

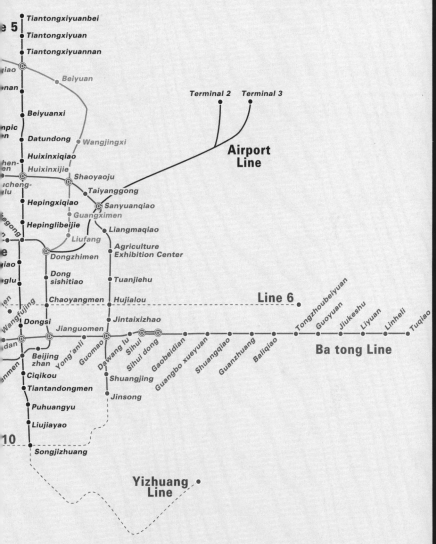

Tiantongxiyuanbei
Tiantongxiyuan
Tiantongxiyuannan
Beiyuan
Beiyuanxi
Datundong
Wangjingxi
Huixinxiqiao
Huixinxijie
Shaoyaoju
Taiyanggong
Hepingxiqiao
Sanyuanqiao
Guangximen
Hepinglibeijie
Liangmaqiao
Liufang
Dongzhimen
Agriculture
Exhibition Center
Dong
sishitiao
Tuanjiehu
Chaoyangmen
Hujialou
Dongsi
Jintaixizhao
Jianguomen
Wangfujing
Guomao
Dawang lu
Sihui
Sihui dong
Gaobeidian
Guangbo xueyuan
Shuangqiao
Guanzhuang
Baliqiao
Tongzhoubeiyuan
Guoyuan
Jiukeshu
Liyuan
Linheli
Tuqiao
Beijing
zhan
Yong'anli
Ciqikou
Shuangjing
Tiantandongmen
Jinsong
Puhuangyu
Liujiayao
Songjizhuang

Terminal 2   Terminal 3

**Airport
Line**

Line 6

Ba tong Line

**Yizhuang
Line**

e 5
10

© AVALON TRAVEL

SIGHTS

3	GARDEN BRIDGE
4	MONUMENT TO THE PEOPLE'S HEROES
7	BUND SIGHTSEEING TUNNEL
9	BUND PROMENADE
11	EAST NANJING ROAD
15	HUANGPU RIVER
29	HUANGPU RIVER CRUISE

RESTAURANTS

12	MR & MRS BUND
13	SUN WITH AQUA
23	M ON THE BUND
26	THE CUPOLA
27	NEW HEIGHTS
31	LOST HEAVEN
32	DAI'S KITCHEN

NIGHTLIFE

1	VUE BAR
6	SALON DE NING
8	BAR ROUGE
16	HAOLEDI
18	M1NT
19	ATANU
21	CAPTAIN'S BAR
24	GLAMOUR BAR
28	HOUSE OF BLUES & JAZZ

ARTS AND LEISURE

5	ROCKBUND ART MUSEUM
25	SHANGHAI GALLERY OF ART
33	SHANGHAI NATURAL HISTORY MUSEUM

SHOPS

| 14 | YOUNIK |
| 22 | SUZHOU COBBLERS |

HOTELS

2	ASTOR HOUSE PUJIANG
10	FAIRMONT PEACE HOTEL
17	SHANGHAI MINGTOWN ETOUR HOSTEL
20	CAPTAIN HOSTEL
30	WALDORF ASTORIA

SEE MAP 9

SEE MAP 8

SEE MAP 10

HAINING LU
QIPU
FUJIAN
SHANYI
TIANTONG LU
BELU
XIAMEN LU
BEIJING DONGLU
NIUZHUANG LU
FUJIAN
TIANJIN LU
ZHONGLU
DONGLU
Xinzha Lu
XINZHA LU
XIZANG
BEIJING XILU
ZHONGLU
NANJING
People's Square
JIUJIANG LU
HANKOU
HUBEI
CHENDU
People's Square
Renmin Park
GUANGXI
BELU
YUNNAN
ZHONG
FUZHOU
ZHEJIANG
ZHONGLU
City Hall
SHANTOU
GUANGDONG LU
Renmin Square (People's Square)
BENHAI
YAN AN
WUSHENG

© AVALON TRAVEL

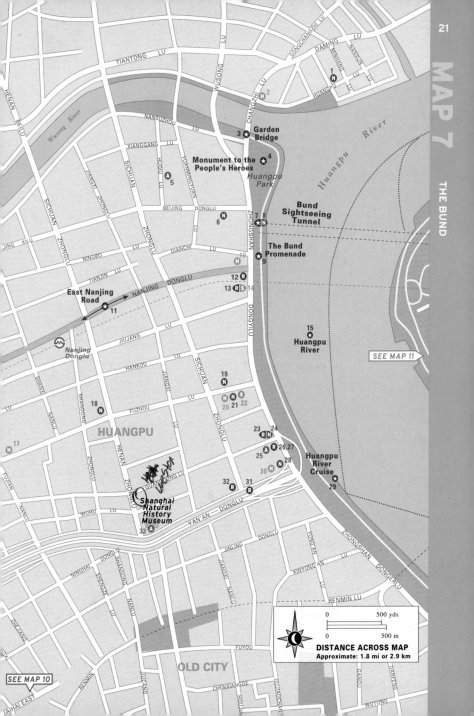

TIANTONG LU

Wusong River

NANSUZHOU LU

XIANGGANG LU

Garden
Bridge

Monument to the
People's Heroes

Huangpu
Park

BEIJING DONGLU

Huangpu

River

Bund
Sightseeing
Tunnel

The Bund
Promenade

East Nanjing
Road

NANJING DONGLU

JIUJIANG

Nanjing
Donglu

HANKOU

Huangpu
River

HUANGPU

FUZHOU

Wusong River

Shanghai
Natural
History
Museum

Huangpu
River
Cruise

YAN'AN DONGLU

JINLING

RENMIN LU

OLD CITY

SEE MAP 11

SEE MAP 10

0   500 yds

0   500 m

DISTANCE ACROSS MAP
Approximate: 1.8 mi or 2.9 km

★ SIGHTS
9 MOORE MEMORIAL CHURCH
17 PEOPLE'S PARK

® RESTAURANTS
2 YANG'S FRIED DUMPLINGS
6 ALLURE
8 GAN GUO JU
11 ELEMENT FRESH
12 CAFÉ DU METRO
13 KATHLEEN'S 5
21 WANG BAO HE

ℕ NIGHTLIFE
15 BARBAROSSA
22 NAPA WINE BAR & KITCHEN
23 CONSTELLATION 3
26 FOCUS CLUB
28 THE FAT OLIVE

Ⓐ ARTS AND LEISURE
1 XINGUANG FILM ART CENTER
14 GRAND CINEMA
16 MOCA SHANGHAI
18 URBAN PLANNING EXHIBITION HALL
24 SHANGHAI GRAND THEATRE
25 SHANGHAI MUSEUM
27 SHANGHAI CONCERT HALL

Ⓢ SHOPS
19 SHANGHAI BOOK TRADERS
20 RAFFLES CITY

Ⓗ HOTELS
3 PARK HOTEL
4 RADISSON NEW WORLD
5 PACIFIC HOTEL
7 LE ROYAL MERIDIEN
10 LANGHAM YANGTZE BOUTIQUE

SEE MAP 9

People's Square

NANJING DONGLU

Shangh Grand The

SEE MAP 12

0 — 250 yds
0 — 250 m
DISTANCE ACROSS MAP
Approximate: 1.0 mi or 1.6 km

© AVALON TRAVEL

1 Ⓐ

NIUZHUANG LU

GUIZHOU LU

GUANGXI BEILU

LIANHE LU

TIANJIN LU

FUJIAN LU

ZHONGLU

XIZANG ZHONGLU

NANJING DONGLU

SEE MAP 7 >

HUBEI LU

4 Ⓗ
5 Ⓗ
6 Ⓡ Ⓗ 7

NANJING XILU

NANJING XILU

XIZANG ZHONGLU

JIUJIANG LU

HANKOU LU

GUANGXI BEILU

Moore
Memorial
Church

10 Ⓗ

9

YUNNAN LU

People's
Square

Renmin

Park

Ⓡ 11

FUZHOU LU

Ⓡ
21

ZHEJIANG ZHONGLU

17 ✪

People's
Park

19 Ⓢ

20 Ⓢ

SHANTOU LU

WUHU LU

Ⓐ 16

GUANGDONG LU

City Hall

18 Ⓐ

BENHAI LU

Renmin Square
(People's Square)

GUANGXI NANLU

YUNNAN NANLU

Ⓐ 25

26
Ⓝ

Ⓐ
27

XIZANG NANLU

YAN'AN DONGLU

ZHONGLU

PUAN LU

Renmin

Park

ZHONGLU

JINLING LU

HUANGPI NANLU

HUAIHAI DONGLU

Ⓜ Da Shijie

HUAIHAI DONGLU

Times
Square

28 Ⓝ

SEE MAP 11 >

✪ SIGHTS

16 JING'AN SCULPTURE PARK
19 JING'AN TEMPLE
26 ⬡ LANE 1025
29 WUJIANG ROAD

ⓡ RESTAURANTS

5 LEGEND TASTE
6 CHIANG MAI THAI CUISINE
10 ⬡ WAGAS
17 TEOTIHUACAN
33 JING'AN
38 MASALA ART
39 HAYA'S
40 LITTLE HUIA
41 MY NYONYA GALLERY
43 NOVA

ⓝ NIGHTLIFE

1 KAIBA
2 CROCUS
4 ⬡ RHUMERIE BOUNTY
11 I LOVE SHANGHAI
15 THE RABBIT HOLE
20 THE SPOT
42 BEEDEES

ⓐ ARTS AND LEISURE

7 IFA GALLERY
9 ONEWELLNESS
18 KUNST.LICHT
25 MAJESTIC THEATRE
32 JING'AN PARK

ⓢ SHOPS

3 GOLDEN RESORT
12 SUGAR & SPICE
14 APSARA
21 GLAMOUR NAILS
22 WEST NANJING ROAD
23 CHATERHOUSE
24 PLAZA 66
28 INPOINT MALL
30 OSCAR'S CLUB
31 ⬡ FENSHINE PLAZA
35 ⬡ CULTURE MATTERS
37 SKIN CITY 5.5

ⓗ HOTELS

8 ⬡ LE TOUR TRAVELER'S REST
13 ⬡ URBN HOTEL
27 ⬡ JIA SHANGHAI
34 PULI HOTEL AND SPA
36 ⬡ HENGSHAN MOLLER VILLA HOTEL

Jing'an Temple
19

32

Jing'an Park

Jing'an Temple

© AVALON TRAVEL

Wusong River

PING LU

HUA LU

XINZHA LU

WUDING XILU

TAIXING LU

SHIMEN ERLU

NANSUZHOU LU

XINHA LU

SHANHAIGUAN LU

DATIAN LU

CHENGDU BEILU

SEE MAP 7

★ 16

BEIJING XILU

Jing'an
Sculpture Park

30 ⓢ

FENGYANG LU

31 ⓢ

ⓢ 14

ⓝ 15

JIANGNING

FENGYANG

NANHUI LU

NANJING XILU

WUJIANG LU

ⓗ 27 ⓢ 28

★ 29
Wujiang
Road

Ⓜ

DINGHAI LU

Nanjing
Xilu

TAIXING LU

SHIMEN YILU

Lane
1025

25 ★ 26
Ⓐ

MAOMING

35 ⓢ

24 ⓢ

BEILU

WEIHAI LU

SHANXI NANLU

SEE MAP 8

nghai
ter

nghai
bition
nter

37 38 39 40 41 42 ⓝ
ⓢ Ⓡ Ⓡ Ⓡ

DAGU LU

Ⓡ
43

Shanghai Second
Polytechnic University

WEIHAI LU

YAN'AN   ZHONGLU

RUIJIN

ⓗ
36

SHANXI NANLU

JULU LU

MAOMING NANLU

0   300 yds

0   300 m

DISTANCE ACROSS MAP
Approximate: 2.1 mi or 3.4 km

JINXIAN LU

SEE MAP 10

SIGHTS

67	SITE OF THE FIRST NATIONAL CONGRESS OF THE CHINESE COMMUNIST PARTY	68	XINTIANDI	77	CITÉ BOURGOGNE
		74	JIASHAN MARKET ECO COMPLEX	78	TIANZIFANG

RESTAURANTS

5	AMOKKA	20	CHARMANT	41	CANTINA AGAVE
6	BAKER & SPICE	21	HAIKU BY HATSUNE	45	EL WILLY
7	MR. WILLIS	22	MADISON	46	SICHUAN CITIZEN
9	HUNAN XIANGCUN FENGWEI	26	THE COTTAGE	47	DAKOTA
10	LA STRADA	27	LA CRÊPERIE	51	OSTERIA
18	CHICHA	29	EL PATIO	52	CITIZEN CAFÉ
19	HOT POT KING	37	NOODLE BULL	54	SOUTHERN BARBARIAN
		38	BISTRO BURGER	75	VIENNA CAFÉ

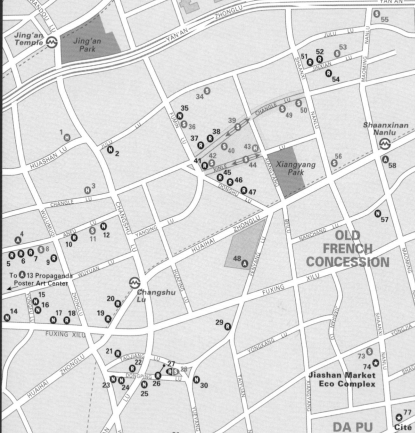

SEE MAP 9

Nanjing Xilu

Shanghai Second Polytechnic University

Jing'an Temple

Jing'an Park

YAN'AN ZHONGLU

Shaanxinan Nanlu

Xiangyang Park

Huashan Lu

Changle Lu

OLD FRENCH CONCESSION

To 13 Propaganda Poster Art Center

Changshu Lu

FUXING XILU

Jiashan Market Eco Complex

DA PU QIAO

Cité Bourgogne

Hengshan Lu

To Cotton's

0   500 yds
0   500 m

DISTANCE ACROSS MAP
Approximate: 2.6 mi or 4.2 km

© AVALON TRAVEL

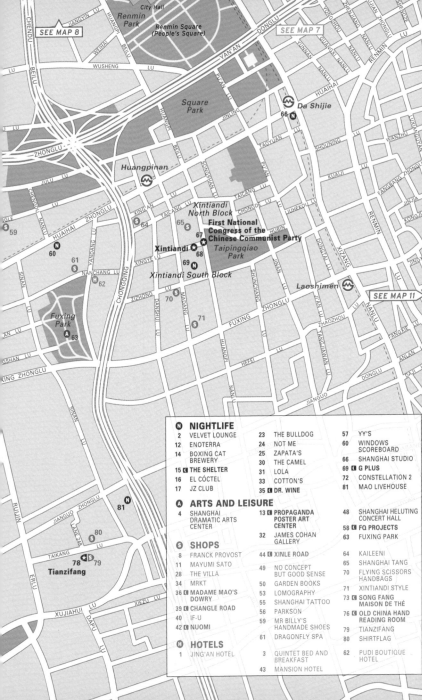

SEE MAP 8

Renmin Park

City Hall

Renmin Square (People's Square)

Square Park

Da Shijie 66

SEE MAP 7

Huangpinan

Xintiandi North Block

First National Congress of the Chinese Communist Party 67

Xintiandi 68

Taipingqiao Park

Xintiandi South Block 69

Laoshimen

SEE MAP 11

Fuxing Park 63

Tianzifang

ⓝ NIGHTLIFE

2	VELVET LOUNGE	23	THE BULLDOG	57	YY'S	
12	ENOTERRA	24	NOT ME	60	WINDOWS SCOREBOARD	
14	BOXING CAT BREWERY	25	ZAPATA'S	66	SHANGHAI STUDIO	
15	THE SHELTER	30	THE CAMEL	69	G PLUS	
16	EL CÓCTEL	31	LOLA	72	CONSTELLATION 2	
17	JZ CLUB	33	COTTON'S	81	MAO LIVEHOUSE	
		35	DR. WINE			

ⓐ ARTS AND LEISURE

4	SHANGHAI DRAMATIC ARTS CENTER	13	PROPAGANDA POSTER ART CENTER	48	SHANGHAI HELUTING CONCERT HALL	
		32	JAMES COHAN GALLERY	58	FQ PROJECTS	
				63	FUXING PARK	

ⓢ SHOPS

8	FRANCK PROVOST	44	XINLE ROAD	64	KAILEENI	
11	MAYUMI SATO	49	NO CONCEPT BUT GOOD SENSE	65	SHANGHAI TANG	
28	THE VILLA	50	GARDEN BOOKS	70	FLYING SCISSORS HANDBAGS	
34	MRKT	53	LOMOGRAPHY	71	XINTIANDI STYLE	
36	MADAME MAO'S DOWRY	55	SHANGHAI TATTOO	73	SONG FANG MAISON DE THÉ	
39	CHANGLE ROAD	56	PARKSON	76	OLD CHINA HAND READING ROOM	
40	IF-U	59	MR BILLY'S HANDMADE SHOES	79	TIANZIFANG	
42	NUOMI	61	DRAGONFLY SPA	80	SHIRTFLAG	

ⓗ HOTELS

1	JING'AN HOTEL	3	QUINTET BED AND BREAKFAST	62	PUDI BOUTIQUE HOTEL	
		43	MANSION HOTEL			

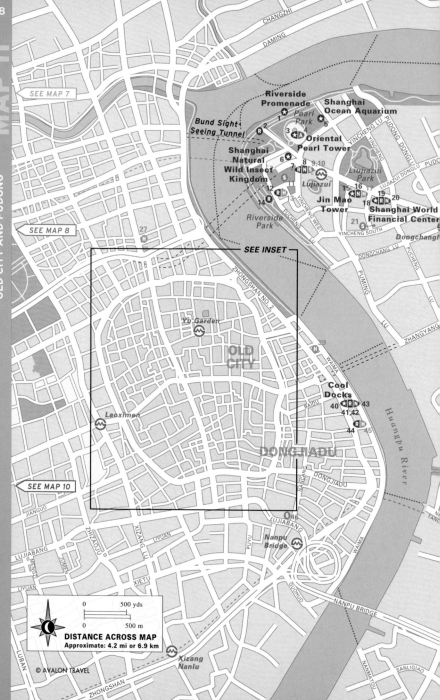

SEE MAP 7

CHANGZHI

DAMING

Riverside
Promenade

Shanghai
Ocean Aquarium

Pearl
Park

Bund Sight-
Seeing Tunnel

Oriental
Pearl Tower

Shanghai
Natural
Wild Insect
Kingdom

Liujiazui
Park

YINCHENG LU   PUDONG DONGLU   PUD

Lujiazui

Jin Mao
Tower

Shanghai World
Financial Center

SEE MAP 8

Riverside
Park

Dongchang L

YINCHENG SOUTH

DONGCHANG LU

SEE INSET

ZHONGSHAN NO. 2

Yu Garden

PUMING

PUCHENG

ZHANGYANG

OLD
CITY

WAIMA

Laoximen

Huangpu River

Cool
Docks

SEE MAP 10

DONGJIADU

DONGJIADU

NANCANG

PUVU

PUJU

LUJIABANG

Nanpu
Bridge

JIANGUO

ZHAOJU

XIZANG LU

LIYUAN

XIETU

LUJIABANG

ZHONGSHAN

TUNNEL

LIYUAN

LUBAN

NANPU BRIDGE

0   500 yds
0   500 m

DISTANCE ACROSS MAP
Approximate: 4.2 mi or 6.9 km

Xizang
Nanlu

© AVALON TRAVEL

ZHONGSHAN

SANLIQIAO

NANMA TOU

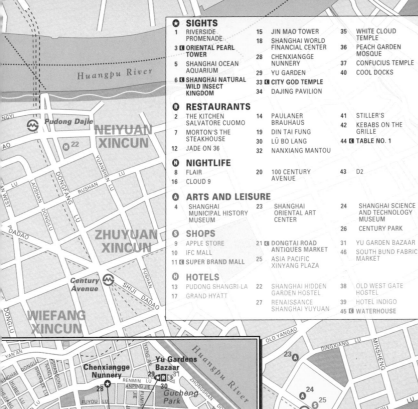

★ SIGHTS

1	RIVERSIDE PROMENADE
3 ◖	ORIENTAL PEARL TOWER
5	SHANGHAI OCEAN AQUARIUM
6 ◖	SHANGHAI NATURAL WILD INSECT KINGDOM
15	JIN MAO TOWER
18	SHANGHAI WORLD FINANCIAL CENTER
28	CHENXIANGGE NUNNERY
29	YU GARDEN
33 ◖	CITY GOD TEMPLE
34	DAJING PAVILION
35	WHITE CLOUD TEMPLE
36	PEACH GARDEN MOSQUE
37	CONFUCIUS TEMPLE
40	COOL DOCKS

® RESTAURANTS

2	THE KITCHEN SALVATORE CUOMO
7	MORTON'S THE STEAKHOUSE
12	JADE ON 36
14	PAULANER BRAUHAUS
19	DIN TAI FUNG
30	LÜ BO LANG
32	NANXIANG MANTOU
41	STILLER'S
42	KEBABS ON THE GRILLE
44 ◖	TABLE NO. 1

® NIGHTLIFE

8	FLAIR
16	CLOUD 9
20	100 CENTURY AVENUE
43	D2

Ⓐ ARTS AND LEISURE

4	SHANGHAI MUNICIPAL HISTORY MUSEUM
23	SHANGHAI ORIENTAL ART CENTER
24	SHANGHAI SCIENCE AND TECHNOLOGY MUSEUM
26	CENTURY PARK

Ⓢ SHOPS

9	APPLE STORE
10	IFC MALL
11 ◖	SUPER BRAND MALL
21 ◖	DONGTAI ROAD ANTIQUES MARKET
25	ASIA PACIFIC XINYANG PLAZA
31	YU GARDEN BAZAAR
46	SOUTH BUND FABRIC MARKET

Ⓗ HOTELS

13	PUDONG SHANGRI-LA
17	GRAND HYATT
22	SHANGHAI HIDDEN GARDEN HOSTEL
27	RENAISSANCE SHANGHAI YUYUAN
38	OLD WEST GATE HOSTEL
39	HOTEL INDIGO
45 ◖	WATERHOUSE

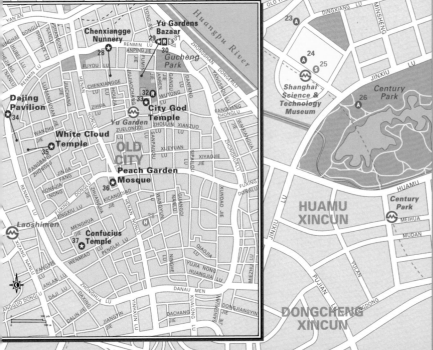

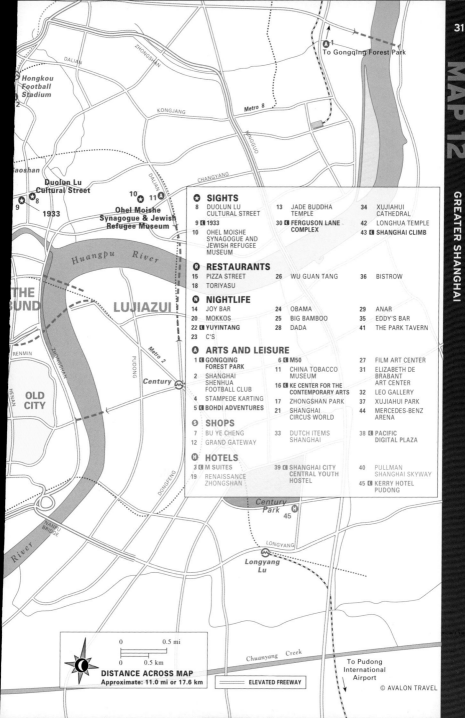

ⓞ SIGHTS

8	DUOLUN LU CULTURAL STREET	13	JADE BUDDHA TEMPLE	34	XUJIAHUI CATHEDRAL
9	1933	30	FERGUSON LANE COMPLEX	42	LONGHUA TEMPLE
10	OHEL MOISHE SYNAGOGUE AND JEWISH REFUGEE MUSEUM			43	SHANGHAI CLIMB

ⓡ RESTAURANTS

15	PIZZA STREET	26	WU GUAN TANG	36	BISTROW
18	TORIYASU				

ⓝ NIGHTLIFE

14	JOY BAR	24	OBAMA	29	ANAR
20	MOKKOS	25	BIG BAMBOO	35	EDDY'S BAR
22	YUYINTANG	28	DADA	41	THE PARK TAVERN
23	C'S				

ⓐ ARTS AND LEISURE

1	GONGQING FOREST PARK	6	M50	27	FILM ART CENTER
2	SHANGHAI SHENHUA FOOTBALL CLUB	11	CHINA TOBACCO MUSEUM	31	ELIZABETH DE BRABANT ART CENTER
4	STAMPEDE KARTING	16	KE CENTER FOR THE CONTEMPORARY ARTS	32	LEO GALLERY
5	BOHDI ADVENTURES	17	ZHONGSHAN PARK	37	XUJIAHUI PARK
		21	SHANGHAI CIRCUS WORLD	44	MERCEDES-BENZ ARENA

ⓢ SHOPS

7	BU YE CHENG	33	DUTCH ITEMS SHANGHAI	38	PACIFIC DIGITAL PLAZA
12	GRAND GATEWAY				

ⓗ HOTELS

3	M SUITES	39	SHANGHAI CITY CENTRAL YOUTH HOSTEL	40	PULLMAN SHANGHAI SKYWAY
19	RENAISSANCE ZHONGSHAN			45	KERRY HOTEL PUDONG

DISTANCE ACROSS MAP
Approximate: 11.0 mi or 17.6 km

ELEVATED FREEWAY

© AVALON TRAVEL

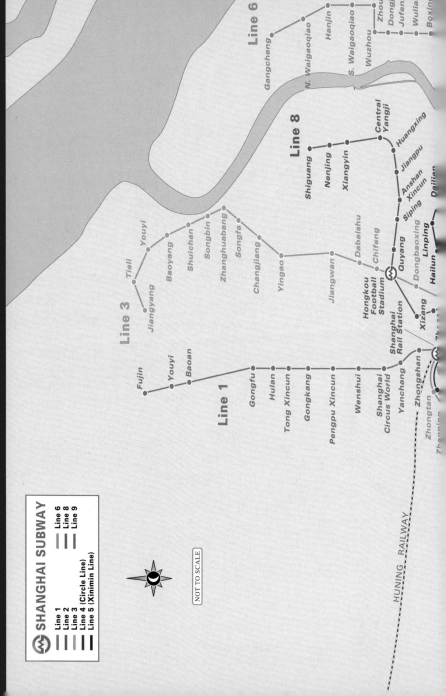

SHANGHAI SUBWAY

Line 1
Line 2
Line 3
Line 4 (Circle Line)
Line 5 (Xinimin Line)
Line 6
Line 8
Line 9

NOT TO SCALE

HUNING RAILWAY

Line 6

Gangcheng
N. Waigaoqiao
Hanjin
S. Waigaoqiao
Wuzhou
Zhouhai
Dongjing
Jufeng
Wulian
Boxing

Line 8

Shiguang
Nenjing
Xiangyin
Central Yangji
Huangxing
Jiangpu
Anshan Xincun
Dailian
Siping
Quyang
Dongbaoxing
Linping
Hailun
Xizang

Line 3

Tieli
Youyi
Jiangyang
Baoyang
Shuichan
Songbin
Zhanghuabang
Songfa
Changjiang
Yingao
Jiangwan
Dabaishu
Chifeng
Hongkou Football Stadium
Shanghai Rail Station

Line 1

Fujin
Youyi
Baoan
Gongfu
Hulan
Tong Xincun
Gongkang
Pengpu Xincun
Wenshui
Shanghai Circus World
Yanchang
Zhongshan
Zhongtan
Zhenping

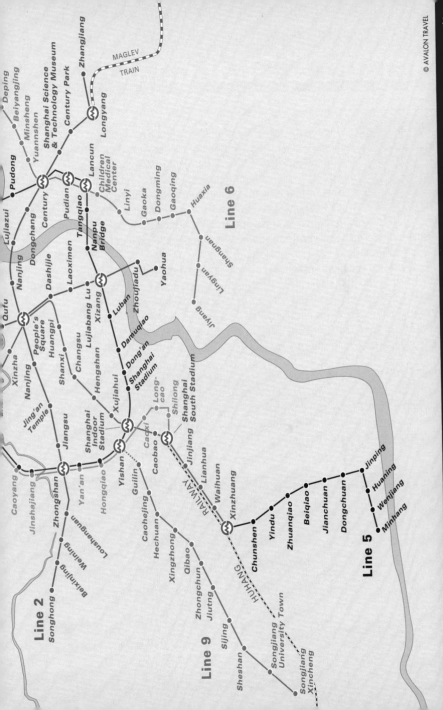

© AVALON TRAVEL

MAGLEV
TRAIN

Line 6

Line 2

Line 9

Line 5

HUHANG RAILWAY

Zhangjiang

Deping
Beiyangjing
Minsheng
Yuannshen
Shanghai Science
& Technology Museum
Century Park
Longyang

Pudong
Century
Dongchang
Pudian
Lancun
Children
Medical
Center

Lujiazui
Nanjing
Laoximen
Tangqiao
Nanpu
Bridge

Linyi
Gaoka
Dongming
Gaoqing
Huexia

Qufu
Dashijie
Changsu
Xizang
Luban
Zhoujiadu

People's
Square
Huangpi
Lujiabang Lu
Yaohua

Xinzha
Nanjing
Shanxi
Hengshan
Dong'an

Jing'an
Temple
Jiangsu
Xujiahui
Shanghai
Stadium
Long-
cao
Shilong
Shanghai
South Stadium
Shangnan

Lingyan
Jiyang

Yan'an
Shanghai
Indoor
Stadium
Yishan
Caoxi
Jinjiang
Lianhua

Caoyang
Zhongshan
Hongqiao
Guilin
Caobao
Waihuan
Xinzhuang

Jinshajiang
Weining
Loushanguan

Beixinjing

Hechuan
Caohejing
Xingzhong
Qibao
Zhongchun
Jiutng
Sijing
Sheshan
Songjiang
University Town
Songjiang
Xincheng

Chunshen
Yindu
Zhuangqiao
Beiqiao
Jianchuan
Dongchuan
Jinping
Huaning
Wenjiang
Minhang

Songhong
Nanjing

Damuqiao
Darnuqiao

Discover
Beijing & Shanghai

Shanghai, the bright Pearl of the Orient, the outward-looking Paris of the East. Beijing, the weaver of China's historical tapestry. It's hard to imagine two cities more different from each other. Beijing's history and political importance bear witness to millennia of Chinese culture, while Shanghai's relentless drive for progress typifies the nation's forward motion on the world stage. Both cities embody the contradictions of a complicated country and at the same time defy the world's expectations.

Shanghai is a city that thrums with life. Its beating heart is the throb of traffic on the highways; its soul is the chatter of human interaction on every street and alley. Old neighborhoods with billowing laundry and street-side noodle shops coexist with a backdrop of skyscrapers. You're never far from a crane or construction site. Shanghai is a work in progress: The passage of time can be seen in areas like the Old French Concession, with its low-rise art deco apartments and villas, and the Old City, with its alleys and bazaars. Things change fast in Shanghai. Every week sees another bar open, another restaurant close. A large expatriate population infuses the downtown districts with an international twist. The shopping malls, designer boutiques, and coffee chains testify to this ever-increasing Westernization.

Beijing is calmer and more confident. A low sprawl of ring roads and straight avenues, its layout is comfortingly uniform. Tucked between the concentric squares are ancient temples and austere monuments that are a historian's dream come true. When you survey the expanse of Tian'anmen Square with the Mao-adorned gate at its helm and monuments to socialism all around, you feel as if you're at the hub of China's nerve center.

China's rocky history and political landscape form the backdrop to outsiders' views of the nation. Closed from the rest of the world for three decades under Mao, China's reputation as a mysterious sleeping dragon captivates observers. It's when the outsider ventures inward that China begins to reveal its true self. Visiting Beijing and Shanghai is the first step to discovering the country as it exists today. It's an opportunity to see two of the most visually, historically, and culturally interesting cities in the world.

Planning Your Trip

▶ WHERE TO GO

Beijing
TIAN'ANMEN
天安门

From the sprawling Forbidden City to the former imperial gardens, the Tian'anmen area is the city's political and historic nerve center. World-changing events took place on the wide expanse of Tian'anmen Square and Chairman Mao's body lies preserved in his austere mausoleum. Some of the city's most important thoroughfares crisscross this district, such as wide Chang'an Avenue and bustling Wangfujing Avenue, with its shops and restaurants. A crop of high-end restaurants overlooks the Forbidden City and streets around the palace provide some great nightlife options.

HOUHAI
后海

The capital's northerly reaches are home to some of the best-preserved *hutong* alleys, the Drum and Bell Towers, and Lama and Confucius Temples—all reminders of a slower time in Beijing's past. As well as these imperial relics, the area is home to a vibrant nightlife scene. Houhai is famous for the neon-lit bars that line its shore, but the hip crowd skips the lakeside in favor of the cafés and *hutong* bars of Gulou Avenue and Nanluoguxiang. The

Tian'anmen Square

Temple of Heaven

area is a cradle of Beijing's famous rock music scene, with a plethora of live music venues, jazz clubs, and smoky bars.

QIANMEN
前门

Home to the Temple of Heaven where emperors prayed for a good harvest, Beijing's southern area also includes districts that retain aspects of their history and tradition even after a spate of modernization. The colonial-era buildings of the Legation Quarter are occupied by contemporary restaurants and art centers. Qianmen pedestrian street, Liulichang, and Dazhalan continue to host merchants and food stalls, as they have since the early Qing Dynasty.

CHAOYANG, THE CENTRAL BUSINESS DISTRICT, AND SANLITUN
朝阳, 国贸和三里屯

There's plenty to do and see in Beijing's eastern quarter. This is one of the city's busiest areas. Sprawling Chaoyang is home to foreign embassies, markets, and shops. Sanlitun is Beijing's longest established nightlife district. The Central Business District (CBD) has some of the city's most striking modern architecture, like the New CCTV Tower.

CAPITAL MUSEUM AND THE TEMPLE OF GREAT CHARITY
首都博物馆和广济寺

Home to Beijing's ever-growing financial district, this area is also blessed with historical treasures like the Temple of Great Charity, White Dagoba Temple, and the Temple of the Ancient Monarchs, as well as the excellent Capital Museum and Lu Xun Museum. The area is bisected by Fuxingmenwai Avenue, the western continuation of Chang'an Avenue, and contains the sprawling Yuyuantan Park.

UNIVERSITY DISTRICT AND THE SUMMER PALACE
海淀区和颐和园

The Univeristy District, Wudaokou, is the epicenter of student life in Beijing, with the cafés and bars to prove it. Farther west and north, the bustle quiets down, with iconic sights like the Summer Palace, where emperors and empresses once retreated for a little rest and relaxation, and the lesser-known ruins of the Old Summer Palace.

GREATER BEIJING

Beijing's outer districts provide an escape from the busy downtown area. Spend an afternoon among the flora at the Botanical Garden, stroll in the Fragrant Hills, check out the iconic Bird's Nest Olympic Stadium, and the hip 798 and Caochangdi Art Districts, then finish off with an evening at one of the trendy bars or restaurants nearby.

Shanghai
THE BUND
外滩

The Bund, Shanghai's historic waterfront, is home to some of the city's most impressive and imposing buildings. Built during the colonial heyday, this stretch of neoclassical and art deco customs houses, bank headquarters, and luxury hotels faces the ultra-modern Lujiazui skyline in Pudong across the river. The pedestrian zone at East Nanjing Road comes alive with neon at night and is one of the city's busiest commercial hubs. Home mainly to Chinese department stores and restaurants, it connects The Bund with People's Square.

PEOPLE'S SQUARE
人民广场

Though Shanghai does not have a true center, People's Square can rightly be called its downtown, with 30-acre People's Park, a former racetrack, as its anchor. Though known for the modern malls and skyscrapers scattered throughout its boundaries, People's Square is also home to buildings designed by the famous Hungarian architect László Hudec, like the Moore Memorial Church.

people walking on The Bund, Shanghai

JING'AN
静安

Shanghai's love of wealth comes face to face with older devotions in the Jing'an district. Despite religion being banned in the People's Republic, Buddhism and folk religions are still widely practiced. Jing'an Temple is Shanghai's oldest Buddhist place of worship. The huge shrine is located on West Nanjing Road, alongside the shopping malls, designer boutiques, and department stores that make this area a haven for consumerism. North of the temple, bars and cafés mingle with residential districts.

OLD FRENCH CONCESSION
法租界

As its name belies, the Old French Concession (OFC) was once controlled by France. Because of this , the OFC has been imbued with a distinctly European atmosphere, with its slower pace, narrow tree-lined lanes, and upscale boutiques, like those on Changle Road and Xinle Road. The architecture, though, is distinctly Shanghainese, with the red-brick Cité Bourgogne and the *shikumen* (stone arch gate) terraces of the Xintiandi district lending a graceful touch to the area.

OLD CITY
古城

Old Shanghai is well preserved in the Old City, with its warren of streets, bustling bazaar, and historic gardens and temples, but development is afoot around the South Bund. Once home to docks and shipyards, this area has recently transformed into a trendy entertainment zone.

PUDONG
浦东

On the eastern side of the Huangpu River, things are brighter, brasher, bolder, and bigger: Pudong New District is everything

street in the Old City of Shanghai

you'd expect from the financial heart of China's economic center. With improbably wide boulevards and modern shopping malls, Lujiazui is Pudong's main artery. Nearby you'll find Century Park, some excellent museums, and sprawling villa complexes that provide a relative calm against the otherwise constant rush.

GREATER SHANGHAI

Shanghai's outlying districts have some hidden gems. Heading away from the main tourist spots takes you to parts of town that the push of progress has left behind: tangles of old streets, fruit for sale on the corner, and ramshackle homes sprawling upwards from old *shikumen* (stone arch gates). It's a side of Shanghai that shouldn't be missed in favor of the glitzier parts. Head a couple of metro stops out to Zhongshan Park. Life here is a world of its own, with tai chi, outdoor ballroom dancing, and kite-flying. The area around Zhongshan Park is a retail haven, with malls and shops galore.

▶ WHEN TO GO

The best times of year to visit both cities are spring and fall, particularly March–May and September–November. Beijing's winters are cruel, with temperatures dropping as low as -10 degrees Fahrenheit. However, if you can bear the cold, it's worth traveling during winter for the clear skies, mild white sunshine, and crisp air. As soon as the warmer months come, so does the worst of the pollution.

Summers are hot and damp, with 60 percent of annual rainfall coming in July and August. Shanghai is a humid furnace between late June and late September, so avoid summer if at all possible. The "plum rains" fall in early- to mid-June, following a pleasant couple of months of springtime. Fall is warm and dry.

Avoid late January to early February if you don't want to get caught up in the Chinese New Year festivities that render many attractions closed. Travel between cities at this time of year is a nightmare, as tens of millions of people are on the move. The holiday is a moveable feast (meaning the dates

modern architecture in Shanghai

change each year), so check dates before you book your trip. Similarly, the Golden Week holiday in the first week of October sees chaotic transportation and overcrowded tourist attractions.

view of Shanghai from Century Park

▶ BEFORE YOU GO

Passports and Visas

All non-Chinese citizens require a visa to enter the country. The tourist visa is known as the L and comes as Single Entry (valid for 3–6 months), Double Entry (valid for 6 months), or Multiple Entry (valid for 6 months or 12 months). Contact your local Chinese embassy or consulate for details. Your passport must have at least six months remaining before it expires.

Transportation

International flights into Beijing come into Capital Airport. It's one of the busiest airports in the world and one of the best equipped. A special branch of the Beijing subway system called the Airport Express line goes to downtown Dongzhimen. If you'd rather take the bus, there are six shuttle bus routes into the city. Or, you can hail a taxi.

Most domestic arrivals into Shanghai usually land at Hongqiao Airport. International flights (and some domestic, depending on the airline) come into Pudong International Airport. This mighty air-hub is connected to the city by the super-fast Magnetic Levitation (Maglev) train, which takes just eight minutes to cover the 30 kilometers (19 mi) to Longyang Road station. Other options for getting into town include a taxi or the metro.

Travel between Beijing and Shanghai got infinitely more convenient with the opening of the High-Speed Railway in June 2011. The train zips between the cities in just five hours. A cheaper option is the regular train, which usually sets off in the evening and arrives early the following morning. Air travel between the cities is fast and convenient, taking just under two hours.

What to Take

The fancier restaurants and bars in Beijing and Shanghai may balk at shorts, sandals, and sneakers, so pack some dressier outfits. Take a waterproof jacket if you're visiting in late spring or summer. Umbrellas can be bought cheaply at most convenience stores. Both cities are populated with shops of all varieties, from pharmacies to clothing shops, so don't panic if you forget to pack something.

flight arriving at Capital Airport in Beijing

Explore Beijing & Shanghai

► THE BEST OF BEIJING AND SHANGHAI

Day 1

You've flown into Beijing, which is laid out around the Forbidden City, so this is a logical place to start. Grab some brunch at the Big Tree Café, just north of the Forbidden City, then spend a couple of hours wandering through the courtyards and pavilions of the Forbidden City. The sprawling former home of China's emperors is a treasure trove of history, with beautifully decorated halls, shady courtyards, and impressive statues. Don't miss the stunning Nine Dragon frieze with its brightly colored tiles, and be sure to admire the opulent former living quarters of the imperial concubines. Behind the palace, there's pretty Beihai Park, with its white dagoba. Take some time to stroll around the park and admire the greenery, then grab lunch at one of the many lakeside eateries around Houhai, like Hutong Pizza.

Next, wander down through Beihai Park to Tian'anmen Square where Mao's portrait watches over the enormous plaza. Check out the chairman's preserved body at the Mausoleum of Mao Zedong, then gawk at macabre relics like photographs of crime scenes and assassinations (plus the guns used by the assassins!) at the Beijing Police Museum. Head west to Wangfujing Avenue and sample some unusual street food—scorpions on sticks, whole barbequed squid, and exotic bugs—at the buzzing night market. Stop by Redmoon bar for a glass of wine, then stay the night at nearby Hotel Kapok for an affordably luxurious experience.

Day 2

After feasting on a hearty German-style breakfast at trendy Zarah, spend your second day at two of Beijing's most important historic

Beihai Park, Beijing

sites. Head up to the Summer Palace in the morning to acquaint yourself with the complex where the imperial court would spend their summers to escape the heat of the city. Explore the stunning Long Gallery, take a boat ride on immense Kunming Lake, and stroll down quaint Suzhou Market Street, where the emperor would pretend he was one of the "common people" by haggling in a marketplace run by his staff.

Head back into town for a nice lunch at The Whampoa Club on Financial Street, spend the afternoon at the Temple of Heaven, which sits inside over 3 million square yards of parkland and was once considered to be the most important of four sacrificial temples in Beijing. Be sure to visit the triple-gabled, vividly colored Hall of Prayer for Good Harvests within the temple compound, which is one of Beijing's most iconic structures.

Next, take your time strolling through the Legation Quarter, which lies directly east of Tian'anmen Square. It was home to many foreign embassies during the latter part of the Qing Dynasty, but the colonial-era buildings of the Quarter are now home to high-end restaurants and art galleries. Take a peek into a few of the galleries, but try to resist venturing into one of the restaurants, as you've got other plans in store for dinner tonight. You can't leave Beijing without trying the city's most famous specialty: Beijing duck. Some of the city's best and leanest Beijing duck can be had at Da Dong; you'll want to make a reservation ahead of time, however, as Da Dong is very popular. For this evening's entertainment, take in a show at Tianqiao Acrobatics Theater and prepare to be amazed by the dexterous members of the Beijing Acrobatic Troupe. Tuck into bed at the well-located and affordable Rainbow Hotel.

Day 3

Start your day with a leisurely breakfast at Alba; if the weather is nice, grab a table on the sunny roof terrace. A trip to Beijing wouldn't be complete without a visit to the Great Wall, so strap on your walking shoes, throw some snacks and water into your bag, and hail a taxi. The accessible but quiet Great Wall at Mutianyu is a great choice for a day trip. The

temple in the Summer Palace in Beijing

FOR THE LOVE OF FOOD

On your vacation to Beijing and Shanghai, you'll be exposed to cuisine unlike any other, whether it's with insanely spicy Hunanese food or a gourmet take on tastes of the West. Take advantage of the range of options available and sample the best of the best, as listed here.

BEIJING
Beijing Duck
This famous dish, also known as Peking duck, is a vacation requirement-you can't leave Beijing without trying it at least once!

- Go local at **Li Qun,** the restaurant with arguably the tastiest roast ducks in the capital.

- **Da Dong** serves Beijing's leanest ducks in sophisticated surroundings.

- It's a hotel restaurant, but **Fat Duck** sacrifices nothing when it comes to the taste and quality of its Beijing duck.

Beijing Cuisine
Dumplings and steamed buns are famous Beijing-style snacks that can be a good lunch or light dinner.

- Try some traditional Beijing dumplings **Shun Yi Fu,** where fillings range from vegetables to shrimp and donkey.

- Grab a steamer of *baozi* at **Goubuli Baozi,** and fill up on the delicious fluffy, pork-filled steamed buns for dinner.

Spicy Regional Fare

- The spicy, Turkish-influenced flavors of the Xinjiang region highlight dishes like lamb, flatbread, and homemade yogurt at **Crescent Moon.**

- Sour and spicy Guizhou cuisine is little known outside of China, so **Three Guizhou Men** is the ideal place to try it. The steamed ribs with pickled greens or sour fish soup are both sure to please your taste buds.

- **Dali Courtyard** is the perfect place to sample Yunnanese food like fried mint leaves and wild mushrooms.

SHANGHAI
Shanghainese
Shanghai's specialties are legion, but while

Peking duck, China's most famous dish

you're in town, be sure to awe your taste buds by trying *xiaolongbao* (soup dumplings) and some of the local seafood, particularly hairy crab.

- Sample *xiaolongbao* at popular **Nanxiang Mantou** in the Old City.

- Locally sourced crab, river fish, and eel are menu highlights at **Lü Bo Lang** inside the Yu Garden.

- If you're in town in the fall, be sure to try the hairy crab at **Wang Bao He,** the city's oldest crab restaurant.

Yunnanese

Yunnanese food is greatly influenced by the region's proximity to Laos, Thailand, and Myanmar. Curry, potatoes, and pork are common ingredients.

- The food of Yunnan Province goes gourmet at chic **Lost Heaven,** where the Dai-style chicken is a sure bet.

- Regional Yunnan specialities like marinated pork and buckwheat cakes are served at the rustic **Legend Taste.**

- At **Southern Barbarian,** there's no topping the fried goat cheese, potato pancakes, or barbeque skewers.

Spicy Regional Fare

- Test your taste buds with some seriously fiery Hunanese food at **Hunan Xiangcun Fengwei.** You can't go wrong with the smoked pork or sizzling beef.

- Eat spice-filled Sichuan fare like authentic kung pao chicken or the intimidatingly named numbing spicy tofu at **Sichuan Citizen.**

- Try traditional dry pot cooking from China's southern Guizhou province at **Gan Guo Ju,** which features flavorful spicy-sour dishes.

Lost Heaven

Wall here is well preserved and perfect for a hike. Explore the watchtowers dating from the Ming Dynasty, and take in the stunning mountain scenery. If, like many before you, you are entranced and enchanted by the Wall and you decide to stay the night, rent a guesthouse from The Schoolhouse at Mutianyu or a room from one of its affiliated hotels like the Brickyard Inn & Eco-Retreat. If you're anxious to get back to experiencing Beijing, however, head back to town in the afternoon to familiar territory: Qianmen's Legation Quarter. There, explore the Urban Planning Exhibition Hall, where you'll find an incredible scale model of Beijing and learn about the city's history and plans for its future.

For dinner, you don't have to go far for a memorable experience. Splurge a little on French fare at nearby Maison Boulud, housed in the former U.S. embassy building. Make sure to grab a drink at the restaurant's bar, Fresco, either before or after dinner. You'll no doubt be tired from your long day of sightseeing, so head up Qianmen Avenue and check into the Capital Hotel for the night. The hotel doesn't look like much from the outside, but the decor and luxurious guest rooms, some with a view of the Forbidden City, belie the hotel's 5-star status.

Day 4

Spend today in the Chaoyang District, starting at Chef Too with a late brunch. After you're full to bursting with eggs Benedict or French toast, cruise over to 798 Art District and lose yourself amid the many galleries. Make sure to check out the Iberia Center for Contemporary Art and the 798 Photo Gallery. If you need to reenergize, grab a latte at nearby AT Café, then browse the excellent selection of books at Timezone 8.

Next up, brave the crowds at the Silk Street Market, where anywhere from 20,000–60,000 people may cross its threshold in a given day. Here, you can practice your bargaining skills and purchase tacky souvenirs, bags, and jewelry, among many other options. After you've gotten your goods and your wallet is verging on empty, relax and recuperate in pretty Chaoyang Park. Stroll around the park and admire the flower gardens or pick a patch of grass and lie down for a while.

Mutianyu section of the Great Wall

Rent a bike or take a boat ride around the lake, then head into the heart of Sanlitun for the evening. Try the deservedly famous hot pot at Hai Di Lao, where you can customize your order at the sauce station, and even get a manicure while you wait for your food! After dinner, check out Babu Space for a taste of Beijing's famous street art. If you fall in love with one of the many paintings, photographs, or illustrations on display, check to see if it's for sale, and you may be able to bring home a one-of-a-kind souvenir of your time in Beijing.

Now it's time to kick back with an expertly concocted drink at Apothecary. Snack on some New Orleans–style bar food as you sip on a whiskey cocktail and soak up the laid-back atmosphere. Tuck in for the night at boutique hotel The Opposite House, known to be among the chicest and trendiest hotels in the city. For the night owls, the hotel is also home to Mesh bar, good for a glass of wine and chatting with friends, or Punk, with its late-night parties.

Day 5

Sleep in a bit and enjoy a lazy brunch at The Vineyard, known for its mouth-watering hot breakfasts. For today's adventure, you'll want to rent a bicycle and explore the picturesque *hutong* alleys of Houhai's Gulou Avenue—but try not to get lost! Cycle over to Zhongwan Hutong and visit the Drum and Bell Towers. These eye-catching structures date from the 1200s and were used as time-keeping devices for the Forbidden City complex.

Head back onto Gulou Avenue and try some tasty Yunnanese food at Dali Courtyard for lunch. Make sure to take a peek at the rooms just off the restaurant's courtyard—they're filled with quirky ornaments and knick-knacks. Make your way to the Penghao Theater to catch a play in the intimate performance space. Penghao specializes in community and youth theater, and is a great way to experience true Beijing culture. If you've got time to kill before the show starts, grab a drink at the theater's rooftop bar.

On your way to dinner, make sure to pass through Nanluoguxiang, the buzzing *hutong* full of unique shops and food vendors. An absolute must here for the ultimate souvenir is Plastered T-shirts. If you can resist the tempting smells from the street food vendors, you can pay homage to your earlier visit to the Drum and Bell Towers by dining at Nanluoguxiang's Drum and Gong. Adventurous eaters can try the kung pao chicken pizza, but the Yunnan mushrooms are always a hit. After dinner, pop in to Mao Mao Chong for a nightcap. If you feel like staying out late, get a taste of Beijing's rock scene at the nearby MAO Livehouse, located in a converted warehouse on East Gulou Avenue. If you're tuckered out, spend the night at the charming Lusongyuan courtyard hotel. Or, get a head start on the second half of your trip by taking the overnight train to Shanghai.

the Oriental Pearl Tower in Shanghai

Day 6

Once you've arrived in Shanghai, spend a morning on the Bund and you'll witness the city's contrasts firsthand. Buy some savory buns for breakfast at Yang's Fried Dumplings, and eat on the go, as you walk east down the Bund Promenade. Go as far as the Cool Docks and you'll see the breathtaking modern skyline of Pudong's Lujiazui financial district across the Huangpu River. Look for the futuristic Oriental Pearl Tower, Shanghai's first skyscraper; the pagoda-esque Jin Mao Tower, which features an octagonal floor plan and is the site of the world's longest laundry chute; and the Shanghai World Financial Center, known commonly as the "Bottle Opener" thanks to the gap near the top of the building.

For lunch, hang out at the Cool Docks and grab a snack at Kebabs on the Grille. Hop on the Huangpu River Cruise and choose the three-hour trip to get to know Shanghai via boat. On your way up to the mouth of the Yangtze River, you'll pass the castle-shaped Yangshupu Water Plant and the Wusong Fort, where the Opium Wars were fought. Treat yourself to a Taiwanese feast at Din Tai Fung, where you'll get the chance to try *xiaolongbao* and *jiaozi* if you haven't already. Soak up Shanghai's streets at night with a stroll, then meander back over to the Jin Mao Tower and stop in for a drink at Cloud 9, one of the world's tallest bars. If you're feeling indulgent, check into the Grand Hyatt for the night—it's expensive, but worth every yuan you'll spend. Luxuriate in the marble-encased bathroom and admire the view from way up high before getting a good night's rest.

Day 7

Grab a smoothie from Element Fresh for breakfast, then spend the morning in the Old City, with its temples and bazaars, and brave the tourist throng at Yu Garden to take in the telltale dark wood, red and gold paint, and upturned eaves indicative of Shanghai's

Jin Mao Tower and Shanghai World Financial Center

A lion guards the gate of the Yu Garden.

Day 8

Have breakfast at the Wagas in Jing'an, then hop on a train and head to the beautiful old canal city of Suzhou. Wander the narrows paths of the Humble Administrator's Garden, one of China's most attractive Ming Dynasty gardens, and admire the quaint pavilions, shaded ponds, and lush trees. Dine at Dain Ti Hill for lunch, then finish off your trip with a visit to Pan Gate, Suzhou's city gate and site of historical importance. Be sure to check out the ancient Ruigang Pagoda and the Wu Gate, both of which date back some 2,500 years. Take the train back to Shanghai and make your way into the Old French Concession. Dine on upscale American food at Bistro Burger; be sure to sample a spiked milkshake while you're there. A few blocks away, you can sleep in comfort at the quirky Hengshan Moller Villa.

Day 9

Start your day in the Old French Concession and enjoy a Viennese breakfast at Vienna Café. Then head over to the Old City, and spend the morning shopping like a true Shanghailander. Visit the Dongtai Road Antiques Market, then haul your bags over to Jing'an's Fenshine Plaza for some faux-designer goods. Head to the edges of the city and spend the afternoon at the M50 art complex in northern Shanghai. The galleries and studios that make up M50 are housed inside an old warehouse complex by Suzhou Creek.

Next, head south across Changshou Road to check out the Jade Buddha Temple with its many lovely statues (including the eponymous Buddha). Start heading back into the heart of the city, stopping off at Pizza Street for a quick bite.

Make a stop at People's Park before the sun sets and take in the urban views around you. If you have the time, take in a concert at the Shanghai Concert Hall, situated on park

historic architecture. Along with the garden after which it's named, the complex includes the City God Temple and a shopping bazaar. Wander around the garden, being sure to visit the rockery and the teahouse. If you're feeling peckish, join the line at Nanxiang Mantou and order some *mantou* buns to snack on.

Next, head over to Tianzifang and immerse yourself in the quaint lanes with their independent boutiques, outdoor cafés, and art galleries. From here, lose yourself in the tree-flanked streets of the Old French Concession. Wind your way up to Xintiandi and learn about Shanghai's old *shikumen* (stone gate) architecture at the Shikumen Open House Museum before dining on Peruvian fare at Chicha. Grab a drink a the lounge-y El Cóctel, where there's always a place to sit. After midnight, night owls will want to make their way to The Shelter, which is known for its till-dawn parties. Once you're partied out, lay your weary head on a pillow at the Pudi Boutique Hotel on Yandang Road, one of Shanghai's pedestrian streets.

incense burner at Jade Buddha Temple in Shanghai

spacious Le Tour Traveler's Rest hostel to save a few yuan for your last day in Shanghai.

Day 10

Start your final day in People's Square, the throbbing heart of Shanghai. Go underground for breakfast at Café du Metro in a below-ground mall under the People's Square Metro Station. Next, take in some contemporary art at MOCA Shanghai, then shop till you drop on West Nanjing Road (stopping off at Plaza 66, one of the giant shopping malls along the road). Once you reach Jing'an Temple, take some time to admire the gilded roofs and the giant copper bell, then hop on the metro to East Nanjing Road and take a walk along the Bund Promenade as night falls.

Treat yourself to dinner at M on the Bund for your final meal and enjoy the view of the glittering skyline. Spend your last night in the lap of luxury at the Bund's Fairmont Peace Hotel and say goodbye to Shanghai as you head to the airport in the morning.

land. Venture over to Dagu Road for dinner and tickle your taste buds with New Zealand cuisine at Little Huia. Check in to the

▶ THE BUSINESS TRAVELER'S WEEKEND

Beijing
FRIDAY

It's been a long week of meetings, and now it's time to unwind a little. Grab a cup of coffee and a bite to eat from your hotel's restaurant and start your day on Financial Street—a modern business thoroughfare that contains many company headquarters, banks, and luxury hotels. Admire the gleaming highrises that form Beijing's commercial heartland as you make your way down the street to Oriental Taipan Massage for a relaxing foot or body massage.

If you're meeting clients or coworkers for lunch, take them to CourtYard for a highend European meal overlooking the imperial

city. After lunch, it's worth the short jaunt to take a look around the Forbidden City, a former place of business, as it were, for China's emperors. Depending on how much time you spend in the Forbidden City, you may have time to take in a show before dinner, so head over to the Beijing Center for the Arts in Qianmen's Chi'enmen 23 complex. Catch a performance at the Center's Black Box theater, or you can simply explore the two-story exhibition hall.

For a dinner sure to impress your clients, stay in the Chi'enmen 23 complex to experience Maison Boulud, one of Beijing's best restaurants. Make your way to Sanlitun and stop at Glen for a nightcap, then check into the Kerry Centre Hotel where you can catch up on your email before turning in for the night.

SATURDAY

Start your morning off with some tai chi or an aimless walk in Ritan Park, Beijing's most peaceful green space, then head east to grab a quick breakfast from Trends Lounge. Get acquainted with the CBD by checking out the unusual contemporary architecture of the New CCTV Tower, designed by Rem Koolhas and Ole Scheeren. Now it's time to pick up a few souvenirs for your family and coworkers back home at the designer shops and boutiques of Sanlitun Village.

For dinner, immerse yourself in culinary tradition at Fat Duck, the Renaissance Beijing Capital Hotel's elegant Beijing duck restaurant. Round off your meal with a drink at Atmosphere, the city's highest bar. Head back to your room at the Kerry Centre Hotel and get a good night's rest in preparation for a busy final day in the capital city.

SUNDAY

Break your fast with the comforts of home at Grandma's Kitchen, then it's time to explore. Wander through Tian'anmen Square and nearby Legation Quarter to get a glimpse of the various places from which Beijing has been ruled over the years, through imperial times to the colonial era, and into the era of Communism.

Have lunch at Ristorante Sadler, another gem of the Chi'enmen 23 development, then head back in the direction of Tian'anmen Square and visit the National Museum of China, the largest museum in the world. Lose yourself among the countless artifacts and exhibits, but be sure you don't miss the Han-era jade burial suit.

Treat your clients to one last dinner, this time at Domus. Feast on the mouth-watering

the Bund Promenade in Shanghai

SHOP AROUND

Shanghai is well-known as a shopping destination, and Beijing is making a name for itself as a shopping mecca as well. With a mix of traditional wares, trendy fashions, and incredibly quirky gifts, both Beijing and Shanghai have a plethora of goods to offer you on your trip, if only you know where to look.

MALLS
Beijing

- **The Malls at Oriental Plaza** sell luxury labels like Boss and Burberry alongside mid-range brands.

- **The Place** is a local landmark, thanks its LED "sky screen." Tourneau, the largest watch shop in China, is located here.

- **Sanlitun Village** is a contemporary development containing Western brands like Armani, Adidas, Mango, Apple, and Diesel. Split into North and South Villages, it's been designed to echo the *hutong* (alleys) that were once on the site of Sanlitun Village.

Shanghai

- The **ifc Mall** in Pudong's Lujiazui district sits among the skyscrapers, and is home to international designer brands and upscale restaurants, as well as Shanghai's flagship Apple store.

- The **Super Brand Mall** is an astonishing 13 stories tall and houses mid-range brands like Uniqlo and H&M.

- In the center of the busy Xujiahui commercial district sits the **Grand Gateway** mall with its distinctive glass exterior, which resembles a golf ball. Grand Gateway is home to international brands and a multiplex cinema.

MARKETS
Beijing

- Beijing's most famous antique market is **Panjiayuan,** which sells everything from Mao memorabilia to Buddha statues.

interior of the ifc Mall in Pudong, Shanghai

- The **Hongqiao Market** is best known for its pearls, so head straight to the third floor to purchase some, but be sure to avoid the obviously fake ones.

- Choose from over 1,700 stalls selling clothes, fake bags and watches, jewelry, fabric, electronics, and more at **Silk Street Market.**

Shanghai

- A great place to bargain for "antiques" and knick-knacks is the **Dongtai Road Antiques Market** close to the Old City.

- Enliven your wardrobe with some bespoke threads from the **South Bund Fabric Market** with its many booths and tailors.

- Brave the crowds at the **Yu Garden Bazaar** and pick up some "traditional" Chinese fans, chopsticks, and postcards to take home.

Mayumi Sato

garments, try **NuoMi,** a label that uses natural fabrics like cotton and bamboo.

CLOTHES
Beijing

- Witness Beijing's love of all things retro at **Mega Mega Vintage,** where the inventory of leather jackets, knitted sweaters, and accessories are carefully selected.

- Take home an ironically sloganed T-shirt from China's famous **Plastered T-shirts.**

- Treat yourself to a piece of Beijing's high fashion at **candy&caviar,** an innovative brand run by Californian designer Candy Lin.

Shanghai

- **Culture Matters** is the best place to pick up a pair of ever-popular Huili or Feiyue sneakers. They'll even customize your new Huilis for an extra fee.

- **Mayumi Sato** is a boutique whose owner, Mayumi Sato, designs gorgeous, contemporary silk and cotton clothing that typifies cool Shanghai.

- If you're looking to buy some eco-friendly

GIFTS AND SOUVENIRS
Beijing

- Quirky **Old-Toxin Tin Toys** sells reproductions of the toys that every Beijing kid played with before the arrival of plastic action figures.

- Browse handmade items from local designers at **Fengguo Box Store,** where indie designers show their goods in a clear display box.

- Pretty, handcrafted notebooks abound at **Xing Mu's Handicrafts,** made from a special type of paper called "niupi."

Shanghai

- Pick up some kitschy, retro souvenirs like ceramics, propaganda art, and old postcards at **Madame Mao's Dowry.**

- Recycled felt is used to craft **mrkt**'s funky, functional accessories and houseware.

- A different kind of tea shop, **Song Fang Maison de Thé** is run by a French expat, and is famous for its pastel-blue tin caddies.

home-cooked European dishes, then relax with a cocktail at the chic XIU lounge before heading back to your hotel (or the airport, if you've booked a redeye).

Shanghai
FRIDAY

Shanghai is China's economic heart, and its main artery is the area around Lujiazui Street in the Pudong district. Make sure to visit the area's three distinctive skyscrapers, the Oriental Pearl Tower, the Jin Mao Tower, and the Shanghai World Financial Center. Each has impressive viewing decks and observatories for awe-inspiring views (and photographs) of the city.

Enjoy a view of the Huangpu River over an Italian lunch at The Kitchen Salvatore Cuomo, then cross the river into the Bund. A walk down the Bund Promenade will introduce you to Shanghai's iconic architecture: the riverfront is lined with colonial-era customs houses, banking headquarters, and shipping buildings dating from the mid-1800s. Be sure to visit historic Garden Bridge, and stop by Huangpu Park to see the Monument to the People's Heroes, a concrete statue honoring China's revolutionary and political martyrs.

Head to the Cool Docks on the South Bund for dinner with clients at Stiller's, a contemporary restaurant helmed by a German chef. If you've got matters of business still to be discussed, there's no better place to do it than over a drink at the glitzy yet refined Glamour Bar. Turn in for the night at nearby Hotel Indigo for a high-end boutique experience.

SATURDAY

You've got a busy day ahead of you, so grab a coffee and a quick bite from a street-side vendor then head to the Xujiahui neighborhood to check out Pacific Digital Plaza where you'll want to stock up on the latest and greatest electronics. If you need to take a minute to

make some calls and check your email, do it over lunch at Element Fresh. Service here is efficient, so you'll be back to sightseeing in no time.

After lunch, head to People's Square and the Urban Planning Exhibition Hall. You'll be greeted by a large sculpture featuring Shanghai's most prominent architecture; be sure not to miss the three-dimensional model of the city upstairs. Next up is People's Park just down the street, and within it, the Shanghai Museum. Home to over 120,000 relics of Shanghai's history, the museum features bronzes, jade halls, and Ming- and Qing-era furniture.

If you've worked up an appetite, it's time for dinner at Kathleen's 5, which is housed in People's Square's former clubhouse. Have a drink with clients at Barbarossa—with its location inside People's Park, it's known as one of the best-situated nightlife spots in Shanghai. Head back to your room at the Hotel Indigo, or, if you don't want to venture far, check out the simple but impressive Pacific Hotel on West Nanjing Road.

SUNDAY

Make the most of your last day in Shanghai with a Huangpu River Cruise. The boat trip takes you through the city's commercial center and up to the mouth of the Yangtze River. Back on dry land, eat lunch at SUN with AQUA, a Japanese restaurant that features a shark-filled aquarium inside.

After lunch, stretch your legs with a walk up the Bund Promenade toward the grand old hotel with the pyramid-shaped roof. This is the Fairmont Peace Hotel, which began life as the legendary Cathay Hotel. Wander around the Fairmont's lobby and admire the yellow marble floors and the domed glass ceiling.

Cross the Huangpu for dinner amidst stunning modern interior design at Jade on 36. Housed within the Pudong Shangri-La, Jade on 36 offers contemporary

French fare; it's bar is open late, so linger over a drink and admire the views of the city below. Finish off your last night in style at Flair, the place to see and be seen in Shanghai. Head back to your hotel and bid adieu to the city in the morning.

► GOING GREEN: ECO-FRIENDLY FUN

Bike

Explore Beijing by bike, and you'll get to know the city like a local. Rent a bike from Bicycle Kingdom in the center of town and venture out to explore the city on two wheels. Bicycle Kingdom offers tours, as well, so you can get a local's take on the best sights in the city. If you want a bike tour of Beijing, and you also want a little extra boost, check out Beijing eBike Tours, a group that will show you the city via a zero-emissions electric bike.

In Shanghai, it's absurdly easy to rent a bike: Just find one of the orange cycles dotted around the city (a good place to try is the junction of Hunan and West Fuxing Roads), use your credit card for the deposit, and the bike is yours for the day. If you'd like something a little more structured, sign up for a tour of city

with BOHDI Adventures. This tour group offers an assortment of options, including nighttime rides around Shanghai.

Eat

In Beijing, check out Saveurs de Corée for organic, locally sourced Korean food. MSG is banned from the kitchen, so you're guaranteed a delicious, healthy, and environmentally friendly meal.

In Shanghai, Wagas is a great place to go if you're craving a healthy breakfast or lunch. In addition to its healthy sandwich and salad offerings, Wagas promotes sustainability by sourcing its breads and pastries from a nearby bakery. For something a little more upscale, head over to Mr. Willis, which features hearty Western-style fare made with organic and locally sourced ingredients.

bikes parked on the street, Shanghai

URBN Hotel in Shanghai

Play

If you're looking to work up a sweat while visiting Beijing, be sure to book a hike with Dandelion Hiking. This eco-travel hiking company will show you how to travel like a local, lessening your impact on China's environment, as well as take you to some off-the-beaten-path spots outside of Beijing.

Century Park in the Pudong district of Shanghai is a great place to take a bike ride or fly a kite for a few easy hours. Century Park also functions as the city's green lung, with its grass and many trees filtering out carbon dioxide and supplying oxygen to the financial district.

Shop

While you're in Beijing, pop into Shanghai Trio in Sanlitun to browse the selection of upcycled bags and purses. In Shanghai, you'll want to visit NuoMi, a small boutique in the Old French Concession. NuoMi stocks womenswear made from soy, cotton, and bamboo, focusing on sustainable materials.

Another eco-friendly shop in Shanghai is mrkt, which sells items like laptop bags, coasters, and hair accessories, most of which are made of recycled felt. The shop is known for its generous donations to local charities.

Sleep

Eco-conscious travelers in Shanghai will want to stay at URBN Hotel. URBN is China's first carbon-neutral hotel, so a stay here means your vacation's carbon footprint is minimized. It's a small hotel, with only 26 rooms, so it's not another behemoth crowded into downtown Shanghai. URBN also boasts a restaurant that features organic ingredients; even the servers' aprons are made from organic fibers!

BEIJING

SIGHTS

Few cities in Asia have so many iconic historical sights as Beijing. The old city was built around the Forbidden City (named so because it was "forbidden" to all but the emperor and his court), with a series of concentric roads fanning out around it, ringed with gatehouses to prevent attacks from enemy tribes. Under various dynasties, China's capital has moved among different cities throughout the country's history, from Xi'an in the northeast to Nanjing and Hangzhou in the south. Beijing was the capital of the Yuan Dynasty that came down from Mongolia under Kublai Khan. The Yuan-era capital was known as Dadu and was renamed Beijing (meaning "northern capital") when the Ming rose to power in 1368.

As you would expect from a city with such a rich and varied history, Beijing is awash with gorgeous old palaces, temples, and imperial buildings. The most important of these is the Forbidden City, but equally famous is the Summer Palace in the northwest part of downtown Beijing, where the emperor took refuge from the heat of the capital. The Temple of Heaven, where he paid tribute to his ancestors and thanked them for the harvest, is another must-see. The Drum and Bell Towers that lie northeast of the Forbidden City form the epicenter of a bustling nightlife and leisure scene. The three lakes behind the palace complex make up the Houhai area, the banks of which are lined with bars and cafés, spilling over into the *hutong* (alleys) behind.

The 20th century was a period of much political turmoil for China and the vestiges of revolution, civil war, and the era of Communism

© SUSIE GORDON

HIGHLIGHTS

LOOK FOR  TO FIND RECOMMENDED SIGHTS.

Best Historic Sight: Home to many of China's emperors, the **Forbidden City** is the centerpiece of historic Beijing, both physically and metaphorically. Sitting at the very center of the capital, the site is the largest surviving palace complex in China, and a treasure trove of imperial history (page 60).

Most Morbidly Fascinating Sight: See the Great Helmsman in person at the **Mausoleum of Mao Zedong** in Tian'anmen Square, as well as memorial halls for other important Chinese leaders like Deng Xiaoping (page 62).

Most Iconic Sight: Scored into the world's memory thanks to the events of 1989, **Tian'anmen Square** should be on your Beijing itinerary. It's the biggest public plaza in the world, covering 440,000 square meters (page 62).

Best Activity for the Kids: If the children are tired of visiting temples, treat them to an afternoon with the fish at **Blue Zoo Aquarium,** home to Asia's longest observation tunnel, and chock full of vibrant marine life and interactive displays (page 68).

Most Surprising Modern Architecture: Nicknamed the "big underpants" due to its unusual shape, the **New CCTV Tower** is a highlight of Beijing's contemporary skyline (page 68).

Hidden Gem: The **Temple of Wisdom Attained** often slips under visitors' radars, but is worth a visit for its tranquil vibe and original Ming-era wood structure (page 68).

Most Surprising Ancient Architecture: The **Five Pagodas Temple** is a refreshing change from other Buddhist and Daoist worship halls in the city. It was modeled on the "diamond throne" temples of Southeast Asia (page 71).

Best Reprieve: Head out west to the **Summer Palace,** following in the footsteps of the emperors who used the lakeside complex to escape the heat of the city (page 72).

Best Greenery: The lovely **Fragrant Hills Park** sits to the west of Beijing, and is a haven for those in search of some fresh air, open space, and attractive scenery (page 73).

Tian'anmen Square

© SUSIE GORDON

can be seen in more modern historic sites like Tian'anmen Square, the mausoleum of Chairman Mao, and the stark, Soviet-style architecture around town.

In sharp contrast to the older structures are the contemporary office buildings, leisure facilities, and hotels of the Central Business District (CBD), the highlights of which are the oddly shaped CCTV building and the nest-like Olympic Stadium. With so many sights both modern and ancient, a trip to Beijing can easily become an exploration of time itself.

Tian'anmen   Map 1

◖ FORBIDDEN CITY
故宫
4 Jingshan Qianjie, 10/6513-2255
HOURS: Daily Apr. 1-Oct. 14 8:30 A.M.-5 P.M.,
Oct. 15-Mar. 31 8:30 A.M.-4:30 P.M.
COST: ¥60 Apr. 1-Oct. 31, ¥40 Nov. 1-Mar. 31
METRO: Tian'anmen West (Line 1)

Probably the most important historic site in Beijing, the Forbidden City lies right in the center of the modern capital, on a central axis from which the rest of the city fans out. With 980 buildings, it is the largest surviving palace complex in the world, and is listed as a UNESCO World Heritage Site thanks to its great historical importance.

Gugong, as the Forbidden City is known in Mandarin, was home to 24 emperors of the Ming (1368–1644) and Qing (1644–1912) Dynasties. Since the emperor was believed to be descended from gods, his palace was strictly out of bounds to the common people, and thus "forbidden." It was also known as the Purple Palace to link it with Polaris, which was known as the purple star and considered to be the center of heaven. The palace complex was built by an estimated one million laborers (many of whom were forced into the work), starting in 1406 and finishing in 1420 during the reign of Yongle, the second emperor of the Ming Dynasty. Yongle's father, the Hongwu Emperor, had burned down the palaces of the defeated Mongol Yuan Dynasty (1271–1368) and moved his capital to Nanjing for a fresh start, but Yongle brought it back to Beijing and decreed that a great palace complex be built on the site of the Yuan court.

The Forbidden City's low roofs and ochre buildings sprawl over 720,000 square meters (7.7 million sq. ft.); their yellow-topped roof tiles symbolize royalty. Only the imperial library has a black roof, signifying the water that would extinguish any fire that threatened the royal books inside.

The Forbidden City is divided into two main sections. The southerly **Outer Court** contains the rooms from which the emperor ruled, while the northerly **Inner Court** was where the royal family lived. It is open to the public as the **Palace Museum** and contains much of its original decoration, although part of the collection was relocated to the National Palace Museum in Taipei after the Communist Revolution.

Enter the palace complex through the **Meridien Gate,** after crossing the 52-meter-wide (171 ft.) moat that separates it from the rest of the city. The gate is also known as the Five Phoenix Tower, and leads onto the marble **Inner Golden Water Bridges** that take you over a small stretch of water towards the **Hall of Supreme Harmony.** The hall is guarded by the **Gate of Supreme Harmony** with its fearsome bronze lions, and is the first of the three halls in the Outer Court. The largest of the three, this building has the Hall of Martial Valor to its southwest and the Imperial Library and Hall of Literary Prowess to its southeast, where crown princes studied. Heading north you'll come to the smaller Hall of Central Harmony where the emperor rested on his way to conduct official business in the Hall of Supreme Harmony. Next is the **Hall of Preserving Harmony**—the final building of the Inner Court—where banquets were held and imperial examinations were supervised by the emperor.

The Inner Court is accessed by the **Gate of Heavenly Purity,** leading to three halls on a central axis that mirror the trio in the Outer Court but are smaller. The **Palace of Heavenly Purity** once contained the bedroom of the emperor, and was the place where he held banquets and official meetings. The **Hall of Celestial and Terrestrial Union** was where the empress received and greeted the royal concubines, and her bedroom was known as the **Palace of Earthly Tranquility.** Behind the palace lies the **Imperial Garden,** echoing the style of the great classical gardens of south China with pavilions, rock formations, pools, and foliage. Its main structure is the **Hall of Imperial Peace.**

On either side of the Hall of Imperial Peace are the **Six Eastern Palaces** and **Six Western Palaces** that made up the living quarters of the emperor's concubines. Each palace has its own courtyard, front and rear halls, and annexes for sleeping. Many of the original furnishings remain. The Six Eastern Palaces now contain displays of art and craftwork from the Ming and Qing Dynasties. Below the Eastern Palaces are the **Hall of Ancestry Worship** and the **Palace of Abstinence,** where the emperor would spend several days before offering sacrifices at the Temple of Heaven and the Temple of the Earth. To the south of the Western Palaces is the **Hall of Mental Cultivation** where state business was carried out.

Head east from the back of the Hall of Ancestry Worship and you'll reach the Outer East Wing through the Gate of Great Fortune and Xiqing Gate. This wing was built for the retirement of the Qing emperor Qianlong (1735–1796), and contains some beautiful halls, chambers, and pavilions, as well as the decorative **Nine Dragons Screen.** Behind the Imperial Garden is the Gate of Spiritual Valor which leads across the moat and out of the palace complex.

The Forbidden City was home to 14 Ming and 10 Qing emperors. With the end of the Qing Dynasty in 1912, the Forbidden City stopped being used as a palace. Puyi, the last emperor, abdicated from the throne as the Xinhai Revolution gathered steam, but was allowed to stay in the Inner Court. The outer part of the Forbidden City was taken over, and the whole of the City was turned into the Palace Museum in 1925 after Puyi was finally evicted. After the Japanese invasion of 1933, much of the palace treasure was removed; some treasure remains in Taiwan, while the rest is part of the Palace Museum collection and can be seen in the Forbidden City today.

The complex suffered minor damage after the Communists came to power in 1949 and was threatened during the Cultural Revolution (1966–1976) until Premier Zhou Enlai sent guards to protect it. The Forbidden City became a UNESCO World Heritage Site in 1987, and so has escaped the fate that befell most of Beijing's old city gates. A Starbucks was opened on the site in 2000, but closed seven years later after complaints of commercialization.

There is a lot to see in the Forbidden City, so it's a good idea to devote at least a morning or afternoon to visiting (if not more). It's most sensible to go first thing in the morning so you have the whole day to explore.

GREAT HALL OF THE PEOPLE
人民大会堂

Tian'anmen Square

HOURS: Dec.-Mar. daily 9 A.M.-2 P.M., Apr.-June daily 8:15 A.M.-3 P.M., July-Aug. daily 7:30 A.M.-4 P.M., Sept.-Nov. daily 8:30 A.M.-3 P.M.

COST: ¥30 adults, ¥15 students

METRO: Tian'anmen West (Line 1)

This imposing edifice on Tian'anmen Square was one of the 10 buildings constructed to mark the 10th anniversary of the founding of the People's Republic. It opened in September 1959 after 10 months of work by volunteers. Covering over 170,000 square meters (1.8 million sq. ft.), the hall is used for Communist Party ceremonies, state banquets, and meetings of the PRC parliament. It is the largest complex of halls in the world, even bigger than the Forbidden City. These halls include the Great Auditorium, Central Hall, Golden Hall, and Congress Hall, as well as a room for each Chinese province. The State Banquet

Hall can hold up to 7,000 guests, and reached its full capacity when Nixon visited in 1972. Look out for the red star detailing on the ceiling of the Great Auditorium.

◖ MAUSOLEUM OF MAO ZEDONG
毛主席纪念堂

Tian'anmen Square

HOURS: Tues.-Sun. 8 A.M.-noon, Sept. 9 and Dec. 26 8 A.M.-11 A.M., 2-4 P.M.

COST: Free

METRO: Qianmen (Line 2)

The body of the Great Helmsman lies in permanent state at this mausoleum on People's Square, despite his lifelong desire to be cremated. The mausoleum was begun after Mao's death in September 1976 and opened on May 24, 1977, by his successor, Hua Guofeng. The edifice is a true work of art, made from Sichuan granite, Guangdong porcelain, Shaanxi pinewood, quartz from the Kunlun mountains, and even a rock from Mount Everest. The addition of water and sand from the Taiwan Straits makes a clear political statement. Mao's preserved body lies inside a crystal coffin that took an unimaginable amount of wrangling to construct. Thankfully, it is earthquake-proof. The mausoleum's 2nd floor contains memorial halls to other political veterans like Deng Xiaoping and Zhou Enlai.

◖ TIAN'ANMEN SQUARE
天安门广场

Central Beijing, south of Chang'an Jie

HOURS: Daily 24 hours

COST: Free

METRO: Tian'anmen West or Tian'anmen East (Line 1)

Tian'anmen Square is etched in world history due to the events that unfolded in June of 1989, the effects of which are felt across China to this day. Located just south of the Forbidden City, Tian'anmen is the largest public plaza in the world with an area of 440,000 square meters (4.7 million sq. ft.). It sits between the Forbidden City's ancient Tian'anmen (Gate of Heavenly Peace) to the north, and Qianmen (Front Gate) to the south, and contains the Monument to the People's Heroes and Mao's

Mausoleum, as well as the Great Hall of the People and the National Museum. It was from the square that Chairman Mao announced the birth of the People's Republic on October 1, 1949. His image now looks out over the plaza from the south wall of the Forbidden City.

There has been a square here since 1651, but it only reached its current dimensions (around four times the size of the original) in the 1950s. It has been the site of many political events, including the anti-Imperialist May Fourth Movement of 1919, during which nationalist rallies and uprisings took place to protest against China's flimsy response to the Treaty of Versailles. Further protests happened in 1976 after the death of Premier Zhou Enlai, but the most infamous were the rallies that ended in tragedy and loss of life in the summer of 1989.

The events leading up to the massacre on June 4, 1989, began on April 15 with the death of former Communist Party official Hu Yaobang. Students and political protesters began to gather and strike, occupying Tian'anmen Square to air their dissatisfaction and call for democracy and economic reform. Prime Minister Li Peng declared a state of martial law on May 20, backing military action to remove the protestors and end the unrest. On June 4, tanks operated by the People's Liberation Army moved into Tian'anmen Square, shooting indiscriminately until the area was clear of dissenters. No one knows for sure how many people lost their lives; the figures range from 400 to tens of thousands.

Many people in the West associate the Tian'anmen Square incident with a poignant image of a man standing in front of a line of tanks. The photograph of "Tank Man," or the Unknown Rebel, was actually taken on June 5, the morning after the massacre. He halted the tanks' progress out of the square before being removed, unhurt, from their path. It is not known what became of the man. The events of June 4 (known as Liu Si Shijian in Mandarin) changed the course of modern Chinese history, auguring an age of strict state control and censorship of the media.

Tian'anmen Square is a requirement for any

Beijing itinerary, and an appropriate starting point for a day of sightseeing. Be prepared for a bag search coming up from the Metro, and tightened security around the anniversary of the June 4 incident.

WORKERS' CULTURAL PALACE
劳动人民文化宫

Southeast corner of Forbidden City,
outside of the moat
HOURS: Daily 6:30 A.M.-7:30 P.M.
COST: ¥2
METRO: Tian'anmen East (Line 1)

Rarely visited by Tian'anmen tourists, the Workers' Cultural Palace is actually well worth a look. Its name is misleading; it's not a palace, but the site of the imperial Great Temple (Tai Miao), which was designated as a place of cultural enrichment by the government in 1951. A sign in Chairman Mao's handwriting welcomes guests into the compound. It is far less crowded than the nearby Forbidden City, but shares its red walls and yellow roof tiles. The central walled section is ringed by a moat spanned by seven stone bridges. Marble steps lead up to the Hall of Worshiping Ancestors. Quieter than the Forbidden City, it's a good introduction to Beijing's imperial architecture. Unfortunately, the three halls (Front, Middle, and Rear) are not open to the public. Fortunately, the site is worth visiting just to see their elaborately decorated exteriors. The Great Temple is accessible, and its large, traditionally decorated halls are a welcome retreat from the city's hum.

Houhai

Map 2

CONFUCIUS TEMPLE
孔庙

15 Guozijian Jie
HOURS: Tues.-Sun. 9 A.M.-5 P.M.
(last ticket sold at 4:30 P.M.)
COST: ¥20
METRO: Yonghegong (Line 2, Line 5)

Confucius is one of the most important figures in Chinese history and his teachings still hold sway over the modern psyche. Confucius was a sage and philosopher who was alive during the Spring and Autumn Period, between 551 and 479 B.C. His philosophies are known as Rujia or Confucianism and focus on the correct ways to behave both personally and within a society. Dating from 1302, Beijing's Confucius Temple is split into two parts. The temple itself is devoted to the worship of Confucius (the Kong Miao) and the old imperial academy (Guozijian), where the highest rank of civil servants were trained. The temple is the second largest of its kind in China, and was used throughout the Yuan, Ming, and Qing Dynasties to pay tribute to Confucius. The temple complex covers 22,000 square meters (236,800 sq. ft.) and includes four courtyards, gates, and halls. The atmosphere is one of quiet contemplation, but the architecture is vibrant. Particularly attractive is the three-arched gate and the stone statue of Confucius with its enigmatic smile. Also of interest is the 700-year-old Chujian Bai, or "Evil Touching Cypress," which apparently knocked the hat off a Ming official who was later discovered to be unscrupulous. In the first courtyard, look out for the 198 stone tablets carved with the 51,624 names of scholars who passed the highest imperial exams during the Yuan, Ming, and Qing Dynasties.

DRUM AND BELL TOWERS
鼓楼 钟楼

41 Zhongwan Hutong, off Gulou Dajie
HOURS: Daily 9 A.M.-5 P.M.
COST: Drum Tower: ¥20, Bell Tower: ¥15
METRO: Guloudajie (Line 2)

Standing out above the low roofs north of the Forbidden City, the Drum and Bell Towers sit on the city's northern axis. They date from 1272 in the reign of Kublai Khan when Beijing was known as Dadu, capital of the Yuan Empire. The Yongle Emperor of the Ming Dynasty moved the towers east of their original site in 1420, and they underwent further

NINE MILLION BICYCLES

In 2005, singer Katie Melua released a song called "Nine Million Bicycles," which was said to be based on the number of bikes in Beijing at that time. The famous song lyrics are probably out of date now – the truer figure is closer to 10 million. No matter the exact number, Beijing's favorite mode of transportation is clearly the humble bicycle. Although the capital has a reputation for bad traffic and an interesting interpretation of road laws, getting around by bike is relatively quick and safe. The layout of the city and its flat topography make it ideal for cycling, and most streets and boulevards have dedicated bike lanes. The traditional *hutong* (alleys) are best seen from the saddle of your bike, anyway.

If you decide to rent or buy a bike (decent models can be picked up at local shops for a few hundred yuan, and many hostels and hotels offer rentals), make sure you get at least two strong locks, as well as a helmet. Few Beijing cyclists use helmets, but accidents can (and do) easily happen, so it's better to be safe than sorry. Theft is rife: Try and lock your bike to a post or fence to deter thieves. If you get a flat, head to one of the repair shops located on almost every road.

renovations in 1800. Originally instruments of time keeping, the drum and bell fell silent for many years after the last emperor, Puyi, finally left the Forbidden City in 1924. The Drum Tower is now used to tell the time again, and both towers are open to the public.

HOUHAI
后海
Part of Shichahai Lake complex
HOURS: Daily 24 hours
COST: Free
METRO: Guloudajie (Line 2)

Houhai, or Back Lake, is the largest section of the Shichahai complex, sitting between Qianhai to the south, and Xihai to the north. The shores of the lake are lined with bars and clubs, but its days at the fashionable end of the nightlife spectrum are behind it. Aside from a handful of venues, most of Houhai's drinking establishments veer on the side of tacky. However, the lake is still worth visiting in the daytime to rent a pedal boat or take a walk. On weekends crowds gravitate to the lakeside paths, but weekday mornings and afternoons are more peaceful. With willow trees, lilypads, and other flora, Houhai is a pleasant green spot in the city center. The *hutong* (alleys) fanning out from the lakeside are worth exploring too, as they are filled with cafés and restaurants.

The Shichahai Lake complex is part of an ancient route that was used to transport grain from the Grand Canal to the Forbidden City. According to local legend, the Qianlong Emperor liked to stand on Yinding Bridge and admire the view of the distant Western Hills.

LAMA TEMPLE
雍和宫
12 Yonghegong Dajie, 10/6404-3769
HOURS: Daily 9 A.M.-4 P.M.
COST: ¥25
METRO: Yonghegong (Line 2, Line 5)

Also known as the Yonghe Lamasery, this beautiful temple is the home of the Geluk School of Tibetan Buddhism. It consists of five main halls built on an axis connected by courtyards, and contains a selection of erotic sculptures and murals as well as several golden Buddhas. Today the Lama Temple is an important Buddhist landmark, but it was originally built as a residence for imperial eunuchs of the early Qing Dynasty. It later became the court of Prince Yong, the son of the Kangxi Emperor. When Yong succeeded his father in 1722, he gave half of the building over to the lamas. The Qianlong Emperor took over in 1735 and turned the whole building into an imperial temple, adding the requisite yellow roof tiles. Zhou Enlai saved the temple from destruction during the Cultural Revolution.

Qianmen

Map 3

FAYUAN TEMPLE
法源寺

7 Fayuan Si Qianjie, 10/6317-2150

HOURS: Thurs.-Tues. 8:30-11A.M., 1:30-4P.M.

COST: ¥5

METRO: Caishikou (Line 4)

Quieter and less tourist-packed than many of Beijing's temples, Fayuan is one of the most important Buddhist centers in Beijing. It was built in 645 by the Tang emperor Li Shimin, and renovated in the early Ming era to cover 6,700 square meters (72,000 sq. ft.). It is home to Ming and Qing Buddhist texts, as well as relics, bronzes, stone lions, and three golden Buddhas. Through the main gate is the Hall of Heavenly Kings, a hall containing prayer sutras, Bell and Drum Towers (similar to the ones in the Gulou district that served the Forbidden City), and a centuries-old gingko tree. The temple was built to honor the memory of loyal soldiers who died in battle, and was originally named Chongfu Si (Temple of Exalted Happiness). It was renamed Fayuan in 1734, which means "source of dharma."

LEGATION QUARTER
东交民巷

Directly east of Tian'anmen Square

HOURS: Daily 24 hours

COST: Free

METRO: Qianmen (Line 2)

East of Tian'anmen Square lies Beijing's Legation Quarter, which held the offices of foreign diplomats between 1861 and 1959. Today the area is dominated by the Chi'enmen 23 complex—a large courtyard of striking colonial-era buildings that were converted into high-end restaurants, galleries, and events spaces. During the Yuan Dynasty, the area was known as East River Rice Lane since it was close to the river port where grain imports arrived from the south of China. Tax offices and customs houses sprang up, and the area began to attract foreign legations (a diplomatic office lower than an embassy) after the second

Opium War in 1860. The quarter was badly damaged in the Boxer Rebellion, but many structures remain. Buildings of particular note include St. Michael's Catholic Church, the Belgian embassy, and the French post office.

MING CITY WALL RUINS PARK
明城墙遗址公园

Chongwenmen Dongdajie, 10/6527-0574

HOURS: Mon.-Fri. 9A.M.-2P.M.

COST: Free

METRO: Chongwenmen (Line 2)

During the Ming Dynasty, Beijing was ringed by a series of walls to keep out intruders. They were built in 1419 during the reign of the Yongle Emperor. The four fortifications were the Forbidden City Wall, Imperial City Wall, and Inner and Outer City Walls. Little still exists of this 140-kilometer (87 mi.) system, except for short stretches of the Inner City Wall at the Huangchenggen Relic Park, and the Ming City Wall Ruins Park. The latter is 70 square kilometers (27 sq. mi.) of lawns, trees, and flowers, and was landscaped in 2002. Rarely busy, it is a great way to see the old city wall while enjoying some inner-city nature in a district that is mainly smog-choked boulevards.

OX STREET MOSQUE
牛街清真寺

88 Niu Jie, 10/6353-2564

HOURS: Daily 8A.M.-4P.M. (avoid Fridays)

COST: ¥10

METRO: Changchunjie (Line 2)

Islam was introduced to China during the Tang Dynasty (A.D. 618–907) and has followers among the Uighur, Hui, and Uzbekh minority groups. Beijing has around 80 mosques, and the most beautiful and interesting is the one on Ox Street. It sits at the center of a Muslim community numbering over 10,000, and is one of northern China's most important places of Islamic worship. The mosque looks typically Chinese from the outside; it's only once you get inside that you notice the Muslim-style decoration. The building dates from A.D. 996 in the Liao Dynasty, but was made to look Chinese in the reign of the Qing Dynasty's Kangxi Emperor (1661–1722). Prayer rooms are closed to non-Muslims, and modest dress is required. Look out for the 300-year-old handwritten Koran.

QIANMEN
前门

Directly south of Tian'anmen Square
HOURS: Daily 8:30 A.M.–4 P.M.
COST: ¥20 Apr.-Oct., ¥10 Nov.-Mar.
METRO: Qianmen (Line 2)

Sitting on the city's north-south axis, Qianmen (meaning "front gate") was used by the emperor when he visited the Temple of Heaven to perform rituals during the winter solstice and first lunar month. The gate was built in 1419 during the Ming Dynasty, and was known as Zhengyangmen, or "the gate facing the sun." At 42 meters (138 ft.) high, it was the tallest gate along the city walls. It survived the 1960s cull of city gates, during which Deshengmen and Dongbianmen were torn down. Along with the archery tower (which is closed to the public), Qianmen formed a barbican to scare off would-be intruders to the imperial city. The gate suffered damage during the Boxer Rebellion, and was occupied by the People's Liberation Army in 1949. Today it forms an imposing backdrop to the newly renovated Qianmen shopping street, and is a beautiful example of Ming architecture. Inside the watchtower is a museum tracing Beijing's history and folk customs.

SOUTH CHURCH
南堂

141 Qianmen Xidajie, 10/6602-6538
HOURS: English mass Sun. 10:30 A.M. and 7 P.M., Chinese mass throughout the week
COST: Free
METRO: Qianmen (Line 2)

Also known as Nantang, Xuanwu Church, and the Cathedral of the Immaculate Conception, this baroque church is the diocesan cathedral of Beijing. It dates from 1904 and holds masses

in English, Latin, and Mandarin. With a beautiful cupola at one end and an imposing front, the cathedral is one of the most interesting pieces of architecture in the capital. Inside, an aisle leads past stone pillars up to an altar below a domed ceiling. The wall behind the altar is dominated by an image of the Virgin Mary. The austere stone-fronted building was built to replace the original, which was destroyed in the Boxer Rebellion. Italian Jesuit Matteo Ricci had established a chapel on the site in 1605 when the Ming emperor Wanli granted him residence nearby. The chapel grew into a thriving church and was expanded in 1650. The cathedral saw the installation of Joseph Li Shan in 2007, the only bishop to be approved by both the Vatican and the Chinese Patriotic Catholic Church.

SOUTHEAST WATCHTOWER
东南角楼

Chongwenmen Dongdajie, 10/8512-1554
HOURS: Daily 9 A.M.–5 P.M.
COST: Free
METRO: Chongwenmen (Line 2)

This early Ming watchtower dates from 1436 and sits on a surviving section of the old city wall. Its double-eaved roof rises 30 meters (98 ft.) higher than the actual wall. It is the largest remaining corner tower of all of China's ancient walls, and a small museum inside explains its history. It was captured in 1900 during the Boxer Rebellion, but survived the attack. Look for the Railway Arch cut into the wall; it was carved in 1915 for the railway that connected to Xizhimen, Chaoyanmen, Andingmen, and Deshengmen gates. Today, modern trains can be seen pulling into Beijing Station from the tower's ramparts. The lower floors house the Red Gate contemporary art gallery.

TEMPLE OF HEAVEN
天坛

Yongdingmen Dajie, 10/6702-8866
HOURS: Park: Daily 5 A.M.–9 P.M.; Temple: Daily 8 A.M.–5:30 P.M.
COST: ¥35 Apr. 1-Oct. 31, ¥30 Nov. 1-Mar. 31
METRO: Tiantandongmen (Line 5)

© SUSIE GORDON

Temple of Heaven

The beautiful Temple of Heaven sits inside 2.7 million square meters (29 million sq. ft.) of parkland, and was used by the rulers of Imperial China to pray for a good harvest. The complex was completed in 1420 in the reign of the Ming Dynasty's Yongle Emperor. It was originally one of four sacrificial temples in Beijing along with the Temples of the Sun, Moon, and Earth, and was the most important. The northern part of the temple compound is semicircular to symbolize the heavens, and the southern part is square to represent the earth. This follows the traditional Chinese principle that the earth is square and heaven is round. The number nine appears regularly in the design of the temple, as this was the number of the emperor.

The temple's buildings are split into three main compounds. The first is the most recognizable and striking. The triple-gabled **Hall of Prayer for Good Harvests** with its blue tiled roof and decorated walls is one of Beijing's most iconic structures. It stands 38 meters (125 ft.) high on a marble plinth, and is adorned both inside and out with vibrant red, blue, green, and yellow patterns. This is where the emperors made offerings to the harvest gods at the winter solstice. The Hall's interior is dominated by 28 columns. The innermost 4 columns symbolize the seasons, while the middle 12 stand for the months of the year. The 12 columns that form the outer ring represent the 12 *shichen* (the ancient method of measuring time). Outside, the roofs are covered with tiles glazed in black, yellow, and green to symbolize heaven, earth, and earth's creations. The original Hall of Prayer for Good Harvests was struck by lightening and burned down in 1889, but an identical replacement was built a year later. No nails were used in construction in accordance with traditional rules of architecture.

Behind the Hall of Prayer for Good Harvests, connected by the **Bridge of Vermilion Steps** (also known as Sacred Way), is the **Imperial Vault of Heaven,** which is smaller and resembles the uppermost gable of the larger hall. The Vault is surrounded by the Echo Wall, which magnifies sound. In imperial times, it amplified the emperor's prayers, helping them reach the heavens. The **Three Echo Stones** stand outside the Imperial Vault. Stand on the first stone and speak in the direction of the vault and you will hear one echo; stand on the second and third, and you will hear two and then three echoes.

Behind the Imperial Vault of Heaven is the white **Circular Mound Altar** where bulls were sacrificed and burned. This ceremony has its roots in early civilization, when sacrifices were made to Shangdi, the creator god. The emperor was held to be the son of heaven, with a bloodline traceable to the deities. Predating Daoism, it was a bloody rite that was ended when Imperial China gave way to the revolutionaries in 1911.

The vast parkland surrounding the temple buildings is a popular place for Beijingers to exercise, socialize, and relax. Wide lawns and paths lined with trees make it a tranquil spot to spend some time after exploring the buildings.

SIGHTS

Chaoyang, the Central Business District, and Sanlitun   Map 4

◖ BLUE ZOO AQUARIUM
北京工体富国海底世界

South Gate of Workers' Stadium, 10/6591-3397,
www.blue-zoo.com

HOURS: Winter daily 8:30 A.M.-6:30 P.M.,
summer daily 8 A.M.-8 P.M.

COST: ¥75 adults, ¥50 children under 12; children
under 1 meter (39 in.) tall free

METRO: Chaoyangmen (Line 2)

Especially fun for children, and great for adults
in need of a change of scenery, the Blue Zoo
was one of the first walkthrough aquariums in
China. It was opened in 1997 by Jim Bolger,
then–Prime Minister of New Zealand, during
a visit to Beijing, and is the largest and most
comprehensive of its kind in Asia. In addition
to its 110-meter-long (360 ft.) acrylic viewing
tunnel, Blue Zoo is home to an artificial eco-
system containing 3.5 million liters (924,600
gal.) of salt water, plus 18 other tanks containing over 6,000 species from every possible
aquatic environment: oceans, rivers, estuaries,
mangroves, and tidal basins. Feeding time happens twice a day.

DONGYUE TEMPLE
东岳庙

141 Chaoyangmenwai Dajie, 10/6551-0151

HOURS: Tues.-Sun. 8:30 A.M.-4:30 P.M.

COST: ¥10

METRO: Chaoyangmen (Line 2)

Not one of Beijing's most visited temples, but
definitely one of its more sinister, thanks to its
ghost and spirit statues, the Dongyue Temple
is named to honor Mount Tai in Shandong
Province—the easternmost holy mountain of
Daoism (*dongyue* means eastern peak). Built
during the Yuan Dynasty in 1319, Dongyue
is the largest temple of the Zhengdi sect. It
contains three halls (Yude, Daizongbao, and
Yuguang) and 376 rooms, many containing
life-sized plaster statues of ghosts, spirits, and
animal deities used in ancestor worship. The
statues are arranged into the "departments" of
the Daoist afterlife. Some of the most macabre

are to be found in the rooms relating to hell and
death, like the evocatively named Department
for Implementing 15 Kinds of Violent Death.
When the temple was originally reopened to
the public in 1995, it was given the moniker
Beijing Folk Customs Museum thanks to the
richness of its Daoist artifacts. The stone "forest" on either side of the main hall contains
hundreds of standing tablets carved with the
temple's history. As you walk up to the temple,
you'll pass walls covered in red prayer charms
affixed by worshippers. The Dongyue complex is in good condition, having undergone
its most recent renovation in 2002.

◖ NEW CCTV TOWER
中央电视台总部大楼

Guanghua Bridge, Dongsanhuan Zhonglu

HOURS: Interior closed to the public

METRO: Guanghua Road (Line)

Not to be confused with the needle-like com-
munications tower on the other side of town
that's also called the CCTV Tower, the New
CCTV Tower is one of the city's most striking buildings. Nicknamed "big underpants"
thanks to its unusual shape, the building was
finished in early 2008 after four years of construction. It was designed by Rem Koolhas
and Ole Scheeren of OMA, and engineered by
Arup. Its unusual design took logistical skill to
execute, such as joining the two towers early in
the morning before the steel had a chance to
swell. A fire gutted the annex containing the
Mandarin Oriental Hotel during Chinese New
Year 2009, and the main building is mostly
unoccupied, awaiting tenancy from China
Central TV. Although entry to the tower is
prohibited, it's worth visiting for some great
photo opportunities.

◖ TEMPLE OF WISDOM ATTAINED
智化寺

5 Lumicang Hutong, Chaoyangmen Nanxiaojie,
10/6525-0072

HOURS: Daily 8:30 A.M.-4:30 P.M.

COST: ¥20
METRO: Chaoyangmen (Line 2)

Known as Zhihua Si in Mandarin, this temple sits behind a low red wall on Lumicang Hutong. A Buddhist temple, it was commissioned by Ming Dynasty eunuch Wang Zhen as an ancestral hall in 1443 during the reign of the Yingzhong Emperor. It is the only wooden building complex to survive from the Ming era and was declared a cultural relic in 1961. Inside the main gate is a series of halls and pavilions, the most impressive of which is the Tathagata

Hall, containing a statue of Tathagata (the name Buddha used to refer to himself), and 9,999 statues in niches on the walls of the 2nd floor. Also interesting are the rare black roof tiles and the 400-ton wooden Tripitaka cabinet containing Buddhist sutras in Chinese. The 20,000-square-meter (215,000 sq. ft.) temple compound contains the Beijing Cultural Exchange Museum, which opened in 1992. Living at the temple is a group of monk musicians: its six members come from 27 generations of players. The monks perform regularly.

Capital Museum and the Temple of Great Charity   Map 5

BEIJING PLANETARIUM
北京天文馆新馆
138 Xizhimenwai Dajie, 10/6835-2453, www.bjp.org.cn
HOURS: Wed.-Sun. 10 A.M.-4 P.M.
COST: ¥15 adults, ¥10 children
METRO: Xizhimen (Line 2, Line 4, Line 13)

If you feel like a change of scenery from Beijing's temples and museums, try its planetarium. When Building A was opened in 1957 it was the first major planetarium in China and the only one in Asia for a considerable length of time. It contains the Celestial Theater and two exhibition halls that feature both permanent and rotating educational displays about the solar system and the history of astronomy. Building B followed more recently, and is home to 3- and 4-D theaters with Carl Zeiss laser projectors, as well as two observatories. The three-dimensional shuttle simulator is an exhilarating experience. The commentary is mainly in Chinese, but the visuals are compelling enough for it not to matter.

FINANCIAL STREET
北京金融街
Jinrong Jie
HOURS: Daily 24 hours
METRO: Fuchengmen (Line 2)

The 35 blocks of modern high-rise office buildings along Jinrong Street make up Beijing's Financial Street. Its origins as a commercial thoroughfare go back to the Yuan

Dynasty, when banks and gold shops flourished. At the start of the People's Republic in 1949, the old Bank of the Qing Dynasty was renamed Bank of China, and other financial establishments began to spring up around it. Today, an average of ¥10 billion flows through Financial Street every day, and its offices are home to Fortune 500 companies. As well as domestic corporations like People's Bank of China and CITIC, international firms such as Goldman Sachs, UBS, and JP Morgan have offices here. The street features a contemporary twist on traditional courtyard architecture, dreamed up by Skidmore, Owings, and Merrill along with SWA landscape architects. As well as offices, Financial Street is home to some excellent restaurants and bars, and is a refreshing contrast to the more ancient parts of Beijing.

TEMPLE OF ANCIENT MONARCHS
历代帝王庙
131 Fuchengmennei Dajie, 10/6612-0186
HOURS: Daily 9 A.M.-4:30 P.M.
COST: ¥20
METRO: Fuchengmen (Line 2)

Built on the site of an old Buddhist temple, this compound was constructed in 1530 for the Ming emperors to worship their ancestors. When it was first built, it had three marble bridges and a wooden memorial arch, but all were destroyed during anti-feudal raids in the 1950s. Further damage was wrought during the Cultural Revolution, but there is still plenty to see. Among the most interesting are the memorial tablets left by emperors down the ages. Be careful not to be conned into paying ¥60 when you go in, unless you want an English-speaking guide, which really isn't necessary.

TEMPLE OF GREAT CHARITY
广济寺
25 Fuchengmennei Dajie, 10/6616-0907
HOURS: Daily 8:30 A.M.–5:30 P.M.
COST: Free
METRO: Xisi (Line 4)

This attractive temple is the headquarters of the Chinese Buddhist Association, and one of the most important places of Buddhist worship in Beijing. It was originally built during the Jin Dynasty (1115–1234), with additions from famous historical architect Liu Wangyu. The temple that stands today dates from the Ming Dynasty under the rule of the Tianshan Emperor between 1457 and 1464. Following traditional Buddhist temple layout, it contains a Hall of the Heavenly Kings, Sutra Hall, and Bell and Drum Towers behind a main gate.

The Sutra Hall is home to over 100,000 volumes of Buddhist scripture as well as Ming-era relics. Look out for the wall of 18 Arhat statues.

WHITE DAGOBA TEMPLE
白塔寺
171 Fuchengmennei Dajie, 10/6616-0211
HOURS: Daily 9 A.M.–5 P.M. (last ticket sold at 4:30 P.M.)
COST: ¥20; free on Wed.
METRO: Fuchengmen (Line 2)

A landmark of this area, this temple's striking white dagoba rises 51 meters (167 ft.) above the low roofs surrounding it. The temple's official name is Miaoying, meaning divine retribution, and the dagoba dates from 1279, in the reign of Kublai Khan in the Yuan Dynasty, when Beijing was known as Dadu. It was designed by the Nepalese architect Arniko, and is topped by a corona containing wind chimes and bells to ward off evil spirits. The dagoba was damaged in the Tangshan earthquake of 1976 and rebuilt two years later. The temple survived the Cultural Revolution at the behest of premier Zhou Enlai. Aside from the dagoba, highlights include the Hall of the Enlightened ones, and a statue of Arniko.

LIFE DOWN THE LANES

When the Forbidden City was built at the start of the 15th century, Beijing's non-aristocratic residents lived around the palace complex in a series of lanes and alleys called *hutong*. The name derives from the Mongolian word for water well, and each *hutong* contained a collection of courtyard residences known as *siheyuan*. The *hutong* of the upper classes were built to the east and west of the Forbidden City, and were elaborate, well-kept complexes with landscaped gardens. Humbler folks, like merchants and laborers, lived to the north and south. Their *hutong* were simpler and not as well tended. Since the *siheyuan* were built facing south to catch the sun, most *hutong* ran from east to west.

When the Qing Dynasty fell to the republicans in 1911, the *hutong* network was expanded. The newer compounds were built with less care, and existing lanes fell into disrepair. By the end of the Qing era there were 978 *hutong*; by 1949 the number rose to 1,330. Many were torn down and replaced by state buildings when the Communists came to power, and the destruction continues to the present day. Despite many heartfelt plans and protests, a huge number of Beijing's *hutong* neighborhoods have been destroyed. However, there are still plenty to see, especially around the Drum and Bell Towers to the northeast of the Forbidden City. Some have become hip neighborhoods in their own right, attracting bars, cafés, and shops, such as Nanluoguxiang, off East Gulou Avenue in the Houhai District.

University District and the Summer Palace   Map 5

◖ FIVE PAGODAS TEMPLE

五塔寺

24 Wutasi Cun, on Changhe River, 10/6217-6058

HOURS: Tues.-Sun. 9 A.M.-4:30 P.M.

COST: ¥20

METRO: National Library (Line 4)

Different from the traditional Beijing temple architecture that characterizes many of the capital's places of worship, the style of the Five Pagodas Temple (Wuta Si) follows Southeast Asian models and looks more Indian or Thai than Chinese. It used to sit far out in the western suburbs until the city encroached and included the temple in its spread. Built in the diamond throne style, or vajrasana, the Ming-era temple was finished in 1473 using plans drawn up by an Indian monk who donated five golden Buddha statues to the emperor. Its bluestone bricks and five towers give it an exotic air with a central pagoda surrounded by four smaller versions. Each of the pagodas is richly decorated with Buddha figures, Sanskrit verses, and bodhi trees; together, the five pagodas represent the five "directions" of the Buddha. The parkland around the temple is peaceful enough to make you forget you're in a capital city. Check out the on-site Museum of Stone Carvings, which displays over 2,000 pieces of (you guessed it) carved stone.

GREAT BELL TEMPLE

大钟寺

31A Beisanhuan Xilu, 10/6255-0819

HOURS: Tues.-Sun. 8:30 A.M.-4:30 P.M.
(last ticket sold at 4 P.M.)

COST: ¥10, plus an extra ¥2 to climb the tower

METRO: Dazhongsi (Line 13)

Named for its giant 46-ton Ming Dynasty bell, this Buddhist temple makes for an interesting excursion. Although the famous bell tolls just once a year (albeit 108 times, and at 120 decibels) to usher in the New Year, there is plenty to see, like the bell itself (located in the rear hall, and carved with 227,000 Sanskrit and Chinese symbols) and a museum full of smaller bells from all around Beijing and the rest of China. The main bell is older than the temple. It was cast during the reign of Ming emperor Yongle (1403–1424) and was brought to the temple during the winter of 1743 on a series of ice sledges. The temple was built in the era of Emperor Yongzheng of Qing in 1733 as the Juesheng Si (Temple of Awakened Life).

OLD SUMMER PALACE

圆明园

28 Qinghua Xilu, 10/6262-8501

HOURS: Daily Apr., Sept.-Oct. 7 A.M.-6:30 P.M.,
May-Aug. 7 A.M.-7 P.M., Nov.-Mar. 7 A.M.-5:30 P.M.

COST: ¥10

METRO: Yuanmingyuan (Line 4)

Less well known than the Summer Palace, the ruins of Yuanmingyuan (also known as the Old Summer Palace) offer a different option than the typical Beijing tourist attractions. Located to the east of the Summer Palace, Yuanmingyuan dates from the reign of Qing emperor Kangxi in 1709. It was built as an alternative to the Forbidden City for Qing government affairs, and contained many beautiful buildings, some in European style. In one of the most shameful events of the Second Opium War of the 1860s, much of the complex was ransacked and destroyed by British and French forces. The specter of humiliation looms even to this day. In its time, Yuanmingyuan (meaning Garden of Perfect Brightness) was known as the Versailles of the East and the Garden of Gardens, and some of its former glory can still be witnessed among the ruins. The site includes three gardens—Perfect Brightness, Eternal Spring, and Elegant Spring, covering 3.5-square kilometers (1.35 sq. mi.). The complex dwarfed the Forbidden City, and was adorned with pavilions, halls, pools, and temples. Among the most beautiful of the buildings still standing or reconstructed are the Huanghuazhen labyrinth and Zhengjue Temple.

◖ SUMMER PALACE

颐和园

Yiheyuan Lu, 10/6288-1144

HOURS: Daily Apr. 1–Oct. 31 7 A.M.–5 P.M., Nov. 1–Mar. 31 6:30 A.M.–6 P.M.

COST: ¥30 (Apr. 1–Oct. 31), ¥20 (Nov. 1–Mar. 31); half price for students

METRO: Beigongmen (Line 4)

Beijing's temperature rises to scorching during the summer months, so the emperors learned early on that getting out of the city was the best way to avoid the worst of it. The Summer Palace became their refuge from the heat and dust. Located 15 kilometers (9 mi.) to the northwest of the Forbidden City, the palace complex construction began in the Jin Dynasty (1115–1234) and reached its current size in 1705 during the reign of Qing emperor Qianlong. It was particularly favored by the last Empress, Dowager Cixi, who spent time there with her nephew, Emperor Guangxu. Three quarters of the complex's 249 hectares (615 acres) are water, including the artificially-made Kunming Lake. Earth from the digging of the lake was used to build Longevity Hill and Nanhu Island, major landmarks in the palace.

A UNESCO World Heritage sight, the palace is split into four main parts: the court, front hill, front lake, and rear area. Many buildings bore the brunt of the Boxer Rebellion in 1860, but plenty remain. Visitors enter the court section through the **East Palace Gate,** emblazoned with the Summer Palace's Chinese name (Yiheyuan) in characters, which means "maintaining energy." In imperial times, the three main arches of the gate were reserved for the emperor, while courtiers, officials, and members of the royal family used smaller entrances at each side.

The first building is the **Hall of Benevolence and Longevity,** dating from 1750. The original was burned during the Boxer Rebellion and rebuilt in 1888. It was the site of imperial administrative duties, and still contains many of the original furnishings. The courtyard contains a large Qilin statue. This mythical chimera was said to

guard against fire and bring prosperity, and was brought to the Summer Palace from the ruined Yuanmingyuan. The **Garden of Virtue and Harmony** was where Empress Cixi watched Peking opera performances. Sitting in the garden's **Hall of Nurtured Joy,** she observed the stage in the **Grand Theater.** The emperor conducted state business, slept, and relaxed in the **Hall of Jade Ripples**—a complex that includes a main chamber and two smaller rooms on either side. Nearby **Yiyun House** was the dwelling of Empress Longyu, the wife of Emperor Guangxu who was cast aside in favor of the concubine Zhen. Most of the royal family lived in the **Hall of Joyful Longevity** when they resided at the Summer Palace. It was built by the Qianlong Emperor as a gift for his mother's 60th birthday, and includes a main hall dominated by a sandalwood throne.

The front hill section of the Summer Palace begins with the stunning **Long Gallery**—the longest of its kind in China. The 728-meter (0.4 mi.) stretch of elaborately decorated pillars and roofs was built by Qianlong in 1755, and connects Longevity Hill with Kunming Lake. The **Hall of Dispelling Clouds** on Longevity Hill was the site of festivals and celebrations, including the birthday of Empress Cixi. Look out for the beautiful red gate that cuts the Long Gallery into an eastern and western section. The highest point on Longevity Hill is the **Tower of Buddhist Incense,** where Cixi made offerings on auspicious days. Standing 41 meters (134 ft.) tall on a 21-meter-high (69 ft.) base, it can be seen from most parts of the palace complex, and is a great vantage point. Climb up for some incredible views of the surrounding area. Be sure not to miss the **Baoyun Pavilion** to the west. Made entirely of bronze, it stands on a marble base, and echoes with the sound of bronze bells. The **Hall of the Sea of Wisdom** sits atop Longevity Hill, and survived the fires of the Boxer Rebellion thanks to its glazed tiles. The hall contains statues of Buddha and the mercy goddess Guanyin.

Vast **Kunming Lake** dominates the Summer Palace complex, and was extended by Emperor

Qianlong. **Nanhu Island** was created from the resulting silt, and is worth visiting for the view from Hanxu Hall, where Empress Cixi liked to spend time. The west bank of Kunming Lake has been landscaped to resemble Hangzhou's much-lauded West Lake, and six bridges span the entrance. The most striking bridge in the Summer Palace is the 17-arch marble structure that connects the eastern bank of the lake with Nanhu Island. Before you cross the bridge, look out for the giant bronze ox statue that is believed to ward off flooding. Another interesting folly is the marble boat that sits on the lake below Longevity Hill. The original was burned down, and the boat seen today was built by Cixi, using money she embezzled from the navy.

The rear hill area contains the **Garden of Harmonious Interests,** modeled after the classical gardens of the Yangtze Delta. Its main features number eight in total: a path, a pavilion, a tower, a room, a house, a hall, a bridge, and a hole. This part of the Summer Palace also contains **Suzhou Market Street,** originally built to give the royal family a taste of common life. Eunuchs, concubines, and courtesans manned the shops and stalls, allowing the emperor and empress to act as normal townsfolk. Today the shops sell souvenirs and curios.

The Summer Palace has countless beautiful scenic spots, pavilions, temples, and gardens, and requires at least half a day to enjoy properly. Go first thing in the morning so that you may have all day to explore.

Greater Beijing   Map 6

BEIJING BOTANICAL GARDEN
北京植物园

Xiangshan Lu, 10/6259-1283, www.beijingbg.com
HOURS: Gardens: Daily 9 A.M.-5 P.M.; Sleeping Buddha Temple, Cao Yueqin Memorial, and Conservatory: Daily 8:30 A.M.-4:30 P.M.
COST: Gardens and Sleeping Buddha Temple ¥5, Cao Yueqin Memorial ¥10, Conservatory ¥50
METRO: Shangdi (Line 13)

A far cry from the busy, traffic-choked avenues of central Beijing, the Botanical Garden is an oasis of greenery and fresh air in the northwestern suburbs. In addition to a stunning array of plants, trees, flowers, and bushes, the garden contains a memorial to Cao Yueqin (author of the famous novel *Dream of the Red Chamber*) and a temple dedicated to a bronze Reclining Buddha cast in the Tang Dynasty. The garden itself contains a hothouse split into three sections—evergreens, tropical aquatics, and commercial plants like cocoa—as well as 11 gardens dedicated to flowers. The most attractive are the peony, lilac, rose, and magnolia gardens. In total, the Botanical Garden contains over 6,000 species of flora. On top of the beautiful foliage and flowers, look out for some lovely bridges, pavilions, and rock gardens among the greenery.

◖ FRAGRANT HILLS PARK
香山公园

1 Xiangshan Lu, 10/6259-1155
HOURS: Daily Apr. 1-June 30, Sept. 1-Nov. 15 6 A.M.-6:30 P.M., July 1-Aug. 31 6 A.M.-7 P.M., Nov. 16-Mar. 31 6 A.M.-6 P.M.
COST: Nov. 16-Mar. 31 ¥5, Apr. 1-Nov. 15 ¥10; Biyun Temple: ¥10; Cable car: ¥50 for single trip, ¥60 at weekends and holidays, ¥20 for children
METRO: Shangdi (Line 13)

The hills in this beautiful park take their name not from their aroma, but from the Incense Burner Peak (Xianglu Feng). Rising 557 meters (1,800 ft.), the hill is crowned with two boulders that resemble an incense censer. The park was an imperial garden during the Qing Dynasty, and covers 160 hectares (395 acres). It was first designated as a park during the Jin Dynasty, undergoing expansions in the Yuan and Ming eras. Qing emperor Qianlong decreed that more pavilions and halls be built; he named those pavilions and halls in the Garden of Tranquility and

© SUSIE GORDON

Beijing's Olympic Stadium

of the sixth Panchen Lama, and the Study of the Reading Heart. The southern route will take you past the Green Tranquility Lake, Shuangqing Villa, Fragrant Temple, and the Incense Burner Peak.

OLYMPIC STADIUM

国家体育场（鸟巢）

18 Beichen Donglu

HOURS: Mon.-Fri. 9 A.M.-6 P.M., Sat.-Sun. 9 A.M.-9:30 P.M., and for sports events and concerts

COST: ¥50

METRO: Olympic Sports Centre (Olympic Line)

An iconic reminder of the 2008 Olympic Games, the Bird's Nest (otherwise known as the National Stadium) was conceived by Swiss architects Jacques Herzog and Pierre de Meuron and Chinese designer Li Xinggang. The building's unusual facade is made up of exposed steel strips around an inner shell. The stadium was used for the unforgettable Olympic opening and closing ceremonies, and for track and field events throughout the Games. There are 91,000 seats, of which 80,000 are permanent and 11,000 temporary. The ground space measures 258 square meters (2,800 sq. ft.), and the stadium cost ¥2,267 (US$33 million) to complete. Since the Olympic Games finished, it has been used as a sports and performance venue and retains its status as a tourist attraction.

Pleasure. Many of the garden's buildings were damaged during the British attacks that ruined the Old Summer Palace in 1860. Fragrant Hills Park is particularly popular in the fall, when the Red Leaf Festival begins. The northern reaches contain Yangjing Lake, the Bright Temple lamasery that was built for the visit

RESTAURANTS

Thanks to its status as a capital city, Beijing is blessed with a vibrant, varied dining scene that has something for every palate and budget. Whether you're happier nibbling lamb kebabs on a street corner, stirring hot pot with a group of friends, or enjoying haute cuisine overlooking a palace, there's something for you in Beijing.

The native cuisine of northern China is different from most outside views of Chinese food. Far from the sticky tropical flavors of Guangdong and the fiery chili dishes of Hunan and Sichuan, *dongbei* (literally "east north") food features potatoes, stodgy dumplings, lamb, and pickled cabbage. There are plenty of *dongbei* restaurants in Beijing, but the city's signature dish is definitely the roast duck. Famous the world over, and served in Chinese restaurants from San Francisco to Sydney, Beijing duck, with its accompanying pancakes, sliced scallions, and plum sauce, is a true classic. Some of the best places to try it in its hometown are Quan Ju De, Li Qun, and Fat Duck.

Beijing has a flourishing street food industry, with vendors setting up shop for breakfast, lunch, and dinner. Egg pancakes and meat-filled buns are popular breakfast dishes, and Xinjiang *chuan'r* (kebabs) make a tasty snack. Head to the Donghuamen night market on Wangfujing Avenue in Tian'anmen for some of the most unusual and varied snack food in the city, including scorpions and parts of animals you wouldn't ordinarily consider eating.

As Beijing leapt into the 21st century, it started to style itself as a modern, cosmopolitan city. This is reflected in both the range of

HIGHLIGHTS

LOOK FOR  TO FIND RECOMMENDED RESTAURANTS.

 **Best Atmosphere:** At the end of a quiet, winding alley, **Dali Courtyard** serves food from China's southern Yunnan province in an open courtyard under the stars (page 79).

 **Best Café:** Houhai's Gulou Avenue is home to plenty of hip cafés, but **Alba** is the coolest of them all, with its kitschy interior, cute roof terrace, and great coffee (page 81).

 **Best Beijing Duck:** With so many great duck restaurants, it's a difficult task to pick a winner, but the unpretentious vibe and family recipe at **Li Qun** put it over the top (page 83).

 **Best Splurge: Maison Boulud** has all the fixings for a memorable splurge: a French celebrity chef, chic decor, immaculate service, and, of course, incredible gourmet food (page 85).

 **Best Hot Pot:** It's worth the line at **Hai Di Lao.** The hot pot here is widely held to be the best in Beijing thanks to its flavorful broth and quality ingredients. A bonus: women can get manicures while they wait (page 86).

 **Best For Something Different:** Try a Chinese cuisine that's not so well known at **Three Guizhou Men,** where the tangy pickles of southwestern China add a distinctive flavor to the dishes (page 87).

 **Best Casual Fine Dining:** Enjoy top-quality brunch favorites like steak, huevos rancheros, and pancakes at chef Billy Bolton's innovative and homey **Chef Too** (page 87).

 **Best Sandwiches:** Grab a Serbian sausage baguette and chill on the terrace at **Kiosk,** one of Sanlitun's most enduringly popular eateries due to its speedy Western fare and striking pink exterior (page 89).

 **Most Authentic Indian:** Residents of Beijing's University District know that the best and most authentic Indian food can be found at **Ganges** (page 94).

 **Best Comfort Food: The Kro's Nest** serves up some of the tastiest Western food in town, so if you're craving the flavors of home, drop in and see how they measure up when it comes to pizza and classic American desserts like funnel cake (page 94).

Alba in Beijing's trendy Houhai district

© SUSIE GORDON

international restaurants and the increase in higher-end establishments. Restaurants like Capital M and Maison Boulud in Qianmen wouldn't seem out of place in New York, Paris, or London. Beijing's expat population has contributed to the rise of mid-range, Western-friendly eateries, and there are, of course, the ubiquitous McDonalds, KFCs, and Pizza Huts.

What's great about Beijing's dining scene is its versatility. Whether you feel like a quick, cheap street snack or a four-course dinner

prepared by a Michelin-starred chef, you'll find it somewhere in the city.

PRICE KEY

$ Entrées less than ¥100

$$ Entrées ¥100–500

$$$ Entrées more than ¥500

Tian'anmen
Map 1

RESTAURANTS

BEIJING DUCK
QUAN JU DE $$
9 Shuaifuyuan Hutong, off Wangfujing Dajie, 10/6525-3310
HOURS: Daily 11 A.M.–2 P.M., 4:30–9 P.M.
METRO: Wangfujing (Line 1)

With over a century of duck-roasting expertise under its belt, the Quan Ju De chain is an obvious choice for a Peking Duck dinner. While other places around town may be more intimate and atmospheric, Quan Ju De never fails to deliver when it comes to taste, crispy skin, and duck-related side dishes. Richard Nixon and Fidel Castro have eaten here, and both apparently left satisfied. Quan Ju De has a secret recipe for the coating on its roast ducks that no other restaurant has managed to replicate. Whole ducks are sliced in front of you at your table. Be sure to book ahead.

REGIONAL CHINESE
SHUN YI FU $
36-3 Ganyu Hutong, off Wangfujing Dajie, 10/6528-1960
HOURS: Daily 10:30 A.M.–10:30 P.M.
METRO: Wangfujing (Line 1)

If you're a fan of dumplings a visit to Shun Yi Fu is a must. Dumplings are what they do best (widely held to be the very best in Beijing) and the options are plentiful. They come either boiled or pan-fried, with fillings ranging from shrimp to donkey, and most things in between. Particularly tasty are the vegetarian

dumplings, and the fresh salads are worth a try too, to offset the heavier flavors. Classic choices like pork and cabbage never fail to hit the spot. The skin of the dumplings at Shun Yi Fu tends to be thicker than the regular variety, adhering to old Beijing traditions. Interior decor is clean and simple, with unfussy furnishings and crockery.

AMERICAN
GRANDMA'S KITCHEN $
47-2 Nanchizi Dajie, near Forbidden City East Gate, 10/6528-2790, www.grandmasbeijing.com
HOURS: Daily 8 A.M.–10:30 P.M.
METRO: Tian'anmen East (Line 1)

An actual grandma owns and runs this casual, American-style café, along with the other four branches in her chain. She started her enterprise in 2003, and has been satisfying Beijing's desire for tasty, hearty, home-style food ever since. This branch opened in 2007 and sits just east of the Forbidden City. It serves an award-winning brunch along with classics like burgers, BLTs, milkshakes, and apple pie. You get free refills of coffee and a choice of omelets, hash browns, and other breakfast treats before 2 P.M. The restaurant has a quiet courtyard and a cozy but airy atmosphere inside. It's strictly casual, with a living-room feel.

CAFÉS
BIG TREE CAFÉ $
10 Jingshan Qianjie, north of the Forbidden City,

10/6407-2092
HOURS: Daily 8 A.M.–8 P.M.
METRO: Dongsi (Line 5)

Perfectly located for brunch before (or lunch after) a trip to the Forbidden City, the Big Tree Café lies at the northeast corner of the palace complex. It's a tourist favorite, but don't let that put you off; it's popular for a good reason. Red lanterns hang from the eaves out front, facing the leafy street. Inside, the decor is bare, slate-brick walls; red accents; and all the traditional trappings. The menu offers a good selection of cheap coffee, tea, juices, and sandwiches, as well as a particularly attractive assortment of cakes.

ZOE'S CAFÉ AND BISTRO $

No. 3, Bldg. 1, Millennium Heights, Oriental Plaza, Dongchang'an Jie, 10/8518-2176
HOURS: Daily 7:30 A.M.–10 P.M.
METRO: Wangfujing (Line 1)

Recharge your batteries after a morning dodging the crowds of Wangfujing at this popular, Western lunch spot in the Oriental Plaza complex. Zoe's is an Australian outfit that expanded into Beijing in 2006. It serves good coffee as well as pizza, gourmet burgers sandwiches, wraps, and pasta. There are bagels and omelets for breakfast and brunch, and an outdoor terrace with umbrellas for an alfresco lunch or snack. Inside, the decor is standard, contemporary café style. On weekday lunchtimes, Zoe's attracts the neighborhood's office workers, but everyone is welcome and the atmosphere is far from corporate.

CONTEMPORARY CHINESE
DONGYANGE $$

76 Donghuamen Dajie, near Nanchizi Dajie, 10/6523-8770
HOURS: Daily 10:30 A.M.–10:30 P.M.
METRO: Tian'anmen East (Line 1)

Just east of the Forbidden City, Dongyange is located in a gray slate building with a traditional up-turned roof. The restaurant serves a mix of imperial, Cantonese, and Hunan food in an atmosphere full of character, involving chandeliers; elaborate, contemporary wall decorations; swirling red ceiling art; and Chinese paintings that guests can buy. As for the food, it's an enlightening mix of regional styles, from Beijing roast duck to dry-wok donkey meat, along with wildcards like snails and Korean duck heads.

FINE DINING
TIANDI YIJIA $$$

140 Nanchizi Dajie, 10/8511-5556, www.tiandigroup.cn
HOURS: Daily 11 A.M.–2 P.M., 5–10 P.M.
METRO: Tian'anmen East (Line 1)

Gorgeous decor and high-end food makes Tiandi Yijia one of the most exclusive restaurants in Beijing. Popular with the city's beautiful people and local celebrities, it serves classic Beijing fare like roast duck and dumplings in an artistic, glamorous environment. Art decorates the walls, and the ceilings are painted lavishly and decorated with fans. Gray walls add a minimalist vibe. The windows look out over the low roofs of the old quarter, while foliage and contemporary water features add to the atmosphere. The menu offers luxury items like foie gras and scallops, along with imperial delights that are cooked well and attractively presented. Tiandi Yijia is, unsurprisingly, pretty expensive.

FRENCH FUSION
SHI $$

Emperor Hotel, 33 Qihelou Jie, 10/6526-5566
HOURS: Daily 7 A.M.–11 P.M.
METRO: Dongsi (Line 5)

The restaurant inside the Emperor Hotel beside the Forbidden City is a destination of its own. Serving imperial food with a twist, Shi offers dishes in which the overriding influence is French. Appetizers include fresh salads, soups, and tasty bites, such as tofu cubes. For entrées, expect "imperial beef" steak, a range of inventive meat dishes, and regularly rotating seasonal specials. Look out for multi-course set meal deals for lunch and dinner. *"Shi"* means "food" in Mandarin, and the decor is as simple as the name. Furniture is all either bright orange or white in block colors, and the feel is minimalist. It's a good reason to visit the Emperor Hotel if you're not a guest.

INTERNATIONAL
COURTYARD $$$
95 Donghuamen Dajie, 10/6526-8883
HOURS: Daily 6–10 P.M.
METRO: Tian'anmen East (Line 1)

CourtYard sets the standard for high-end European food in Beijing, and has been featured in *The New York Times*. Its windows look out onto the moat of the Forbidden City, while the interior decor is beautiful but understated. Silver service, white drapes on the ceiling, and a downstairs lounge and gallery add up to a chic and luxurious atmosphere. The wine list features over 600 bottles and has won CourtYard the Wine Spectator Restaurant Award of Excellence every year since 2002. The restaurant looks just as attractive from the outside with its slate stairway and outer walls illuminated. The owner Handel Lee, an American attorney, also developed Beijing's Legation Quarter and 3 on the Bund in Shanghai.

DOMUS $$$
115 Nanchizi Dajie, near Dongchang'an Jie,
10/8511-8015
HOURS: Mon.–Sat. 6 P.M.–1 A.M.
METRO: Tian'anmen East (Line 1)

Just next door to the Forbidden City, this classy Euro restaurant and lounge is a 60-seat, casual fine-dining venue with a great reputation and central location. The ground floor is a bar and café, serving fresh oysters and gourmet burgers, while the lower level contains the main restaurant area. The decor consists of bare slate walls, painted white eaves, Minotti furniture, and soft, cream-colored furnishings inside a renovated historical building. The menu focuses on home-cooked European staples like bouillabaisse, risotto, goat cheese, and pan-fried meats. The wine list is comprehensive. A meal at Domus won't be cheap, but the quality and atmosphere are top notch.

ITALIAN
RISTORANTE SADLER $$$
Chi'enmen 23, 23 Qianmen Dong Dajie, 10/6559-1399
HOURS: Tues.–Sun. 11:30 A.M.–2 P.M., 6–10:30 P.M.
METRO: Qianmen (Line 2)

Another solid choice for high-end Western food in this area is Ristorante Sadler. The man behind the name is two-star Michelin chef Claudio Sadler, whose menu includes Italian pasta and meat dishes, inventive salads, and his special Naples sponge and Tiramisu for dessert. The dining area is bright and sunny, with simple white furniture. Wine comes from the Cantina Sadler cellar downstairs, and you can pick up gourmet goods at the Sadler food store. The 12-seat chef's table can be booked for private dinners. Ristorante Sadler is part of the Chi'enmen 23 complex in the Legation Quarter, which contains the best examples of Beijing's colonial-era architecture.

RESTAURANTS

Houhai

Map 2

REGIONAL CHINESE
◖ DALI COURTYARD $$
67 Xiaojingchang Hutong, off Gulou Dongdajie,
10/8404-1430
HOURS: Daily 11 A.M.–2 P.M., 6–11 P.M.
METRO: Guloudajie (Line 2)

One of Houhai's most atmospheric restaurants, Dali Courtyard serves up traditional Yunnan food under the stars. It's tricky to find it (head all the way up the *hutong* and turn left when you see the red lantern), but well worth the search. Tables are arranged in the open-air courtyard, and the food comes in set menus. Choose a set price option, and sit back as your food is delivered dish by dish. The menu is seasonal, but staples include fried mint leaves, meat jerkies, sautéed wild mushrooms, and fried goat cheese. Vegetarians are catered for, but it's often a case of picking your way around the meat, so it might not be the best option for strict no-meat diners. The courtyard tends to be covered between November and April, though that doesn't take away from the atmosphere. The rooms off the courtyard are filled with traditional furniture and quirky ornaments.

DRUM AND GONG $

104 Nanluogu Hutong, off Gulou Dongdajie, 10/8402-4729
HOURS: Daily 10 A.M.–noon
METRO: Guloudajie (Line 2)

This popular Nanluoguxiang restaurant benefits from a great location on the area's most vibrant *hutong*. It serves reasonably priced North Chinese cuisine as well as Sichuan food and some interesting fusion experiments (kung pao chicken pizza, for example), and has a comprehensively written menu that explains the spices and tastes of each dish. Thanks to its expat co-owner, Drum and Gong's menu is largely trilingual (Chinese, French, and English), making things even easier for visitors. The menu specifies which dishes are more appealing to foreign tastes, advice that you can choose to follow or ignore depending on your preferences. Top choices are the Yunnan mushrooms and beef stir-fry. Both the roof terrace and the indoor dining area tend to get busy on weekends.

HOT BEAN COOPERATIVE $

Chaodou Hutong, Jiaodaoukou Nandajie, near Kuan Jie, 10/8401-6165
HOURS: Daily 11 A.M.–10 P.M.
METRO: Zhangzizhonglu (Line 5)

Cheap and cheerful, this trendy *chuan'r* (meat kebab) place is run by a group of young locals with a penchant for spice and quirky interior design. It's best known for its chicken wing skewers, and the spice level goes from the mildly tangy to the perversely piquant. The concrete walls are hand-painted and chalked, and the snack bar's blue alien mascot features widely among the designs. Your wings will arrive two to a skewer balanced on a small tin bucket. Choose from a variety of toppings, and go as spicy as you dare. There's an open courtyard in the middle for warm days.

LAO HANZI HAKKA $

12 Qianhai Nanyan, east bank of Qianhai, 10/6404-2259
HOURS: Daily 10:30 A.M.–2 P.M., 5–11 P.M.
METRO: Guloudajie (Line 2)

The Hakka people know how to cook good seafood, and this lakeside restaurant does a great line in shrimp kebabs, grilled fish, and other Fujianese specialties. Sit (or stand) outside at street level, or take a table on the 2nd floor—either way, you get to watch the world go by while you drink cold beer and enjoy some seafood done the Hakka way. For a more laid-back experience, avoid the midday and 5 P.M. rushes, and go either for an early lunch or a late snack. Service is quick to the point of being brusque when it's busy.

NO NAME RESTAURANT $$

1 Dajinsi Hutong, between Qianhai and Houhai, 10/8328-3061
HOURS: Daily 10:30 A.M.–2 A.M.
METRO: Guloudajie (Line 2)

The enigmatically monikered No Name Restaurant is a sister venue of No Name Bar. Manager Bai Feng opened it in 2005 to serve Yunnanese food in a quiet *hutong* courtyard set back from the noisy lakeside bar scene. It's not the easiest place to find, but once you get there it's worth it. The rooftop terrace has a view over to the Drum and Bell Towers. No Name Restaurant is only a handful of meters from busy Yinding Bridge, but it seems like a world away. Feast on South Chinese dishes like mint beef and Yunnan cheese as you drink frozen cocktails and admire the eclectic furniture and ornaments. It may not be the best Yunnanese food in Beijing, but it's a great all-around experience.

SOUTH SILK ROAD $$

Unit 12-13, 19 Shichahaiqian Haixiyan (Lotus Lane), 10/5971-6388
HOURS: Daily 10:30 A.M.–10 P.M.
METRO: Pinganli (Line 4)

This branch of famous Beijing-based artist Fang Lijun's uber-hip restaurant group is a hangout for local art dealers, painters, sculptors, and the like who come for Yunnan food and homemade rice wine. The walls are decorated with art, and the atmosphere is strictly bohemian. The original South Silk Road is in Sanlitun, but this branch is just as charming. Yunnan classics, like smoked ham, mushrooms, and sausages, are all represented, and there are some intriguing dishes like tree bark salad that are worth a try for intrepid eaters. Fang Lijun's enterprise wins awards for its food and general ambiance.

AMERICAN
HUTONG PIZZA $$
9 Yindingqiao Hutong, 10/8322-8916
HOURS: Daily 11 A.M.-11 P.M.
METRO: Guloudajie (Line 2)

This small courtyard pizza restaurant is a Beijing legend and the first place most people think about when craving mozzarella. American-style pizzas are served up on wooden slabs, with the added novelty of being square-shaped. Choose from meat and veggie options, and add side dishes like filled potato skins. As well as the usual Tsingtao beer, they also serve Leffe and Corona, which makes for a nice change. There's also some decent wine by the glass. Hutong Pizza is located in a converted traditional house and is simple and unpretentious with a cozy vibe. Proximity to Houhai means that you can work off your pizza with a post-meal walk around the lake.

CAFÉS
⬛ ALBA $
70 Gulou Dongdajie, 10/6709-1383
HOURS: Daily 10 A.M.-2 A.M.
METRO: Guloudajie (Line 2)

As well as live music and quirky shops, Gulou is famous for its artsy café scene. Alba is possibly the best of the bunch, and has everything you'd expect: free Wi-Fi, a menu scrawled on blackboards, worn wooden furniture, and cheap, tasty food. A sunny café by day, Alba morphs into a laidback bar when night falls. There's a small rooftop area for warm nights and a front room with beat-up easy chairs for reading and chatting. Smoking is permitted throughout, adding to the bohemian atmosphere. The menu was designed by a chef from

a nearby Italian restaurant, and runs the gamut of Western sandwiches, pastas, and salads.

CAFÉ DE SOFA $
12 Yindingqiao Hutong, 10/6203-2905
HOURS: Tues.-Sun. 11 A.M.-midnight
METRO: Guloudajie (Line 2)

This trendy Houhai café is a quiet oasis set back from the busy Yinding Bridge area. Serving Lavazza coffee in a bohemian environment, the café has fewer sofas than you might imagine from its name, but is blessed with a great roof terrace and a resident dog named Zhuzhu. On the food menu are Western sandwiches, burgers, breakfasts, and pasta, along with Taiwanese-style desserts. The star of the drinks list is the special ice-dripped coffee that takes 48 hours to prepare. If the day's supply has been exhausted by the time you get there, the regular iced coffee is a good alternative. Decor is simple, with touches of kitsch among the pale wood and brick.

CAFÉ ZARAH $
42 Gulou Dongdajie, 10/8403-9807
HOURS: Daily 10 A.M.-midnight
METRO: Guloudajie (Line 2)

Slicker than Alba but with a similar bohemian vibe, Café Zarah sits a few doors down on the same street. Its wide windows look out onto East Gulou Avenue, so you can watch the hipsters pass as you sip your Gaggia coffee. Café Zarah is favored in the daytime by laptop users who love its minimalist decor and trendy vibe. The walls are decorated with rotating photography exhibitions, adding to the artsy feel. As for food, a reasonably priced German-style breakfast is served all day. In case you were wondering, the café is named after the baby daughter of the German owner's friends.

FRENCH
CAFÉ DE LA POSTE $$
58 Yonghegong Dajie, 10/6402-7047
HOURS: Daily 11 A.M.-1:30 P.M., 6-11:30 P.M.
METRO: Beixnqiao (Line 5)

This atmospheric French restaurant is located inside a restored *hutong* building and has all the rustic charm of a village bistro. The menu is written on a blackboard, and candlelight adds to the Gallic atmosphere. Chef and manager Yannick Gauthier aimed for a local feeling, and he has definitely succeeded. Watch your steak sizzling in the open kitchen while you work your way through the wine list. Café de la Poste is a regular recipient of awards from the Beijing press, and its popularity means that it fills up quickly, especially on weekends. If you fancy something different from rice and noodles, this is a great option.

INTERNATIONAL
THE VINEYARD $$

31 Wudaoying Hutong, west of Lama Temple, 10/6402-7961

HOURS: Tues.-Sun. 11:30 A.M.-11:30 P.M.

METRO: Yonghegong (Line 2, Line 5)

The Vineyard is located in trendy Wudaoying Hutong close to the Lama Temple. On the menu is a selection of homemade European dishes like moussaka, pasta, quiche, and stufffed baked potatoes, and a weekend brunch attracts a crowd on Saturdays and Sundays. Classic British sandwich fillings include coronation chicken and tuna mayo, and there's also a selection of pizza and burgers to choose from. Craving a Western-style hot breakfast? This is the place to come to. If you're here for lunch, look out for special deals on set menus. With beer and wine as well as soft drinks, it's a good dinner option, too. The decor fits the boho Gulou vibe, with wooden tables, exposed brick, and that all-important courtyard.

KOREAN
SAVEURS DE CORÉE $$

29 Nanluogu Hutong, off Gulou Dongdajie, 10/6401-6083

HOURS: Daily 11 A.M.-11 P.M.

METRO: Guloudajie (Line 2)

The food of China's near neighbor South Korea is well executed at this Nanluoguxiang restaurant. There are around 100,000 Koreans in Beijing, and Saveurs de Corée is their best option for luxury cuisine at reasonable prices. Stylish decor with glass walls and wood accents

creates a funky, contemporary atmosphere to enjoy classics like kimchi and *bibimbap*. A tranquil, slate-tiled, rooftop seating area overlooks the low *hutong* roofs. The food is organic and locally sourced wherever possible, and MSG is banned from the kitchen. Set menus are available. If you're looking for a barbecue-style meal you will be disappointed, but for other Korean dishes this is a great choice.

RUSSIAN
TRAKTIRR PUSHKIN $$

1 Xiyangguan Hutong, off Dongzhimennei Dajie, 10/6403-1690

HOURS: Daily 10 A.M.-10:30 P.M.

METRO: Dongzhimen (Line 2)

Thanks to its relative proximity to Russia, Beijing has a long history of Soviet restaurants. In fact, Russian eateries were among the first foreign restaurants to open in the capital. Traktirr Pushkin's two branches are probably the most famous. The original is located beside the Russian Embassy. The branch on Xiyangguan Hutong is its second incarnation, and is equally well loved. Prices are reasonable, and the food is authentic. You'll find borscht, chicken Kiev, and dumplings on the menu, accompanied by infused vodka, Baltika beer, and plenty of black and red caviar. Russian food is known for its stodgy, comforting textures and Traktirr Pushkin does a great job of recreating them. The elaborate Russian decor extends from the grand entrance to the mosaic murals on the walls inside and the grand arches and light fittings. Despite this, Traktirr manages to remain unpretentious, with simple cutlery and crockery and homestyle servings.

SOUTHEAST ASIAN
CAFÉ SAMBAL $$

43 Doufuchi Hutong, Jiugulou Dajie, 10/6400-4878

HOURS: Daily noon-midnight

METRO: Guloudajie (Line 2)

Such is Café Sambal's popularity that it has recently expanded its operations in Shanghai. The Beijing branch continues to attract a loyal clientele thanks to its consistently good

Malaysian food, *hutong* location, and atmospheric courtyard. The restaurant takes its name from *sambal,* a type of chili sauce made with brown sugar and salt. On the menu at Café Sambal are classics like *gado gado, rendang* curry, *satay, kapitan* chicken, and sweet *kuih dadar pandan* crepes for dessert. It is one of the longest established restaurants in Beijing's dining scene and a firm favorite. Prices tend to reflect its quality and reputation, and it attracts a client base that doesn't mind paying a little more for their Malaysian food. That being said, the atmosphere is classy without being exclusive.

Qianmen
Map 3

BEIJING DUCK
LI QUN $$

11 Beixiangfang Hutong, Zhengyi Nanlu, Qianmen Dajie, 10/6702-5681

HOURS: Daily 10 A.M.-10 P.M.
METRO: Qianmen (Line 2)

If Quan Ju De in Tian'anmen sounds too touristy for your taste, try Li Qun for a taste of duck instead. It's a completely different experience thanks to its somewhat run-down but full-of-character location in an old *hutong* house. The menu offers various non-duck dishes, but these are nothing compared to the main attraction. Li Qun himself cooks the duck to his own recipe in a brick oven, and the walls are decorated with photos of celebrities and dignitaries who have enjoyed his handiwork over the years. It's a world away from the big, production-line

RESTAURANTS

THE LEGENDARY PEKING DUCK

If there's one dish that is synonymous with China's capital, it's Beijing *kaoya,* commonly known as Peking or Beijing duck. Roasted in stone ovens until crispy, then wrapped in wafer-thin pancakes, Beijing's signature dish is well known and loved all around the world. But what's the story behind the delicacy?

Ducks have been roasted in China since ancient times. The first written mention of *kaoya* came during the Yuan Dynasty when a cook book was published in 1330 detailing the emperor's fondness for duck. The Ming emperors who succeeded the Yuan took on the imperial recipe, and the first duck restaurant opened in Qianmen in 1416. The reign of the Qing Dynasty's Qianlong Emperor saw roast duck filtering down from the aristocracy to the middle classes, and poets began to write about its flavor and charm. Yang Quanren, who invented a special sort of oven to hang ducks, opened the now-famous duck restaurant Quan Ju De in 1864.

Originally, the birds used to make *kaoya* were wild ducks from the canals of Nanjing, but the breed was later domesticated and named "Pekin ducks." They are first allowed to roam free-range for 45 days before being fattened up to 5-7 kilograms (11-17 lbs.) through four meals a day. After a duck is killed, its de-feathered body is pumped with air to separate the skin from the flesh, then basted with maltose syrup and left to hang for 24 hours. It is then roasted in a special oven for 30-40 minutes at 270 degrees Celsius (518°F) until brown. The duck is served in two parts: first the skin is brought out, and eaten with a sugary dipping sauce. Next, the rest of the bird is carved at the table and wrapped in pancakes with scallions, sliced cucumber, and a sweet sauce.

Such is the importance of *kaoya* that Richard Nixon's historic visit to China is attributed to a duck banquet between the Chinese and Henry Kissinger in Beijing. Since then, international leaders, including Fidel Castro, Helmut Kohl, and Bill Clinton, have enjoyed its flavors.

Although it's available in Chinese restaurants across the globe, nothing beats trying authentic *kaoya* in its city of origin. Top restaurant choices are Li Qun, Fat Duck, and Quan Ju De.

duck restaurants elsewhere in town. If you're here in winter, wrap up warm, as it tends to get chilly.

REGIONAL CHINESE

DUYICHU $

38 Qianmen Dajie, 10/6702-1671
HOURS: Daily 8:30 A.M.-8:30 P.M.
METRO: Qianmen (Line 2)

Another Beijing *laozhihao* (well-loved, legendary establishment), Duyichu serves up *shaomai* dumplings. Unlike the fatter, fluffier *baozi* and slim *jiaozi, shaomai* are made of very thin dough with frilly, pleated edges. They are filled with pork, chicken, vegetables, or a mix of all three, and eaten with a special sour cabbage. It takes 16 individual processes to create a single *shaomai,* and a lot of care goes into each one. As well as dumplings, Duyichu serves noodles, soups, meat dishes, and appetizers. A picture menu makes it easy to order.

The restaurant dates from 1738 when the young Qing emperor Qianlong was struck by hunger upon his return to the Forbidden City. He stopped with his entourage and ate a hearty meal. He asked the owner for the restaurant's name, and when the owner said that it had none, he sent him a sign saying "the only restaurant in the city," or Duyichu.

GOUBULI BAOZI $

29-31 Dazhalan Xi Dajie, 10/6353-3338
HOURS: Daily 8:30 A.M.-6 P.M.
METRO: Qianmen (Line 2)

The name of this well-loved savory bun shop means "dogs don't come near." The origins of the name are unclear, but Goubuli's buns are good enough to attract long queues come lunch and dinnertime. The shop on Dazhalan pedestrian street has an elaborately decorated facade painted red and blue and adorned with lanterns. Inside, the traditional decor features gold dragons and red doors. Goubuli's Tianjin-style *baozi* (steamed buns) contain a variety of fillings, most usually pork but also often vegetables, and have a thicker, fluffier skin than most. You get around 10 buns per steamer. Incidentally, Chinese legend attributes

the invention of these buns to the 3rd century military strategist Zhuge Liang.

LITTLE SHEEP $

Northwest corner of Caishikou, Lin 43, Guangnei Dajie, 10/6316-6668, www.littlesheep.com
HOURS: Daily 11 A.M.-midnight
METRO: Caishikou (Line 4)

Get your dose of hot pot at this well-known and well-loved chain. Hailing from Inner Mongolia in 1999, Little Sheep now has a worldwide empire spanning North America, Japan, and China. The secret to its success is the fact that it uses meat from grassland sheep, which provide better texture and flavor. As is customary, the hot pot cauldron is divided into two halves, one containing mild, cream-colored broth and the other with spicy red soup. Each table gets a single pot, and meat and vegetables are added as they arrive on dishes from the kitchen. Hot pot is a communal experience and great fun. Wash it down with a cold beer for extra authenticity. Little Sheep restaurants tend to be bright, often rowdy affairs with a great local atmosphere.

TAN FISH HEAD HOT POT $$

25 Zhushikou Xi Dajie, 10/6301-8885
HOURS: Daily 10:30 A.M.-10 P.M.
METRO: Caishikou (Line 4)

Don't let the name put you off. Although fish heads form a major part of Tan's charm, they are not the only item on the menu. If you're keen to try this Sichuanese delicacy, be prepared for some serious spice. Traditional Sichuan hot pot comes in a split bowl, with mild broth in one half and spicy soup in the other. Meat, seafood, vegetables, and mushrooms arrive at your table, separately, to be dunked in the bubbling hot pot and cooked. One portion equals half a head, which means that you can try it without committing to a whole. Other menu highlights are meatballs and coagulated duck and chicken blood (this tastes better than it sounds). The restaurant is busy and loud, with a convivial atmosphere.

XINCHENG NOODLE HOUSE

Liangshi Dian Xiejie, no phone

HOURS: Daily 5:30 A.M.–8:30 P.M.
METRO: Qianmen (Line 2)

If you're tired of overpriced pretentious restaurants and want to see exactly how locals eat, head to this noodle house behind Qianmen Avenue. There's grass growing on the roof and no fixed telephone number, but rickshaw drivers, local shopkeepers, and *hutong* dwellers flock here for shots of *baijiu* (a distilled alcoholic beverage) by the yuan and simple, tasty noodles. Xincheng is a *guo ying* (state-run restaurant) and has hardly changed over the years. Five yuan gets you a bowl of noodles (just ask for *"mian"* or point to what other diners are eating) and probably a fair number of curious looks from regulars and passersby.

FRENCH
C MAISON BOULUD $$$

Chi'enmen 23, 23 Qianmen Dongdajie, 10/6559-9200, www.maisonboulud.com
HOURS: Mon.–Fri. 11:30 A.M.–2 P.M., 6–10 P.M., Sat.–Sun. brunch 11 A.M.–4 P.M., dinner 6–10 P.M.
METRO: Qianmen (Line 2)

Regularly voted as Beijing's best restaurant in local magazines, Maison Boulud provides one of the classiest, French fine-dining experiences to be found in the capital. The domain of Michelin three-starred French chef Daniel Boulud opened in 2008 to wide acclaim, and executive chef Brian Reimer keeps the kitchen standards high. The restaurant is housed inside the former U.S. Embassy, which now forms part of the luxury Chi'enmen 23 complex. The interior decor of both the restaurant and the Fresco bar is tasteful, with modern takes on classical red screens and dark wood. Maison Boulud frequently wins awards for its service, and it is matchless among Beijing's restaurants.

INTERNATIONAL
CAPITAL M $$$

3/F Qianmen Dajie
HOURS: Lunch: Mon.–Fri. 11:30 A.M.–2:30 P.M.; dinner: daily 6–10:30 P.M.; brunch: Sat.–Sun. 11:30 A.M.–5 P.M.; afternoon tea: Sat.–Sun. 3–5 P.M.
METRO: Qianmen (Line 2)

The beautiful Capital M provides one of the best dining experiences in all of Beijing. It's run by Michelle Garnaut, the Australian restaurateur and businesswoman behind M on the Bund in Shanghai and M on the Fringe in Hong Kong. Capital M is located inside a gorgeous traditional building at the entrance of Qianmen Pedestrian Street, and its terrace and windows overlook the old-style roofs of the surrounding district. Attention to detail (such as the black-and-white floor patterning) lifts Capital M above the competition. The food is Euro-based, with head chef Rob Cunningham cooking up suckling pig, gourmet soups, and the famous M pavlova. If you want to treat yourself to a gourmet meal in gorgeous surroundings, this is a good pick. Sit inside by a roaring fire in winter or enjoy the view of the old city from the terrace in summer.

VEGETARIAN
GONGDELIN $

58 Qianmen Dajie, 10/6702-0867
HOURS: Daily 11 A.M.–9 P.M.
METRO: Qianmen (Line 2)

Finding a decent meal can be difficult for vegetarians in Beijing, as many restaurants just don't get why you wouldn't want to eat meat. If you're tired of picking through limp cabbage, try Gongdelin. The chain was established in 1922 and quickly gained a reputation for tasty meat-free dishes. The food is mainly Buddhist and includes tofu and protein-based meat substitutes fashioned to look like actual chicken, duck, beef, fish, and pork. Tucking into a "lamb" kebab can be something of a surreal experience. This branch of Gongdelin sits inside an ornate building on Qianmen Avenue. Service can be hit and miss, but that doesn't take away from its popularity.

BEIJING DUCK

DA DONG $$

5/F Jinbao Tower, Jinbao Jie, 10/8522-1111

HOURS: Daily 11 A.M.–10 P.M.

METRO: Dengshikou (Line 5)

Da Dong claims that its ducks are the leanest in Beijing, so if you're watching your weight, this might be something to bear in mind. Ducks run a little more expensive than other places, but Da Dong's award-winning status accounts for the discrepancy. The 160-page menu is daunting, but apart from a foray into fried oysters, I recommend sticking to the *kaoya* (Beijing duck). The interior decor is simple and contemporary, with bamboo accents and subtly decorated screens. Make sure you reserve a table, as Da Dong tends to fill up fast. And, if you're tired of Beijing's love affair with tobacco, this place is a good bet: Smoking is not permitted in the restaurant.

FAT DUCK $$

Renaissance Beijing Capital Hotel, 61 Dongsanhuan Zhonglu, 10/5863-8241

HOURS: Daily 11:30 A.M.–2:30 P.M., 5:30–10:30 P.M.

METRO: Shuangjing (Line 10)

A good alternative to the city's other Beijing duck options, Fat Duck shouldn't be overlooked just because it's a hotel restaurant. It's certainly not a rip off: The whole-duck price is very affordable. Also on the menu are regional favorites from Sichuan and Guangdong, like bird's nest soup, abalone, suckling pig, and duck hearts. The open kitchen, smart red drapes, dark wood fittings, and gorgeous wall decorations lift Fat Duck above the competition when it comes to interior decor. A wood-burning oven makes roasts each duck to perfection. Complement your meal with something from the generous, red-heavy wine list.

REGIONAL CHINESE

BELLAGIO $$

6 Gongti Xilu, 10/6551-3333

HOURS: Daily 24 hours

METRO: Chaoyangmen (Line 2)

This trendy Taiwanese mega-restaurant is open late for post-clubbing sustenance, and its bright lights aren't exactly conducive to a relaxing dinner. However, if you're feeling buzzy and don't want your night to end, it's a fun experience. Always busy, always smoky, and even slightly manic, Bellagio is a great way to end a night on the tiles. Good choices from the menu are the *san bei ji* ("three-cup chicken"), noodles with XO sauce, and taro soup. The monumental shaved-ice desserts are also worth a try. Bellagio provides some interesting people-watching opportunities, not least the wait-staff with their funky hairstyles.

CRESCENT MOON $

16 Dongsi Liu Tiao, 10/6400-5281

HOURS: Daily 10 A.M.–11:30 P.M.

METRO: Zhangsizhanglu (Line 5)

Xinjiang food is one of the most interesting and unusual Chinese cuisines thanks to the Turkish influence of the region's Uighur ethnic group, and an emphasis on lamb dishes. Crescent Moon is among Beijing's finest Uighur restaurants and is less rowdy and touristy than the popular Red Rose in Sanlitun. The welcome lack of belly dancers and gimmicky music lets the quality of the food speak for itself. Tasty Xinjiang dishes include lamb with Uighur-style flatbread, lamb with noodles, and lamb with pretty much any adornment and accompaniment. Crescent Moon's *hutong* location and green decor add to its charms. Don't miss the Sinkiang black beer and homemade yogurt.

◖ HAI DI LAO $

2A, Baijiazhuang Lu, near Nansanlitun Lu, 10/6595-2982

HOURS: Daily 24 hours

METRO: Gongtibeilu (Line 10)

Famous for its hand-pulled noodles, Hai Di Lao is much more than just a hot pot joint. With many locations dotted around Beijing, it's widely held to serve the best hot pot in town. As well as good-quality meat and vegetable ingredients, Hai Di Lao has a sauce station where guests can create their own condiments, and fun extras like manicures while you wait for a table. If you want to try hot pot, this is a good place to do it. It has all the atmosphere of a traditional hot pot house and is clean and relatively well organized too. The decor is smarter than cheaper hot pot restaurants, with wood fittings and gold accents.

HERBAL CAFÉ $

B02, 17 Wanda Plaza, 93 Jianguo Lu, 10/5820-4679
HOURS: Daily 8 A.M.-4 A.M.
METRO: Dawangqiao (Line 1)

Cantonese food with all its gloopy goodness and MSG flavors isn't generally considered to be healthy, but Herbal Café proves that it doesn't always have to be a nightmare for your arteries. Here, MSG is banned and the emphasis is on low-fat Hong Kong and Cantonese fare like soups, stir fries, sweet and sour pork, and dim sum, with egg tarts and coconut puddings for dessert. Drinks include a range of tea with some interesting medicinal varieties. Prices are very reasonable, and the interior design is more contemporary bohemian than Kowloon chophouse, with wooden tables and exposed brick walls. Retro touches like booth seating and a replica British telephone booth add to the quirky vibe. There's a second branch in Sanlitun Village.

KARAIYA SPICE HOUSE $$

3/F, Bldg. 8, Sanlitun Village South, 19 Sanlitun Lu, 10/6415-3535
HOURS: Daily 11:30 A.M.-2 P.M., 5:30-10 P.M.
METRO: Tuanjiehu (Line 10)

Fiery Hunan food is known for its liberal use of red chilies. The cuisine of Chairman Mao's native province is brought up to date at this sleek spice house, from the same management as Hatsune and Kagen Teppanyaki. Manager Alan Wong's wife is from Hunan Province and she keeps an eye on the menu's authenticity. Sliding glass doors guarded by stone lions welcome you in. The attractive modern decor is an unusual but conducive setting to regional food that's more often enjoyed in roadside restaurants. Dishes come beautifully presented on slates and in pots, and the signature whole steamed mandarin fish with red and yellow chilies is a good choice. The fried tofu and pork stir-fry are also worth a try.

(THREE GUIZHOU MEN $$

8 Gongti Xilu, inside West Gate of Workers' Stadium, 10/6551-8517
HOURS: Daily 24 hours
METRO: Chaoyangmen (Line 2)

Set up by three men hailing from China's southerly Guizhou, this restaurant showcases the cuisine of their native province. Guizhou food is characterized by the piquant *paocai* pickle, which plays a part in many dishes. Try the mashed potato, steamed ribs with picked greens, and the enigmatically named Ants on a Tree—rice noodles with minced pork and peppers. Other top picks include *xiangbai bohe* (peppermint salad) and *suantang yu* (sour fish soup). There are three branches of Three Guizhou Men in Beijing, and this one is the most laid back and bohemian. It's open around the clock and is a good post-clubbing option if you don't fancy braving the noisier Bellagio.

AMERICAN
(CHEF TOO $$

Chaoyang Gongyuan Xilu, opposite West Gate of Chaoyang Park, 10/6591-8676
HOURS: Tues.-Sun. 11 A.M.-2 P.M., 5-10 P.M., Sat.-Sun. brunch 9:30 A.M.-3 P.M.
METRO: Tuanjiehu (Line 10)

Situated opposite Chaoyang Park, this American restaurant serves burgers, salads, award-winning Australian steaks (chilled, not frozen during import), and an impressive brunch that includes eggs Benedict, French toast, huevos rancheros, and pancakes. Chef William "Billy" Bolton runs the kitchen, insisting that his restaurant is smoke-free. Peach-toned walls, white tablecloths, and silver service give it a reassuringly solid feel—more of a fine-dining neighborhood joint than diner. Prices reflect the quality, but they're far from

RESTAURANTS

EATING ON THE HOOF: STREET SNACKS AND NIGHT MARKETS

Grabbing a bit to eat on the street is part of life for most Beijingers. Breakfast, especially, is a meal that's most often eaten on the go. If you're up and about early, you'll see office workers rushing for the subway clutching flimsy plastic bags containing steaming egg pancakes, or biting into *baozi* buns as they wait for the bus. Street vendors peddle their wares on most corners, dishing out *youtiao* (fried dough sticks), sealed bowls of *zhou* (congee, or rice porridge), and plastic cups of soy milk.

When night falls, food sellers pull up their carts and start to cook noodles on hot woks, or expertly turn meat skewers and vegetable kebabs on narrow, portable barbecues. Often, *yang rou chuan'r* (pronounced yang-roe-chwar), or lamb kebabs, are cooked on special barbecue grills outside Uighur restaurants, giving off the tempting scent of cumin and crackling fat. Another tasty street treat is the *roujiamo* (pronounced roe-jah-moe) – also known as the Chinese hamburger. It's a warm pita bread stuffed with a mixture of cilantro and cumin-spiced pork, lamb, or chicken, and originates in Xi'an.

exorbitant. Be sure to try the homemade ice cream for dessert if you have room.

LET'S BURGER 🟢🟢

D101a, Nali Patio, 81 Sanlitun Beilu, 10/5208-6036
HOURS: Daily 11:30 A.M.–midnight
METRO: Tuanjiehu (Line 10)

If you've been in China long enough to be craving Western food, head to Let's Burger at Sanlitun's Nali Patio for a gourmet feast. Choose from Wagyu beef or regular-style, and watch your food being cooked on the open grill. French fries come in cups with a choice of 12 sauces for dipping. The order-at-the-counter system gives the place the feel of a classy diner. Also on the menu are sliders, salads, milkshakes, and smoothies. Burger toppings range from simple relish to foie gras. The managers have recently branched out, with Let's Seafood now in their portfolio.

CAFÉS
COLIBRI 🟢

Sanlitun Village North, Level LG-51, 11 Sanlitun Lu, 10/6417-0808, www.colibricupcakes.com
HOURS: Daily 10 A.M.–10 P.M.
METRO: Tuanjiehu (Line 10)

This sleek, modern café is one of Beijing's most contemporary. Glass walls, wooden floors, and slick white furniture form the backdrop for a great selection of cupcakes and light meals. Sit outside to admire Sanlitun Village's beautiful people heading to the nearby Armani store, or take your laptop inside to surf while you sip. There are 10 varieties of cupcake on offer at a time, ranging from simple chocolate to more unusual flavors like green tea. Opt for takeout and watch as your cupcake is boxed up in a beautiful cardboard container, which is almost as pretty as the cake itself.

TRENDS LOUNGE 🟢

L214, 2F, Trends Tower, The Place North Wing, 9 Guanghua Lu, 10/6587-1999, www.trends.com.cn
HOURS: Daily 10 A.M.–10 P.M.
METRO: Jintaixizhao (Line 10)

Trends by name and trendy by nature, this stylish café and lounge is run by the Trends media group that has its offices in the same building. Curved white bookcases run from floor to ceiling, and chairs, tables, and counters are dotted around. With a selection of English books and Western magazines to read and buy, tote bags, notebooks, and other hip accessories for sale, and some surprisingly tasty food on offer, Trends attracts the wealthier bohemian sort. The well-priced menu focuses on Chaozhou food from Guangdong Province (although there are Western options too).

CONTEMPORARY ASIAN
BEI 🟡🟡

B1/F, The Opposite House Hotel, Bldg. 1, Sanlitun
Village, 11 Sanlitun Lu, www.beirestaurant.com
HOURS: Daily 5:30–10:30 P.M.
METRO: Tuanjiehu (Line 10)

David Laris is a name more usually linked
with Shanghai's high-end restaurant scene,
but his Beijing endeavor at the Opposite
House Hotel brings his innovative style to
the capital. Designed by architects Neri &
Hu, Bei has won awards for both its decor
and its food. On the menu is an artful mix of
Japanese, North Chinese, and North Korean
dishes, with a focus on fresh, natural ingredients. The tasting menu and seasonal set
menu are both good ways to get a feeling
for its style. Chef Max Levy heads up the
kitchen, and his sushi masters were trained
in Tsukiji. Top picks from the menu are the
unagi (eel) roll with foie gras, Wagyu beef,
and mochi dessert. After the excellent food,
the interior design is Bei's strongest draw.
Contemporary lines, purple neon, and light
fittings hanging from the ceiling create a designer look.

CONTEMPORARY CHINESE
XIAO WANG FU 🟡🟡

Ritan Park North Gate, 10/8561-5985
HOURS: Daily 11 A.M.–2 P.M., 5:30–10 P.M.
METRO: Yonganli (Line 1)

Of Xiao Wang Fu's four locations in Beijing,
this one inside Ritan Park is the most pleasant. It's also slightly more expensive, but it's
worth the extra yuan for the park setting. An
English picture menu makes things easier for
non-Mandarin speakers, and the wine list is
surprisingly thorough. The menu reads like
a who's who of Chinese food, with dishes
like kung pao chicken, hong shao pork, roast
duck, cashew chicken, and sweet and sour
pork. You get to escape the bloating though,
as MSG is banned from the kitchen. The outdoor space situates you among the trees and is
ideal for warm afternoons and evenings, while
the interior is equally attractive with a bright,
sunny lounge.

FRENCH
BRASSERIE FLO 🟡🟡

2/F, Rainbow Plaza, 16 Dongsanhuan Beilu,
10/6595-5135
HOURS: Daily 11 A.M.–3 P.M., 6–11 P.M.
METRO: Tuanjiehu (Line 10)

This lovely French brasserie has all the art nouveau charm of a Parisian bistro. In fact, the
Flo brand began in Paris in 1901. Jean-Paul
Bucher brought it to Beijing in 1999, and it
has been a valued part of the fine dining scene
ever since. The interior is decorated in classic
brasserie style with brass fittings, art deco ornaments, and warm lighting. The terrace outside is shaded by white parasols. Stop in on a
weekday for a two- or four-course lunch deal.
Fresh local produce is used alongside imported
Brittany oysters and French foie gras.

INTERNATIONAL
🟡 KIOSK 🟡

1 Xingfu Yicun, 10/6416-3068
HOURS: Daily 10 A.M.–10 P.M.
METRO: Tuanjiehu (Line 10)

This bright pink building is a big hit among
Beijingers seeking a fast food fix at a budget
price. Burgers and sandwiches are served on
crusty baguettes accompanied by thick cut
fries. Quirkier menu offerings include grilled
Serbian sausage sandwiches and paprika salad,
and the wine list includes both glasses and
bottles. The outdoor space on the 2nd floor is
popular when the weather is fine, and you can
watch your food being grilled while you wait.

ITALIAN
ANNIE'S 🟡

Ritan Highlife 2-3-93, 39 Shenlu Jie, opposite Ritan
Park North Gate, 10/8569-3031
HOURS: Mon.–Fri. 9 A.M.–2 P.M.
METRO: Chaoyangmen (Line 2)

For good-value Italian cuisine, Annie's is a
solid choice. Now with multiple venues around
the city, Annie's started as a café in Sanlitun
in 1996 and opened its first restaurant near
Chaoyang Park in 1999. The price of a small
margarita pizza has stayed at ¥28 since 2000,
and the rest of the menu isn't much more

expensive. The top pick from the menu is the well-stuffed calzone. The interior design takes after a homestyle Italian eatery with a warm, friendly atmosphere and cream-toned walls. The restaurant is named after Annie Lee, the general manager, and staff members run their own magazine called *Sharing,* which features career advice and tips.

JAPANESE
HATSUNE ⓢⓢ
S8-30, Bldg. 8, Sanlitun Village South, 19 Sanlitun Lu, 10/6415-3939
HOURS: Daily 11:30 A.M.-2 P.M., 5:30-10 P.M.
METRO: Tuanjiehu (Line 10)

A Beijing staple when it comes to good quality sushi, Hatsune now has sister branches in Shanghai and Hangzhou, as well as teppanyaki, grills, and hot pot spinoffs in the capital. Opened in 2001, the original Hatsune serves California-influenced sushi as well as Japanese staples like tempura and grilled meat. The chief sushi designer is Alan Wong, whose pedigree stretches back to some of California's finest Japanese restaurants. Many of his rolls, like the legendary Moto-roll-ah are copied in sushi joints all around China. From an original menu of 10 maki, Hatsune's list now runs to 50 varieties. The beautifully designed, minimalist interior, with its glinting fish mobiles and clean lines, is the perfect setting.

LATIN FUSION
MOSTO ⓢⓢ
3/F, Nali Patio, 81 Sanlitun Beilu, 10/5208-6030
HOURS: Daily noon-3 P.M., 6-10:30 P.M.
METRO: Tuanjiehu (Line 10)

This attractive, contemporary fusion restaurant is one of Sanlitun's most fashionable locales. Opened in 2008 by Daniel Urdaneta (formerly of SALT), it serves well-conceived dishes with a Latin influence, like seviche and rib-eye steak, as well as Chinese tweaks, such as chocolate soufflé with Sichuan peppercorn ice cream. Receiving awards across the board from Beijing's lifestyle magazines, Mosto looks great both inside and out, with balcony seating, a courtyard with a fountain, and brick indoors

walls dotted with tea lights. The wine list is comprehensive and the service is top-notch, creating an overall dining experience that's chic but laidback.

MEXICAN
THE SADDLE CANTINA ⓢⓢ
Nali Patio, 81 Sanlitun Beilu, 10/5208-6005
HOURS: Sun.-Thurs. 11:30 A.M.-2 A.M., Fri.-Sat. 11:30 A.M.-4 A.M.
METRO: Tuanjiehu (Line 10)

Cheery yellow exterior walls and a terrace overlooking the courtyard below are just some of Saddle Cantina's charms. The others include the Cinco de Drinko deal on the fifth of every month, where drink prices are halved. There are beer and tacos on the ground floor, and a larger menu of good quality Mexican fare upstairs. Homebrewed beer and margarita cocktails are the highlights of the drinks menu. The interior design gives a nod to Mexico without being gimmicky, endearing Saddle to Sanlitun's crowds, especially on weekends when it gets very busy. Weekday afternoons are quiet and you'll probably have the terrace to yourself.

NORTH KOREAN
HAITANGHUA PYONGYANG COLD NOODLE RESTAURANT ⓢ
12 Chaoyangmenwai Dajie, 10/6502-3557
HOURS: Daily 11:30 A.M.-2 P.M., 5:30-8:30 P.M.
METRO: Chaoyangmen (Line 2)

The Hermit Kingdom may be a mystery to the outside world, but outsiders can experience its cuisine at this noodle house. A slightly surreal experience thanks to the traditionally clad waitresses in their voluminous dresses, KTV tunes on the stereo, and plenty of soju. The restaurant itself is pretty sober-looking, with a gray brick exterior and red neon signboard. Inside it's equally unassuming. The small menu includes barbecue items, kimchi, and the cold noodles that give the place its name. North Korean food isn't much different from South Korean, in fact. If you're there at 7 P.M., you'll be treated to a performance of songs in honor of Kim Jong-Il.

PIZZA
NEARBY THE TREE 😊😊
32A Nansanlitun Lu, 10/6413-1522
HOURS: Daily 10 A.M.-midnight (kitchen closes at 10 P.M.)
METRO: Tuanjiehu (Line 10)

This popular, two-floor pizzeria and bar is a spinoff from the even more popular Tree around the corner. The decor is almost identical to the original, with pale wood floors, brick walls, and a modern pub feel. Best known for its huge pizzas, Nearby The Tree branched out into pasta too. Its Belgian beer selection is strong, with Chimay, Hoegaarden, and Koninck topping the menu. There's live music on Saturday nights, and a daily happy hour 6–9 P.M. Nearby the Tree is a place you go to for dinner upstairs and then end up staying all night in the bar downstairs.

TAPAS
MODO 😊😊
S10-31, 3/F, Bldg. 8, Sanlitun Village South, 19 Sanlitun Lu, 10/6415-7207
HOURS: Daily 11 A.M.-11 P.M.
METRO: Tuanjiehu (Line 10)

Mosto's trendy little sister down the street is the funkily decorated Modo, headed up by Daniel Urdaneta and Alex Molina. The menu consists of a series of small dishes that arrive as soon as they're ready. The concept is European tapas, with cheese provided by local cheesemaker Liu Yang. A 16-bottle enomatic machine allows guests to try a variety of wines while they admire the eye-catching black and white patterned walls. Prices are in the mid-range. The restaurant's motto is "No smoking, no gossiping, no bullsh*tting, no backstabbing." You've been warned!

THAI
PURPLE HAZE COURTYARD 😊😊
1 Dongsi Liu Tiao, 10/6501-9345
HOURS: Daily 10:30 A.M.-midnight
METRO: Dongsishitiao (Line 2)

Serving creative food and good value drinks, Purple Haze Courtyard is a great option for Thai food in this part of town. The original Purple Haze is in Gongti. This new branch attracts a trendier crowd thanks to its eponymous courtyard and clean interior design. Purple accents prevail throughout on the walls and furniture. With two dining rooms, a bar, and a courtyard, Purple Haze is spacious yet intimate. The menu contains Thai classics like curries, cold appetizers, and noodles, as well as more imaginative fusion dishes. There's live jazz on Thursday nights and good deals on set lunches.

VIETNAMESE
MUSE BRASSERIE 😊😊
1/F Tongli Studio, 43 Sanlitun Beilu, 10/6415-6388
HOURS: Daily 10 A.M.-4 A.M.
METRO: Tuanjiehu (Line 10)

Popularly held to be the best Vietnamese restaurant in Beijing, Muse Brasserie adds a French twist to its menu. Generous portions of pho bring a regular stream of customers to the Tongli Studio eatery, with its boxy exterior and red signboard. The *banh mi* (Vietnamese sandwich), spring rolls, and papaya salad are solid choices. Finish your meal with a cup of authentic Vietnamese coffee. Service is fast, so it's great for a quick bite on the go. Muse's cozy interior is decorated in simple red, white, and black. An outdoor area fills up during the warmer months.

RESTAURANTS

Capital Museum and the Temple of Great Charity Map 5

REGIONAL CHINESE
JINYANG $$

2 Yuetan Xilu, 10/6803-5839
HOURS: Daily 10:30 A.M.-2 P.M., 5-9 P.M.
METRO: Fuchengmen (Line 2)

This courtyard restaurant was the first Shanxi eatery to open after the 1911 revolution. Shanxi Province (not to be confused with neighboring Shaanxi that has Xi'an as its capital) sits to the west of Beijing and Hebei Province, and is known for its hearty bread, mutton, and vinegar. Very different from the lighter dishes of south China, Shanxi food is part of the *dongbei* (northeastern) cuisine that involves heavy noodles, breads, and soups. Jinyang restaurant is best known for its cat ear pasta with meat and vegetables (made from pasta, not real cats!), pork dipped in hot oil, and sour, vinegary flavors.

CONTEMPORARY CHINESE
THE WHAMPOA CLUB $$$

23A Jinrong Jie, 10/8808-8828
HOURS: Daily 11:30 A.M.-10 P.M.
METRO: Fuchengmen (Line 2)

This Shanghai transplant is named after the Huangpu River, and is a byword for high-end Beijing cuisine. The attractive courtyard restaurant sits among the skyscrapers of Financial Street and serves classic Chinese dishes deconstructed and put back together with a modern touch. The building was designed by Shanghai firm Neri & Hu and modeled after a traditional Beijing courtyard. The menu is the handiwork of chef and restaurateur Jereme Leung. Although this Whampoa Club is lower-key than the original in Shanghai, it is visually stunning, especially the chandelier that covers most of the ceiling. Don't miss the exquisitely decorated toilets and illuminated birdcages.

FRENCH
OH! MARCO $$

9 Jinchengfang Jie, Jinrong Jie, 10/6622-0566
HOURS: Daily 8 A.M.-10 P.M.
METRO: Fuchengmen (Line 2)

This cozy French brasserie is decked out like an art nouveau painting by Alphonse Mucha, and is a somewhat surprising contrast to the chrome grandeur of the surrounding financial district. A French enterprise dating back to 1930, the Beijing outpost was opened in 2007. Oh! Marco now has 13 branches across six Chinese provinces. A 2009 reworking of this branch by French designer Philippe Grande saw the addition of a generous wine cellar, containing over 100 varieties. As for food, it's French all the way, with cheese and charcuterie plates, bistro fare like quiche Lorraine, and even *macarons*.

ITALIAN
CEPE $$

Ritz-Carlton Financial St., 1 Jinchengfang Dongjie, Jinrong Jie, 10/6601-6666
HOURS: Daily 11 A.M.-2:30 P.M., 6-10:30 P.M.
METRO: Fuchengmen (Line 2)

An homage to the humble (and not so humble) mushroom, the Ritz-Carlton's fine dining restaurant is dedicated to serving quality Italian food with a strong emphasis on fungus. Cepe takes its name from a type of mushroom, and has a humidor on-site to keep the specimens fresh. Even the private dining room is named after a mushroom—the Porcino. Cepe has been listed among Forbes.com's Top Power Dining Spots thanks to the quality of the food, décor, and service. The kitchen is helmed by Umbrian master chef Eugenio Iraci, who dishes up mainly Northern Italian dishes. If you're not a fan of mushrooms, don't be put off; there are plenty of other options on the menu.

University District and the Summer Palace | Map 5

REGIONAL CHINESE
BAI FAMILY MANSION 💲💲
15 Suzhou Jie, 10/6265-4186
HOURS: Daily 11 A.M.-10:30 P.M.
METRO: Suzhoujie (Line 10)

For something out of the ordinary, try Bai Family Mansion. It's worth the trip up to Suzhou Street. The restaurant is located in the former garden of Prince Li, along the old route from the Forbidden City to the Summer Palace. As you traverse the stone path up to the pavilion-style main building across a little bridge, ladies in traditional Manchurian costume from the Qing Dynasty will greet you with an ancient welcome. Once inside, pick from a menu of imperial dishes as you soak up the lavish decor. Wooden pillars painted red and gold hold up the intricately patterned ceiling. Among the most interesting dishes to order are *lu rou* (braised donkey meat), flower petal salad, and peanut cakes that were a favorite of the Empress Dowager Cixi.

GOLDEN PEACOCK 💲
16 Minzu Daxue Beilu, Weigoncun, 10/6893-2030
HOURS: Daily 11 A.M.-10 P.M.
METRO: Weigoncun (Line 4)

Little known outside of China, but one of the tastiest and most interesting regional cuisines, food from southerly Yunnan Province is well represented in Beijing. One of the cheapest yet most authentic places to try it is the Golden Peacock. The food comes mainly from Dai minority recipes from the area around Dali. Highlights of the large menu are pineapple fried rice (which comes inside a hollow pineapple), fried potato balls, and rice wine. The Golden Peacock sits among many regional restaurants and stalls on a stretch of street close to the Central University for Minorities. Its bamboo decor creates an authentic, unpretentious atmosphere.

MIDDLE 8TH 💲💲
R17 Zhongguancun Plaza Buxing Jie, 10/5172-1728,
www.middle8th.com
HOURS: Daily 10 A.M.-10 P.M.
METRO: Zhongguancun (Line 4)

Beijing has no shortage of Yunnan restaurants, but Middle 8th vies for the top spot with its award-winning food and warm, tasteful decor. Following a recent trend of gentrifying regional Chinese cuisine, Middle 8th takes the food of Yunnan Province and serves it in an intimate, contemporary setting complete with spot-lit tables and wood-paneled walls. If you're in this part of town, it's worth giving it a try for unusual entrées like worms (four different types!), and Yunnanese favorites like "crossing the bridge noodles" and fried mushrooms. Thankfully, prices aren't exorbitant. Middle 8th has two more branches, one in Sanlitun and one in the CBD.

AMERICAN
HOLY FRIES 💲
Chengfu Lu, 158/0151-3518
HOURS: Daily noon-late
METRO: Wudaokou (Line 13)

If you're craving junk food, head to Holy Fries—a street booth in the heart of Beijing's student district that serves hot dogs, bagels, and churros, as well as the eponymous French fries. These are made from imported potatoes and are thick and crispy, available with an array of sauces and toppings, like grilled bacon, cheese, mayo, and chili. Holy Fries is a great option if you're running low on cash, and it's a reincarnation of the much-missed Crazy Hot Dogs. The sausages on its menu hark back to the glory days. There's even a veggie option for non-meat eaters.

CAFÉS
BRIDGE CAFÉ 💲
1, Bldg. 12, Huaqing Jiayuan, Chengfu Lu, 10/8286-7026
HOURS: Daily 24 hours
METRO: Wudaokou (Line 13)

Loved by laptop-toting students and freelancers, the Bridge Café is a Wudaokou staple when it comes to decent coffee around the clock, hearty but healthy food, and a bohemian atmosphere that is quintessentially Beijing. The ¥30 breakfast is a perennial favorite, along with the almost legendary carrot cake and assorted pies. The café is spread over three floors with a roof terrace that's open in the daytime. There are separate areas for smokers, and no one will mind if you install yourself at a table with a book for a whole afternoon. A word of advice if you order food: The sandwiches are widely held to be a cut above the pasta dishes.

INDIAN
€ GANGES ⑤⑤

160 Chengfu Lu, San Cai Tang, 10/6262-7944
HOURS: Daily 10 A.M.-3 P.M., 5-10:30 P.M.
METRO: Wudaokou (Line 13)

For arguably the most authentic Indian food in Beijing, head to Ganges in Wudaokou. Located opposite the south gate of Qinghua University, it's a popular student haunt. Ganges regularly wins prizes at the local magazine awards for authenticity, and its excellent kormas, *rogan josh,* naan breads, and tandoori meats attest to its quality. There are plenty of non-meat options on the menu too, so it's a good choice for vegetarians. Kingfisher beer and *kulfi* ice-cream desserts make a good accompaniment to your meal. The restaurant's interior is as colorful as a Bollywood movie. Ganges has been open since 2005 and now has three other branches around town.

MIDDLE EASTERN
FALAHFEL ⑤

1/F, Bldg. 12, Dongshengyuan, 10/6252-8188
HOURS: Daily 1 P.M.-midnight
METRO: Wudaokou (Line 13)

For a glimpse into northwestern Beijing's Arab community, have dinner at Falahfel. As well as a convivial, homey atmosphere, you get tasty, authentic, and reasonably priced Middle Eastern food, fresh fruit juice, and a flavored Shisha pipe if you feel like it. The Turkish coffee with cardamom is particularly good. For food, good bets include hummus, salads, *shawarma,* and (of course) falafel, and the menu is in English and Arabic. The restaurant is located on a quiet part of Wudaokou's main bar street and is a focal point for local Arabs who meet up to chat, eat, and smoke Shisha.

Greater Beijing   Map 6

AMERICAN
€ THE KRO'S NEST ⑤⑤

35 Xiaoyun Lu, 10/8391-3131
HOURS: Daily 11 A.M.-midnight
METRO: Sanyuanqiao (Line 10)

After a thorny saga involving closures and takeovers, The Kro's Nest reopened in the northeastern suburbs. The new venue has the same giant American-style pizzas and Western snacks that made the original branch famous, along with cool nest-themed decor, including slightly menacing cartoon bird statues and wooden decorations. The huge space is hard to miss from the outside due to a multi-story painting of the black bird mascot. The Kro's Nest is popular thanks to its reliable Western menu, including nostalgic desserts like funnel cake. The arcade games add to its charm, and the exposed brick interior keeps things hip.

PARKSIDE BAR AND GRILL ⑤⑤

6-9 Jiangtai Xilu, Lido, 10/6444-6555, www.parksidebeijing.com
HOURS: Daily 10 A.M.-late
METRO: Sanyuanqiao (Line 10)

See how Beijing's expat community lives and eats at this Lido restaurant and bar. Parkside is a popular venue for the foreign families and individuals who live in this part of town. It has a modern, bright interior with clean wooden floors and facilities like a pool table and terrace. The food is classic Western pub fare, with steaks from the grill, fries, sandwiches, and salads. Drinks are reasonably priced for an expat-oriented area. Along with SALT and Frank's Place nearby, Parkside is one of the Lido area's top destinations. Look out for the cheekily named ladies' and gents' toilets.

CONTEMPORARY ASIAN
WISH RESTAURANT AND LOUNGE $$

6 Fangyuan Xilu, Lido Garden South Gate, 10/6438-8883
HOURS: Daily 10 A.M.–10 P.M.
METRO: Sanyuanqiao (Line 10)

A café by day, a restaurant for lunch and dinner, and a live music venue on Fridays and Saturdays, Wish is a chameleon of a venue that does everything well. The trendy space is filled with wicker chairs, pastel green cushions, and purple velvet sofas. The two-story venue is spacious and airy thanks to liberal use of glass. The health-conscious menu contains modern takes on traditional Chinese dishes like Beijing Duck and kung pao chicken. A dish to try is the curry ingeniously contained inside bread; appetizers come highly recommended. Details like the scroll-style menu are nice touches.

KOREAN
AI JIANG SHAN $$

Si'de Park North Gate, 39 Jiangtai Xilu, 10/8456-9511
HOURS: Daily 11 A.M.–11 P.M.
METRO: Sanyuanqiao (Line 10)

Beijing has its fair share of Korean restaurants, but Ai Jiang Shan is the venue of choice for those in search of top-quality kimchi and stone pot rice dishes. It is particularly good for Korean barbecue, and tables have their own grills and ventilation systems. Shabu-shabu–style hot pots are also available, and the meat and seafood is among the best you'll find in Beijing's Korean restaurants. *Bibimbap* and a generous selection of kimchi varieties complete the menu. The decor is smart without being overly elaborate, and the atmosphere tends on the busier side of sedate.

LATIN-MEDITERRANEAN FUSION
SALT $$

1/F, 9 Jiangtai Xilu, 10/6437-8457
HOURS: Mon.-Sat. noon–3 P.M., 6–10 P.M., Sun. noon–4 P.M.
METRO: Sanyuanqiao (Line 10)

Treat yourself to some gourmet fare at this local favorite. Venezuelan chef Ana Esteves, who brings her mixed Lebanese heritage to the menu, leads SALT's kitchen. The food ranges from Mediterranean to South American, and the two- and three-course menus change daily depending on what is in season. The wine list is particularly comprehensive. Sunday brunch attracts the weekend crowds. The interior is all clean lines, white walls, and smart contemporary furniture, and the open kitchen lets you watch the chefs at work. The park-facing balcony, with its vibrant red parasols, is a summer staple in this area.

NIGHTLIFE

Beijing is a great place to party, with every imaginable permutation of bar, club, and pub. The scene might not yet be as sophisticated as Shanghai's, but there is enough variety to guarantee a memorable night out. The city's major nightlife hub is the Sanlitun area and nearby Workers' Stadium. Sanlitun started to fill up with bars in the late 1990s, and the action spread to the stadium area. The SARS outbreak of 2003 encouraged revelers to move outside, and they did just that, migrating to the Houhai district.

The shores of Houhai Lake, just northwest of Workers' Stadium, soon began to hum with life. The bars that flank the lakeside tend toward the glitzier end of the nightlife spectrum and are good for a loud and energetic night.

More discerning drinkers may not find the Houhai scene to their liking. However, it's worth a trip to visit the East Shore Live Jazz Café, one of the city's best jazz venues.

Sanlitun is still hugely popular, and the west gate of Chaoyang Park is on the rise as a new social center. The CBD is now home to some classy bars and lounges, while Gulou Avenue in Houhai is your best bet for a cheap, laidback night with a bohemian vibe.

Beijing's legendary live music scene can be enjoyed at several excellent venues, like Yugong Yishan and MAO Livehouse. The gay scene is slowly picking up here with a selection of bars and lounges catering to the LGBT crowd, but Destination is really the only option for late-night dancing.

HIGHLIGHTS

LOOK FOR ◖ TO FIND RECOMMENDED NIGHTLIFE.

◖ **Best Live Music:** Witness Beijing's thriving live rock music scene at **MAO Livehouse.** Local bands cut their teeth here, and it's sure to be a stop for international indie, rock, and punk groups on tour (page 100).

◖ **Best-Kept Secret:** Hidden away down a narrow alley off Gulou Avenue in Houhai, **Amilal** is a cozy little bar with a great whiskey list (page 101).

◖ **Best Cocktails:** Enjoy a cocktail like the "Martinez" martini prepared by expert mixologists using only the best ingredients at **Apothecary** (page 101).

◖ **Most Beautiful View:** Admire the distant mountains while you drink at **Atmosphere,** Beijing's highest bar (page 102).

◖ **Best *Hutong* Atmosphere:** Among the warren of alleys in a trendy part of town, **El Nido** is a tiny, unpretentious bar that represents the *hutong* vibe that Beijing nightlife is famous for (page 103).

◖ **Hidden Gem:** Beijing's first (and only) Prohibition-style speakeasy, **Fubar** lies behind a secret wall in a hot dog restaurant (page 103).

◖ **Best Snacks:** Sate your mid-party hunger pangs with some of **Luga's** hearty Mexican bar food (page 104).

◖ **Most Upscale Bar: XIU** is pronounced "show" in Mandarin, and it's certainly a place to show off. Pricy drinks keep things exclusive; make sure to check out the gorgeous roof terrace (page 107).

◖ **Best People-Watching:** Arguably one of Beijing's best-known clubs, the **World of Suzie Wong** is a nightlife staple in the capital city, and a great place to observe the clubbing scene in action (page 108).

◖ **Best Concept:** In the Houhai district, **Bed Bar** combines drinking with lounging, allowing you to recline on actual beds as you enjoy your beverage (page 109).

© DERRICK NEILL/123RF.COM

Beijing has nightlife venues to suit everyone, like quiet Amilal and exclusive XIU.

NIGHTLIFE

Live Music

ALANTING LIVE BAR AND CAFÉ

1/F, Forte International Apt., 235 Chaoyang Beilu, 10/8571-5168

HOURS: Mon.-Thurs. 8 A.M.-midnight, Fri.-Sun. 8 A.M.-late

COST: No cover charge

METRO: Hujialou (Line 10)

Map 4

Alanting is a great all-around venue for drinks, live music, and café-style relaxation. The place comes alive on Friday with live Latin American music 9 P.M.–midnight, and Saturdays see a variety of bands take to the stage. Sunday is groove improvisation 7 P.M.–midnight. As well as being a funky, laidback place to go for a drink and some tunes, Alanting is well-liked for its reasonable prices. The interior is casually decorated, with exposed ceiling pipes and a bare brick wall.

CD BLUES LIVE MUSIC

16 Dongsanhuan Beilu, 10/6506-8288

HOURS: Daily 4 P.M.-late

COST: No cover charge

METRO: Nongyezhanlanguan (Line 10)

Map 4

This bar is the hub of Beijing's blues and jazz scene. It opened as the CD Jazz Café in 1995 and reopened in spring 2010 with its current name. The founder is Liu Yuan, former horn player for Chinese rock legend Cui Jian. Liu also manages the East Shore Live Jazz Café in Houhai and has played with Wynton Marsalis, Kenny Garrett, and Herbie Hancock's band. The manager is Zhang Ling—bassist for Rhythm Dogs and founder of Beijing's blues scene. CD Blues Live Music bar is known for its great atmosphere, unpretentious decor, quality live music, and cheap drinks. Try the CD Blues signature cocktail: a potent mix of gin, vodka, rum, and blue curaçao.

D-22

242 Chengfu Lu, 10/6265-3177, www.d22beijing.com

HOURS: Daily 8 A.M.-2 A.M.

COST: No cover charge

LIVE LOUD: BEIJING ROCKS

Young Beijingers are rightfully proud of their thriving rock and punk scene. With more live music venues than any other Chinese city, there's a gig on virtually every night. Beijing has always been the epicenter of rock music in China, dating back to the late 1980s. It all started when Cui Jian released his single "Nothing To My Name" in 1986, influenced by the Northwest Wind movement that mixed Shaanxi folk melodies with Western rock beats. The style was picked up by the post-Tian'anmen youth and became even more attractive when rock was banned by the government after Chi Zhiqiang released music in the "prison song" genre. Rockers like Dou Wei developed the genre with his band Black Panther, and three major groups were formed in the wake of the Tian'anmen Square incident. They were Breathing, Cobra, and Nineteen Eighty Nine, and they helped to push rock music forward. In February 1990, a huge concert was staged at the Capital Gymnasium – the first of its kind in China. Cui Jian's band ADO performed, along with big names like Tang Dynasty. Although Mandopop has always been more commercially successful, Beijing rock music gained popularity both in China and abroad in 2003 when Cui Jian played with the Rolling Stones. The Beijing Midi School opened in 1993 to teach rock, jazz, and other contemporary styles, and launched the Midi Festival in 1999. Now the city teems with venues and bands, from the divey D-22 in student-centric Wudaokou to the ever-popular MAO Livehouse in Gulou.

METRO: Wudaokou (Line 13)
Map 5

Wudaokou is known fondly as "Wu" by its student population, and there is no more legendary Wu music venue than D-22. Around since 2006, D-22 is a great place to go if you want to witness Beijing's punk and rock scene at its rawest and most real. D-22 is about as no-nonsense as it gets. If you're not a fan of smoke, humidity, and live music, go somewhere else. Cheap drinks, graffiti-covered walls, and a strong sense of community make it a great place to hang out if you like that sort of thing. Check the website to find out what's going on when you're in town.

EAST SHORE LIVE JAZZ CAFÉ

2/F, 2 Qianhai Nanyan, near Di'anmenwai Dajie, 10/8403-2131
HOURS: Daily 3 P.M.–2 A.M.
COST: No cover charge
METRO: Guloudajie (Line 2)
Map 2

One of the only Houhai bars that's truly worth a look is the East Shore Live Jazz Café. It's run by Liu Yuan, one-time accompanist to jazz trumpeter Wynton Marsalis and former saxophonist for China's first rock star, Cui Jian. The venue is small and intimate, with wood-paneled walls, New Orleans–style chandeliers, and display cases of old musical instruments from Liu's collection. He opened the club in 2006 after managing the CD Jazz Café, and has a loyal client base. Drinks are surprisingly cheap here. A small roof terrace looks out over the lake, but the best view is of the stage inside when there's a live jazz band playing.

HOT CAT CLUB

46 Fangjia Hutong, off Andingmen Dajie, 10/6400-7868
HOURS: Daily 10 A.M.–midnight
COST: No cover charge
METRO: Beixinqiao (Line 2)
Map 2

This small but lively music venue on up-and-coming Fangjia Hutong is a good weekend option. On weeknights it serves as a quiet place

for a beer, among a smattering of mismatched sofas, and then really comes to life on Friday, Saturday, and Sunday nights when local jazz acts come to woo the crowds. There's the odd international act, too, as well as DJ sets. There's room for about 300 revelers at a squeeze. You'll be rubbing shoulders with some of the hippest kids in town. Music videos and indie films play on the back wall when there's no music, contrasting with the psychedelic murals.

JIANGHU BAR

7 Dongmianhua Hutong, off Jiaodaokou Nandajie, 10/6401-5269
HOURS: 7 P.M.–2 A.M.
COST: No cover charge
METRO: Zhangzizhonglu (Line 5)
Map 2

This live music venue, which attracts some of the city's best bands, is an unpretentious bar in an unassuming *hutong* (alley). It is run by musicians from local group Shazi. Jianghu is well loved for its no-frills decor, cheap beer (including Western brews on tap), and improvisation sessions that go on late into the night. Even better, there's never a door charge. The schedule includes regular jazz nights as well as performances by local folk groups and more established bands. There's foosball too, along with a quieter area for chatting and chilling out.

MAKO LIVE HOUSE

Hongdian Art Factory, 36 Guangqu Lu, 10/5205-1112, www.mako001.com
HOURS: Daily noon–8 P.M., 9 P.M.–2 A.M.
COST: No cover charge
METRO: Shuangjing (Line 10)
Map 6

Opened in 2010, Mako Live House is a relative newcomer to Beijing's live music scene but is already attracting the city's best rock talent. A large dance floor and excellent acoustics keep the venue rocking until late. A bar runs the length of one wall, serving Tsingtao beer and cocktails. Mako also includes a dance studio and art gallery, as well as a 300-seat theater. A giant transformer statue and a coffee bar are

NIGHTLIFE

unexpected but welcome additions. Check the website for upcoming gigs. Mako is slightly difficult to find: courtyard 36 is 500 meters south of Carrefour on Guangqu Road.

⬛ MAO LIVEHOUSE

111 Gulou Dongdajie, 10/6402-5080, www.maolive.com
HOURS: Open for performances
COST: No cover charge
METRO: Guloudajie (Line 2)
Map 2

Beijing's rock music scene is the strongest in China, and MAO Livehouse is where all the top bands play. It's a mid-sized converted warehouse behind an unassuming frontage on East Gulou Avenue, and its logo is the forehead of the eponymous Chairman. The Livehouse is backed by a Japanese record label called Bad News, which manages famous Beijing punk outfit Brain Failure. MAO's sound system is one of the best in town and the musical equipment comes from Yamaha, Marshall, and Zildjian. The industrial vibe is a perfect backdrop to the music. MAO Livehouse is a raw, unpretentious venue that is well worth a look if there's an event that takes your fancy. Check the website for the schedule.

THE ONE CLUB

Bldg. 5, 718 Art & Culture Zone, 19 Ganluyuan, 10/5914-8087
HOURS: Daily 11 A.M.-1 A.M.
COST: No cover charge
METRO: Sihuidong (Line 1)
Map 6

If you want to experience Beijing's famous live music scene but don't fancy slumming it in one of the dive-ier venues, try The One Club. It's perfect for fans of live music that would rather sit down than dance or mosh, and its table seating makes for a more sedate experience. The club is housed in an unusually shaped white building designed by Percy Law, protégé of I.M. Pei. The venue also contains an art gallery, recording studio, and VIP area, and is something of a hub for the East 4th Ring Road's creative crowd.

2 KOLEGAS

21 Liangmaqiao Lu, inside Maple Drive-in Movie Theater, 10/6436-8998, www.2kolegas.com
HOURS: Daily 9 P.M.-late
COST: No cover charge
METRO: Liangmaqiao (Line 10)
Map 6

Established by two good friends, hence the name, 2 Kolegas is a bit of a trek from downtown, but worth the trip if you've exhausted the live houses in town. It's one of the mainstays of Beijing's live music scene, and its regular crowds prove that the city's rock fans don't mind traveling. Join them for cheap drinks, a friendly atmosphere, and the most authentic rock, punk, and jazz that Beijing has to offer. The bar is located inside a drive-in movie theater; look out for the bright yellow painted logo on the outside. Check the website for upcoming events.

VA BAR & CAFÉ (VANGUARD)

13 Wudaoying Hutong, near Lama Temple, 10/5844-3638
HOURS: Daily 2 P.M.-late
COST: ¥20 cover when bands play
METRO: Yonghegong (Line 2, Line 5)
Map 2

This bar makes a good stop-off after an afternoon at the nearby Lama and Confucius Temples. Wudaoying Hutong is the ultimate in Gulou hip, and VA oozes boho charm. There's live jazz on weekends, and jazz DVDs the rest of the time. Warm red lighting and comfortable sofas add to a laidback vibe. If you're looking for a quiet place for a drink on a weeknight, this is it. When there's no live act, VA is quiet.

WHAT? BAR

72 Beichang Jie, near the west gate of the Forbidden City, 133/4112-2757
HOURS: Mon.-Thurs. 3 P.M.-midnight, Fri.-Sat. 3 P.M.-2 A.M.
COST: No cover charge
METRO: Tian'anmen West (Line 1)
Map 1

Sitting in the shadow of the Forbidden City's West Gate, the What? Bar is a cozy local live music venue that attracts new talent as well as more established bands. Many of the city's most famous and popular rock and punk groups started their careers here, watched by a small but discerning audience. What? Bar fits a maximum of 50 people, so the atmosphere is intimate but convivial when there's a band playing. The decor is as simple and unpretentious as you'd expect from a Beijing live rock music venue, with a bombed-out wall providing access to the bar from the main room.

YUGONG YISHAN

3-2 Zhangzizhong Lu, 10/6404-2711, www. yugongyishan.com
HOURS: 7 P.M.-late
COST: No cover charge

METRO: Zhangzizhonglu (Line 5)
Map 2

Another good option for live music is Yugong Yishan. The venue takes its name from an old saying meaning "an old man moves mountains" and is located behind an imposing gray wall on the site of Republican warlord Duan Qirui's short-lived government between 1916 and 1920. Yugong Yishan attracts acts from both China and abroad thanks to its Meyer sound system and decent acoustics. The medium-size venue has a lounge upstairs for anyone who doesn't fancy moshing. This is actually its second location. Between 2004 and 2007 it was up near the Workers' Stadium in Sanlitun. Films are often screened on nights when there's no live music.

Bars

ALFA

6 Xingfu Yicun, 10/6413-0086
HOURS: Daily 11 A.M.-late
METRO: Dongsishitiao (Line 2)
Map 4

This attractive bar in Sanlitun is popular with Beijing hipsters and laidback professionals alike. Open for nearly 10 years, it's one of the longest established bars in the capital. Alfa is very gay-friendly despite not being an LGBT bar; the regular Disco Inferno nights draw the crowds.

Suffused in warm yellow light, Alfa's decor is subtle, with floor-to-ceiling drapes and low banquette seating as well as a dance floor. The enclosed outdoor seating area is great on warm evenings, and the mezzanine floor is perfect for people-watching. The bar is well stocked with spirits, which go into Alfa's excellent cocktails. The sake cocktails are particularly good.

⟨ AMILAL

48 Shoubi Hutong, off Gulou Dongdajie, 10/8404-1416
HOURS: Daily 6 P.M.-late
METRO: Guloudajie (Line 2)
Map 2

Hard to find but worth the look, Amilal is nestled down narrow Shoubi Hutong, off the main East Gulou drag. The owner comes from Inner Mongolia, and has another venue called Aluss down the road. Amilal is dedicated to whiskey in all its forms, especially Scotch. There's also a list of imported Belgian, Dutch, and German beers to peruse, along with South American wine. Amilal is small and intimate, with nooks and anterooms suffused with warm amber light. Black and white photographs adorn the walls, and secondhand furniture keeps things hip.

⟨ APOTHECARY

D302, 3F, Nali Patio, 81 Sanlitun Beilu, 10/5208-6040, www.apothecarybj.com
HOURS: Tues.-Sat. 7 P.M.-late, Sun. 6 P.M.-late
METRO: Tuanjiehu (Line 10)
Map 4

One of the most innovative and interesting venues in Beijing, the Apothecary is a world away from the identikit bars of Houhai or the commercial clubs elsewhere in Sanlitun. Designed as a molecular cocktail bar with New Orleans–style bar food, Apothecary has award-winning chef Max Levy in the kitchen and Beijing's best mixologists creating the drinks. Simple decor

NIGHTLIFE

allows the flavors to speak for themselves. The whiskey cocktails are especially good, and a good value for Beijing. Apothecary only takes bookings before 9 P.M., so be prepared not to get a table if you turn up later on Friday or Saturday night.

◖ ATMOSPHERE

80/F China World Summit, 1 Jianguomenwai Dajie, 10/6505-2299 ext. 6432
HOURS: Daily noon-2 A.M.
METRO: Yonganli (Line 1)
Map 4

The highest bar in Beijing sits on the 80th floor of the World Summit building, with views (on clear days) all the way out to the distant mountains that ring the city. Atmosphere is the lounge bar that grew up, with some of the best cocktails in town and a restrained atmosphere that suits a leisurely drink that you don't mind paying top brass for. The high ceiling, contemporary glass accents, and purple seats stay just the right side of minimalist. There are expert mixologists to prepare your drinks and live jazz to entertain you while you sit and admire the constellation-style light fittings.

BEIJING OKHOTSK BEER

7 Shangye Jie, Phoenix City, Shuang Xili, 10/5866-8552
HOURS: Daily 11 A.M.-12:30 A.M.
METRO: Sanyuanqiao (Line 10)
Map 6

If Tsingtao just isn't hitting the spot and you feel like a stronger, tastier beer, head to Okhotsk. It's a bit of a trek out of downtown, but well worth it for a selection of home-brewed pilsners, stouts, and white beer brewed in professional-standard copper vats. Beer is served in portions of three sizes: 300 milliliters, 500 milliliters, and a huge 1,000 milliliters (one liter). Go on a Tuesday and enjoy all-you-can-drink for a set price (though it costs nearly twice as much for men as it does for women). The beer is the main attraction at Okhotsk, but the food is decent too, consisting of pizza, pasta, and salads. A pale wood bar, floor, and furniture give an airy but cozy feel.

THE BRICK

Unit 2-11, Bldg. 2, Tianzhi Jiaozi, 31 Guangqu Lu, 159/0149-7008
HOURS: Mon.-Sat. 5 P.M.-2 A.M., Sun. noon-2 A.M.
METRO: Shuangjing (Line 10)
Map 6

This neighborhood bar is the lynchpin of the slowly growing Shuangjing nightlife scene. The Western manager styled it as a comfortable, laidback pub-style venue, with a daily happy hour 5-8 P.M. The beer menu features regularly rotating international brews on draft and by the bottle. Food and bar snacks are home-made, and three big screen TVs broadcast sport games or movies. The Brick has a relaxed feel on weeknights, whereas weekends get more crowded. There's a nice mix of locals and expats, many of whom live and work in the surrounding CBD.

THE DEN

A4 Gongti Donglu, 10/6592-6290
HOURS: Daily 24 hours
METRO: Tuanjiehu (Line 10)
Map 4

One of the longest standing and most (in)famous of Sanlitun's nightlife venues, The Den is a sports bar with a difference. A red neon dragon beckons customers inside, where two floors of tables, booths, screens, and pool tables await the eager drinker. Many are attracted by the generous happy hour: Between 5 and 10 P.M., pizza and drinks are half price. The Den is open 24 hours a day, every day, making it a popular choice for post-clubbing sustenance. The clientele tends to be mainly expat, with numbers swelling whenever there is a major game on.

D LOUNGE

Courtyard 4, Gongti Beilu, 10/6593-7710
HOURS: Daily 7 P.M.-late
METRO: Tuanjiehu (Line 10)
Map 4

D Lounge certainly scores points for amazing interior design. The white Gaudi-esque bar curves out from the bare brick walls, running from floor to ceiling and creating an almost futuristic look. Oddly-shaped chairs and funky furniture add to the effect. Li Bo, ex-manager of several Japanese bars, and Warren Pang, from Punk at the Opposite House Hotel, run the bar. D Lounge offers a stylish, artsy atmosphere to enjoy good quality, well-mixed drinks. It's one of those Beijing venues that got people talking when it first opened, and is managing to hold onto its cachet thanks to its consistent quality. It's a haven for Beijing's beautiful people who want to see and be seen; so dress smartly.

EARL BAR

1 Dongdan Bei Dajie, 10/8511-6646
HOURS: Daily 7 P.M.-2 A.M.
METRO: Dengshikou (Line 5)
Map 1

This no-frills dive bar and basement hangout is an island of neon and cheap beer in an area not known for its thriving nightlife scene. Local DJs spin to a casual crowd who are more interested in getting tipsy and dancing than posing and preening. There's also a foosball table for drunken tournaments. The walls are painted red, and there's a definite dingy vibe that adds to the divey atmosphere. Dress code is strictly casual. Earl Bar is a popular bar for evening beers as well as late-night partying on the weekend. If you don't mind the down-and-dirty vibe, you'll almost definitely like it.

(EL NIDO

59 Fangjia Hutong, off Andingmennei Dajie, 10/8402-9495
HOURS: Daily 4 P.M.-late
METRO: Andingmen (Line 2)
Map 2

This tiny bar is hidden down Fangjia Hutong near the Hot Cat Club. El Nido is notable not just for its size, but for its surprisingly thorough selection of imported beers and wines. Imported beers tend to be expensive in Beijing, but El Nido's owner refuses to give in to ludicrous price markups. There are only two tables inside, so chances are that you'll strike up a conversation with your neighbors, as well as the owner, and anyone else who happens to be there. In the warmer months, the outdoor benches are your best bet.

FRANK'S PLACE AT TRIO

8 Jiangtai Xilu, 10/6437-8399
HOURS: Daily 9 A.M.-late
METRO: Sanyuanqiao (Line 10)
Map 6

Frank's Place is the oldest sports bar in Beijing, and has been a firm favorite among the capital's expat community since it opened back in 1989. Located in front of Si'de Park opposite the Rosedale Hotel, it is decked out with televisions showing sports, a pool table, and a big central bar serving imported beers. The Western food menu can be hit and miss, but the snacks are fairly reliable. What's best about Frank's is the atmosphere and the homey decor of warm wood, exposed brick, and cast-iron light fittings. It's a home away from home for tourists and expats alike.

(FUBAR

Inside Stadium Dog, Gate 10 of Workers' Stadium, 10/6593-8227
HOURS: Sun.-Thurs. 2 P.M.-2 A.M., Fri.-Sat. 2 P.M.-4 A.M.
METRO: Dongsishitiao (Line 2)
Map 4

When it first opened a couple of years ago, Fubar caused quite a stir thanks to its secret location. Now everyone knows where it is, but it's still fun to find. Located behind a false wall inside a hot dog shop at the Workers' Stadium, it's a Prohibition-style speakeasy decorated in red and black, with jazz on the sound system. It sounds gimmicky, but it's actually pretty classy. Fubar appeals both to the party crowd and more laid-back drinkers, and it's a good place to start a night out. Cocktails come served in ceramic Buddhas, which you get to keep when you're done, and have quirky names like Fu-jito and Fu-tini. The Dizzy Buddha is a tropical fruit cocktail with a punch, and the potent Fu-Manchu comes in a mug with Fu Manchu himself emblazoned on it. Happy hour runs 3–9 P.M. daily.

GEORGE'S

Gate 12, Workers' Stadium East Side, 10/6553-6299
HOURS: Daily 3 P.M.-2 A.M.
METRO: Dongsishitiao (Line 2)
Map 4

NIGHTLIFE

Mixologist George Zhou learned the fine art of cocktail making at many of Beijing's top bars. He took over the First Café and named it Midnight before setting up Q Bar with his partner Echo to show off his skills. His most recent endeavor is the self-titled George's. What's great about this place is that most of the cocktails cost less than ¥50. His bar is well designed but unpretentious, with an unassuming gray facade, wooden floors, and a sunken area and mezzanine. He has amassed one of the most comprehensive whiskey collections in Beijing, rivaling some of the bigger names like Glen. His cocktails are unsurprisingly well put together, with quality ingredients and expert mixing.

GLEN

203 Taiyue Suites, 16 Nansanlitun Lu, 10/6591-1191
HOURS: Mon.-Fri. 6 P.M.-2 A.M.
METRO: Tuanjiehu (Line 10)
Map 4

Beijing's best stocked whiskey bar is a rare beacon in a city that subsists on a diet of Johnnie Walker and Jameson. Using Japanese mixology techniques and handcrafted ice, Glen's bar staff are meticulously trained in the art of pouring their single malts. The bar is named after the many "glen" varieties of Scotch whiskey, like Glenfarclas, Glenfiddich, and Glenmorangie. The interior of the bar is comfortable and just dark enough to make you feel as if you're in a cozy British pub (although way fancier). The green velvet bucket seating is a nice touch, as is the artwork on the walls.

GREAT LEAP BREWERY

6 Doujiao Hutong, off Fangzhuan Chang Hutong, off Di'anmenwai Dajie, 135/5223-7655, www.greatleapbrewing.com
HOURS: Thurs.-Sat. 3 P.M.-late
METRO: Zhangzizhonglu (Line 5)
Map 2

In a nation not known for the quality of its domestic beer, an outfit like Great Leap Brewery is a valuable asset. If you've had enough of weak, watery Tsingtao, head over to Carl Setzer's craft microbrewery close to Qianhai for a pint of something stronger and tastier. Great Leap operates inside a cute *hutong* building with a sunny seating area. Setzer's seasonal brews usually include Indian pale ales and stouts, with the addition of unusual ingredients like Sichuan peppercorns and pumpkin.

ICHIKURA

36 Dongsanhuan Beilu, 10/6507-1107
HOURS: Daily 6 P.M.-1:30 A.M.
METRO: Hujialou (Line 10)
Map 4

One of Beijing's best "hidden gem" Japanese whiskey bars, Ichikura has all the important details, like the perfect spheres of ice in your drink to the piping hot towel you get when you first sit down. Unsurprisingly popular with the capital's Japanese community, Ichikura has a great collection of single malts and bourbons. The bar bristles with bottles, and the bar staff know a thing or two about mixing classic cocktails and more innovative drinks. The vibe is intimate and slightly serious thanks to the dedicated whiskey aficionados who filter through. Finding Ichikura can be tricky; go under the archway and head up the stairs on the side of the building.

LAGOON

36 Dongsanhuan Beilu, 10/6507-1013
HOURS: Mon.-Sat. 6 P.M.-2 A.M.
METRO: Hujialou (Line 10)
Map 4

Work your way through 84 varieties of mojito at this sleek but understated Japanese cocktail bar. It's classy without straying into bling territory, and has a neighborhood feel. The chandeliers that hang above the red bar are subtle rather than striking. Still something of a hidden corner, it never gets too busy. There's beer and Guinness on tap, as well as virgin mojitos. Resident mixologist Kyohei Fujita prepares the cocktails; bar snacks come in the form of pizza and nachos.

(LUGA'S

41 Sanlitun Beilu, 10/6415-4005
HOURS: Daily 10:30 A.M.-3 A.M.

METRO: Tuanjiehu (Line 10)

Map 4

The Luga name has become a Mexican empire in Beijing, with the Luga's Villa and Luga's Basement bars, and Vietnamese restaurants Luga's Banh Mi and Luga's Pho Pho. The bar snacks at the original venue in Sanlitun are widely held as being the best in town, with burritos, tortilla soup, guacamole, and banana chimichangas at the top of the list. As for drinks, there's Corona beer, the famous frozen Margaritas, shooters, and other cocktails. The interior's dark orange walls give a passably authentic Mexican feel. Luga's is a popular stop on Sanlitun bar crawls thanks to its reasonable prices, outdoor space, and the daily happy hour that runs 4–9 P.M.

LUSH

2/F, Bldg. 1, Huaqing Jiayuan, Chengfu Lu, 10/8286-3566

HOURS: Daily 24 hours

METRO: Wudaokou (Line 13)

Map 5

Another student favorite, Lush is open 24 hours a day, seven days a week, and morphs from a breakfast bar to a café in the daytime, and a restaurant, bar, and club when night falls. It was the first foreign-oriented bar in Wudaokou when it was opened by a New Zealander in 2003, and it maintains a loyal following. Wednesday night is quiz night from 8 P.M., and there's an open mic music session on Sunday evening. Happy Hour runs nightly 8–10 P.M., with two drinks for the price of one. The food menu includes waffles, focaccia sandwiches, and all-day breakfast options. Expect to share the venue with students hard at work during the day, or hipsters if you're there in the evening.

MAO MAO CHONG

12 Banchang Hutong, off Nanluogu Hutong, 10/6405-5718, www.maomaochongstore.com

HOURS: Wed.-Mon. 6:30P.M.-midnight

METRO: Zhangzizhonglu (Line 5)

Map 2

Mao Chong means caterpillar in Mandarin (literally "furry insect"), and this award-winning bar in a *hutong* (alley) off Nanluogu is something of an institution. It's run by a husband and wife team and is a haven for local artists and hipsters who come for well-mixed drinks and cheap, tasty pizza. There's modern art by co-owner Steven Rocard on the walls and funky decorations throughout, like the swirly writing on the blackboard above the bar. Wednesday nights see cocktail prices slashed, with innovative concoctions like Tail of the Dragon and African Queen. Mao Mao Chong creates its own infused vodka using ingredients like lemongrass, honey, ginger, and cinnamon.

MESH

The Opposite House Hotel, Sanlitun Village, 11 Sanlitun Beilu, 10/6417-6688

HOURS: Daily 5P.M.-1A.M.

METRO: Dongsishitiao (Line 2)

Map 4

The Opposite House Hotel in Sanlitun Village is something of a byword for boutique chic, and its on-site bar (one of six food/drink venues) does not fall short. Mesh is great for chatting and chilling over a decent wine or cocktail; its atmosphere is classy and relaxed. Mesh drapes hang from the ceiling, and the interior decor is all clean lines and low leather seats. The music is muted electronica, more conducive to conversation than to dancing. The cocktail list is one of the most thoughtful and best executed in town. If you feel like staying on after Mesh closes at 1 A.M., head downstairs to Punk where the party carries on late into the night.

NO NAME

3 Qianhai Dongyan, 10/6401-8541

HOURS: Daily noon-2A.M.

METRO: Guloudajie (Line 2)

Map 2

It might lack a name, but this bar makes up for it in character. It was the first bar to set up on the Houhai lakeshore, sparking a nightlife scene that is still alive and kicking today. No Name takes up the front room of an old

NIGHTLIFE

hutong house, and recreates the homey atmosphere with wood-burning stoves, potted plants, photos on the wall, and a resident cat. While many of Houhai's bars are characterless, neon-fronted nightmares, No Name retains its friendly, laidback atmosphere, winning popularity among those in the know. The drinks list is long and plentiful, and the lake view is a winner.

PADDY O'SHEA'S

28 Dongzhimenwai Dajie, 10/6415-6389, www. paddyosheas.com
HOURS: Daily 11 A.M.-2 A.M.
METRO: Dongzhimen (Line 2, Line 13)
Map 4

If you're familiar with Irish bars and aren't keen on the customary levels of rowdiness and gimmicky decor, don't be put off—Paddy O'Shea's is different. While it's most certainly Irish, it's less in-your-face than most and is actually a sports bar. A consistent winner at the local magazine awards, Paddy's is a great place to relax with a pint of Guinness while watching sports on the big screens. It can certainly get busy though, and when there's a big game on, the atmosphere is jovial and most definitely high-spirited. Quiz night is on Wednesday, and an Irish singer takes to the stage on Friday evening.

Q BAR

6/F Eastern Inn Hotel, 6 Baijiazhuang Lu, 10/6595-9239, www.qbarbeijing.com
HOURS: Daily 6 P.M.-3 A.M.
METRO: Hujialou (Line 10)
Map 4

Opened by local mixology hero George Zhou (of George's bar fame) and his partner Echo, Q Bar is a favorite among the city's cocktail connoisseurs. The rooftop terrace is dotted with big, rectangular brick arches, while the indoor area is decked out with simple wooden floors and brick walls. Warm orange lighting and understated furniture add to the unpretentious vibe. Go on Wednesday evening 6–11 P.M. for martini night, and be sure to try their tasty appletini.

RED YARD

95 Donghuamen Dajie, 10/6403-1584
HOURS: Daily 6-10 P.M.
METRO: Tian'anmen East (Line 1)
Map 1

Despite cheap drinks and friendly service, this popular courtyard bar to the east of the Forbidden City never gets too rowdy. It's the ideal place for a quiet drink after an afternoon in the Forbidden City; it's even quiet enough for a reading session to plan your next day of sightseeing. Red Yard, appropriately outfitted with a generous coat of red paint throughout, has the same management and similar laidback vibe as popular Huxley's bar in Houhai. It is a cheap, relaxed alternative to the fancier bars in the Tian'anmen area. The drink list covers wine, beer, spirits, and soft drinks.

SALUD

66 Nanluogu Hutong, off Gulou Dongdajie, 10/6402-5086
HOURS: Daily 3 P.M.-late
METRO: Guloudajie (Line 2)
Map 2

This multi-level Spanish-themed bar on Nanluoguxiang is a great live music spot as well as a regular drinking venue with decent wine, beer, and spirits. You get a free plate of tapas with your beer, along with the chance to see local musicians jamming on the small crow's nest stage on the 2nd level. Salud's specialty is its selection of house rums, and you can get a tasting paddle of 10 shots to sample them all. The atmosphere is pumped on weekends and convivial during the week. The bar is run by the managers of Café de la Poste, and the vibe is similarly casual. Get there early to secure one of the tables up in the rafters that look out over the bar below and the stage opposite.

SCHOOL

53 Wudaoying Hutong, 10/6402-8881
HOURS: Daily 8 P.M.-late
METRO: Yonghegong (Line 2, Line 5)
Map 2

Wudaoying Hutong near the Lama Temple is firmly on the rise as the new "go to" alley, with hip new venues sprouting up all the time. School is a Wudaoying mainstay, and is one of the best places to go if you want to hear decent electro and alternative music. The epicenter of a collaboration between Beijing and Shanghai music crews, School was founded by Liu Hao, an ex-member of well-known band Joyside. The ambience is chill, with a minimalist white bar, courtyard, and murals. Upstairs is the dance floor where things tend to be louder. Friday nights see local and international DJs taking over the decks.

TAO YAO

39 Beiguanfang Hutong, south shore of Houhai, near Yinding Bridge, 10/8322-8585
HOURS: Daily 2 P.M.-2 A.M.
METRO: Guloudajie (Line 2)
Map 2

Another diamond in the Houhai lakeshore rough, Tao Yao is the opposite of brash and tacky. Tibetan-themed, it has the atmosphere of a funky youth hostel, full of handcrafted ornaments, patterned sofas, and beat-up charm. Go on a Friday and drink as much as you like for ¥50, with unlimited food as well for ¥100. They call this event "Yak Tipping." It's one of the best drink deals in town and is not-surprisingly popular. Weeknights are quieter but no less enjoyable, and regular drink prices are very affordable.

THE STUMBLE INN

S3-31, Level 3, South Village Sanlitun, 19 Sanlitun Lu, 10/6417-7794, www.stumbleinnbeijing.com
HOURS: Sun.-Thurs. 10 A.M.-2 A.M., Fri.-Sat. 10 A.M.-late
METRO: Tuanjiehu (Line 10)
Map 4

A favorite among Beijing's expats thanks to its friendly pub atmosphere, great beer selection, and solid food menu (including the legendary Jenga fries), Stumble Inn is now in its second location after the first branch closed down. The new incarnation is spread over two floors and has over 100 beers on tap and by bottle—one of the best collections in the city. Western staff will happily tune the TV screens to sports matches, and there are pool tables and dart boards for you to hone your skills. Glenn Phelan and Shane O'Neill, who are the brains behind many of the capital's most successful bars, founded the Stumble Inn.

【 XIU

6/F, Beijing Yintai Center, 2 Jianguomenwai Dajie, 10/8567-1838
HOURS: Sun.-Wed. 6 P.M.-2 A.M., Thurs.-Sat. 6 P.M.-3 A.M.
METRO: Guomao (Line 1, Line 10)
Map 4

This beautiful contemporary bar in an annex of the Park Hyatt Hotel looks like a traditional Chinese pavilion. The various rooms and bars are separated by outdoor terraces, alleys, and water features, and the indoor area contains a wine room, lounge, and five bars. Outside is a grill for cooking food in summer. The cocktails are innovative, and there's a wood-fired oven for roasting Beijing Duck. The martini and vodka bar runs a weekly Ladies' Night on Thursday 10 P.M.–1 A.M., offering free vodka for women. (In case you were wondering, *xiu* means "bloom" or "flourish" in Mandarin.)

Dance Clubs

THE HOUSE

Workers' Stadium North Gate, 138/1188-2479
HOURS: Mon.-Fri. 9 A.M.-2 A.M.
METRO: Dongsishitiao (Line 2)
Map 4

If you're looking for a place to dance that doesn't play endless hip-hop, house, and R&B, try The House. Run by techno record label

Acupuncture, it's Beijing's only dance-oriented nightclub and attracts local producers and international DJs to play techno until the small hours. The new, modern space has a huge LED screen and a lounge area on the ground floor that's similar to Acupuncture's other venue, Lantern. The main dance floor is upstairs, and the decks are almost always tuned to electronic

NIGHTLIFE

house. Chinese clubbing elements, like fruit platters and green tea mixers, are a part of the scenery, and while bottles don't come cheap, spirits by the glass are affordable.

LAN CLUB

4/F, LG Twin Towers, B12 Jianguomenwai Dajie, 10/5109-6012
HOURS: Daily 11 A.M.-late
METRO: Yonganli (Line 1)
Map 4

Much more than just a club, Beijing's LAN (there's one in Shanghai too) contains a restaurant, oyster bar, cocktail lounge, cigar room, and dance floor. Philippe Starck designed the bar with plush fabrics, opulent drapes, and glamorous chandeliers, creating a chic ambiance. Prices reflect this; it's definitely not cheap. Each of the 35 private rooms is decorated with valuable oil paintings, but entrance to the main club is free. Frequented by high rollers from the surrounding CBD, LAN Club is definitely a place to see and be seen. For visitors, it provides an opportunity

to see a side of Beijing that's a world away from the *hutong.*

WORLD OF SUZIE WONG

1A Nongzhanguan Lu, west gate of Chaoyang Park, 10/6500-3377
HOURS: Daily 8:30 P.M.-late
METRO: Tuanjiehu (Line 10)
Map 4

It may come under fire among locals and expats for its tacky charms, but Suzie Wong's is a mainstay of Beijing's nightlife scene. Situated on the cusp of Chaoyang Park, it was responsible for kick-starting the bar industry in this part of town. It's well known as a pick-up joint, to which the opium den decor, canopy bed, and red lighting all attest. The club is split into a basement nightclub playing mainly house music, a lounge, and a roof terrace, and is prime people-watching territory. It takes its name from the 1957 novel by Richard Mason in which a British artist falls in love with a Chinese prostitute in Hong Kong, and is as glamorous and vice-driven as its eponymous heroine.

Gay and Lesbian

DESTINATION

7 Gongti Xilu, opposite west gate of Workers' Stadium
HOURS: Sun.-Thurs. 8 P.M.-2 A.M., Fri.-Sat. 8 P.M.-late
METRO: Tuanjiehu (Line 10)
Map 4

Pretty much the only really happening gay nightclub in Beijing, Destination's motto is "anything can happen." The clientele is predominantly male, but club-loving *lalas* (Mandarin slang for lesbians) make an appearance too. Look out for the gorgeous waterfall of lights behind the bar that glows with

the colors of the rainbow. A mix of concrete walls, red couches, traditional kang-style beds, and birdcage light fixtures create a funky, stylish atmosphere, along with portraits of gay icons like Madonna and Marilyn Monroe. Step into the neon blue lighting around the bar area while you wait for your cocktail to be made, or dance in one of the themed rooms. Destination gets packed on Friday and Saturday nights, as it's the first choice for many gay people in search of a drink and a dance.

Lounges and Karaoke

◖ BED BAR

17 Zhangwang Hutong, Jiugulou Dajie, 10/8400-1554
HOURS: Daily 2 P.M.–3 A.M.
METRO: Guloudajie (Line 2)
Map 2

Ever felt so sleepy in a bar that you dreamed of a bed to lay down on? At Bed Bar, it's a reality. It's a *hutong* bar with a difference. Along with the regulation courtyard and beat-up furniture are actual beds within the interconnected rooms. The trappings are cushions instead of pillows and duvets, but it's still plenty comfortable enough to get some shut-eye. If you don't feel like sleeping, there's a small area for dancing, along with outdoor courtyard space, table seating, and a menu of cocktails to work your way through. Snacks come in the form of Asian tapas.

HAOLEDI

Shunmai Jinzuan Tower, 52B Dongsanhuan Nanlu, 10/6772-6311
HOURS: Daily 24 hours
METRO: Jinsong (Line 10)
Map 6

Karaoke (referred to as KTV in China) in the West is the preserve of drunken nights in bars, but it is taken way more seriously in China. Alcohol still plays a part in many KTV evenings, but the emphasis is on singing well instead of purposefully badly. In Chinese KTV halls, each party has a private room with its own screen and microphones, and waitresses deliver drinks and snacks. Haoledi is one of the best-known chains in China and tends to be clean and well run, with English songs on the list as well as Mandopop. KTV has a reputation as a cover for the sex trade, and while it's true that some KTV girls double as escorts, it's easy to have a night at Haoledi and not notice.

TOUCH

2/F, The Westin Beijing Chaoyang, 7 Dongsanhuan Beilu, 10/5922-8880
HOURS: Tues.–Thurs. 9 A.M.–1 A.M., Fri.–Sat. 9 A.M.–2 A.M.
METRO: Liangmaqiao (Line 10)
Map 6

The Westin Beijing Chaoyang's lounge bar is an attractive venue with some of the most imaginative vodka cocktails in town. The decor is a cool array of black and fluorescent green, with leather, glass, and marble fittings. Vodka dominates the drink list with 88 different varieties and a huge selection of vodka cocktails. Wednesday evening is Ladies' Night, when female drinkers get to choose from a special menu of free cocktails 9 P.M.–midnight. Touch is a good example of a hotel bar done well, and one that is worth going to even if you're not a guest at the Westin. Look out for interesting touches like interactive tabletops.

NIGHTLIFE

Wine Bars

ENOTERRA

D405 Nali Patio, 81 Sanlitun Lu, 10/5208-6076, www.enoteca.com.cn
HOURS: Daily 10 A.M.–2 A.M.
METRO: Tuanjiehu (Line 10)
Map 4

Imported wine tends to be expensive in China, but Enoterra bucks the trend. Wines are organized into "emotions" instead of varietals, with a choice of Hedonist, Sensualist, Evocative, and Playful flavors. As with the brand's Shanghai branches, the Beijing Enoterra has red velvet chairs, smart European-style decor, and walls decorated with unopened bottles of wine. There is inside and outside seating to choose from, and a menu of French charcuterie, cheese, and sandwiches. Happy hour runs daily 4–8 P.M., and Fridays see special deals. There's often live music in the evenings.

REDMOON

1/F Grand Hyatt Hotel, Beijing Oriental Plaza, 1 Dongchang'an Dajie, 10/8518-1234 ext. 6366

HOURS: Sun.-Thurs. 5 P.M.-1 A.M., Fri.-Sat. 5 P.M.-2 A.M.

METRO: Wangfujing (Line 1)

Map 1

Hotel bars often suffer from a distinct lack of character, but Redmoon at the Grand Hyatt is a striking exception. The walls are lined with shelves of wine bottles and a fire burns in a contemporary hearth in winter. Take a seat on one of the sumptuous red and purple sofas or chairs and choose from a menu of sushi (with hand-grated wasabi) to accompany your wine (of which there are 20 varieties served by the glass, and many more by the bottle). Attention to detail and excellent service, along with a dedicated cigar lounge and stylish atmosphere, make Redmoon extra special. It's a favorite among visiting businesspeople, but the atmosphere is far from corporate.

ARTS AND LEISURE

Beijing has a long and well-deserved reputation for being China's most culturally advanced city. While Shanghai has the style, the money, and the attitude, Beijing has a thriving contemporary art scene of the city's hot art spots are located slightly outside central Beijing. The most famous art complex is the 798 District, but lesser-known Caochangdi Art District is catching up in popularity.

When it comes to green space, the capital is blessed with plenty of parks. While Beijing may appear at first glance to be a mass of concrete and asphalt, the urban spread is actually interspersed with a good collection of open spaces. Many of the city's parks contain interesting historical sites, like the sacrificial altars in Ritan Park and the temples and pavilions in Zhongshan Park. Others, like Chaoyang Park and Tuanjiehu Park,

have great facilities for children, like swimming pools and amusement parks.

Beijing boasts more museums than you'll ever be able to visit, covering an astounding variety of subjects. There's traditional art at the Beijing Art Museum, countless historical artifacts at the National Museum of China, and Chinese literature at the Lu Xun Museum; view offbeat exhibitions at the Beijing Police Museum and discover how the capital city developed in the modern era at the Urban Planning Exhibition Hall.

Stage performances abound in Beijing, with offerings ranging from traditional Peking opera and kung fu in beautiful old theaters, to dance shows, contemporary dramas, and concerts from international musicians at modern performance venues and stadiums.

HIGHLIGHTS

LOOK FOR ◖ TO FIND RECOMMENDED ARTS AND ACTIVITIES.

◖ **Best Way to Get to Know Beijing:** See the city laid out beneath your feet at the **Urban Planning Exhibition Hall** (page 115).

◖ **Best Place to See Contemporary Art:** Established by controversial artist Ai Wei Wei, **Caochangdi Art District** contains some of Beijing's best contemporary galleries (page 116).

◖ **Best Art Complex: 798 Art District** is the epicenter of Beijing's ever-growing contemporary art scene. This former electronics factory has been transformed into a series of galleries, cafés, and shops (page 117).

◖ **Best Kung Fu Fighting:** Head to the **Red Theater** near the Temple of Heaven to watch martial artists in action (page 118).

◖ **Best Place to Watch Opera:** The beautiful **Huguang Guild Hall,** with its Qing-era decor, hosts regular performances of traditional Chinese opera (page 119).

◖ **Best Community Show:** Watch homegrown, Beijing-based talent onstage at the intimate **Penghao Theater** (page 119).

◖ **Most Festive:** Falling on the last day of Spring Festival (also known as Chinese New Year) celebrations, the **Lantern Festival** honors Buddha lantern lightings and fireworks shows across the city (page 122).

◖ **Best Escape: Ritan Park** is a great spot to relax among the flowers, ponds, and trees, admire a Ming-era temple, and learn some tai chi (page 124).

◖ **Most Historic Park:** As well as being a pleasant place to enjoy nature and the site of the Forbidden City Concert Hall, **Zhongshan Park** contains the emperors' ancestral temples (page 125).

◖ **Best Children's Activity:** A trip to the **Beijing Zoo** provides a reprieve for families who need a change from visting the city's temples (page 125).

◖ **Best Tour:** Electric scooters are almost as popular in Beijing as the standard pedal bike. See the city like a local with **Beijing eBike Tours** (page 126).

spring cherry blossoms in Zhongshan Park

© SUSIE GORDON

The Arts

MUSEUMS

ARTHUR M. SACKLER MUSEUM OF ART & ARCHAEOLOGY

Peking University, 5 Yiheyuan Lu, 10/6275-1667
HOURS: Daily 9:30 A.M.-4:30 P.M.
COST: ¥5
METRO: Yuanmingyuan (Line 4)
`Map 5`

A visit to this excellent museum is a great reason to explore the leafy, sprawling campus of Peking University. The museum owes its name to the American philanthropist, entrepreneur, and psychiatrist who commissioned it to be built in 1986. It didn't open until 1993, by which time Sackler had died, but it remains an important legacy. The museum contains over 10,000 artifacts from the collections of Peking and Yanjing Universities, charting Chinese history from Paleolithic times to the 17th century. The major highlight among the jade, bronze, and bone relics is Jiuniushan Man who dates back 280,000 years.

BEIJING CAPITAL MUSEUM

16 Fuxingmenwai Dajie, 10/6337-0491
HOURS: Tues.-Sun. 9 A.M.-5 P.M.
(last ticket issued at 4 P.M.)
COST: Free with prior reservation; ¥20 for temporary exhibitions
METRO: Muxidi (Line 1)
`Map 5`

This behemoth of history and culture is second only to the National Museum of China in Tian'anmen Square when it comes to scope and size. The Capital Museum's collection moved to its current, specially built location in 2001, having inhabited part of the Confucius Temple for the previous 20 years. Although it is a contemporary building, traditional architecture is echoed in the overhanging roof. The unusual bronze cone jutting from the side of the six-floor museum is the Bronze Exhibition Hall, one of several display rooms. There are nearly 200,000 pieces in the museum's collection, charting the history of Beijing and China

through art, calligraphy, opera, culture, and folk customs.

BEIJING POLICE MUSEUM

36 Dongjiaomin Hutong, 10/8522-5018
HOURS: Tues.-Sun. 9 A.M.-4 P.M.
COST: ¥5
METRO: Qianmen (Line 2)
`Map 1`

One of the city's most interesting and offbeat museums, this cornucopia of crime and punishment is located inside the old New York City Bank building with the imposing columns. It displays 1,500 relics from a 70,000-strong collection, including guns and batons, Qing torture and execution devices, graphic photographs of crime scenes, and the stuffed body of Feisheng, the famous German Shepherd police dog. Look out for the formerly top-secret map charting Kim Il-Sung's journey around Beijing from his 1987 visit and the guns used in the robberies of notorious criminal Lu Xianzhou. The gift shop sells oddly sinister souvenirs, like toys made from gun shells.

BEIJING WORLD ART MUSEUM

9A Fuxing Lu, 10/5980-2990 (individual reservations), 10/5980-2199 (group reservations), 10/5980-2222 (general inquiries)
HOURS: Tues.-Sun. 9 A.M.-5 P.M.
COST: Free
METRO: Military Museum (Line 9)
`Map 5`

Opened with the purpose of introducing foreign art to Chinese audiences, the Beijing World Art Museum is part of the Century Monument, which was built to commemorate the new millennium. The museum covers 20,000 square meters (215,000 sq. ft.) and includes several display rooms including the Permanent Exhibition Hall, Special Exhibition Hall, and Digital Art Gallery. Although there is excellent work in each, the latter is probably the most interesting if you are pushed for time. The Great Century Hall contains a huge frieze charting Chinese history, which is also worth a look. Call at least a day in advance to make sure you get a ticket.

LU XUN MUSEUM

19 Gongmen Er Tiao, Fuchengmen, 10/6616-4168
HOURS: Tues.-Sun. 9 A.M.-4:30 P.M.
COST: ¥5, ¥3 students
METRO: Fuchengmen (Line 2)
Map 5

Lu Xun was a prominent figure in the nationalist May 4 movement of 1919. He is known as the father of modern Chinese literature thanks to the depth and reach of his work. A visit to this museum is a good way to learn more about him. The most influential Chinese writer of the 20th Century spent most of his career in Shanghai and its environs, but spent a crucial period of his life in Beijing. The house he lived in near Fuchengmen between 1924 and 1926 has been converted into the Lu Xun Museum and pays tribute to his life and work. It was opened in 1956 and contains over 20,000 historical items, including Lu's book collection, private journals, and letters.

MILITARY MUSEUM

9 Fuxing Lu, 10/6686-6114
HOURS: Daily 8:30 A.M.-4:30 P.M.
COST: ¥5, ¥2 students
METRO: Military Museum (Line 9)
Map 5

War buffs will love this large-scale temple to all things military, from weapons belonging to the People's Liberation Army to the tools of modern warfare. An enormous ballistic missile dominates the hangar-like Hall of Weapons, and Soviet tanks from the Cold War number among the exhibits, along with artillery seized during the Sino-Japanese War. There are U.S. weapons taken by the Kuomintang in the Chinese Civil War, as well as American war goods from Korea. Lesser-known struggles are also represented, like the Agrarian Revolutionary War fought between 1927 and 1937. The quaintly named Friendly Hall showcases the many hundreds of gifts bestowed upon China by foreign armies and governments.

NATIONAL ART MUSEUM OF CHINA

1 Wusi Dajie, 10/6400-6326 (tickets), 10/8403-3500 (general inquiries), www.namoc.org/en
HOURS: Daily 9 A.M.-5 P.M.
COST: Free
METRO: Dongsi (Line 5)
Map 1

With 17 exhibition halls over five floors, this comprehensive museum gives a great overview of Chinese art, with 100,000 individual pieces on display. The National Art Museum of China (NAMOC) is housed in a lovely traditional building with upturned eaves and colorful outer decoration. It was opened in 1963 by Chairman Mao and renovated in 2003 in time for its 40th anniversary. The art on show is mainly contemporary, but there are some great examples of Ming, Qing, and early Republican art. Visiting exhibitions of Western greats like Chagall, Picasso, Dalí, and Miró achieve the gallery's aim of educating Chinese audiences about foreign art. NAMOC also contains a restaurant, café, and bookstore.

NATIONAL MUSEUM OF CHINA

16 Dongchang'an Jie, east side of Tian'anmen Square, 10/6511-6400
HOURS: Tues.-Sun. 9 A.M.-5 P.M.
(last ticket issued at 4 P.M.)
COST: Free
METRO: Tian'anmen East (Line 1)
Map 1

The newly refurbished National Museum on Tian'anmen Square is the biggest in the world and contains a comprehensive overview of Chinese history, geography, politics, and society from prehistory to the end of the Qing Dynasty. Renovations, including the addition of 28 new halls, were completed in April 2011. The museum originally opened in 1959 for the 10th anniversary of the founding of the People's Republic and is owned and curated by the Ministry of Culture. Inside the imposing column-fronted building are 200,000 square meters (2.1 million sq. ft.) of floor space. Highlights include the remains of Yuanmou Man dating back 1.7 million years, the Simuwu Ding cooking pot from

FOR ART'S SAKE: AI WEIWEI AND CONTEMPORARY ART IN BEIJING

While Beijing's contemporary art scene has grown in scope and international acclaim over the past decade with several big sales at Sotheby's in New York, there is one man who stands as a symbol of artistic output, political activism, and the fight against censorship across all of the arts. His name is Ai Weiwei and he was born in Beijing in 1957. The enfant terrible of China's contemporary arts, he is famous for his strong statements and relentless fight against what he perceives to be injustices peddled by the state. At the same time as his "Sunflower Seeds" installation was on display at the Tate Modern in London, he was busy investigating a government cover-up over unsafe buildings that collapsed during the 2008 Sichuan earthquake, killing children. Ai's father was sent to a labor camp during the

Cultural Revolution, no doubt impacting Ai's political awareness from an early age.

Despite being at the helm of contemporary art in China, Ai Weiwei dislikes the way it is becoming commercialized in line with Western standards. He mounted a protest to the Shanghai Biennale in 2000 with an exhibition entitled "F*CK OFF." In 1981-1993, Ai lived in New York City and studied at Parsons School of Design. On his return to Beijing, he set up an artists' commune called East Village, followed by a studio in Caochangdi. In 2006, he helped design a residential building in New York. Seen as a huge threat by the Chinese government, he is lauded outside of his home country, so much that an asteroid has been named after him. His frequent government-led disappearances are viewed with concern in the West.

the ancient Shang Dynasty, and a Han jade burial suit. The museum's front has been used to display important countdowns, such as the 2008 Olympics, 2010 Shanghai Expo, and the handover of Hong Kong in 1997.

◖ URBAN PLANNING EXHIBITION HALL

20 Qianmen Dongdajie, 10/6701-7074
HOURS: Daily 9 A.M.-5 P.M.
COST: ¥150
METRO: Qianmen (Line 2)
Map 3

This excellent and informative exhibition hall opened in September 2004 to tell the story of Beijing in the context of urban development. Like Shanghai's museum of the same name, Beijing's has an impressive scale model of the city that you can walk around; the model mimics day and night with a real-time lighting system. The parts of the city that aren't represented by 3D buildings are laid out with aerial photographs, so you get a comprehensive overview of the city from above. The exhibition hall also contains detailed and interesting information about Beijing's impressive

transportation system. Getting so many people from A to B is quite a feat. The museum is housed in a modern building close to the old railway station, and is worth the rather steep entry cost just for the scale model.

ART DISTRICTS AND GALLERIES

BABU SPACE

Unit N2-40, North Sanlitun Village, 11 Sanlitun Beilu, 10/6415-8616, www.babu-art.com
HOURS: Daily 10:30 A.M.-9 P.M.
METRO: Tuanjiehu (Line 10)
Map 4

For something a little different from the contemporary art on display at most galleries in the capital, visit Babu Space to see work by some of the most talented Beijing-based street artists. The gallery in Sanlitun is a non-elitist space designed for displaying and selling urban art and design, illustrations, and photographs. Some of the most prolific artists whose work is showcased at Babu are German graffitist Seak, French Ceet (pronounced "city"), and a street-art duo called Graphic Airlines. The spacious

ARTS AND LEISURE

white gallery has a concrete floor and separate areas for displaying and selling work.

BEIJING CENTER FOR THE ARTS
Chi'enmen 23, 23 Qianmen Dongdajie, 10/6559-8008, www.beijingcenterforthearts.com
HOURS: Tues.-Sun. 10 A.M.-10 P.M.
METRO: Tian'anmen East (Line 1)
Map 3

Part of the Chi'enmen 23 complex in the Legation Quarter, the Beijing Center for the Arts occupies the Qing Dynasty U.S. Embassy building, built by Sid H. Nealy in 1903. The two-floor exhibition hall covers 1,600 square meters (17,000 sq. ft.), and there's an on-site repertory theater called Black Box that holds regular performances. Art expert Weng Ling, the partner of developer Handel Lee, curates the space. The pair also developed the Shanghai Gallery of Art at Three on the Bund. Beijing Center for the Arts opened in 2008 and aims to join China's art community with the general public.

◀ CAOCHANGDI ART DISTRICT
Caochangdi Village, Wuhuan Beilu
HOURS: Most galleries open Tues.-Sun. 10 A.M.-6 P.M.
METRO: Sanyuanqiao (Line 10)
Map 6

Farther off the tourist trail from the 798 Art District is Caochangdi, a collection of galleries and artist studios near the North 5th Ring Road. The village is made up of low brick buildings and quiet walkways, and was established in 2000 by contemporary artist and bête noire of the authorities, Ai Wei Wei. Caochangdi is home to some excellent galleries, like Pekin Fine Arts, PKM, Galerie Urs Miele, and the Caochangdi Work Station. There is also an offshoot of Shanghai-based ShanghART. Caochangdi came to international attention in 2007 thanks to an article in the *New York Times* travel section, but it's still far enough off the beaten track to remain free of crowds.

C5ART CENTER
Bldg. F, 5 Sanlitun Xi Lu, 10/6460-3950, www.c5art.com
HOURS: Tues.-Sun. 10 A.M.-7 P.M.

METRO: Agricultural Exhibition Center (Nongye Zhanlanguan) (Line 10)
Map 4

The C5Art Center is a gallery devoted to nurturing upcoming talent in Chinese contemporary art. Promoting gifted young artists with a passion and understanding of the past, the gallery shows work across a range of media; you'll see photography, sculpture, painting, and mixed media. C5 likes to focus on a small number of artists, the better to nurture their talents. If you're interested in collecting Chinese art, this is a great place to pick something up. It may be worth a lot of money if the artist becomes well known. Unassuming from the outside with its low gray wall, the gallery is white and airy inside.

CREATION ART GALLERY
Ritan Donglu, at corner of Ritan Beilu, 10/8561-7570, www.creationgallery.com.cn
HOURS: Tues.-Sun. 10 A.M.-7 P.M.
METRO: Yonganli (Line 1)
Map 4

Founded by Li Xiaoke, artist and son of master painter Li Keran, the Creation Art Gallery displays contemporary pieces by artists whose work is informed by the past and traditional methods of creating art. If you're a fan of traditional Chinese art but want to take home something more meaningful than a mass-produced scroll from the silk market, a trip to Creation Art Gallery might give you some inspiration. There are also more conventional contemporary art works on display and on sale. The Creation name covers several galleries and organizations, like the Li Keran Foundation and the Creation Space.

89 PROMENADE DES ARTS GALLERY
Rm. 1010, Block D, Lanbao Bldg., 3A Dawang Xilu, 10/8599-9974, www.89-gallery.com
HOURS: Wed.-Fri. and Sun. 2-9 P.M.
or daily by appointment
METRO: Jinsong (Line 10)
Map 4

If you've seen enough Chinese contemporary art and fancy a change, head to 89 Promenade des Arts Gallery. Owned and run by an artistically-named Frenchman, Valery Vauban de Montaudon, it mounts exhibitions from Western greats like Joan Miró, Salvador Dalí, and Pablo Picasso. You might not immediately think of coming to Beijing to pick up a piece of fine art from a great modern master, but 89 Promenade makes it a distinct possibility. Even if you're not in the market to buy a Picasso, the gallery provides a welcome change from the rest of the galleries in town.

EM-ART

8 Liangjiayuan Hutong, 10/5208-3787
HOURS: Tues.-Sun. 10 A.M.-10 P.M.
METRO: Dawang Road (Line 1)
Map 4

With a sister branch in Seoul, this contemporary art gallery focuses on promoting the work of Asian artists. Past exhibitions have included work by painters, photographers, and sculptors from India, Vietnam, China, and Korea. A striking black and silver signboard welcomes visitors to the gallery, which is down a *hutong* in the CBD. EM-Art opened both of its branches in the run-up to the 2008 Olympics. The Beijing branch launched with an exhibition of work from Chinese artists who studied at the Central Academy of Fine Art, the China Academy, Luxun Academy, and Xi'an Academy.

QIN GALLERY

Bldg. 1, Rm. 1E, Huawei Li, 10/8779-0461,
www.qingallery.com
HOURS: Tues.-Fri. 9:30 A.M.-7 P.M., Sat.-Sun. 10 A.M.-7 P.M.
METRO: Jinsong (Line 10)
Map 6

The focus of the Qin Gallery is promoting work by recently graduated artists whose work embodies the traditions of classical Chinese art. While not solely classical in theme and appearance, the art displayed at Qin is all influenced by ancient techniques. The gallery opened in 1996 as a platform for academic and cultural exchanges in the realm of art, displaying mainly oil paintings, but also watercolors, sculpture, and folk art produced in China,

across group and solo exhibitions. Works are framed using Italian techniques. The gallery interior is simple, with wood floors and white walls.

RED GATE GALLERY

Levels 1 and 4, Dongbianmen Watchtower,
Chongwenmen Dongdajie, 10/6525-1005
HOURS: Daily 9 A.M.-5 P.M.
METRO: Beijingzhan (Line 2)
Map 3

Intriguingly located inside the Ming Dynasty Southeast Watchtower, the Red Gate Gallery was opened by Australian Brian Wallace in 1991 as the first privately-run contemporary art gallery in China. Wallace's aim is to nurture up-and-coming artistic talents, and he runs a special residency scheme to promote their work, as well as exchange programs with foreign artists. He studied at Beijing's Central Academy of Fine Arts 1990–1991 before setting up the gallery with the support of the Chinese Bureau for the Preservation of Cultural and Historical Relics. Outside of the 798 complex, Red Gate is the hub of Beijing's contemporary art scene.

◖ 798 ART DISTRICT

4 Jiuxianqiao Lu, www.798district.com
HOURS: Most galleries open daily 10 A.M.-6 P.M. with various late-night events and openings
METRO: Sanyuanqiao (Line 10)
Map 6

Beijing's contemporary art scene has its epicenter in the 798 Art District. Also known as Dashanzi, this complex of galleries, exhibition spaces, cafés, and shops takes up what was the state-owned North China Wireless Joint Equipment factory in the 1950s. Artists began to move into the abandoned warehouses in 2002, and now there are over 400 galleries and venues onsite. Notable among them are the 798 Photo Gallery, 798 Space (inside a Bauhaus-style hangar), the Iberia Center for Contemporary Art, and the Ullens Center for Contemporary Art. The AT Café (owned by artist Huang Rui) is a good choice for refreshments, and the Timezone 8 bookshop stocks some excellent international titles. If you have even a passing interest in China's emerging art scene, a trip to 798 should be on your itinerary.

ULLENS CENTER FOR CONTEMPORARY ART

4 Jiuxianqiao Lu, 798 Art District, 10/6438-6675, www.ucca.org.cn
HOURS: Tues.-Sun. 10 A.M.-6 P.M.
METRO: Sanyuanqiao (Line 10)
Map 6

This contemporary art gallery is one of the most striking and best-known inside the 798 complex. Ullens Center for Contemporary Art (UCCA) is based inside a striking Bauhaus-style factory dating from the 1950s and is widely held to be the best modern art gallery in China. Covering 8,000 square meters (86,000 sq. ft.) in a hangar-like building, the gallery helps to promote connections between China and the rest of the world in the field of contemporary art. It was established as a nonprofit organization by Belgian art collectors Guy and Myriam Ullens in 2007 and holds forums and lectures as well as exhibitions. Check out the shop for books, clothes, and gifts.

DANCE, ACROBATICS, AND KUNG FU

BEIJING LDTX MODERN DANCE COMPANY

Dongcheng Cultural Center, 111 Jiaodaokou Dongdajie, 10/6405-4842, www.beijingldtx.com
HOURS: Open for performances
COST: ¥60-100
METRO: Beixinqiao (Line 5)
Map 2

This contemporary dance company is based at the Dongcheng Cultural Center and was established in 2005 by Willy Tsao, former artistic director of the Beijing Modern Dance Company and Hong Kong's City Contemporary Dance Company. The troupe's full name is Lei Dong Tian Xia, meaning "thunder under the sky," and it has toured Asia, Europe, and North America under a team of veteran choreographers. Willy Tsao hosts the annual Beijing Modern Dance Festival every spring and holds

regular classes and performances throughout the year with some of China's most talented dancers. Check the website for events when you're in town.

🎭 RED THEATER

44 Xingfu Dajie, inside Workers' Cultural Palace, 10/6710-3671 (discount hotline: 10/6400-0300)
HOURS: Performances at 5:15 P.M.-6:35 P.M. and 7:15 P.M.-8:35 P.M.
COST: ¥150-300
METRO: Tiantandongmen (Line 5)
Map 3

This venue started out as the Workers' Cultural Palace Theater and is the location for one of Beijing's best long-term kung fu performances. The martial art practiced by the likes of Jet Li, Jackie Chan, and Bruce Lee, kung fu is almost synonymous with China. The Legend of Kung Fu at the Red Theater showcases the talents of a team of young martial artists (whose average age is around 17). In six 10-minute segments, they tell the story of a young boy who leaves his parents to go and study at the temple under a great kung fu master. The theater is easy to find thanks to its glowing neon-red facade.

TIANQIAO ACROBATICS THEATER

95 Tianqiao Shichang Jie, 10/6303-7449, www.tianqiaotheater.com
HOURS: Performances at 5:30 P.M. and 7:30 P.M.
COST: ¥180-380
METRO: Qianmen (Line 2)
Map 3

Taking in an acrobatics show is a time-honored tradition among visitors to Beijing. The Tianqiao Acrobatics Theater is one of the best places to do it. Not to be confused with the nearby Tianqiao Theater at 30 Beiwei Road, the acrobatics house is a white-fronted building with a century of history. It is home to the famous Beijing Acrobatic Troupe, the members of which entertain two nightly crops of spectators with their tumbling, balancing, leaping, and springing. The show changes every season, but you're guaranteed to see gravity-defying human pyramids, impressive contortions, and some tricky work with a diabolo (a spool-shaped juggling prop).

MUSIC, THEATER, AND OPERA
BEIJING CONCERT HALL
1 Beixinhua Jie, Liubukou, 10/6605-7006,
www.bjconcerthall.cn
HOURS: 9 A.M.–5:30 P.M.
METRO: Tian'anmen West (Line 1)
Map 1

Opened in 1985, this venue was Beijing's first modern, professional concert hall. It's a contemporary glass-fronted cube of a building that looks particularly attractive at night, and sits just over 1,000 people inside a well-designed performance space. The hall is home to the China Philharmonic Orchestra, and the ensemble plays regular concerts of Western classical music throughout the year. Visiting luminaries have included Yo-yo Ma, Yehudi Menuhin, and Plácido Domingo. The annual performance schedule includes an opera season, piano season, and chamber music season, as well as regular concerts and guest appearances.

CHANG'AN GRAND THEATER
7 Jianguomennei Dajie, 10/6510-1309,
www.changantheater.com
HOURS: Open for performances
METRO: Jianguomen (Line 1, Line 2)
Map 4

This striking silver-fronted building might not look like a theater at first glance, but its unlikely exterior holds one of the city's finest performance spaces. Visitors enter the 800-seater, through an incongruous Chinese-style gate, to watch Beijing opera performances. Although waning in popularity somewhat in recent years, Jingju opera still has a strong following in the capital, and Chang'an Grand Theater is a good place to experience it. Even if you don't understand a word of what is being sung, the vibrant costumes and exaggerated gestures help to tell the story. The first floor of the theater contains a shop selling Chinese paintings and handicrafts, which make good (if a little unimaginative) souvenirs.

FORBIDDEN CITY CONCERT HALL
Xichang'an Jie, inside Zhongshan Park, 10/6559-8285,
www.fcchbj.com
HOURS: Open for performances
METRO: Tian'anmen West (Line 1)
Map 1

Well known for its beautiful surroundings as well as for the quality of the performances it hosts, the Forbidden City Concert Hall sits inside Zhongshan Park in the south west of the Forbidden City. It hosts visiting musicians and groups from around the world, and offers film screenings, children's events, and concert seasons all year round. Its annual Christmas performance of Handel's *Messiah* is a Beijing staple. The building is contemporary both inside and out, with top-notch sound equipment. Get seats in the stalls for the best acoustics. Tickets are available online and from the Friendship Store on Jianguomen Wai Avenue, opposite the Scitech Building.

◖ HUGUANG GUILD HALL
3 Hufang Lu, near Luomashi Dajie, 10/6351-8284
HOURS: Performances daily at 7:30 P.M.
COST: ¥150–240
METRO: Caishikou (Line 4)
Map 3

Another popular Beijing pastime is Peking opera. While not everyone likes the strangled vocals that characterize this form of opera, the costumes are impressive and the background music attractive. If you fancy checking out a performance, the Huguang Guild Hall is a good place. As well as quality performances by talented opera singers and musicians, the hall is a beautiful example of Qing Dynasty wooden architecture. It was built in 1807 and was one of the capital's four great theaters in its heyday, attracting celebrated performers like Mei Lanfang. It was at the Huguang that the nationalist Guomindang (KMT) party was formed on August 25, 1912.

◖ PENGHAO THEATER
35 Dongmianhua Hutong, off Nanluogu Hutong,
10/6400-6452
HOURS: Café: daily 10 A.M.–midnight, Theater: daily

2:30–9:30 P.M.
METRO: Guloudajie (Line 2)
`Map 2`

This small theater is a world away from Beijing's large-scale performance venues. Situated in a converted courtyard complex behind the Central Academy of Drama, the Penghao Theater takes its name from a type of chrysanthemum that also symbolizes the "common people." Dedicated to nurturing young talent, it hosts the annual Beijing Youth Theater Festival, as well as the Beijing Actors' Workshop and Beijing Improv Group. The 80-seat performance space is outfitted with professional sound and lighting equipment and is a community theater hub. The rooftop bar and café are popular outside of performing hours.

POLY THEATRE

Poly Plaza, 14 Dongzhimen Nandajie, 10/6500-1188 ext. 5126, www.polytheatre.com
HOURS: Open for performances
COST: ¥50–100
METRO: Dongsishitiao (Line 2)
`Map 4`

With a capacity of 1,500, the Poly Theatre hosts regular performances of theater, as well as opera, ballet, and classical music from international and local groups. The interior is simple and contemporary, with wood-paneled walls and purple velvet seats. Built in 1991, the theater was designed by British firm TT International Stage Design Company with top-quality acoustic equipment and stage setup throughout. It was classified as a Type A theater by the ministry of culture and is a hub for the arts in Chaoyang district. Its striking exterior features two parallel towers rising on either side of the entrance.

PERFORMANCE VENUES
WORKERS' STADIUM

Gongti Beilu, 10/6501-6655, ext. 503
HOURS: Dependent on games and performances
METRO: Dongsishitiao (Line 2)
`Map 4`

Known for being the epicenter of Beijing's major nightlife scene, the Workers' Stadium functions as both a sporting arena and a concert venue. The 350,000-square-meter space (3.7 million sq. ft.) has room for 64,000 spectators and was used as a location for events at both the 1990 Asian Games and the 2008 Olympics. The stadium was built in 1959 as one of the 10 great structures that were designed to celebrate the 10th anniversary of the People's Republic of China. It was strengthened and renovated in 2004 in preparation for the Olympics. The stadium is used mainly for football matches, but it hosts concerts too, such as the Beijing leg of Bob Dylan's China tour in spring 2011.

CINEMA
CNEX SALOON CAFÉ

Jing Yuan, 2/F, Bldg. 1, 3 Guangqu Donglu, 10/8721-5576, www.cnex.org.cn
HOURS: Daily 2–9 P.M.
COST: Most screenings free
METRO: Sihui East (Line 1)
`Map 6`

Documentary maker Ben Tsiang is the brains behind this cinema-café that screens movies and documentaries by filmmakers from the mainland, Taiwan, and Hong Kong to tell the story of modern China. It's a nonprofit organization that promotes Chinese filmmaking while bringing together fans and proponents of the genre. Each year, CNEX adopts a different theme for its screenings and talks, each theme pertains to Chinese social issues. The theme for 2011 is youth and 2012 is education. Screenings are accompanied by cheap beer (¥20–25) and mixed drinks (starting from ¥30), with two-for-one drinks 6–9 P.M. Even if there's no movie on, you're welcome to hang out and have a drink. Check the website for screenings.

DAGUANLOU CINEMA

36 Dazhalan Xijie, 10/6303-0878
HOURS: Daily 9 A.M.–8:30 P.M.
COST: Tickets start at ¥80
METRO: Qianmen (Line 2)
`Map 3`

The Daguanlou Cinema and Drama House

on Dazhalan is the oldest operating movie theater in the world and the oldest cinema in China. It opened in 1905 inside an attractive granite-fronted building, which entrepreneur and film enthusiast Ren Qingtai had bought in 1902. The first shows were the silent movies that had first been shown in Shanghai in 1896. Since there was no Mandarin word for them, the term *dianying* (electric shadows) was coined. The ground floor China Film Gallery with its plain brick walls and 40 individual chairs is more atmospheric than the modern screen rooms upstairs. Eat cheap popcorn and sandwiches and sip Tsingtao beer while you watch. Most films are in Mandarin, but it's worth going for the experience.

WANDA INTERNATIONAL CINEPLEX
3F, Bldg. 8, Wanda Plaza, 93 Jianguo Lu,

10/5960-3399, www.wandafilm.com
HOURS: Daily 11 A.M.–11 P.M.
COST: Tickets ¥60, half price for students
METRO: Dawang Road (Line 1)
`Map 4`

If there's a blockbuster out that you just can't miss, watch it at Wanda International Cineplex. If you're traveling with children, Wanda's activity arcade will provide welcome entertainment, and there's a café to satisfy pre- or post-movie munchies. Go on a Tuesday and it's half price for everyone. Wanda is your typical big-bucks commercial movie theater, so if it's art house or history you're looking for, go elsewhere. Also bear in mind that only a certain number of Hollywood movies are sanctioned to be played in Chinese cinemas each year, so you might have to wait until you go home to see the latest blockbuster.

Festivals and Events

WINTER
CHINESE NEW YEAR
Known to Westerners as Chinese New Year and to the Chinese as Spring Festival, the major national holiday in China is a time when families get together to usher in the new lunar year. It usually falls in late January or early February, and workers get a week off to celebrate. Spring Festival sees one of the largest human migrations in the world, as millions of workers go back to their home cities. The train and road networks are jammed, and getting a ticket is nigh-on impossible.

On New Year's Eve, the skies light up with fireworks and the rattle of firecrackers goes on until the early hours, designed to frighten off spirits, and the mythical Nian monster. The wealth god is welcomed three nights later, and the chaos starts again. Then, on the last day of the festivities, people gather to watch lanterns contrasted against the night sky. Children traditionally receive red hongbao envelopes stuffed with money and are treated to a new outfit. Families visit relatives and feast on lucky food like oranges, fish, tofu, and dumplings, greeting each other with *gong xi fa cai* (pronounced gong-shee-fah-tseye), meaning "happiness and prosperity."

Shop fronts and public spaces are adorned with auspicious characters and depictions of

SPRING FESTIVAL (CHINESE NEW YEAR) DATES

The dates for Spring Festival change every year. The festival's starting date is always the first day of the first month of the Chinese calendar, which is not concurrent with the Gregorian calendar.

- January 23, 2012
- February 10, 2013
- January 31, 2014
- February 19, 2015

ARTS AND LEISURE

whichever zodiac animal has risen to prominence that year. Beijing and Shanghai tend to empty out over Spring Festival, with local businesses shutting up shop for the duration of the week. Larger enterprises remain open, and it can be a pleasantly chaos-free time to visit if you don't mind being woken by fireworks or navigating a busy transport system at each end of the holiday.

LANTERN FESTIVAL
The Lantern Festival falls on the last day of the week-long Chinese New Year holidays, and is one of the highlights of the festivities. People gather to watch lanterns being lit in parks and temples across the cities and eat rice balls stuffed with black sesame. The festival dates to the time of the Han emperor Ming Di, who decreed that lanterns be lit to honor Buddha.

SPRING
BEIJING BOOKWORM LITERARY FESTIVAL
www.bookwormfestival.com
COST: Author events ¥50
In a nod to the capital's ever-growing literary scene, the Bookworm café and bookshop runs a festival every March to promote reading and writing across all genres, from children's literature to historic biography. Events run across several weekends, and include literary lunches, author talks, panel debates, and discussions. A ticket to an author event entitles you to a drink. Similar festivals run concurrently in Suzhou, Chengdu, and Shanghai.

BEIJING QUEER FILM FESTIVAL
www.bjqff.com
Mainland China's only LGBT film festival is slowly gathering momentum after something of a rocky, drawn-out start. The inaugural event took place in 2001, organized by members of the Peking University Student Cinema Association with a movie enthusiast named Yangyang at its helm. Around working in Europe for the Belgian Film Archive, Yangyang has developed the festival through

several incarnations into a major event that screens LGBT-related films from China and abroad. The festival tends to happen every two years, so check the website to find out if it's going on when you visit Beijing.

MEET IN BEIJING ARTS FESTIVAL
www.meetinbeijing.com.cn
An international festival for the arts, this event has run every year since 2000, backed by the Ministry of Culture, Beijing Municipal Government, and the State Administration of Radio, Film, and Television. Based around a different theme each year (such as opera, drama, or folk dance), the festival is held late April–late May at various locations around Beijing. It attracts professional acts from all around the world. It is one of China's best known and best-respected arts festivals, and is always well attended.

TOMB SWEEPING
Outlawed by the Communists during the Cultural Revolution, this ancestor-honoring festival may not be a public holiday, but it is observed by a growing number of people. Falling in early April, it is a time for solemn remembrance, tending graves, and burning paper money and other goods to provide deceased relatives with everything they need in the afterlife. These days, it's not uncommon to see paper iPads, laptops, and even cars being sold on the street to burn as offerings.

SUMMER
BEIJING MIDI FESTIVAL
www.midifestival.com
Rock fans flock from all around China to attend the super popular Midi Festival in early May. Running over four days, it attracts bands from Beijing and abroad to play for an enthusiastic crowd at one of several outdoor venues, including Haidian Park. Run by the Midi School (which teaches rock, punk, jazz, and other modern genres of music), the festival has become the most popular and best known in China since it launched in 1997, and has even spread to Shanghai.

DRAGON BOAT FESTIVAL

On the fifth day of the fifth lunar month, China celebrates the life and commemorates the death of the ancient poet Qu Yuan, who killed himself in 278 B.C. in protest of corruption in the imperial court during the Warring States Period. Since Qu died by drowning, dragon boats are raced on rivers and lakes, and *zongzi* (rice balls) are eaten. Dragon Boat is celebrated across Asia, and is known as Tuen Ng Jit in Cantonese. As with many traditional festivals, Dragon Boat was banned during the Cultural Revolution, and it was only recognized officially again in China in 2008.

FALL
BEIJING MUSIC FESTIVAL

www.bmf.com

Running from mid-September to early October, the Beijing Music Festival gathers classical talent from around the world to play at various performance venues in the city. In 1998, the Ministry of Culture and the Beijing Municipal Government launched the event, which attracts big names like José Carreras and Julian Lloyd Webber.

NATIONAL DAY

If you're in Beijing on October 1, head down to Tian'anmen Square at sunrise to watch flags being raised in celebration of the People's Republic of China—established by Chairman Mao right there on October 1, 1949. On decade anniversaries, the celebrations are especially florid, but even regular October 1 festivities are impressive. Portraits of the great Chinese Communist leaders are displayed in Tian'anmen Square, and fireworks are set off around the city. National Day is the last public holiday of the year, meaning that Beijingers have a tough few months of winter to get through before Spring Festival comes around.

Recreation

PARKS
BEIHAI PARK

1 Wenjin Jie, 10/6403-1102

HOURS: Nov.-Mar. daily 6:30 A.M.-8 P.M., Apr.-May and Sept.-Oct. daily 6 A.M.-9 P.M., June-Aug. daily 6 A.M.-8 P.M.
COST: ¥10 Nov. 1-Mar. 31, ¥5 Apr. 1-Oct. 31
METRO: Ping'anli (Line 4)
Map 1

This 10th-century imperial garden lies to the northwest of the Forbidden City and was connected to the palace complex prior to 1911. It opened to the public in 1925 and is popular for its huge lake and pretty white dagoba stupa. The lake covers over half of the park's area. The white stupa is perched on Qionghua Island, which sits in the middle of the lake. The 40-meter (131 ft.) stupa was rebuilt in 1976 after the Tangshan earthquake, and it houses Buddhist relics. Beihai Park's lakes and pavilions were built in the styles of Hangzhou and Yangzhou, while its landscaped gardens copy the Suzhou style. Don't miss the Nine Dragon Wall—a beautiful glazed frieze dating from 1402.

CHAOYANG PARK

1 Nongzhan Nanlu, 10/6506-5409
HOURS: Daily 6 A.M.-10 P.M.
COST: ¥5
METRO: Tuanjiehu (Line 10)
Map 4

Beijing's equivalent to New York City's Central Park, Chaoyang is the city's largest urban green space and the biggest city park in the whole of Asia. Measuring 2.8 by 1.5 kilometers (1.7 by 0.9 mi.), the park opened in 1984 and has been solidly popular ever since. Even better, it is one of the few parks in Beijing that actually allows visitors to play ball games and sit on the grass. In addition to flower gardens, lawns, lakes, and ponds, Chaoyang Park also contains leisure facilities like rental boats and bikes. A giant ferris wheel was under construction in 2008 but sadly never opened due to lack of funds. The

ARTS AND LEISURE

park has hosted the annual Beijing Pop Festival since 2005.

JINGSHAN PARK
44 Jingshan Xijie, 10/6404-4071
HOURS: Daily 6 A.M.–10 P.M.
COST: ¥2
METRO: Dongsi (Line 5)
Map 1

The imperial gardens that surround the Forbidden City provide some of Beijing's most interesting park space. Jingshan Park is located directly north of the palace complex's north gate and was part of the Forbidden City until the early 1900s. A royal landscaped garden, it dates from the Yuan Dynasty and covers 230,000 square meters (2.4 million sq. ft.). The park is also known as Coal Hill, thanks to the coal that was once stored at the base of its peak. The hill was made with the soil excavated during the digging of the Forbidden City moat. Inside the park, the scenic spots have appealing names like Pavilion of Accumulating Fragrance and Pavilion of Admiring Summer. The park is the site of the last Ming emperor's suicide; he hanged himself from a tree when the Manchu invaders approached.

LONGTAN PARK
8 Longtan Lu, 10/6714-4336
HOURS: Mon.–Fri. 9 A.M.–2 P.M.
COST: ¥2
METRO: Tiantandongmen (Line 5)
Map 3

Longtan (Dragon Pool) Park sits east of the Temple of Heaven, and the body of water from which it takes its name covers over half of it. It was established and landscaped in 1952, and is said to contain 100 carved dragons on its various bridges, pavilions, and monuments. Whether you find all of them or not, the park provides a pleasant space for a stroll. The most notable building is also the least attractive. The Yuandushi Temple was constructed to commemorate a military hero named Yuan Chonghuan who defended the Great Wall from invaders. Longtan Park also

contains a popular outdoor bird market and holds an annual Spring Festival fair in early February.

◖ RITAN PARK
6 Ritan Beilu, Chaoyangmenwai Dajie, 10/8563-5038
HOURS: Daily 6 A.M.–9 P.M.
COST: ¥1
METRO: Yonganli (Line 1)
Map 4

Pretty Ritan Park, close to the Jianguomen embassy area, is one of Beijing's most pleasant and peaceful (as well as one of its oldest) parks, with something for everyone. There are amusement facilities and activities for children, early morning tai chi lessons for Zen-seekers, and some Ming Dynasty architecture for history buffs. The rectangular park takes its name from the Temple of the Sun that it surrounds. This is a special altar built in 1530, where the Ming and Qing emperors made offerings to the solar deity. The corresponding Temple of the Moon is farther west in Fuchengmen. Ritan Park provides a break from the busy CBD and a good spot for children to work off some energy by playing mini-golf or bouncing on inflatable play structures.

TAORANTING PARK
19 Taiping Jie, 10/6353-2385
HOURS: Daily 6 A.M.–9:30 P.M. (last ticket issued at 9 P.M.)
COST: ¥2
METRO: Taoranting (Line 4)
Map 3

Most of Beijing's inner-city parks started out as imperial gardens, but Taoranting has a more scholarly past. It was established in 1695 by the Qing emperor Kangxi as a stamping ground for the local literati, and named after a line in a poem by Tang Dynasty wordsmith Bai Juyi. He recommended being carefree and joyful (taoran) when the chrysanthemums are yellow. The pretty park covers 240,000 square meters (2.5 million sq. ft.), and contains the tombs of several famous writers as well as a Qing pavilion that is among the most famous in China. This pavilion, called the Taoran, is part of the Temple of Mercy (Cibei) on the Yuan Dynasty island in Taoranting's lake. The China Garden of Famous Pavilions is worth a look.

TUANJIEHU PARK

16 Tuanjiehu Nanlu, Sanhuan Donglu, 10/8597-3603
HOURS: Daily 6:30 A.M.-7 P.M.
COST: Beach: ¥20 adults, ¥15 children; boat rides: ¥30-60/hr.; skating: ¥5 (¥10 for skate rental)
METRO: Hujialou (Line 10)
Map 4

If you're traveling with children, Tuanjiehu Park in Chaoyang is a great choice in summer thanks to its water park and 4,500-square-meter (48,400 sq. ft.) sandy beach. With water-slides, wave pools, and inflatable rings, it's great relief for kids who are exhausted of sightseeing. Dry activities include skating and bumper cars. Go during the week if you can, as weekends get uncomfortably busy. Even if you don't have children, Tuanjiehu Park is worth a look if you need a change of scenery. The rest of the park contains lakes, bridges, and traditional buildings like the Evening Glow (Yiwan) Pavilion.

YUYUANTAN PARK

Xisanhuan Lu, south entrance behind China Millennium Monument, 10/8865-3804
HOURS: Dec.-Mar. daily 6:30 A.M.-7 P.M., Apr.-May and Sept.-Nov. daily 6 A.M.-8:30 P.M., June-Aug. daily 6 A.M.-9:30 P.M.
COST: ¥2 (¥10 during Cherry Blossom Festival in late Mar.-Apr.)
METRO: Military Museum (Line 9)
Map 5

Yuyuantan, meaning Jade Lake, is a gorgeous public space famous for its annual spring-time Cherry Blossom Festival. The lake in the park's name connects to the Summer Palace, which is accessible by boat from the pier near the south gate. The original cherry trees were sent over from Japan in 1973, and now number over 3,000 from a batch of 180. The area has been a popular scenic spot since the Jin Dynasty (1115–1234) but has been known as Yuyuantan only since 1960. One of Beijing's 11 municipal parks, it is used by kite flyers, nature seekers, and tai chi practitioners all year round. The lake is open to swimmers in high summer. Look out for the porcelain screen wall and Qing-era pine forest by the south entrance.

◖ ZHONGSHAN PARK

4 Zhonghua Lu, 10/6605-2610
HOURS: Winter 6:30 A.M.-8 P.M., summer 6 A.M.-9 P.M.
COST: ¥3
METRO: Tian'anmen West (Line 1)
Map 1

Almost every Chinese town and city has a road or a park named Zhongshan after Sun Yat-sen, the founder of Republican China. Beijing's Zhongshan Park sits southwest of the Forbidden City and contains the emperors' ancestral temples, where Ming and Qing rulers made offerings to ensure a good harvest. The Altar of Earth and Harvests was built by the Ming Dynasty Yongle Emperor in 1421 inside the imperial garden. Open to the public since 1914, the park is now a popular spot for match-making parents seeking to marry off their adult children. It was originally known as Central Park before taking the Mandarin name of Sun Yat-sen in 1928. The park also contains the Forbidden City Concert Hall.

AMUSEMENT PARKS AND ZOOS
◖ BEIJING ZOO

137 Xizhimenwai Dajie, 10/6831-4411, www.bjzoo.com
HOURS: Daily winter 7:30 A.M.-5 P.M., summer 7:30 A.M.-6 P.M.
COST: ¥10 adults, ¥5 children
METRO: Beijing Zoo (Line 4)
Map 5

The Beijing Zoo has nearly 15,000 animals spread over 89 hectares (220 acres), of which 5.6 hectares (14 acres) are water. Its huge aquarium is the biggest in China. The zoo is home to rare animals like the giant panda, snub-nosed monkey, Chinese alligator, and Pere David's deer, as well as lions, jaguars, and 13 types of cranes. The zoo is one of the oldest in China, and was established in 1906 by the Empress Dowager Cixi to house a collection of exotic animals brought from abroad. It took over a Ming Dynasty manor and garden, the ponds and pavilions of which can still be seen.

ARTS AND LEISURE

CITY SEAVIEW

1 Xiedao Lu, Lido, 10/8433-9689, www.cityseaview.net
HOURS: Daily summer 9 A.M.-10 P.M.
COST: ¥60 adults, ¥40 children under 1.4 m. (55 in.)
METRO: Sunhe (Line 15)
Map 6

Spend a day getting wet and wild at this 60,000-square-meter (645,800 sq. ft.) water park inside the Crab Island Resort out near the airport. Built in 2000, it has the biggest artificially constructed beach in China, and is surprisingly cheap to get into compared to similar attractions in the West. City Seaview has everything you need to have fun in the water, from a variety of slides to wave pools, whirlpool tubs, and beach volleyball for the less adventurous. If you get hungry there are barbeque grills available for use, as well as places to buy food. As with most Beijing attractions, avoiding weekends and public holidays will make for a less chaotic and more enjoyable experience.

BIKING

◖ BEIJING EBIKE TOURS

Unit 1202, Bldg. A, Tower 2, 6 Guang'anmennei Dajie, 186/0120-1141, www.bjebiketours.com; meeting point Novotel Beijing Xin Qiao, 1 Chongwenmen Xidajie, 10/6513-3366
COST: ¥275-700/person
METRO: Tian'anmen East (Line 1)
Map 3

Along with bicycles, electric scooters are the most popular way of getting around the city for local Beijingers. This tour group helps you experience the city from the back of an e-bike, visiting the *hutong,* and powering down the capital's wide avenues and boulevards. You'll see important sights like the Forbidden City, Tian'anmen Square, and Qianmen before eating in a courtyard restaurant. Managed by Canadian expats, eBike Tours is environmentally friendly: The bikes are zero-emission. They are classified as bicycles and reach a top speed of 28 kilometers per hour (17 mph). Riding a scooter is great during summer when the weather is hot since you don't work up the same sweat you would on a pedal bike.

BICYCLE KINGDOM

60 Donghuachenggen Nandajie, east of Beiheyan Dajie, 133/8140-0738, www.bicyclekingdom.com
HOURS: Daily 8 A.M.-8 P.M.
COST: ¥100-400/day
METRO: Wangfujing (Line 1)
Map 1

There are nine million bicycles in Beijing, according to the 2005 song "Nine Million Bicycles" by Katie Melua. Get your hands on one of them at Bicycle Kingdom and see the best bits of the city and beyond from the saddle. Operating since 2005, Bicycle Kingdom runs *hutong* tours around Beijing, as well as forays into the countryside for off-road cycling expeditions. The one-day city tour takes in the sights and sounds of the capital before heading out of town to the Fragrant Hills and Miyun Reservoir. Since Beijing's road systems are extremely bike-friendly, cycling is a fun and easy way to get around and see the sights. Bicycle Kingdom also organizes rides to the Great Wall.

HIKING

BEIJING HIKERS

Rm. 601, Bldg. 2, Xinhualian Ligang, 26 Jiuxianqiao Zhonglu (meet for hikes at Lido Starbucks, 6 Jiangtai Lu) 10/6432-2786, www.beijinghikers.com
HOURS: Office open Mon.-Fri. 9 A.M.-6 P.M.
COST: ¥200-300 pp
METRO: Sanyuanqiao (Line 10) for meeting place
Map 6

Get out of town and see some of the incredible countryside that surrounds the capital with Beijing Hikers. Operating since 2001, they are experts in crafting a great trip, minus the annoying detours to jade factories, silk markets, and bad restaurants that typify most organized tours. Hikes are graded in difficulty from 1 to 5, with 5 being the most taxing. Choose from walks to Ming villages, nearby peaks, and little-known parts of the Great Wall. Private tours can be designed if you give at least five days notice. The cost of a hike includes transportation, water, and snacks.

DANDELION HIKING

156/5220-0950, www.chinahiking.cn

COST: ¥400/person

Get out of town and see some of the gorgeous scenery that surrounds Beijing with this eco-travel hiking company. Run by an Inner Mongolian walking enthusiast and a Belgian expat who loves the great outdoors, Dandelion meets regularly to go off the beaten path in search of beautiful China. Their aim is to eat, sleep, and travel like locals, avoiding clichéd tourist spots and well-known areas. The company's Great Wall hikes and bike trips are particularly good, going to out-of-the-way spots like Woushan and Longquanyu that are rarely visited by tourists. Tours meet at various points around the city; you will be given the details when you book your tour.

GYMS AND YOGA
OM YOGA 42

1/F, Bldg. 9, Lido Apartment Bldg., Fangyuan Xilu, 10/6437-8810, www.omyoga42.com

HOURS: Daily 10 A.M.-9:30 P.M.

COST: ¥200 drop-in

METRO: Sanyuanqiao (Line 10)

Map 6

Yoga buffs who don't want to give up on their hobby while away on vacation should try some classes at Om Yoga 42. Named for the degrees to which the yoga studios are heated for bikram yoga (107.6°F), the studio is clean, well-decorated, professionally run, and welcoming to newcomers. You can pick up a card for 30 sessions if you're going to be staying in Beijing for a while. As well as "hot" bikram yoga, Om runs classes in hatha, vinyasa, and ashtanga. With four classes a day during the week and two on Saturday and Sunday, there are plenty of choices.

PACIFIC CENTURY CLUB

5/F, Pacific Center Palace, Tower E, 2A Gongti Beilu, 10/6539-3434

HOURS: Mon.-Fri. 6 A.M.-10 P.M., Sat.-Sun. 7 A.M.-10 P.M.

COST: Day pass ¥110

METRO: Tuanjiehu (Line 10)

Map 4

This reputable gym on Gongti Road offers short-term memberships and day passes, so even if you're only in Beijing for a few days, you don't have to abandon your workout regime. The gym has excellent management and modern facilities with Wi-Fi access throughout, and English- and Japanese-speaking staff. The Pilates equipment is some of the most advanced in China, and the gym is affiliated with an authorized "hot" bikram yoga studio. The gym also offers a swimming pool, outdoor tennis and basketball courts, and group classes that include salsa, aerobics, and tai chi. Pacific Century Club can be a little hard to find; when you get to Pacific Century Place, go to the south side and look for the club entrance, then take the elevator to the 5th floor.

GUIDED TOURS
HIAS GOURMET

308, 6 Ritan Lu, Sunjoy Mansion Annex, 10/6400-9199, www.hiasgourmet.com, info@hiasgourmet.com

COST: ¥350/person

METRO: Jianguomen (Line 1)

Map 4

Mix eating with sightseeing on one of Hias Gourmet's food walks, or learn how to prepare local dishes at a cooking class. Run by a Chinese Malaysian, Hias means "decorate" in Malay, and its aim is to give an introduction to Beijing that's embellished by local flavors. Each group has a maximum of six people, and private tours are available too. The options include Hutong Eats, Night Markets, Tea Tasting Safari, and Breakfast and Farmers' Market, as well as cultural tours of the Great Wall, south Beijing, and north Beijing. At the cooking classes you can learn how to make Sichuan, Cantonese, and Beijing-style food.

ARTS AND LEISURE

SHOPS

Beijing's mix of history, culture, and modernity make it an interesting and varied city for shoppers. If you're on the hunt for traditional Chinese souvenirs like calligraphy wall-hangings, tea sets, chopsticks, fans, or jade bangles, you'll find them in abundance at places like the Silk Market (which, contrary to its name, is a sprawling, multi-story emporium and not a quaint bazaar). Quirkier knick-knacks can be found at the outdoor street markets on Dazhalan and Liulichang, but most of the "antiques" on offer are rather newer than the vendors would have you believe. If you want something a little more unusual than the regular glut of Chinese souvenirs, the antique markets are rife with kitsch Mao statues, propaganda-style artwork, and retro ornaments.

Thanks to its rapid modern development, Beijing has no shortage of sleek, contemporary shopping malls. The pedestrian stretch of Wangfujing Street, east of the Forbidden City, is flanked with shopping centers; Financial Street and the CBD have their fair share as well.

Somewhere in between the antique markets and the malls lie the more bohemian shops on and around East Gulou Avenue. The area is known for its artsy, wall-worn feel, the street is lined with funky boutiques, vintage clothing shops, and stores selling one-off designs. Head down Nanluogu Hutong for the highest concentration of independent stores.

© YULIA ZHUKOVA/123RF.COM

HIGHLIGHTS

LOOK FOR ◖ TO FIND RECOMMENDED SHOPS.

◖ **Most Old-School Atmosphere:** The beautiful Qing-era buildings of the **Dazhalan** shopping district house traditional shops selling silk, calligraphy, and antiques (page 130).

◖ **Best All-Around Shopping Experience: Wangfujing Avenue** has every retail option imaginable, from modern malls to traditional shops, with the famous Donghuamen street-food market at the north end of the street (page 131).

◖ **Best Books:** Enjoy a coffee while you browse the titles on offer at **The Bookworm,** which stocks the best collection of English books in the capital city; it's also home to Beijing's annual literary festival (page 135).

◖ **Best Local Designer:** Pick up a piece of Beijing's fashion scene at **candy&caviar,** where Chicago-born designer Candy Lin is famous for her hooded blazers and smart-casual dresses (page 135).

◖ **Most Vintage Clothes:** Keep abreast of Beijing's craze for retro fashion at **Mega Mega Vintage,** which features carefully chosen garments and accessories (page 136).

◖ **Best T-Shirts: Plastered T-Shirts** sells just that: T-shirts emblazoned with classic Chinese images like Chariman Mao, the double happiness symbol, and lucky number 8 (page 136).

◖ **Best Souvenirs:** Check out images of Beijing in days gone by with a visit to **Beijing Postcard.** The shop sells copies of old postcards and photos that make great gifts and souvenirs (page 138).

◖ **Best Concept:** Looking for a funky gift? It's literally in the box at **Fengguo Box Store,** where vendors rent clear displays to sell their handmade crafts (page 138).

◖ **Best Retro Toys:** Quirky **Old-Toxin Tin Toys** sells replicas of the hollow metal toys that every pre-'80s Beijing child played with. The toys here make great souvenirs for kids and kids at heart (page 138).

© BEIJING POSTCARD

Beijing Postcard

Shopping Districts

⟨ DAZHALAN

Outside of the Qianmen Gate
HOURS: Most shops open daily 9 A.M.-10 P.M.
METRO: Qianmen (Line 2)
`Map 3`

Enter Dazhalan through the filigree archway off Qianmen Pedestrian Street, and wander the length of a Qing Dynasty bazaar. Pronounced "Da'sh'larr" in the local accent, this stretch of road has been a trading point since the Yuan Dynasty. When a curfew was imposed on the city in 1488 during the Ming Dynasty, fences were erected at each end of Dazhalan to stop thieves from looting the shops and stalls within. During the 1960s, the street was the first in Beijing to receive an asphalt coating. These days it is a bustling (if a little touristy) pedestrian road lined with some elaborately decorated restaurants and shops. The best for silk are Ruifuxiang at No. 5 and Xiangyihao at No. 7. There's Nei Lian Sheng for shoes at No. 34, and hats at Majuyuan. Also noteworthy are the famous Tongrenting Traditional Chinese pharmacy, Daguanlou Cinema, and Ten Fu Tea shop.

LIULICHANG CULTURAL STREET

Liulichang Jie, near intersection with Nanxinhua Jie
HOURS: Daily dawn-dusk
METRO: Hepingmen (Line 2)
`Map 3`

The 750-meter (0.5 mi.) stretch of Liulichang Street on either side of the crossing with South Xinhua Road is an old-style menagerie of curios, antiques, art supplies, and books. This is the place to come for unusual gifts and as much retro Mao memorabilia as you can carry. In the Yuan and Ming Dynasties it was the site of a *liuli* (colored glaze) factory that made tiles for the imperial palaces and temples. Liulichang became a gathering place for Ming poets and academics, and shops sprang up to supply them with scholarly goods like calligraphy ink, brushes, and paper. The modern cultural street still has several bookshops

and stationery stores, such as Rongbaozhai and China Bookshop. Don't forget to bargain hard.

NANLUOGUXIANG

Off Gulou Dongdajie
HOURS: Most shops open daily 9 A.M.-late
METRO: Guloudajie (Line 2)
`Map 2`

Running for nearly a kilometer between East Gulou Avenue in the north and Di'anmen Avenue in the south, this *hutong* buzzes with life at all hours of the day and night. Along both sides of the street are low buildings that contain shops and stalls selling T-shirts, traditional handicrafts, and quirky gifts. The best are Plastered Tshirts at No. 61, the Pottery Workshop at No. 23, Grifted at No. 32, and Kodo homewares at No. 31. Food vendors cook meat skewers and fried chicken, while cafés and restaurants do a roaring trade. By night, the action continues as the bars fill up with people. Nanluoguxiang is also home to several hostels and lodging houses.

QIANMEN PEDESTRIAN STREET

Between Archery Tower (Jianlou) and Tiantan Park
HOURS: Most shops open daily 9 A.M.-late
METRO: Qianmen (Line 2)
`Map 3`

Qianmen Pedestrian Street stretches for 840 meters (0.5 mi.) from the Jianlou archery tower in the north to Tiantan Park in the south. It is lined with Qing-style buildings, many of which are replicas from the 2008 pre-Olympic spruce up. Behind the old facades are modern Western brands like Sephora, H&M, and Haagen-Dazs, as well as local staples such as Quan Ju De roast duck restaurant and Duyichu dumplings. Trams ran the length of the stretch from 1924 to 1966; now a pair of 84-seater sightseeing trolleys relive the glory days. The street was known as Zhengyangmen until 1965, in accordance with the alternative name for Qianmen Gate.

WANGFUJING AVENUE

Wangfujing Dajie, btwn. Wangfujing Nankou and Sun Dong'an Plaza
HOURS: Most shops open daily 9 A.M.-late
METRO: Wangfujing (Line 1)
Map 1

The buzzing pedestrian section of Wangfujing Avenue is one of Beijing's busiest commercial stretches. Starting at Oriental Plaza at Wangfujing Nankou to the south and ending at Sun Dong'an Plaza in the north, the wide street is lined with Western brand shops, malls, and traditional Chinese department stores. Around 300 Beijing brands are represented, including tea shops, shoe stores, and milliners. West encroaches on East with the likes of Starbucks, Haagen-Dazs, and Nike. Wangfujing Avenue has been a place of commerce since the Yuan, Ming, and Qing Dynasties. The street was named for the *jing* (well) of sweet water that was discovered close to a *wangfu* (prince's residence). Dong'an Market was established in 1903, when trolley buses traversed the avenue. The nightly food market on Donghuamen Avenue, toward the north end of the pedestrian area, is famous for its unusual snacks, like seahorses on sticks.

Department Stores, Malls, and Markets

ALIEN STREET MARKET

Yabao Lu, south of Full Link Plaza
HOURS: Daily 9:30 A.M.-7 P.M.
METRO: Chaoyangmen (Line 2)
Map 4

This unusually named market is less crowded and manic than Silk Street, and is frequented by Russian traders. This means that the clothes tend to run bigger, and the coats, belts, and hats are of slightly better quality, if a little tacky. Alien Street used to be a haven for fur sellers, but they have mostly been shut down. It's still home to plenty of wacky costume stores that locals and expats plunder for fancy dress parties, as well as some surprisingly good tea stalls. If you want the market experience without the chaos of Silk Street, this could be the place for you.

HONGQIAO MARKET

46 Tiantan Lu, 10/6711-8984
HOURS: Daily 8:30 A.M.-7 P.M.
METRO: Tiantandongmen (Line 5)
Map 3

This vibrant and often chaotic market is a fish bazaar on its three basement levels and a pearl retailer and wholesaler on the 3rd to the 5th floors. The stories in between are home to silk and clothes vendors; the 1st floor sells fake bags, digital goods, and tacky chinoiserie gifts. If you have the patience to make it up to the 5th floor balcony, you will be rewarded with a beautiful view of the Temple of Heaven. When it comes to buying pearls, the best are to be found on the 5th floor. All types are on offer, from freshwater and seawater to the very obviously fake. Hongqiao is the largest pearl distribution center in China, so you're very likely to find something you like.

JOY CITY

131 Xidan Beidajie, 10/6651-7777
HOURS: Daily 10 A.M.-8 P.M.
METRO: Xidan (Line 1, Line 4)
Map 5

Joy City isn't just any shopping mall: In addition to 13 floors of dizzying retail options, it has the world's longest escalator, the largest digital cinema in China, and the largest branch of Sephora in Beijing. It opened in 2007, and now has a sister mall in the Chaoyang District. The glass-fronted shopping center houses an array of international brands like Zara and Uniqlo, and a multitude of food and drink options. The huge 13-screen digital cinema is worth a look if you plan on catching a movie while you're in town.

PANJIAYUAN

West of Panjiayuan Bridge, 10/6775-2405
HOURS: Mon.-Fri. 8:30 A.M.-6 P.M., Sat.-Sun.

BARGAINING: THE DOS AND DON'TS OF GETTING A GOOD DEAL

The idea of haggling can seem anathema to people who aren't used to doing it, but it's a necessity in Beijing if you don't want to be ripped off. Where can you bargain? Almost anywhere that isn't a mall, a chain, or a restaurant. Markets are fair game, as are independent stores (that don't display "No Bargaining" signs). Here are some tips:

- **Do** chop a third off the asking price. The vendor will act horrified, and you'll end up paying more than that in the end, but it's a good starting point.

- **Don't** be afraid to walk away if you don't get the price you want. Have a set amount in mind that you're willing to spend and say goodbye if you can't bargain a vendor down. The chances are that you'll see the exact same item in the stall next door.

- **Do** be nice. Market vendors can seem like

sharks, but there's no need to be rude to them. They're just doing their job.

- **Don't** be too nice. You don't have to be overly aggressive, but neither should you come across as a pushover.

- **Do** learn a few phrases for asking prices and suggesting lower amounts.

- **Don't** get emotional. No vendor will sell for a price that's too low to make a profit, so don't feel guilty about haggling.

- **Do** carry the right money in smaller denominations. Waving wads of hundred notes around isn't a good look, and can be unsafe in a busy market.

- **Don't** agree to a price and then refuse to buy. It's bad form and a waste of everyone's time.

4:30 A.M.–6 P.M.
METRO: Jinsong Road (Line 10)
Map 6

Although the antiques you'll find at Panjiayuan might not be as old as their sellers would have you believe, the market is a great source of quirky souvenirs and gifts. It's best to go on weekends when it opens at 4:30 A.M. Weekdays the market operates inside a warehouse from 8:30 A.M. and is less interesting. Pick your way through stall upon stall of Peoples' Liberation Army memorabilia, Tibetan trinkets, statues, old books and magazines, and every other curio imaginable. This area was a printing and textile hub in the Qing Dynasty, and its name refers to the clan village of the Pan family. Make sure you bargain, and keep your eyes peeled for a true gem among the bric-a-brac.

SANLITUN VILLAGE

19 Sanlitun Lu, 10/6417-6110 (South Village), 10/6417-7110 (North Village)
HOURS: Daily 10 A.M.–10 P.M.

METRO: Tuanjiehu (Line 10)
Map 4

Sanlitun Village is a contemporary architectural development containing luxury and Western brands, like Armani, and mid-range names, like Adidas, Mango, Apple, Diesel, and Steve Madden. The open-plan mall is made up of 19 glass-walled buildings split into the North and South Villages, with alleys and courtyards that are clearly supposed to represent the *hutong* (alleys) that were torn down to construct the mall. Food options include healthy salad and sandwich chain Element Fresh and 30 other restaurants, covering a range of cuisines. The development was designed by Tokyo architect Kengo Kuma and bankrolled by Swire Properties.

SILK STREET MARKET

8 Xiushui Dongjie, Jianguomen Dajie, 10/5169-8800
HOURS: Daily 9 A.M.–9 P.M.
METRO: Yonganli (Line 1)
Map 4

Around 20,000 visitors step through the

portals of Silk Street Market every day, swelling to 60,000 on weekends. If you're here during the peak hours, you'll feel like you're rubbing shoulders with all of them. Spread across seven floors and three basements, the market sells clothing, bags, watches, jewelry, fabric, electronics, and traditional (i.e., tacky) souvenirs. With 1,700 stalls and vendors to choose from, it can get confusing. The market was built in 2005 to replace the old alleys of Xiushui Market that were razed for a new development. As well as shops, there's also a branch of the Quanjude duck chain, a Subway, and a Lavazza café. Expect to be fleeced, and don't forget to haggle.

THE MALLS AT ORIENTAL PLAZA
1 Dongchang'an Jie, 10/8518-6363
HOURS: Daily 9:30 A.M.-10 P.M.
METRO: Wangfujing (Line 1)
Map 1

This enormous shopping arcade is part of Wangfujing's multi-use Oriental Plaza complex that also includes the Grand Hyatt Hotel, office space, and several entertainment venues. The Malls cover 130,000 square meters (1.4 million sq. ft.) and gather luxury Western brands like Boss and Burberry to

trade alongside mid-range names like Mango and Sisley. The shopping zone is split into five distinct areas, ranging from entertainment on the 5th floor, style on the 4th, luxury brands and contemporary fashion on the 2nd and 3rd, and family-oriented venues on the 1st floor. The Malls are connected to the Grand Hyatt Hotel by a skywalk.

THE PLACE
9 Guanghua Lu, 10/8595-1755
HOURS: Daily 10 A.M.-10 P.M.
METRO: Jintaixizhao (Line 10)
Map 4

Another modern mall, The Place is a local landmark thanks to the LED "sky screen" that runs the length of the entrance walkway. Split across two four-story buildings, the mall brings together Western fashion brands like Zara, H&M, Miss Sixty, and Vero Moda with ubiquitous food venues like Starbucks. It also contains Tourneau—the largest watch shop in China; if you're in the market for a new time piece, make this your first port of call. If it's an authentic Old Beijing shopping experience you're looking for, go elsewhere, but if you want to see capitalist China on the rise, definitely stop by.

Bath, Beauty, and Massage

AIBOSEN
A11 Liufang Beili, 10/6465-2044
HOURS: Daily 10 A.M.-1:30 A.M.
METRO: Liufang (Line 13)
Map 6

In China, it is common for blind people to train as masseurs in order to have a career, and blind massage parlors provide no-frills treatments that are usually much cheaper than the fancier salons. Aibosen is at the upper end of the blind massage spectrum with 12 treatment rooms and space for 30 people for food and body massages. Masseurs here use traditional Chinese massage techniques that tend to be deeper and stronger than Thai or Balinese styles. You remain clothed for the body

massage, which consists of pressing, kneading, and unknotting influenced by a principal called *tui na.* If you find the pressure uncomfortable, say *"tong le"* (painful) and the masseur will ease off. As well as your massage you get free juice, coffee, and fresh fruit.

BANYAN HOUSE BODY & MIND
5/F Haiyuncang International Plaza, 1 Haiyuncang
Hutong, 10/6501-2881, www.banyanhouse.cn
HOURS: Daily 11 A.M.-midnight
METRO: Dongsishitiao (Line 2)
Map 3

A sanctuary within the city, Banyan uses beauty products imported from France and Italy for massages, facials, nail treatments, and body scrubs. Also available are waxing and slimming treatments, and an array of massage techniques like Thai, Swedish, hot stones, reflexology, sports, Ayurveda, and lymph draining. Scented candles and soft music set the mood for relaxation. The salon is impeccably clean. Each treatment room has a private shower and a sauna attached. The staff is well trained to international standards and most speak English well. There are couple rooms if you want to have a massage with a friend or partner.

BODHI

17 Gongti Beilu, 10/6413-0226, www.bodhi.com.cm
HOURS: Daily 11:30 A.M.–12:30 A.M.
METRO: Tuanjiehu (Line 10)
Map 4

If your body is crying out for a bit of TLC, take some time out from sightseeing and book yourself a massage or facial at Bodhi. Clean, professional, and reasonably priced, it's a step up from street parlors but without the extravagance (and attached price tags) of fancier hotel spas. Bodhi offers a range of massage treatments and techniques, such as hot stone therapy, aromatherapy, traditional Chinese massage, and Thai style body rubs. Relax amid the Southeast Asian–style decor while your muscles are pummeled and pressed, or opt for a cleansing facial to strip your skin of Beijing's pollution.

DRAGONFLY RETREAT

60 Donghuamen Dajie, near Forbidden City East Gate,
10/6527-9368, www.dragonfly.net.cn
HOURS: Daily 10 A.M.–10 P.M.
METRO: Tian'anmen East (Line 1)
Map 1

Dragonfly is a well-established massage chain with branches in China, Dubai, and Norway. You'll find cheaper massage parlors everywhere in Beijing, but if you want to be sure of quality (and absence of sleaze), Dragonfly is a good choice. Unlike street-side massage joints where the standards can be sketchy, at Dragonfly you know exactly what you're going to get: Zen-like

massage rooms with soft lighting, relaxing atmosphere, expert techniques, and cleanliness throughout. Choose from Chinese, Shiatsu, and oil massage styles for feet or full body. Dragonfly's signature Top-to-Toe massage involves two masseurs working on you at the same time.

ERIC PARIS SALON

43 Sanlitun Beilu, 135/0137-2971. www.ericparis.com
HOURS: Daily 10 A.M.–8 P.M.
METRO: Tuanjiehu (Line 10)
Map 4

Unsurprisngly for a brand that has styled hair for Chanel and Louis Vuitton fashion shows, Eric Paris Salon knows how to deal with Western hair. If you need a trim or a color job while you're in Beijing, this is the place to go. The eponymous Eric hails from Provence, France, where he established the successful Studio 54 chain. He came to China in 1996 to spread his empire and now has salons in Beijing and Paris. His teams consist of both Western and local stylists, all trained to Eric's exacting standards. Ask for a senior stylist for the best possible result.

ORIENTAL TAIPAN MASSAGE

B/1-3F Shuncheng Hotel, 26A Jinrong Jie,
10/6621-8622
HOURS: Daily 11:30 A.M.–11:30 P.M.
METRO: Lingjing Hutong (Line 4)
Map 5

If the commotion of city life gets too much, take the weight off and relax at Oriental Taipan Massage. In a city chock full of massage parlors of all description, this is a solid choice. It's a little pricier than some, but worth the extra money for the standard of service. Expect to pay upwards of ¥150 for a 90-minute foot massage, and around ¥400 for a "four hands" body treatment. As well as professional massage techniques you get complimentary soft drinks and fruit and a choice of healthy meals and snacks. The atmosphere is chilled, and the treatment rooms clean and comfortable.

Books

BEIJING FOREIGN LANGUAGES BOOKSTORE
235 Wangfujing Dajie, 10/6512-6917
HOURS: Daily 9 A.M.–9 P.M.
METRO: Wangfujing (Line 1)
Map 1

If you've worked your way through your stash of holiday reading, or fancy browsing some China-focused literature, this well-stocked bookshop is a good bet. It's the biggest and most comprehensive foreign language bookstore in Beijing and sells a wide variety of literature, including travel guides, English fiction, and Mandarin study aids. There's also a nice selection of bookmarks, greeting cards, and traditional paper-cuttings, as well as cookbooks, translated Chinese literature, and maps. You'll find locally published foreign books on the 1st floor, sheet music on the 5th floor, and a teashop on the 6th floor.

THE BOOKWORM
Bldg. 4, Nansanlitun Lu, 10/6586-9507,
www.beijingbookworm.com
HOURS: Daily 9 A.M.–2 A.M.
METRO: Tuanjiehu (Line 10)
Map 4

Beijing's bohemians and literati gather at the Bookworm, which triples as a bookshop, café, and bar. With sister branches in Suzhou and Chengdu, the Bookworm hosts an annual literary festival every spring. Grab a coffee and a book and head up to the roof terrace if the weather is fine, or hunker down with a glass of wine and a magazine. There are over 15,000 books for sale and lending. The Bookworm was founded by an expat named Alexandra Pearson who wanted to create a space for Beijing's book lovers to meet, work, relax, and find good literature.

Clothing and Shoes

BRAND NEW CHINA
NLG-09a, North Sanlitun Village, 11 Sanlitun Lu, 10/6416-9045
HOURS: Daily 10 A.M.–10 P.M.
METRO: Tuanjiehu (Line 10)
Map 4

This Sanlitun design and fashion store is run by Hong Huang, who is known as the "Chinese Oprah" thanks to her media empire. The daughter of Chairman Mao's English teacher, Hong is CEO of the China Interactive Media Group and opened Brand New China to promote Chinese designers to international levels. She also runs *iLook* fashion magazine, so she knows plenty about style. This 547-square-meter (5,890 sq. ft.) store showcases work from over 100 designers across clothing, accessories, furniture, and graphic art. Brands like Plastered and HiPanda are represented, as well as solo Chinese designers like eco-designer Wei Minghui.

CANDY&CAVIAR
Rm. 921, Bldg. 16, China Central Place, 89 Jianguo Lu, 10/5203-6581, www.candyandcaviar.com
HOURS: Mon.-Fri. 9 A.M.–5:30 P.M.
METRO: Dawanglu (Line 1)
Map 4

Treat yourself to a piece of Beijing high fashion at candy&caviar, an innovative brand run by Californian Candy Lin. Born in Chicago but raised on the west coast, Lin launched her fashion line in 2009. She specializes in versatile pieces with creative flare, like her sought-after hooded blazers and gilets, smart casual wear, and flattering dresses. Candy takes part in the whole process, from designing collections to choosing fabric and executing her designs. Prices are low enough to be affordable, but high enough to feel indulgent.

ELDI
B1/F, NLG-21, North Sanlitun Village, 11 Sanlitun Lu, 10/6416-1762

HOURS: Daily 11 A.M.–7 P.M.
METRO: Tuanjiehu (Line 10)
Map 4

Stylish Dana Li is originally from Shanghai and had a successful career in marketing and fashion-buying before she opened Eldi in North Sanlitun Village. Using fabrics from Italy, Japan, and France to execute her designs, she concentrates on simple, unfussy, and highly wearable garments that flatter the Asian shape and skin tone. Dana studied fashion buying in Milan and has an eye for what works when it comes to style. Tailoring is available as well as the off-the-rack options. With wood floors, rounded shelves, and curved racks, the store has a modern, luxurious feel.

GOOD GOODS COMMUNE

141 Gulou Dongdajie, 10/8400-2628
HOURS: Daily 10:30 A.M.–10:30 P.M.
METRO: Beixinqiao (Line 5)
Map 2

This two-story boutique in the Gulou area sells goods by local designers as well as its own brand. In addition to clothing items, it is popular for its reasonably priced gifts. These include jewelry, mugs, wallets, photo albums, and decorated laptop bags, as well as cloth bags and wool scarves. The wide range of designers represented means that there's something for every pocket, so even if you're short on cash at the end of your trip, you'll almost definitely find something that you can afford. The shop's 2nd floor hosts art and design exhibitions.

◖ MEGA MEGA VINTAGE

241 Gulou Dongdajie, 10/8404-5637, www.mmvintage.
blogbus.com
HOURS: Daily 11 A.M.–midnight
METRO: Guloudajie (Line 2)
Map 2

Vintage clothing is growing ever more popular in Beijing, especially among the hipster crowd that hangs out in the Gulou *hutong*. Mega Mega Vintage is one of the best known and best loved vintage stores in the city, gathering garments, shoes, and accessories from Thailand, Japan, and Korea. Each piece is carefully chosen for its stylistic merit and quality, and the leather jackets are particularly good. Look out for one-off dresses and knitted sweaters, as well as plaid shirts and 1980s-style denim. Gulou is chock full of vintage shops now, but Mega Mega is the original and still the best.

PIG BALANCE

63 Wudaoying Hutong, 10/8403-5498, www.
pigbalance.com
HOURS: Daily 11 A.M.–6 P.M.
METRO: Andingmen (Line 2)
Map 2

The owner of this shop explains that its rather odd name comes from two concepts: the contentment of a pig and the balance needed for true beauty. Through an eclectic mix of vintage garments and her own designs, she hopes to embody both concepts. The shop has a blue exterior and stands behind a white picket fence on trendy Wudaoying Hutong. Half of the stock is made up of vintage clothes and accessories sourced in Japan, Europe, and the United States, while the remainder is designed by the owner. Her work includes simple garments with a hint of attitude.

◖ PLASTERED T-SHIRTS

61 Nanluogu Hutong, 10/6407-8425, www.
plasteredtshirts.com
HOURS: Daily 10 A.M.–10 P.M.
METRO: Guloudajie (Line 2)
Map 2

No self-respecting Beijinger would be seen dead without a Plastered T-shirt. Designs range from retro Mao prints and pandas to slogans and road signs, and their distinctive style makes them easily recognizable by people in the know. Plastered was set up in 2006 in Nanluoguxiang by a British expat named Dominic, and it now has several branches across China. Dominic's aim is to celebrate "everything beautiful about China" from karaoke halls to acrobats. His designs have appeared in *Vogue* and *Elle,* so he's clearly doing something right. Plastered also sells badges, posters, and calendars, all emblazoned with Dominic's unmistakable designs.

RED PHOENIX CLOTHING STUDIO

1/F, 30 Sanlitun Beilu, 10/6417-3591
HOURS: Daily 9 A.M.–9 P.M.
METRO: Tuanjiehu (Line 10)
Map 4

This gorgeous shop is part studio and part fabric store. Satisfied customers include Hillary Clinton. The owner and manager, Gu Lin, cuts and designs every piece herself. If you want to have something made, make sure you visit right at the start of your trip; Gu Lin's handiwork can take up to several weeks to finish, depending on the complexity. If you don't have time to wait, there are always her off-the-rack garments to choose from. Her exquisite embroidery on Jiangnan silk is some of the finest and most detailed in Beijing. A simple jacket will cost around ¥500, with elaborate dresses and cheongsams selling for tens of thousands. The Red Phoenix Clothing Studio has been operating for over a decade.

ROUGE

108B, Tower 2, Sanlitun SOHO, 8 Gongti Beilu, 10/5785-3010
HOURS: Daily 11 A.M.–8:30 P.M.
METRO: Tuanjiehu (Line 10)
Map 4

Pick up some Asian fashion pieces at Rouge's SOHO store. While the Nali Patio branch in Sanlitun sells items sourced on mainland China, this one gets its garments and accessories from Hong Kong and South Korea. Owner and manager Maggie Leung travels to Seoul once a month to buy new items, and her stores are magnets for local fashion fans who come back regularly to see what's new. Clothes make up most of the merchandise, with tops, skirts, jackets, and dresses available for purchase. There's also a good range of one-off bags, belts, and hats to complement your look.

SHANGHAI TRIO

B1, NLG-38, Sanlitun Village North, 11 Sanlitun Lu, 10/6417-3606, www.shanghaitrio.com
HOURS: Daily 10 A.M.–10 P.M.
METRO: Tuanjiehu (Line 10)
Map 4

French designer Virginie Fournier moved to Beijing in 1998 and with two friends set up Shanghai Trio: a socially responsible brand selling homeware, accessories, and gifts. The brand now has stores as far afield as South Africa and Belgium. Among this Beijing branch's most popular items are industrial-chic electrician bags, percale duvet covers, and home accessories made of cotton, bamboo, and linen. Shanghai Trio's bags and purses make great, unusual gifts that are eco-friendly too. Fournier uses old fabric to create her designs. Shanghai Trio's clothing items are mostly modern takes on traditional Chinese garments, and the children's wear is particularly covetable.

TRIPLE MAJOR

81 Baochao Hutong, 10/8402-0763, www.triple-major.com
HOURS: Tues.-Sun. 1-10 P.M.
METRO: Guloudajie (Line 2)
Map 2

Triple Major's mission is to reinvent popular culture with a mix of vintage clothing and work from 20 designers from 15 different countries. The two-story store sells everything a hipster needs, from retro knitted sweaters to neon rucksacks. Racks of clothes and tables of accessories stand among traditional-style calligraphy and light fixtures, and the entrance on Baochao Hutong is draped with blue hangings. The store organizes worldwide events, like the White T-Shirt Project, in which avant-garde designers gave their take on the garment. Triple Major's video game–inspired fashion line has been presented at Paris fashion week, so snap up some pieces before it goes stellar.

Gifts and Souvenirs

BEIJING POSTCARD

85-1 Nanluogu Hutong, 135/0109-8794,
www.beijing-postcards.com
HOURS: Daily 11 A.M.–9 P.M.
METRO: Guloudajie (Line 2)
Map 2

If you're interested in the history of Beijing, this shop is a great place to find copies of vintage postcards that show the city in its former glory. Danish expats Simon Rom Gjeroe and Lars Ulrik Thom collect old postcards from the 1890s to 1940s and reprint them onto postcards, calendars, and framed prints. They find the originals in antique shops, auctions, and flea markets. Their most significant haul came from the family of Danish missionaries who had lived and worked in the capital. The pair run lectures and talks at the shop and are more than willing to chat to customers about their collection.

FENGGUO BOX STORE

G13, Zhongguancun Mall, 12 Zhongguancun Nandajie, 10/6357-6004, www.fengguo.com.cn
HOURS: Daily 10 A.M.–9 P.M.
METRO: Zhongguancun (Line 4)
Map 5

A fun concept that's a world away from the jostling and haggling of the markets, Fengguo Box Store is a brick-and-mortar version of the e-commerce craft website Etsy. For a couple of hundred yuan a month, vendors can rent a display box to showcase their goods. The only stipulation is that everything must be made by hand. What's being sold depends on when you go, but the mainstays are quirky and original. You'll find anything from ornaments, stationery, and artwork to items of clothing and hand-sewn notebooks. Fengguo is a treasure trove of kitschy, unusual gifts that make for a refreshing change from the norm.

OLD-TOXIN TIN TOYS

46 Fangjia Hutong, south of Guozijian Jie,
138/1091-6465
HOURS: Daily 10:42 A.M.–1:06 A.M.
METRO: Beixinqiao (Line 5)
Map 2

This quirky shop sells reproductions of the tin toys that every Beijing kid played with before the arrival of plastic Transformers in 1989. The shop owner, a Beijinger named Gao Lu, is in his early thirties and moonlights as an art teacher. He hasn't allowed anything but retro-style toys since it opened in summer 2009. He also has some of his own childhood toys on display. The shiny wind-up reproductions range from small and simple to bigger, more complicated designs. Note the shop's rather unconventional opening hours—they're not typos!

SPIN CERAMICS

6 Fangyuan Xilu, 10/6437-8649
HOURS: Daily 10 A.M.–9 P.M.
METRO: Sanyuanqiao (Line 10)
Map 6

Spin's creations might not be what you had in mind when you imagined taking Chinese porcelain home with you, but the shop's quirky designs and reasonable prices make it a great choice for some unusual gifts and souvenirs. Set up by Chinese-American interior designer Gary Wang, Spin recruits its potters from Jingdezhen, the birthplace of Chinese porcelain. The Beijing shop is a neat, well-lit treasure trove of tea sets, vases, paperweights, mugs, and plates. Everything here is handmade. The store often offers free gifts with purchase, and limited edition collections are frequent. Spin opened in 2004 and now operates in Shanghai and Melbourne, too.

XING MU'S HANDICRAFTS

11 Yandaixie Jie, 10/8402-1831
HOURS: Daily 10 A.M.–midnight
METRO: Gulou (Line 2)
Map 2

If you want to take home something a bit different from the regular China souvenirs (chopsticks, fans, silk dressing gowns, jade statues), try Xing Mu's Handicrafts near Houhai. The shop specializes in handcrafted notebooks bound in leather of various colors and textures, filled with special brown paper called *niupi*. It also offers a range of card-backed books

decorated with Peking opera masks, goldfish designs, and dragons, as well as hemp products. Xing Mu has many imitations around town, but it is the original and the best. All items are fixed price (no haggling), but the prices are very reasonable for the quality and craft.

Jewelry and Accessories

BELITA JEWELRY

1/F, Eric Paris Salon, 43 Sanlitun Beilu, 10/8576-8836, www.lizamjewelry.com

HOURS: Daily 10 A.M.-7 P.M.

METRO: Tuanjiehu (Line 10)

Map 4

Belita Jewelry is run by Elizabeth Genetti, a Californian designer who used to operate under the name Liza M. Her handmade pieces are delicate but sturdy, crafted from sterling silver and plated with platinum or rhodium. Her earrings, bangles, bracelets, and rings are decorated with gemstones in unusual colors, and her clean, white store is a pleasure to browse in. Belita designs have been worn at the Cannes Film Festival and have appeared in Chinese *Harper's Bazaar*. An affordable luxury, Genetti's jewelry makes an unusual souvenir that's bound to be a talking point when you get home.

MADE IN PARADISE

41 Dazhalan Jie, 10/6303-7218

HOURS: Daily 9 A.M.-10 P.M.

METRO: Qianmen (Line 2)

Map 3

If you're looking to take home something a little different from the usual array of red fans, jade trinkets, and decorative chopsticks, try Made in Paradise. A family-run shop with nearly a decade in the trade, this Tibetan treasure trove sells silver jewelry, patterned scarves

and bags, tapestries and leather items, and most things in between. Shop owner Luo Sang's father is a renowned Tibetan silversmith and makes all of the items by hand. Choose from his finely crafted rings, bracelets, earrings, pendants, and bangles, or go for a Tibetan lantern if there's room in your suitcase. The interior of the shop is typically Tibetan, with Buddha statues and the evocative scent of incense in the air.

PALOMA SANCHEZ

Shop A115, Nali Patio, 81 Sanlitun Beilu, 10/6501-2706, www.palomasanchez.com

HOURS: Daily 11:30 A.M.-8:30 P.M.

METRO: Tuanjiehu (Line 10)

Map 4

Take home a souvenir with a difference from Paloma Sanchez's jewelry boutique in Sanlitun. Trained as a gemologist and designer, Paloma hails from Madrid and has been in Beijing since 2006. Her pieces are characterized by a rough-cut aesthetic and use of unusual precious and semi-precious stones. She sources her gems in Montana, Arizona, Vietnam, Morocco, and Madagascar, and uses techniques she learned while working at prestigious jewelry brands like Patek Philippe. Her rings, bracelets, earrings, and necklaces are displayed behind glass like rare exhibits at a zoo. The white color scheme of the shop exterior is continued inside with eye-catching "knobbly" walls.

HOTELS

Thanks to the 2008 Olympics, Beijing now has a hotel industry befitting international standards. From the big-name 5-stars to the coziest of hostels, there is a bed here to suit every budget and every taste. Depending on what sort of vacation you want, your choice of hotel will make a huge difference to your Beijing experience. If you prefer the glitz and glamour of a luxury, big-name hotel, there's no shortage of Hyatts, Westins, Intercontinentals, and Shangri-Las. For visitors who want the more individuality and charm, a boutique hotel like the ultra-stylish Opposite House or Hotel G is worth considering. Travelers on a budget should consider staying in a hostel: Beijing's hostels are generally clean and have a reputation for friendliness.

CHOOSING A HOTEL

Beijing is a sprawling city, so it's worth staying as close to the Forbidden City as you can if you have limited time, as this will place you close to the main attractions. If you're here on business but want to do some sightseeing too, a hotel in the CBD or on Financial Street (between the Capital Museum and the Temple of Great Charity) is your best bet. Don't want to stay in the smoggy city? If you don't mind a longer metro trip into town, Aman at the Summer Palace is an excellent choice.

Standard rooms in Beijing hotels usually have either a double bed or two singles and a bathroom en suite. Breakfast is usually included in the room price, or is available separately at the hotel restaurant or café. Note that

HIGHLIGHTS

LOOK FOR ☾ TO FIND RECOMMENDED HOTELS.

☾ **Best Design:** Top architects from Studio Pei Zhu designed the contemporary **Hotel Kapok,** a modern take on the traditional court-yard hotel setup (page 142).

☾ **Most Central Location:** Just east of the Forbidden City, 5-star hotel **The Emperor** offers affordable luxury in the heart of the his-toric capital (page 143).

☾ **Most Hip Hostel: Downtown Back-packers** sits right on trendy Nanluoguxiang, close to some great bars, cafés, shops, and his-torical hot spots (page 143).

☾ **Best *Hutong* Atmosphere: Lusongyuan** offers a quaint courtyard atmo-sphere close to the sights and sounds of bohe-mian Gulou Avenue (page 144).

☾ **Best Place for a Party:** Sleep in the heart of Sanlitun's nightlife scene at the con-vivial **Friendship Youth Hostel,** where you're sure to make a few friends (page 146).

☾ **Best Decor: Hotel G** in Sanlitun is beau-tiful both inside and out, with its glowing fa-cade and retro interior design (page 146).

☾ **Best Place for a Business Trip:** Shangri-La's recently renovated **Kerry Centre Hotel** in the CBD is a great choice for those who are in Beijing on business (page 146).

☾ **Best Boutique Luxury: The Opposite House** in Sanlitun Village mixes modern Japanese design, amazing facilities, and top-quality, on-site restaurants and bars that are destinations in their own right (page 146).

☾ **Most Luxurious:** The **Ritz-Carlton Financial Street** has all the top-class facili-ties you'd expect from a 5-star hotel, as well as some great international dining options (page 147).

☾ **Best Resort:** Relax away from the bus-tle of the city at **Aman at the Summer Palace** (page 148).

HOTELS

© THE OPPOSITE HOUSE

The Opposite House

most hotels below a 3-star rating are forbidden by law to admit foreigners.

Many hostels are on par with 3- and 4-star hotels when it comes to cleanliness and facilities, so it's wise to consider staying at a hostel if you're on a tight budget. A bed in a dormitory will usually cost less than ¥100 a night; private rooms tend to cost only a little more. Hostel rooms may not be as well stocked with amenities and may be lower on creature comforts, but most private rooms are equipped with toiletries and sometimes feature televisions. Aside from the price, the biggest benefit of a hostel is the convivial atmosphere and opportunities for socializing with other travelers.

PRICE KEY

$	Under ¥100 per night
$$	¥100-500 per night
$$$	¥500-1,500 per night
$$$$	Over ¥1,500 per night

HOTELS

Tian'anmen

Map 1

HILTON BEIJING $$$

8 Wangfujing Dajie, 10/5812-8888, www.hilton.co.uk/wangfujing

METRO: Dengshikou (Line 5)

The name Hilton needs little introduction, and the Beijing Wangfujing branch has all the luxury and glamour you'd expect from the chain. Simply put, it is one of the best hotels in the whole of China and a great pick if you're looking for high-end accommodations. Standard rooms include 42-inch LCD televisions, sumptuous decor, rainfall showers, and super-comfortable beds. Food and beverage options include Vascos for Macanese fare, Chynna for high-end Chinese, Library for breakfast, and Flames for cocktails. The hotel is decorated with contemporary luxury throughout, including bronze accents and marble floors.

■ HOTEL KAPOK $$$

16 Donghuamen Dajie, 10/6525-9900, www.kapokhotelbeijing.com

METRO: Tian'anmen East (Line 1)

This hotel has an excellent location close to the Forbidden City and Wangfujing Avenue, as well as top-notch services and a glowing green grid exterior designed by architects from Studio Pei Zhu in 2006. The hotel is a modern take on the traditional courtyard setup, and the 89 rooms have either a city or a courtyard view. The Xianjiangba restaurant serves Western and Chinese food, while the funky Bookbar in the basement has free Wi-Fi. Hotel Kapok has a 5-star look and feel, but its prices are very reasonable.

PEKING INTERNATIONAL YOUTH HOSTEL $

5 Beichizi Ertiao, Beichizi Dajie, 10/6526-8855, www.peking.hostel.com

METRO: Tian'anmen East (Line 1)

If you want to stay right in the city center, try the Peking International Youth Hostel. It's slightly more expensive than hostels farther out of town but if you're here to see the main sights like the Forbidden City and Tian'anmen Square, it's worth paying a little extra to be in such close proximity. The *hutong* hostel has plenty of greenery despite its inner-city location, and the comfortable common area looks out over the courtyard. The decor has that pleasant, well-worn feel that's common to Beijing hostels, with traditional accents, lanterns, and plenty of red.

TANGYUE $$

50-54 Donghuamen Dajie, 10/6525-2502, www.tangyuehotelbeijing.cn

METRO: Tian'anmen East (Line 1)

This 66-room 3-star hotel looks like a traditional *hutong* lodging house from the outside, but once you get closer you'll notice a contemporary golden grid decoration across the front of the low-rise building. The intrigue continues inside, with guest rooms decorated in bright, swirling murals and quirky, contemporary furniture. The management recruited a team of hotel experts to design the interior, and each room is equipped with a TV, Internet access, and the customary conveniences. The restaurant serves Western and Asian food along with Fair Trade coffee.

🔳 THE EMPEROR 💲💲💲💲

33 Qihelou Jie, 10/6526-5566, www.theemperor.com.cn
METRO: Dongsi (Line 5)

The 5-star Emperor Hotel is a member of the Design Hotels network due to its boutique status, modern design, and high-end facilities. Built in 2008, the Emperor Hotel is a great choice for proximity to the Forbidden City and for modern, affordable luxury. It is located at the east of the Forbidden City, close to where the Emperor had his sleeping quarters in dynastic times. Each of the 55 rooms in the hotel is named after a different emperor in Chinese history. The hotel's restaurant, Shi, is a destination in and of itself, serving modern fusion food against a backdrop of striking orange furniture.

THE PENINSULA BEIJING 💲💲💲💲

8 Jinyu Hutong, off Wangfujing Dajie, 10/8516-2888, www.beijing.peninsula.com
METRO: Dengshikou (Line 5)

The Peninsula Beijing may be part of a chain, but it has enough character to set it apart from the rest. The facade is a deft mix of traditional and modern, with a decorated Chinese-style gate sitting against a contemporary front. The modern interior design extends from the marble lobby to the well-appointed guest rooms and dining options. These are Huang Ting (serving imperial cuisine), Jing (fusion fare), and the Lobby Lounge for drinks. All rooms are decorated in neutral cream tones, with simple but sumptuous furniture and bedding, and wide windows looking out over the city.

Houhai   Map 2

BAMBOO GARDEN 💲💲

24 Xiaoshiqiao Hutong, 10/5852-0088, www.bbgh.com.cn
METRO: Guloudajie (Line 2)

Before it was a hotel, this beautiful old bamboo-filled courtyard complex was the residence of Andehai, the chief eunuch of the imperial court. It was later home to a minister of the late Qing Dynasty. Nowadays it is a great mid-range lodging option in the heart of the Gulou area. The decor is very much Chinese, with dark wood interiors, red accents, upturned eaves, and gray slate roofs. There are three options for rooms: standard, single, and suite. All guest rooms have a fridge, Internet access, and modern conveniences. On-site is a tea house and several restaurants serving imperial cuisine.

🔳 DOWNTOWN BACKPACKERS 💲

85 Nanluogu Hutong, off Gulou Dongdajie,
10/8400-2429, www.backpackingchina.com
METRO: Guloudajie (Line 2)

Another budget choice, Downtown Backpackers puts you right in the middle of Nanluoguxiang, the heart of Houhai's Gulou area. Many of the neighborhood's best bars and restaurants will be right at your doorstep. Downtown Backpackers is widely touted as being the best hostel in Beijing thanks to its spotless rooms, super-friendly staff, and great location. Rooms are simple but comfortable. On-site activity group A-CLUB organizes sports and activities, and there's a fully equipped games room, bike rental, and luggage storage.

IMPERIAL COURTYARD 💲💲

16 Huayuandong Hutong, 10/6708-5978, www.imperialcourtyard.com
METRO: Andingmen (Line 2)

This 24-room Chinese style boutique hotel has

HOTELS

a striking interior, with a red-painted gallery level overlooking a central courtyard. Prices are mid-range, but look out for special online deals that slash prices significantly. The outdoor area is just as attractive as the interior, with a pleasant courtyard to chill in with a beer or a coffee. The hotel is well placed for all of Gulou's best bits, with plenty of cafés and restaurants in the vicinity. For meals on-site, there's the Imperial Traveler Café and Restaurant that serves both Asian and Western food.

LAMA TEMPLE INTERNATIONAL YOUTH HOSTEL ●

56 Beixinqiao Toutiao, Yonghegong Dajie, 10/6402-8663

METRO: Beixinqiao (Line 5)

This hostel places you among the traditional *hutong* alleys and hip social scene of the Gulou and Yonghegong areas (northeast of the Forbidden City) and is well located close to a subway station for easy transport. With drawings on the walls and Chinese-themed decor in the rooms, it's a cozy spot with a friendly atmosphere. The common room has a pool table and several guitars, and the bar is a great place to meet other travelers and exchange stories. It's really cheap, too.

◖ LUSONGYUAN ●●

22 Banchang Hutong, near Kuan Jie, 10/6404-0436, www.lusongyuanhotelbeijing.cn

METRO: Zhangzizhonglu (Line 5)

Lusongyuan's 50 rooms may not be the most luxurious in town, but for the price you pay, you won't get any better or more charming. The pretty courtyard is dotted with birdcages and was once used by the Qing Dynasty general who owned the property. Many guest rooms contain traditional wood-framed kang beds and all have private bathrooms. The lobby lounge serves tea and coffee all day, as well as Continental breakfast in the morning and Beijing-style food for lunch and dinner. Lusongyuan is well located for exploring Houhai, Gulou, and the Imperial city. The hotel was nominated for the most distinctive courtyard in 2009 by the Beijing Tourism Industry Association.

BOUTIQUE BOOM

Staying in big-brand hotels is great if you're in town on business and your company is paying, but the standard 5-star names can get a little boring after a while. That's why Beijing's recent boutique hotel boom is something to be thankful for. No longer are your options limited to inferior guesthouses and super-pricey luxury chains. With one-off boutiques popping up around town, there's no reason why your stay should be dull. The trend began in the United States in the 1980s and has gradually spread across the world. Boutiques tend to be small (some with only a handful of rooms) and are unique because they're not tied to a chain or brand. Decor is often ultra-modern or in some way interesting and unusual, like Beijing's Hotel Kapok and The Opposite House. Unlike the capital's big hotels, where you're basically just a number, boutiques are small enough for you to be treated like an individual.

RED LANTERN HOUSE ●

5 Zhengjue Hutong, off Xinjiekou Nandajie, 10/8328-5771, www.redlanternhouse.com

METRO: Xinjiekou (Line 4)

A budget option it may be, but the Red Lantern House doesn't skimp on cleanliness, character, or quality. Located in a series of *hutong* courtyards, the hostel is made up of East Yard, West Yard, and Temple Court. The staff speak English well and will arrange tours and airport pickups. Food options are decent but unremarkable, with a variety of breakfast sets, Asian dishes, and Western sandwiches and pastas. It's a good idea to communicate with the staff to find out which branch your room will be in, as West Yard is a couple of metro stops away from the main hostel. All three branches share traditional decor, good air-conditioning and heating, and convivial common space. Expect to pay more for a single room with a private en suite bathroom.

© SUSIE GORDON

Beijing's Red Lantern House

Qianmen

Map 3

CAPITAL HOTEL ⑤⑤⑤

3 Qianmen Dongdajie, 10/5815-9988

METRO: Chongwenmen (Line 2)

Each of Capital's 596 guest rooms is fitted with smart, modern decor, true to its 5-star status. Perfectly located within walking distance of Qianmen's sights, as well as Tian'anmen Square and the Forbidden City, it's a good choice for business travelers and an affordably luxurious option for tourists. The building may look decidedly gray and brutalist from the outside, but its two towers contain excellent guest rooms and suites (some of which overlook the Forbidden City), as well as solid dining options, a chandeliered club lounge, a spa, and a gym.

FAR EAST INTERNATIONAL YOUTH HOSTEL ⑤

90 Tieshuxie Jie, 10/5195-8811, www.fareastyh.com

METRO: Hepingmen (Line 2)

A member of the Utels group, Far East is one of the best hostels in Beijing, with a strong reputation for cleanliness, friendliness, and budget prices. Some of the private rooms are decorated traditionally, with dark wood furniture; others are more modern. The food options are the Western-style Travellers' Den in the courtyard and the Taste of Home restaurant on the 1st floor.

LEO'S HOSTEL $

Guangjuyuan, 52 Dazhalan Xijie, 10/6303-1595, www. leohostel.com

METRO: Qianmen (Line 2)

Opened in 2004, Leo's is one of the most popular hostels in Beijing and is well located on Dazhalan close to Qianmen, Tian'anmen Square, and the Forbidden City. It's a typical *hutong* hostel with a courtyard, common room, and café, offering amenities like bike rental, laundry, and tour booking, as well as more unusual services like tai chi and kungfu. The convivial atmosphere means that it's easy to make friends if you're looking for travel buddies.

RAINBOW HOTEL $$

11 Xijing Lu, 10/6301-2266, www.rainbowhotel.com
METRO: Caishikou (Line 4)

Located in the Tianqiao artistic quarter with its theaters and parks, the Rainbow Hotel is a little more shiny, corporate, and contemporary than its name suggests. Nevertheless, it is a solid choice for a mid-range budget. It benefits from its proximity to the Temple of Heaven, Dazhalan, and Qianmen Pedestrian Street, and is just a short subway trip away from other interesting parts of town. Rainbow has 366 rooms, all with Internet, minibar, fridge, and en suite bathrooms. There are Chinese and Western restaurants on-site and business facilities like conference and meeting rooms. If you're a business traveler, the hotel's proximity to many company headquarters could be an advantage.

Chaoyang, the Central Business District, and Sanlitun Map 4

FRIENDSHIP YOUTH HOSTEL $

43 Sanlitun Beilu, 10/6417-2632, www.poachers.com.cn
METRO: Tuanjiehu (Line 10)

Attached to the popular Poachers Inn bar in Sanlitun, this is definitely a hostel for party lovers. If you don't fancy being woken in the night by returning revelers, this probably isn't the right place for you. However, if you want to make friends and stay up late exchanging travel stories, you'll fit right in. The Friendship hostel contains 20 twin rooms and 15 dormitories of four beds each. It's right in the center of the Sanlitun action and is clean and well kept despite having a well-worn look and feel. Breakfast and laundry is included in your room price.

HOTEL G $$$

A7, Gongrenti Lu, 10/6552-3600, www.hotelg.com
METRO: Dengshikou (Line 5)

This retro, 1960s-inspired hotel in Sanlitun has 110 luxury rooms, which are referred to as good (standard), great (deluxe), and greatest (suite). Designed by Mark Lintott, the hotel's striking facade glows with illuminated neon window panels. Inside, a wellness center, Scarlett wine bar and tapas restaurant, and a Japanese eatery called Morio add to the metropolitan feel. Guest rooms come with high-speed wireless Internet, plasma televisions, and MP3 docking stations. Buffet breakfast is included in the room rate. Hotel G is the ideal place to stay for travelers who can't face another soulless chain. It's modern, vibrant, unique, and brilliantly located for Beijing's nightlife and culture.

KERRY CENTRE HOTEL $$$

1 Guanghua Lu, 10/6561-8833, www.shangri-la.com
METRO: Jintaixizhao (Line 10)

Renovations to the Kerry Centre are set to be complete in early 2012, unveiling a new and improved hotel. Well located in the middle of the CBD, it is one of three Shangri-La properties in the vicinity. With the Shangri-La name comes quality and luxury. The Manchester United football team stayed at the Kerry Centre when they visited Beijing. The Kerry Sports facility, Centro Bar, and family-friendly Horizon restaurant are added benefits. Conceived as a hotel for both business and leisure guests, it's a good, top-end choice.

THE OPPOSITE HOUSE $$$

Bldg. 1, Sanlitun Village, 11 Sanlitun Beilu, 10/6417-6688, www.theoppositehouse.com
METRO: Tuanjiehu (Line 10)

The Opposite House is one of the trendiest boutique hotels in Beijing. Located in chic Sanlitun Village, it was designed by Japanese architect Kengo Kuma and Shanghai firm Neri & Hu. It's the flagship hotel of the Swire group, and no expense has been spared when it comes to detail and quality. The six food-and-beverage venues include Bei restaurant, Mesh bar, and Punk club, each of which is a destination in itself. The Opposite House is one of the most modern and attractive hotels in Beijing, and one of the most expensive. Its atrium reception leads through to stylish, simply decorated guest rooms. If you've got the money to spend, this one comes highly recommended.

ZHAOLONG INTERNATIONAL YOUTH HOSTEL $

2 Gongrenti Beilu, 10/6597-2299, ext. 6111, www.
zhaolonghotel.com.cn
METRO: Tuanjiehu (Line 10)

One of Beijing's longest established youth hostels, Zhaolong opened in 2000. It benefits from an amazing location (close to the subway) and decent interior. With 35 rooms containing 2–6 beds each, it's a solid choice for budget travelers. It takes its name from the neighboring Great Dragon Hotel and offers discounts to members of Hostelling International. Hostel staff can organize trips for you to nearby attractions, like the Great Wall and Ming Tombs. There's also a restaurant, bar, bike rental, outdoor area, laundry, common space, and the use of a nearby fitness center.

Capital Museum and the Temple of Great Charity   Map 5

KELLY'S COURTYARD $

25 Xiaoyuan Hutong, off Bingmasi Hutong,
10/6611-8515, www.kellyscourtyard.com
METRO: Lingjing Hutong (Line 4)

This cozy courtyard hotel in the Financial District is a good budget choice if you don't mind paying slightly more than you would at a youth hostel. Note that there's a 15 percent surcharge, but you get plenty of services for your money. As well as clean, well-decorated rooms, Kelly's Courtyard has a friendly atmosphere that is reminiscent of a hostel. There's Wi-Fi throughout and coffee, tea, and snacks available in the 2nd floor loft and roof terrace. A Continental breakfast is served every day in the courtyard. There are DVDs and bikes to rent and a friendly staff to help you book trips. Kelly herself is a Beijing-born fashion designer and travel fan who manages the premises with her husband.

◉ RITZ-CARLTON FINANCIAL STREET $$$$

1 Jinchengfang Dongjie, 10/6601-6666, www.
ritzcarlton.com
METRO: Fuchengmen (Line 2)

Another 5-star option in Beijing's modern quarter, the Ritz-Carlton Financial Street has an eye-catching, curved-edge exterior made up of glass and chrome panels. The guest rooms and suites mix contemporary design with sumptuous furnishings and contain all the conveniences you would expect from a luxury hotel. Dining options include a Chinese restaurant and a modern Italian trattoria called Cepe. The on-site spa offers nail and hair treatments as well as massages. If it's an authentic boutique experience you're looking for, this might not be the hotel for you, but it's great as a luxury choice if money isn't an issue.

THE WESTIN BEIJING FINANCIAL STREET $$$$

B9 Jinrong Jie, 10/6606-8866, www.starwoodhotels.
com
METRO: Fuchengmen (Line 2)

This part of town is replete with top-end hotels, and the Westin is one of the most luxurious. If you're looking for a 5-star option, this is a good choice thanks to its great location close to the inner-city sights and easy access to the rest of town. Its 486 guest rooms and suites take up one of the complex's twin towers, while the other contains 205 luxury residences for longer stays. Each guest room is blessed with a flat-screen television, Wi-Fi, a "rainforest" shower, and a special trademarked Heavenly bed. Relaxation is the name of the game, with a spa, gym, and indoor pool. Room rates reflect the luxury amenities—this hotel is pricey.

HOTELS

University District and the Summer Palace   Map 5

HOTELS

ALOFT BEIJING $$

Tower 2, 25 Yuanda Lu, 10/8889-8000, www.
starwoodhotels.com/alofthotels
METRO: Renmin University (Line 4)

Ideally placed for visiting the Summer Palace and exploring the vibrant student-centric Wudaokou neighborhood, Aloft Beijing is a mid-range hotel from Starwood's boutique brand. A standard Aloft room covers 32 square meters (344 sq. ft.) that features a comfortable yet contemporary decor. Their larger Corner Rooms feature floor-to-ceiling windows for stunning views of the city. The hotel offers free wired and Wi-Fi internet, as well as a 24-hour pantry to appease late-night snackers. There is a bar, lounge, and café on-site as well.

AMAN AT THE
SUMMER PALACE $$$$

15 Gongmenqian Lu, 10/5987-9999, www.amansara.com

METRO: Xiyuan (Line 4)

Staying this far out of town may not be everyone's bag, but if you detest the noise of traffic and thick air of car fumes, Aman at the Summer Palace may be your dream resort. Incorporating the pavilions used by the guests of the last empress, Dowager Cixi, by the east gate of the Summer Palace complex, Aman is a luxury boutique hotel with beautifully decorated rooms and exteriors. The pavilion roofs are covered in Jin clay tiles, and the wood detailing on the walls is painted red, green, and blue. Ming-style gardens separate the buildings. Despite its historic appearance, it contains a Pilates studio, modern luxury fittings, and three excellent restaurants. Aman appeared on Condé Nast's 2011 Gold List—clearly, luxury is guaranteed here.

Greater Beijing   Map 6

COURTYARD BY MARRIOTT BEIJING
NORTHEAST $$$

101 Jingshun Lu, 10/5907-6666, www.marriott.com
METRO: Sanyuanqiao (Line 10)

The Courtyard by Marriott is a good choice for business travelers, but equally suitable for leisure seekers who don't want to stay in the city center. The decor is a step beyond sterile corporate hotels, with dashes of color and interesting patterns to liven things up. Each of the 258 rooms and suites is fitted with a desk and high-speed Internet, and there are extensive business facilities in the hotel itself. For food there's MoMo café for international breakfast, lunch, and dinner and the MoMo 2 go deli for takeout. The 101 Lounge serves dinner and drinks in the evening.

ROSEDALE HOTEL $$$

8 Jiangtai Lu, 10/5960-2288, www.rosedalehotels.com
METRO: Sanyuanqiao (Line 10)

The Rosedale Hotel benefits from a great location close to pretty Si'de Park and some decent drinking and dining options. Staying in this part of Beijing is a different experience from downtown, and the 4-star Rosedale places you within easy reach of the 798 Art District and Wangjing business zone. Its 400 rooms range from standards to luxury suites, and dining options include Chinese restaurant Cheena and European and Asian eatery Sonata. For drinks on-site there's the Serenade Lounge and the Polo Bar.

TRADERS UPPER EAST $$

2 Dongsihuan Beilu, 10/5907-8888, www.shangri-la.
com/en/property/beijing/tradersuppereast
METRO: Sanyuanqiao (Line 10)

A spin-off of the Shangri-La group, the Traders brand is aimed at business and leisure travelers who want luxury and comfort without an exorbitant room rate. Located near the 798 Art District, Wangjing Hi-Tech Park, and China International Exhibition Center, Traders Upper East Side has 419 rooms and suites along with top-notch business facilities. A glass-fronted lobby that overlooks parkland connects the hotel's twin towers. On-site dining options are Chinese food at Wu Li Xiang and international fare at Café Noir. Take afternoon tea at the lobby lounge and evening drinks at the Collage Bar. For leisure and fitness there's an indoor swimming pool, sauna, whirlpool, and gym.

YI HOUSE $$$

706 Hou Jie, Unit 1, 798 Art District, Jiuxianqiao Lu, 10/6436-1818, www.yihouse.com

METRO: Sanyuanqiao (Line 10)

Stay right in the heart of the 798 Art District at the funky Yi House. This boutique hotel occupies an old crystal factory, and its name is a play on the Mandarin word that means both guesthouse and unequaled. A small hotel with 30 rooms, Yi House is bright and contemporary, with thoughtfully decorated rooms. The Fennel Restaurant and Gossip Bar are venues in their own right. Skip out on the costly airport pickup; a taxi costs no more than a couple of hundred yuan.

HOTELS

THE GREAT WALL

The Great Wall stretches across the northern reaches of China from the ocean at Shanhaiguan in Hebei Province to Lake Lop in the autonomous Xinjiang region in the west, close to the Taklamakan Desert. It was built to protect the nation from nomadic warlords coming down from the north, including Mongolian invaders. The structure was begun in the Qin Dynasty (220–206 B.C.), but most of what survives today was built during the Ming Dynasty (A.D. 1368–1644). The construction of the Great Wall was the longest building project in world history. The actual wall stretches for 6,259 kilometers (3,889 mi), but trenches and natural barriers like hills take its length to the official figure of 8,851 kilometers (5,500 mi). Even though it is not visible from space as the legend claims, it is one of the most impressive sights you will see in China. Photographs or postcards cannot properly capture the beauty of the neat, sand-colored watchtowers winding off into the distance or the sun going down beyond the Wall's crenellations.

One of the most iconic structures on earth, the Great Wall of China should definitely be included in your Beijing itinerary. Many of the Wall's best-preserved and most interesting points lie within easy reach of Beijing. If you want a quick stop and don't mind crowds and souvenir hawkers, try tourist-favorite Badaling that lies 70 kilometers (43 mi) outside of Beijing and has convenient transportation links. Equally well connected and meticulously restored is Mutianyu—another popular spot for visitors. To see the wall at its craggiest and

HIGHLIGHTS

LOOK FOR ☾ TO FIND RECOMMENDED
SIGHTS, ACTIVITIES, DINING, AND LODGING.

☾ **Best Whistle-Stop: The Great Wall at Badaling** is great for visitors with a limited time frame: This portion of the Wall is located only 70 kilometers (43 mi) away from downtown Beijing and can be explored in just a few hours (page 156).

☾ **Best History Lesson:** Learn about the Great Wall in detail at the **China Great Wall Museum** at Badaling. The museum boasts an assortment of exhibits covering the Wall's purpose, construction, and upkeep (page 156).

☾ **Best Luxury Hotel:** The sprawling **Commune by the Great Wall** features beautifully furnished rooms and a luxurious spa, and is easily the most opulent choice for an overnight visit to the Wall (page 158).

☾ **Best Value:** You'll get your money's worth (and then some) at **Great Wall Box House,** a cozy courtyard hostel with friendly staff, good facilities, and a welcoming atmosphere (page 158).

☾ **Best Hiking:** Snake through craggy peaks and steep passes for the 10 kilometers (6 mi) between **the Great Wall at Jinshanling** and Simatai; climb a few watchtowers to cap off a strenuous, but rewarding hike (page 159).

☾ **Best Scenery:** The stunning views around **the Great Wall at Mutianyu** make it a treat for the eyes in all four seasons. This part of the Wall is at its most gorgeous in fall, when the trees turn orange (page 161).

☾ **Most Natural Beauty:** Lakes, forests, and undulating hills make **the Great Wall at Huanghuacheng** a good choice for nature lovers and photographers alike (page 164).

© YULIA ZHUKOVA/123RF.COM

the Great Wall at Jinshanling

THE GREAT WALL

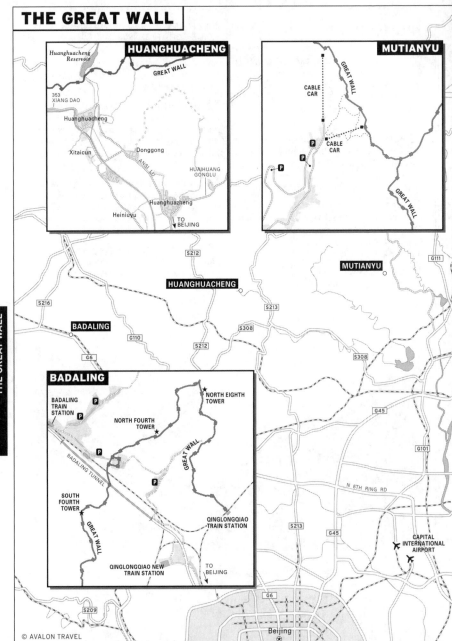

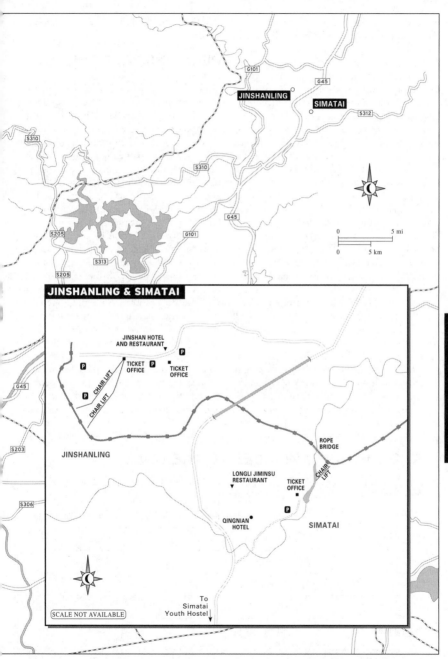

THE GREAT WALL

JINSHANLING & SIMATAI

JINSHAN HOTEL
AND RESTAURANT

TICKET
OFFICE

TICKET
OFFICE

CHAIR LIFT

CHAIR LIFT

JINSHANLING

LONGLI JIMINSU
RESTAURANT

TICKET
OFFICE

ROPE
BRIDGE

CHAIR
LIFT

QINGNIAN
HOTEL

SIMATAI

To
Simatai
Youth Hostel

SCALE NOT AVAILABLE

JINSHANLING

SIMATAI

G101

G45

S312

S310

S310

G45

G101

S205

S313

S205

0 — 5 mi
0 — 5 km

G45

S203

S306

most remote, head to Jinshanling instead. It's farther out of town and great for hiking, but not as well-kept as the stretches of wall closer to Beijing. The Wall at Simatai used to be one of the most beautiful and natural, but has been closed for renovation since June 17, 2010, and the authorities have yet to specify when it will be reopened. Jinshanling is a good alternative, with similar terrain and equally good hiking opportunities. The Wall at Huanghuacheng takes its name from the yellow blossoms that flower in summer; its lake and reservoir add to the scenic beauty of the spot.

Much of the most-frequented parts of the Wall date from the Ming Dynasty and reflect the architectural style of the period. Watchtowers, forts, and beacons occur at regular intervals and the Wall's parapets are indented with crenellations designed for archers to shoot through. Garrisons of armed soldiers guarded the towers, while men on horseback patrolled the Wall itself, watching for invaders. The terrain surrounding the Great Wall posed challenges to the armies that constructed it, as they worked to build the Wall up among hills, mountains, and ridges. Goats were used to transport bricks up the craggy peaks and millions of laborers worked on the Wall throughout its construction. In terms of scope, skill, and history, there's no doubt

that the Great Wall of China is a true wonder of the world.

PLANNING YOUR TIME

It's best to set aside a whole day to see the Great Wall. It's workable in half a day if you go to the sections that are nearest to downtown Beijing, but once you get there, you'll probably want to stay as long as physically possible, just to soak up the scenery and exhilaration of actually being there. Set off as early as you can and take snacks in case you're caught short and need refueling at the Wall. There are snack vendors and restaurants to varying degrees of plenty, depending on which part of the Wall you visit, but it's best to come prepared.

Public transportation is your best option, with comfortable and reliable buses traveling regularly from downtown Beijing to the various sections of the Wall. Bus travel is cheap, too, with most trips costing under ¥15 each way. The only problem is keeping to the timetables, which can sometimes be restrictive. If money isn't an issue, a taxi is a convenient choice and allows you more flexibility. Taxis can be hailed from the street in downtown Beijing to take you to the Wall, but it's a better idea to get your hotel or hostel to book one for you: Explain to the driver where you want to go and whether you want him or her to wait

ROUND-TRIP TAXI RIDES TO THE WALL

The following are rough guidelines for what you can expect to pay for a round-trip taxi ride, including a 2-3-hour waiting time for the driver.

Section of Wall	Distance from Beijing	Approximate Cost of Taxi Ride
Badaling	70 km. (43 mi.)	¥500
Jinshanling	140 km. (87 mi.)	¥800
Simatai	120 km. (75 mi.)	¥700
Mutianyu	85 km. (53 mi.)	¥600
Huanghuacheng	60 km. (37 mi.)	¥600

for you while you tour the wall. It's a good idea to get the driver to wait, as you won't have to worry about finding another taxi when you're ready to head back.

Visiting the Wall on an organized tour is another option and one that is logistically easier than going it alone. If you don't speak Mandarin or read Chinese, it can be a challenge to navigate public transportation. However, if you do go on an organized trip, be aware that companies will invariably take you to some sort of shopping emporium, be it a jade market or calligraphy gallery, and encourage you to buy souvenirs at inflated prices. You'll usually be limited to whichever restaurant they are getting commission from, too. Most hotels and hostels organize tours, but if you want to book one yourself, a reputable tour company that eschews commission-based detours is **Great Wall Hiking** (139/1136-1359, www.greatwallhiking.com). They offer walks at Jinshanling, Mutianyu, Huangyahuan, Gubeikou, and Jiankou and provide pick-ups and drop-offs at your hotel in Beijing. One-day tours start at around ¥500 and a two-day hike with an overnight stop on the Wall starts at around ¥1,300. Another reputable company is **Great Wall Adventure** (138/1154-5162, www.greatwalladventure.com). Established in 1992 and now run by a Canadian company, it offers short and long hikes on the Wall at Jinshanling, Gubeikou, Mutianyu, and Jiankou as well as overnight trips (travelers make camp in watchtowers). Most day hikes cost under ¥500.

Beware of tour solicitors recruiting business in downtown Beijing: There have been situations where such people are running scams. Only book your trip with a reputable agency that can be verified online or over the phone. The **Beijing Hub of Tour Dispatch** (10/6601-5622 or 10/5298-0138) was set up by the government in 2005 to replace the old tourist bus system. It runs routes to various parts of the Wall, some include lunch and entry tickets. The service runs to Badaling daily, and to Mutianyu and Huanghuacheng only on weekends April 7–October 15. (Note: When the Simatai approach was open, it was a part of the weekend service. It is presumed that upon reopening, the same schedule will be resumed.) The Hub's official website is exclusively in Chinese and difficult to navigate, but BeijingTrip.com offers timetables and other helpful information at www.beijingtrip.com/transport/sightseeing-bus.htm.

Staying overnight at the Great Wall is a good idea only if you are interested in longer hikes. Otherwise, seeing the Wall in a morning or a day is more sensible, since the hotel options are limited. Many cater only to Chinese guests, lacking the license that would allow them to accept foreigners. Notable exceptions include the Schoolhouse at Mutianyu—a series of private guesthouses arranged around a central venue in Mutianyu Village—and the luxury Commune at the Great Wall near Badaling.

Weather Considerations

Winter temperatures on the Great Wall can dip well below freezing. This part of North China is known for its biting winds and chilly frosts. Since the Wall is particularly high and exposed, you will need to bring warm, well-insulated clothing if you plan to visit during the colder months. Even if the weather in downtown Beijing seems temperate, it's likely that it will be several degrees colder (and certainly windier) on the Wall. Layer up with thermal underwear, short- and long-sleeve T-shirts, fleece jackets, and windbreakers, and don't forget a warm hat, scarf, and gloves. If it's raining when you visit the Wall, be extra careful, as the stone gets slippery. Sturdy shoes with good traction are recommended whatever the season. If it's raining on the day you plan to visit the Wall, consider postponing your trip.

In sharp contrast to the chills of winter, summer on the Wall is blisteringly hot, with little protection from the sun. The hottest months are July and August, but June and September can get uncomfortably warm too. Make sure you take brimmed hats, shades, sunscreen, and plenty of fluids. (Water and other drinks are widely available on the Wall, especially at Badaling and Mutianyu, but vendors often inflate prices.)

Safety Considerations

Veering off the beaten path can be fun, but it's unwise to try to climb off the Wall outside of the designated areas. With unstable rocks and boulders, the terrain can be dangerous and if you get into trouble in remote areas, it can be impossible to get help. When it comes to conservation, don't take stones from the Wall as souvenirs and respect the landscape by not throwing litter. Beware of vendors pushing you to buy overpriced postcards and souvenirs: They can be very persistent, so make it clear right away that you're not interested by saying *"Bu yao."*

Badaling 八达岭

◖ THE GREAT WALL AT BADALING

The Great Wall at Badaling (Yanqing County, 10/6912-1737, www.badaling.gov.cn, Apr. 1–Oct. 31 daily 6 A.M.–8 P.M., Nov. 1–Mar. 31 daily 7 A.M.–6 P.M., ¥45 Apr. 1–Oct. 31 ¥40 Nov. 1–Mar. 31) attracts hoards of tourists thanks to its proximity to Beijing (70 km./43 mi. northwest of the city) and its well-preserved towers and ramparts. Open to the public since 1957, it has received hundreds of foreign dignitaries over the years, including Richard Nixon in 1972. Chairman Mao was also fond of Badaling (claiming, "If you haven't been to Badaling, you are not truly a man"), which served to raise its profile.

This section of the Wall became a UNESCO World Cultural Heritage site in 1988, four years after Deng Xiaoping launched a renovation effort. It was named one of the New Seven Wonders of the World in 2007. The name Badaling means "reaching eight ridges" and refers to the peaks and points that it traverses. The section of the Wall that is open to the public runs for 3.7 kilometers (2.3 mi) and features 19 towers. Its highest point is Beibalou at 1,015 meters (3,330 ft.).

The Wall at Badaling was constructed in 1505 during the reign of Ming emperor Hongzhi to protect the Juyongguan Pass and the city of Beijing beyond. The site was built on walls from the earlier Warring States Period (475–221 B.C.). The Jiajing emperor continued the project, but it wasn't until the era of Emperor Wanli (A.D. 1563–1620) that a large-scale project was undertaken to shore up the Wall between Shanhaiguan on the coast to Juyongguan, north of Beijing.

Thanks to the renovations of the early 1980s, the Wall at Badaling is now visitor-friendly and easily walkable. Cable cars (one-way ¥40, round-trip ¥60) and funicular-style pulleys (one-way ¥30, round-trip ¥60) are available to take you up to the Wall and back. The cable cars terminate at the North 8th Watchtower, while the pulleys drop visitors at the North 4th. The North 4th is closer to the ticket office, so the hike back is shorter.

Hiking the full length of the Badaling section takes 3–4 hours. The terrain on the Wall is easy on the feet, thanks to extensive renovation. The scenery on either side of the parapets is stunning, with forest-clad crags and peaks undulating into the distance. In winter, the view over the snowy hills is breathtaking. Badaling's proximity to the capital is both a blessing and a curse: While it's close enough to visit in a morning or an afternoon, it is almost always crowded and dotted with the sort of Western chain restaurants and cafés you'd probably rather not see at a site of such historical significance. Go on a weekday in low season, if you can, and you'll miss most of the crowds. Holidays are to be avoided at all costs, as you will traverse the Wall literally shoulder to shoulder with other people, if you can get onto it at all.

◖ CHINA GREAT WALL MUSEUM

This well-laid-out museum (10/6912-1890, Apr. 1–Oct. 31 Tues.–Sun. 9 A.M.–5 P.M., Nov. 1–Mar. 31 Tues.–Sun. 9 A.M.–4:30 P.M., admission included with price of Wall ticket) at the base of Badaling gives a good overview of

THE WALL THROUGH HISTORY

The Great Wall of China has its origins in the Warring States Period, which was the last era of Chinese history before Emperor Huangdi began the first imperial dynasty. The states of Zhongshan, Qu, Wei, Qi, Yan, and Zhao each built walls to protect themselves against the others, using techniques developed in the earlier Spring and Autumn Period. These rudimentary fortifications were constructed by packing earth between wooden boards. When Huangdi unified the states into the Qin Dynasty in 221 B.C., he called for all of the walls to be dismantled apart from the ones that protected the northern reaches of the empire from enemy nomads from the Xiongnu tribe. These early incarnations of the Wall have mostly succumbed to the erosion of time.

The Han Dynasty replaced the Qin in 206 B.C. and the Wall was forgotten until 130 B.C., when the Wudi Emperor recognized the importance of defending the state against Mongol invaders. The Wall was extended westwards through Gansu Province and into Xinjiang, down the Hexi Corridor that was part of the Silk Route. During the Three Kingdoms era that followed the Han Dynasty, only the Kingdom of Wei was concerned with maintaining the Wall, since they needed to defend against the Rouran and Qidan tribes. When the Tang Dynasty rose in A.D. 618, the Great Wall was again abandoned and fell out of use until the simultaneous Liao and Song Dynasties that followed. The Liao controlled the north of China and used the wall to keep out marauding tribes. Unfortunately, their efforts were in vain and the Mongol-led Yuan Dynasty established itself in 1276.

The Wall fell into dereliction once again until the Ming took power in 1368. In order to keep out the Manchus and Mongols once and for all, the Hongwu Emperor pushed for a comprehensive renovation and extension of the Wall. The most famous sections were built between 1569 and 1583. Since they were built from brick and stone instead of earth and packed sand, they are also some of the best preserved. The Wall was effective until the start of the 17th century when attacks from Manchu tribes began once again. The Chinese empire held fast until 1644 when a treacherous guard named Wu Sangui allowed the Manchus to enter the country at heavily fortified Shanghaiguan Pass, in protest against the Shun peasant uprising that was threatening Ming power from Xi'an. Wu's actions cemented the fall of the Ming and the rise of the Manchu Qing Dynasty – China's last dynasty. During the Qing era, the Wall was partially dismantled for other building projects and fell into disrepair once again.

The Communist Cultural Revolution saw some damage to the Wall, but Chairman Mao was a fan, allowing it to open publically in 1957 at Badaling. It wasn't until the 1980s that tourists began to add the Wall to their itineraries, following Deng Xiaoping's restoration efforts of 1984. The Great Wall was declared a UNESCO World Cultural Heritage Site in 1987 and is now one of China's most popular and iconic sites.

From the appearance of the Wall close to Beijing, it would be easy to imagine that the structure is equally well-preserved all along its length, but sadly this isn't the case. The watchtowers and passes in Hebei province and the Beijing municipality have been restored to attract tourists, but much of the Wall's length is derelict. In Gansu Province, vast sections are at risk of disappearing altogether, with just two meters (6.5 ft.) remaining of the original five (16 ft.).

THE GREAT WALL

the history of the Great Wall and is well worth a look. Opened in 1994, it traces the history of the Wall from the fortifications of the Spring and Autumn Period (one of the final eras before China was unified in 221 B.C.) and the early Qin Dynasty to the Ming period when much of the structure was built. The exhibition is laid out across seven different sections, including the Wall of the early dynasties, the Ming Wall, construction equipment, warfare on the Wall, and repair and reconstruction. Relics found on and around the Wall are also on display. The museum's layout echoes the winding nature of the Wall itself, with a zig-zag path leading between the exhibition rooms.

RECREATION
Anantara Spa

The on-site spa facility of Commune at the Great Wall, Anantara Spa (Badaling Expwy., Shuiguan exit, 10/8118-1888, www.spa.an-antara.com) is a luxurious venue offering massages and spa treatments in beautiful surroundings. Take the weight off your feet after a day on the Great Wall with their signature treatment: 2.5 hours of foot and body massage, a body scrub, aromatic flower bath, and hydrating lotion rub. Massage styles include acupressure, hot stones, and ayurveda; there's a range of facial and body treatments to choose from as well. The spa covers a huge 1,000 square meters (10,764 sq. ft.) across three levels, with six suites and nine rooms for couples, as well as a hair and beauty area. The decor is luxury minimalist, with all the dim lighting, neutral colors, and relaxing atmosphere you would expect from a 5-star hotel spa.

HOTELS
◖ Commune by the Great Wall

If you want to spend a night at the Great Wall, one of the most attractive (and expensive) options is Commune by the Great Wall (Badaling Expwy., Shuiguan exit, 10/8118-1888 ext. 5706, www.communebythegreatwall.com, ¥2,500 d, ¥12,500–23,000 villas). Its 42 villas were designed by 12 of Asia's best and most innovative architects. Eleven of the villas can be rented only as a unit, but the others contain 190 individual rooms and suites. The exterior of the hotel is box-like and modern, with the villas arranged on the mountainside like futuristic pods. The interior is equally contemporary and the clientele are those that don't mind paying top dollar. The hotel is surrounded by stunning mountain scenery and is close to some of the most hike-able stretches of the Great Wall. Refuel at one of the four on-site restaurants or recharge in the spa after a day of walking. If you're travelling with children, you can book them into the kids' club while you explore the surrounding area.

◖ Great Wall Box House

A more affordable choice is the Great Wall Box House (Jia 18A, Xidui Main St., Gubeikou Village, Miyun County, 10/8105-1123, www.boxhotel.com, ¥750 private, ¥150 mixed dorm). An outpost of a popular downtown Beijing hostel, the Great Wall Box House is a cozy courtyard lodging with friendly staff, good facilities, and a pick-up service from the city center.

Great Wall Courtyard

Another option is the Great Wall Courtyard (5 Chadaogucheng, Badaling Village, Yanqing, 10/6912-1156, www.courtyard.cc, ¥480), a Ming-style courtyard hotel at the base of the Wall. With its traditional red and black decor, lanterns, and wall-hangings, the atmosphere is welcoming. Amenities include a choice of Western breakfasts and Chinese food, free Wi-Fi, a travel desk, and a lending service for books and DVDs.

GETTING THERE AND AROUND

Bus line 919 has three routes: The quickest gets you to the Great Wall in an hour and leaves from the parking lot to the north of Deshengmen Tower (30 Huayan Beilijia, Deshengmenwai Ave., 10/8284-6760 or 10/6336/0283, ¥12 one-way). This bus is comfortable and air-conditioned. If you have a Beijing Transport Card, the journey will cost just ¥4.8. Buses run to Badaling 6 A.M.–noon; the last return bus leaves the Wall at 4 P.M.

A **tourist train line** (10/6563-6733, ¥7 hard seat, ¥14 soft seat) runs from Beijing North Railway Station to Badaling: Train 6427 departs at 8:29 A.M. and arrives at Badaling at 11:07 A.M. Two **regular train lines** go from Beijing North Railway Station to Badaling: the Y567 (leaves at 9:33 A.M. and arrives at 10:42 A.M.) and the Y575 (leaves at 1:19 P.M. and arrives at 2:28 P.M.). Badaling Station is about a 25-minute walk from the entrance to the Wall and is clearly signposted.

Taking a taxi from downtown Beijing to Badaling will cost in the region of ¥500 round-trip, with the driver waiting for you while you're on the Wall. Taxis can be hailed from downtown, but it's a good idea to ask your hotel to book one for you and explain to the driver that you want him or her to wait and bring you back to Beijing.

Jinshanling and Simatai 金山羚和司马台

◖ THE GREAT WALL AT JINSHANLING

The Jinshanling section (Gubeikou, Miyun County, 10/8402-4628, daily 8 A.M.–5 P.M., ¥50 Mar.15–Nov.15, ¥40 Nov. 16–Mar.14) as it stands today dates from A.D. 1567 when Ming generals Tan Lun and Qi Jiguang were commanded to build fortifications against enemy attacks. General Qi worked for 15 years on 1,200 kilometers (746 mi) of the Wall, including the Jinshanling portion.

Jinshangling is your best bet if you want to see the Wall without hoards of other visitors. It is located 140 kilometers (87 mi) northeast of Beijing on the border of Miyun County and Luanping in Hebei Province. It's a longer journey from downtown, but it's well worth the extra trek. The Wall is very steep in parts and isn't so well preserved as Badaling and Mutianyu, but is manageable as long as you watch your step and are in good health. Visitors who aren't so good on their feet or suffer poor health should not be dissuaded from visiting Jinshanling, as the Wall can be reached by cable car (¥50 adults, ¥30 students) and once you arrive on it, there is no obligation to hike the full length.

Jinshanling means "gold mountain ridge" in Mandarin; it sits between two peaks, Big Jinshan and Small Jinshan. The Wall here lies 10 kilometers (6.2 mi) north of Gubeikou (Old Northern Pass), which was used by the Qing royal family to get to their summer palace at Chengde. It runs for about 10 kilometers (6.2 mi) between the Wangjing Tower in the east and Longyukou in the west, crossing rugged terrain. The Wall is studded with watchtowers along its length, many with two floors that were used as soldiers' barracks. Jinshanling was part of the Gubeikou defense line protecting Beijing in the south, with the Wangjinglou watchtower as its highest point. This tower is said to have been built from blocks of stone carried by Er Lang Shan, the nephew of the mythical Jade Emperor. The structure of the Wall here is slightly different from Badaling and Mutianyu, as it is narrower and has an extra fortification along the parapet. Among the many watchtowers are the Black Tower and the Taochun Tower, named after two girls who were involved with the construction of the Wall. The General Tower was built in memory of Wu Guihua, a Ming-era woman who sacrificed herself to guard the Wall against invaders from the north.

The walk from Jinshanling to Simatai takes around four hours. Before the closure of the Simatai site in summer 2010, one of the best ways to see the Wall was to hike along it from Simatai to Jinshanling. The two sections are joined and there was a fee of ¥5 to cross from one to the other. This is a wonderful way to explore the Wall; check with local tour groups to see if the Simatai site has reopened upon your visit to Beijing. Another option for hiking is the six-hour trek in the opposite direction to Gubeikou. The terrain around the Wall at Jinshanling is bleaker than other parts and is more barren than the verdant Badaling and Mutianyu. It is particularly attractive in wintertime, though, when the scrub is dusted with frost.

THE GREAT WALL AT SIMATAI

Lying 120 kilometers (75 mi) outside of Beijing, the Great Wall at Simatai (Gubeikou, Miyun County, 10/6903-1051) has 35 watchtowers in varying degrees of ruination dotted along its winding, often vertiginous path. The Wall connects to Jinshanling and traversing from one site to the other was a popular hiking choice.

The Wall at Simatai is famous for the density of its watchtowers. It has the most towers of any individual section of the Wall. The Wall is split into eastern and western sections by the Mandarin Duck Lake that is fed by hot and cold springs. The section to the west has the most watchtowers, but the most famous

© SUSIE GORDON
Great Wall at Simatai

ones are on the eastern part. The most famous tower is the Wangjing Tower that rises 986 meters (3,235 ft.) and overlooks the lights of the capital in the distance (its name means "watching Beijing"). Also notable is the Fairy Tower (Xiannulou), named after the legend of an antelope that turned into an angel and fell in love with a shepherd. The story comes from a myth about a lotus flower fairy, which explains the lotus flowers carved above the tower's doorways. Xiannulou is reached by a narrow 80-degree path known as the Heavenly Ladder and connects to Wangjing Tower by the equally vertigo-inducing Stairway to Heaven.

Like most sections of the Wall in this part of China, Simatai was constructed at several points during the Ming Dynasty, most notable under General Qi Jiguang, using primitive foundations laid in the Northern Qi period. Many of the bricks that make up the Wall are inscribed with dates and the names of the work units that laid them. Before Simatai closed, the terrain was extremely rocky and often dangerous, but renovations will most likely shore up the Wall and make future hiking easier.

It is unclear what sort of renovations are taking place at Simatai, although rumors have circulated that a luxury golf club and resort are being built nearby, much to the horror of conservationists. According to official information from the Administration Office of Simatai Great Wall Scenic Area, the project will take at least two years. Check www.simataigreatwall.org to get the latest information available on the renovations at Simatai.

HOTELS

The modest but comfortable **Jinshan Hotel** (Great Wall at Jinshanling, Gubeikou, Miyun County, 10/8402-4628, ¥320), a 2-star guesthouse, is your best bet for accommodations if you want to stay close to the Great Wall at Jinshanling. The hotel is split into three sections. In the main complex, the standard rooms with courtyards are the cheapest and the rooms around the quadrangle are the newest. The apartment suites (complete with separate lounges) lie behind a gray wall topped with an elaborate red-roofed gate. Rooms are modestly decorated and although the amenities are basic, the hotel is clean and comfortable. Decent food is available on site.

Before the closure of Simatai, the **Simatai Great Wall Youth Hostel** (10/8188-9323, ¥320) was a popular spot, thanks to its outdoor patio overlooking the lake and the Wall, courtyard setting, and clean, cozy rooms. It is not known whether the hostel will reopen, but it's worth calling to check.

GETTING THERE AND AROUND

A three-hour journey on the 980 bus from Dongzhimen Long Distance Bus Station (45 Dongzhimenwai Ave., 10/6467-1346, ¥15) gets you to Miyun County; from the Miyun

County stop, take a waiting cab to the foot of the Wall.

The L671 tourist train goes between Beijing's North Railway Station (A1 Beibinhe Rd., Xizhimenwai Ave., 10/5186-6223) and the town of Gubeikou daily mid-April–October. The train departs from Beijing at 7:25 A.M. The journey takes 2.5 hours and costs ¥20 each way. Outside of peak season, the L815 train leaves from Beijing at 8 A.M. (returning to the city at 3:05 P.M. and 4:15 P.M.) and costs ¥10 per ticket. From the Gubeikou station, you'll take a half-hour trip to the Wall in a comfortable minibus, which costs an additional ¥20.

A taxi will cost around ¥800 round-trip, if the driver waits for you as you explore the Wall. Otherwise, you can expect to pay ¥400–500 each way.

Mutianyu 慕田峪

◖ THE GREAT WALL AT MUTIANYU

The Great Wall at Mutianyu (Huairou County, 10/6162-6873, www.mutianyu-greatwall.com, daily 8 A.M.–4 P.M., ¥45 adults, ¥25 children under 1.5m/4'11" tall, free for children under 1.2m/3'11" tall) connects the Juyongguan Pass in the west with the Gubeikou section of the Wall in the east. Slightly less populated by tourists but no less popular than Badaling, Mutianyu is easily accessible from downtown Beijing. Famous for its scenic beauty and dense forests, it is located 85 kilometers (53 mi) from the center of the capital. After evaluating the popularity of the Badaling Wall, the government decided to restore Mutianyu and open it to the public in 1987. It is well preserved and easy to navigate, with cable cars (¥45–65 adults, ¥25–35 children) available to take you up to the Wall and a fun 1,500-meter (0.9 mi) luge slide (¥55 adults, ¥40 children) to get back down, once you've finished walking the Wall.

The Great Wall at Mutianyu was begun during the Northern Qi Dynasty (A.D. 550–557)

and runs for 22 kilometers (14 mi), making it the longest stretch of Wall that's open to the public. Generals Tan Lun and Qi Jiguang strengthened the Wall during the middle Ming Dynasty with 22 watchtowers and granite fortifications. Aside from being made of granite, what sets Mutianyu apart from the other sections of the Great Wall is its double crenellations. On most other sections of the Wall, only the side facing enemy territory has merlons (the gaps between crenellations), but at Mutianyu, they appear on both parapets for extra security. In total, the Wall is around seven meters (23 ft.) high and five meters (16 ft.) wide at the top.

Each of the four seasons brings a different color to the surrounding pine-covered landscape: the white of winter snow; vibrant red and orange in fall; green from the summer grass; and purple with wildflowers in springtime.

HOTELS

For those choosing to stay overnight, Mutianyu has the best and most interesting options near the Wall. Accommodations here are courtesy

THE GREAT WALL

GREAT WALL LORE: MYSTERIES, HOAXES, AND THE VIEW FROM THE MOON

The Great Wall's worldwide fame has been the source of several hoaxes and false claims over the years, along with myths and legends dating back into history. Here are some of the most interesting (and eyebrow-raising).

THE TALE OF THE EXTRA BRICK

During the construction of the Jiayuguan Pass at the Wall in Gansu Province during the Ming Dynasty, a worker named Yi Kaizhan was put in charge of calculating the exact number of bricks needed to complete the Pass. Something of a mathematician, he told the foreman that 99,999 bricks were required. The construction materials were gathered and the Pass was built. When the foreman came to inspect the work that Yi Kaizhan had overseen, he noticed a brick sitting on a ledge and accused Yi of miscalculating. The punishment was three years' hard labor for him and his troops. Yi explained that the extra brick had been placed there by a supernatural force; if it was removed, the whole structure would fall down. Not willing to test this theory, the foreman let Yi off and the brick can still be seen on the Jiayuguan Pass today.

THE DENVER HOAX

The most notorious prank associated with the Great Wall of China originated in the United States. It started as a prank among four reporters in Denver, Colorado, who plotted to raise readership figures by fabricating a story that an American company planned to knock down the Great Wall and replace it with a road. The story was published in 1899 at a time when foreign colonalism was rife in China. The British had just secured a 99-year lease on Hong Kong's New Territories and German troops had taken over Shandong Province in the north of China. Tensions eventually led to the Boxer Rebellion of 1900, when the Chinese rose up against imperial powers. While not a direct cause of the Rebellion, the fake news story certainly did nothing to help diplomatic relations. It spread from Denver to the East Coast and then to Europe and persisted thanks to an ersatz quote from a Chinese official. It wasn't until 10 years later that one of the reporters admitted that the original article had been a hoax.

VIEW FROM THE MOON

One of the most persistent legends surrounding the Great Wall is that it's visible from the Moon. The myth is based on an extremely shaky statement made in 1754 by a British archaeologist and historian named William Stukeley, who said that the Wall "makes a considerable figure on the terrestrial globe and may be discerned at the Moon." During the 19th century, notable scientists backed up his rather ambitious claim, based on the belief that canals could be seen on Mars. It wasn't until modern technology allowed humankind to travel into space that the claims were debunked. Viewing the Wall from the Moon with the naked eye would be like seeing a human hair from three kilometers (1.9 mi) away. Neither Neil Armstrong and the Chinese astronaut Yang Liwei were able to pick out the Great Wall on Earth during their space missions. However, a photograph taken from the International Space Station by Chinese-American Leroy Chiao shows a very indistinct image of the Wall, but this is due to heavy magnification.

of The Schoolhouse at Mutianyu, a complex featuring a collection of properties that caters to many different tastes.

The Schoolhouse at Mutianyu

Converted from an old village elementary school, The Schoolhouse at Mutianyu (Mutianyu Village, Huairou County, 10/6162-6506, www.theschoolhouseatmutianyu.com, office open daily 7–10 A.M., 3–5 P.M.) is a restaurant, art center, and hub that will fix you up with accommodations in one of 11 private guesthouses and small hotels around Mutianyu. If privacy is your priority, the guesthouses in the Schoolhouse complex may be up your alley—guesthouses must be rented in full; individual rooms are not available for rent. All prices include breakfast at the Schoolhouse restaurant.

Depending on your preferences for number of rooms and bathrooms, there are some great options. **Grandma's Place** (www.grandmasplaceatmutianyu.com, ¥2,000) is located in the former courtyard of a Qing Dynasty official; the current building was constructed by a Western expatriate for his mother. Rustic but comfortable, this private guesthouse has two bedrooms, two bathrooms, and a spacious living room, all with wood-beam ceilings and stone walls. The courtyard is dotted with fruit tress and inside the villa, funky ornaments contrast with the rural decor.

Also part of the Schoolhouse is the secluded **Pavilion** (www.thepavilionatmutianyu.com, ¥3,000), with two large bedrooms, an open fire, modern conservatory, and rustic interiors. A spacious patio looks out onto the surrounding scenery. A good choice for larger groups is **The Red Door** (www.thereddooratmutianyu.com, ¥4,200). Formerly the ancestral temple of the village farm, it contains four bedrooms and 3.5 bathrooms (one of which is en suite), as well as a terrace and an open fire in the living room.

The beautiful **Brickyard Inn & Eco-Retreat** (Yingbeigou Cun, Huairou County, 10/6162-6506, www.brickyardatmutianyu.com, Mar.–Dec., ¥1,300) is also under Schoolhouse management and offers individual rooms, rather than a guesthouse. The building used to be a glazed tile factory, the remnants of which can be seen decorating the outer walls and indoor murals. Staying at the Brickyard is a tranquil experience, with no televisions or telephones provided (there's Internet access though). The hotel's common room is in the old kiln room and the main lodge has a lovely fireplace and café. The French managers provide free soft drinks and homemade cookies in the lodge and a country-style breakfast is available every morning. Each of the 16 guest rooms has a floor-to-ceiling window and a private terrace. The vibe is simple yet comfortable and there's a spa, whirlpool tub, and outdoor pool.

GETTING THERE AND AROUND

You can take bus 936 at Dongzhimen Outer (10/6467-1346, ¥16 one-way) to Mutianyu Great Wall, which runs every hour on the hour, 7 A.M.–3 P.M. The last bus back from Mutianyu leaves at 5:30 P.M. Make sure you check with the driver that the bus is going to Mutianyu; there are several branches of the line. Get off at the Mingzhu Square bus station by the Huairou International Conference Center. From here, minibuses ferry visitors to the Wall for ¥25.

On weekends and public holidays, a special Line A bus (10/6467-1346) runs to Mutianyu 6:30–8:30 A.M. It leaves from outside the South Cathedral at Xuanwumen (141 Qianmen Xi Ave.) and the Beijing Sightseeing Bus Centre (10/8353-1111) at Qianmen.

During the Golden Week national holiday at the start of October, a tourist train (10/5186-6223) leaves Beijing North Railway Station (A1 Beibinhe Rd., Xizhimenwai) at 7:10 A.M. for Beizhai Station, after which a minibus ferries visitors up to Mutianyu. The Beijing-bound return train leaves Beizhai at 4 P.M.

If you want to take a taxi, expect to pay around ¥250 from downtown Beijing to Mutianyu.

THE GREAT WALL

Huanghuacheng 黄花城

◖ THE GREAT WALL AT HUANGHUACHENG

This section of the Wall (Chengguan Town, Huairou County, 10/6165-1004, www.huanghuacheng.com, daily 8:30 A.M.–5 P.M., ¥25 adults, ¥12.5 students, free for children under 1.2m/3'11" tall) dates from the Ming Dynasty and snakes through some beautiful mountains and lakes. The yellow flowers that carpet the hills around the Great Wall give the village of Huanghuacheng its name: *huang* means "yellow" and *hua* means "flowers" in Mandarin. This section of the Wall isn't the best preserved, but it's well worth a look if you want something a little more unusual than Badaling and Mutianyu. It's only 60 kilometers (37 mi) out of town, so it's not actually too remote. This 11-kilometer (6.8 mi) stretch of the Wall crosses six passes and includes six forts, 12 beacon towers, and 32 guard towers. It gets steep in parts, so prepare for shin splints. Look out for two large carved characters on the cliff face below the Wall. They are *jin* and *tang,* which mean "strong"—a reference to the sturdy construction of the Wall.

GETTING THERE AND AROUND

Bus 916 from Dongzhimen (10/6467-1346, ¥11 bus with a/c, ¥6 bus without a/c) will get you to the Huairou Local Tax Bureau (Huairou Dishui). Say *"kong tiao?"* ("aircon?") to the driver to find out which type of bus it is. When you get to the Tax Bureau, look for the bus to Shuichangcheng that leaves nearby. A ticket from here to the wall is ¥3. A taxi to Huanghuacheng will cost around ¥150 each way.

SHANGHAI

SIGHTS

One of the fastest-paced, most exciting cities on earth, Shanghai defies expectations at every turn. The cliché goes that it's a city of contrasts, but it's the truest description. Where else on earth would you see Ming-era temples and pavilions sharing a skyline with neoclassical bank headquarters, super-skyscrapers, and art deco theaters? Shanghai's mottled history has left its Technicolor marks on the metropolis, making it an entrancing city to visit.

Contrary to what you might expect from a Chinese city, there is relatively little traditional architecture to be found in Shanghai outside of the Old City. The austere neo-classical houses that line the Bund bear witness to the era when Shanghai was under foreign control; the art

deco villas and European-style apartment blocks in the Old French Concession speak of the city's days as a treaty port inhabited by Westerners.

Shanghai might not have as many ancient buildings as Beijing, but it possesses some rare gems. Spend an afternoon in the Old City for a glimpse of Ming Dynasty temples and gardens, dating from the time when a city wall was built to keep out marauding Japanese pirates. The Old French Concession is best explored on foot or by bike, while Line 2 of the Metro will take you to Jing'an Temple, Nanjing Road, People's Square, and the Bund. Across the river in Pudong lies the city's financial heart, with Fortune 500 companies and banks occupying the jungle of skyscrapers.

HIGHLIGHTS

LOOK FOR  TO FIND RECOMMENDED SIGHTS.

◖ Best View of the Skyline: Take in one of Asia's most stunning cityscapes from the **Bund Promenade,** a raised pedestrian walkway (page 167).

◖ Best Local Color: Immerse yourself in alley life down **Lane 1025,** off West Nanjing Road, with its small cafés and shops (page 172).

◖ Best People-Watching: Watch hipsters, artists, and tourists wander the alleys of **Tianzifang,** a district built around a former candy factory, while relaxing at one of the area's many cafés (page 173).

◖ Best Historic Sight: See the ancient side of Shanghai at the Ming-era **City God Temple** with its Daoist deities (page 175).

◖ Best Vantage Point: At nearly 500 meters tall, the **Oriental Pearl Tower** provides incredible views of the city from each of its giant pink spheres (page 178).

◖ Best Activity for the Kids: Kids will love the vast array of animals at the **Shanghai Natural Wild Insect Kingdom** that, despite its name, has goats, owls, turtles, and much more (page 178).

◖ Best Introduction to the Old French Concession: Kick off your OFC explorations at the charming **Ferguson Lane Complex** with its cafés, galleries, and restaurants (page 180).

◖ Most Unusual Architecture: At one time Asia's largest slaughterhouse, the eerily gorgeous **1933** is now a lifestyle complex featuring upscale shops, restaurants, and cafés (page 181).

◖ Most Adrenaline-Pumping: Get a different view of the city from the top of the Lupu Bridge with **Shanghai Climb.** Don't worry: the staircase isn't as strenuous or vertigo-inducing as it seems (page 182).

The Oriental Pearl Tower is a symbol of Shanghai.

The Bund

Map 7

◖ BUND PROMENADE
外滩
Zhongshan Dongyilu, btwn. Garden Bridge and Yan'an Lu
METRO: East Nanjing Road (Line 2, Line 10)

One of Shanghai's most iconic streets, the Bund stretches along the Huangpu riverfront and is lined with gorgeous colonial-era buildings. It was known as the Wall Street of Asia during the boom of the 1920s and 1930s and it must have been a hive of activity with ships unloading, laborers rushing by, and merchants haggling. Start at the Garden Bridge in the north, and work your way down the promenade all the way to the Shiliupu Docks. The view from the raised pedestrian walkway is unforgettable: On one side are the old customs houses, art deco hotels, and imposing bank headquarters, and on the other are the bristling skyscrapers of the modern financial district across the river. The Bund promenade can get rammed on weekends, so keep an eye on your belongings and don't be inveigled into having your photo taken by dubious "professionals."

BUND SIGHTSEEING TUNNEL
外滩观光隧道
300 Zhongshan Dongyilu, near Nanjing Donglu, 21/5888-6000
HOURS: Mon.-Thurs. 8 A.M.-10:30 P.M.
COST: ¥40 round trip, ¥30 one way
METRO: East Nanjing Road (Line 2, Line 10)

If the name puts you off, don't be discouraged. Far from being a dry historical relic, the Bund Sightseeing Tunnel is a short train ride of pure weirdness. Of all the options the developers could have chosen for this subterranean journey from Puxi to Pudong, this is the least likely. Oddly robotic assistants lead you into your pod before shutting the door and propelling you into the unknown. Surreal puppets rise up on either side of you and a veritable disco of neon lights pulsates in every direction. There is nothing even vaguely educational or historical about the experience, and it's more expensive than the ferry, but it's worth it just for the "huh?" factor.

EAST NANJING ROAD
南京东路
Nanjing Donglu, btwn. Xizang Lu and The Bund
METRO: East Nanjing Road (Line 2, Line 10)

One half of the mighty Nanjing Road, this section of street between The Bund to the east and People's Park to the west was one of Asia's first ever modern commercial boulevards. East Nanjing Road started life in 1845 as Park Lane in the International Settlement, extending from the Bund to Henan Road. It was lengthened over the years until it reached Xizang Road in 1862 and was renamed Nanking Road (the old postal spelling of Nanjing). Thanks to its many shops and restaurants, locals called it Da Ma Lu (Main Street). In the early 1900s, a series of

eight department stores sprang up, followed by countless franchise shops and stalls. In a cruel twist of fate, over 600 shoppers died on August 23, 1937, when a Chinese airplane offloaded a bomb before flying off to fight the Japanese. Much of East Nanjing Road was made into a pedestrian zone in 2000 and entered a twinning agreement with Paris's Champs Élysées in 2007. Nowadays, East Nanjing Road thrums with life, neon, and commerce. Vendors will, no doubt, pester you along the way. Be careful not to fall for any scams (for example, some "students" may approach you to have tea to practice their English and then leave you with the bill).

GARDEN BRIDGE
外白渡桥
Zhongshan Dongyilu, near Huangpu Park
METRO: East Nanjing Road (Line 2, Line 10)

This bridge might not be one of the prettiest sights in Shanghai, but it is definitely one of the most historically interesting. It is the only camelback truss bridge of its kind in Asia; it was built by the engineering firm responsible for the Victoria Bridge over the Zambezi River. It also offers a view of both the Bund and the Pudong skyline. Until 1856 the only way to get from the Bund to Hongkou district was to hop on a rickety ferry, so a bridge was commissioned to span the Suzhou Creek. The original wooden viaduct was replaced in 1908 by the latticed bridge you see today (known as Waibaidu by locals), which carries over three million vehicles per day.

HUANGPU RIVER
黄浦江
Btwn. Puxi and Pudong
METRO: East Nanjing Road (Line 2, Line 10)

The wide stretch of water that cuts Shanghai in two is the Huangpu Jiang (Yellow Bank River). The Huangpu slices the city into easterly Pudong (where the skyscrapers are) and westerly Puxi (with People's Square, Jing'an Temple, and the Old French Concession). It starts life in Dianshan Lake and flows for 97 kilometers (60 mi.) before emptying into the mighty Yangtze River at Wusongkou, 29 kilometers (18 mi.) north of Shanghai. Measuring 400 meters (0.25 mi.) across at its widest point, it is the last major tributary of the Yangtze. The Huangpu is responsible for Shanghai's dizzying rise to international fame. It brings cargo through the city to the East China Sea from as far afield as Sichuan Province in China's interior.

HUANGPU RIVER CRUISE
黄浦游船
219 Zhongshan Dongyilu, 21/6326-3693, www. pjrivercruise.com
HOURS: Long cruise daily 2–5 P.M.; short cruises daily 9:30 A.M., 10:45 A.M., 1 P.M., 2:30 P.M., 3:15 P.M., 4 P.M., and 4:30 P.M.; short cruises nightly every half hour 7–8:30 P.M.
COST: ¥50-150
METRO: East Nanjing Road (Line 2, Line 10)

The best way to see both the river and the city it divides is on a cruise. The Shanghai Huangpu River Cruise Company (Shanghai Pujiang Youlan) is the major provider of river boat trips and offers either a three-hour jaunt up to the mouth of the Yangtze at Wusongkou, or a leisurely one-hour sail past the main city sights between the Nanpu and Yangpu bridges. There's also an evening option to take in the glitz of the skyline at night. The three-hour cruise is a great way to gain a thorough understanding of what makes Shanghai tick. After cruising past the colonial buildings of

the Bund to the left and the Lujiazui skyline to the right, you'll travel past the wharves and docks of Hongkou district before passing into industrial territory. Sights include the castle-like Yangshupu Water Plant, built by the British in 1883, and the Wusong fort, where the Opium Wars were fought. Finally, you'll reach the meeting point of the Huangpu, the Yangtze, and the East China Sea, where the waters mix.

MONUMENT TO THE PEOPLE'S HEROES
人民英雄纪念塔
Inside Huangpu Park, Zhongshan Dongyilu, near Garden Bridge
HOURS: Daily 24 hours
COST: Free
METRO: East Nanjing Road (Line 2, Line 10)

Commemorating China's revolutionary and political martyrs of the turbulent 20th century, this unusual concrete statue is the centerpiece of the small Huangpu Park and offers unimpeded views of the skyline across the river. The monument is an abstract representation of three rifle heads arranged with their tips together, symbolizing both strength in numbers and an end to fighting. The statue was designed and erected by the Shanghai Municipal Government in the 1990s and stands 24 meters (79 ft.) tall. Although not particularly attractive, it is a good location for photographing the surrounding buildings and nearby Garden Bridge.

People's Square   Map 8

MOORE MEMORIAL CHURCH
沐恩堂
316 Xizang Zhonglu, near Jiujiang Lu, 21/6322-5069
HOURS: Tues.-Sun. 9 A.M.–6 P.M., Sun. services 7:30 A.M., 9 A.M., 2 P.M., 7 P.M.
COST: Free
METRO: People's Square (Line 1, Line 2, Line 8), exit 20

Among the modern malls and skyscrapers that flank People's Square is a building that stands apart. The red brick Moore Memorial Church (known as Mu'en Tang in Mandarin)

was designed by Hungarian architect László Hudec in the early 1930s. The modest building stands on the site of an older church that was constructed by American missionaries in 1887. Moore Memorial Church started out as a place of Methodist worship but is now nondenominational. It was closed but remained intact during the Cultural Revolution, reopening for worship in 1979. Evangelist Billy Graham preached here in 1988, and two bishops were consecrated on-site the same year.

© SUSIE GORDON

Moore Memorial Church

PEOPLE'S PARK
人民公园
231 Nanjing Xilu, inside People's Square
HOURS: Daily 6 A.M.–6 P.M.
COST: Free
METRO: People's Square (Line 1, Line 2, Line 8), exit 10

When Shanghai was a treaty port back in the 1800s, this part of town fell inside the International Settlement. The 30-acre plot of land that is now People's Park used to be the British racecourse and its gray brick clubhouse is now the Shanghai Art Museum. When the Communist Party outlawed gambling in 1949, the racetrack was given over to parkland. The modern park sits inside People's Square and contains some of the city's most famous buildings, like the Urban Planning Exhibition Hall, Municipal Government building, Shanghai Grand Theatre, Shanghai Concert Hall, and Shanghai Museum. The park is ringed by gleaming malls and skyscrapers and sits on top of a 2.5-million-square-meter (27 million sq. ft.) underground shopping and snack arcade. Inside the park, pathways wind between lawns and over ponds, and there are plenty of benches for visitors to rest and admire the urban landscape.

Jing'an   Map 9

JING'AN SCULPTURE PARK
静安雕塑公园
128 Shimen Erlu, near Beijing Xilu, 21/5228-9562
HOURS: Daily 5 A.M.–9 P.M.
COST: Free
METRO: West Nanjing Road (Line 2)

Part outdoor art gallery and part urban park, this newish attraction has yet to garner too much attention. This means that you'll probably have it all to yourself. Despite its location close to some of Shanghai's busiest streets, the Sculpture Park is 30,000 square meters (323,000 sq. ft.) of pure tranquility. Trees, flowers, and sprawling lawns form a

HUDEC'S LEGACY: ART DECO SHANGHAI

© SUSIE GORDON

art deco apartments on Shanghai's Wukang Road

One of the things that makes Shanghai so interesting is the mix of styles that characterizes its architecture. The sleek skyscrapers of Lujiazui stand in stark contrast to the lower, colonial-era edifices that line the Bund. They are a world away from the upturned eaves of the Old City and the pastel-toned stucco villas of the Old French Concession. Many of the city's most interesting and storied buildings date from the art deco period and lots have survived despite mass demolition in other parts of town. The man who gave Shanghai much of its early modernist architecture was Slovakia-born Ladislav (László) Hudec. Working in Shanghai in 1918-1945, he was responsible for the stunning Park Hotel, Grand Theater, Moore Memorial Church in People's Square, and countless villas and apartment blocks.

Hudec's life reads like an epic. He was born in the former Czechoslovakia in 1893 to a Slovak father and a Hungarian mother and studied architecture at the University of Budapest. After volunteering to fight in World War I, Hudec was captured by the Russians in 1916 and sent to a labor camp in Siberia. He managed to escape from a train near the Chinese border and made his way to Shanghai where he got a job with an American architecture firm called R. A. Curry. He left in 1925 to start his own company and spent the years until 1941 designing nearly 40 buildings. Art deco was all the rage in the 1930s, spreading from America and Europe where it was admired for its simple lines, optimistic colors, and smooth curves.

Shanghai also has local designers to thank for its rich art deco heritage. As well as Hudec and the French architecture firm Leonard, Veysseyre & Kruze, Chinese architects contributed to the trend. Trained at the University of Philadelphia in the 1920s, Benjamin Chih Chen, Shen Chao, and Chuin Tung founded the Allied Architects firm and built the Chekiang First Commercial Bank in 1948. Their countryman Dong Dayu was the talent behind the famous Chinese Aviation Association building, designed to look like a 1930s airplane.

backdrop for the giant art installations. There are 300 trees in total, including gingko, camphor, beech, and hackberry, as well as 124 cherry trees. Sculptures are changed on a rotating basis, so expect to see anything from outsized bulls to enormous human figures. The trees of Sculpture Park are said to cancel out the energy of 1,500 air-conditioning units.

JING'AN TEMPLE
静安寺
1686 Nanjing Xilu, near Huashan Lu, 21/6256-6366
HOURS: Daily 8 A.M.–5 P.M.
COST: ¥30
METRO: Jing'an Temple (Line 2, Line 7)

Squatting among downtown's neon-lit shopping malls and flashy high-rise office blocks, Jing'an Temple is a slice of history and devotion among monuments to capitalism. The gilded roofs and lotus-topped pagoda make an arresting sight from the elevated highway. Inside you'll find a 3.5-ton copper bell dating from the early Ming Dynasty (1368–1644), the biggest sitting jade Buddha in China, a camphor statue of the female bodhisattva, and stone Buddhas from the Southern and Northern Dynasties. The relics are spread across three main halls located around a courtyard. The temple's name means "peace and tranquility." It was originally located near Suzhou Creek. Dating from A.D. 247, it is Shanghai's oldest temple. It was moved to its current location in 1216 during the Song Dynasty and has undergone extensive (and expensive) renovation since 1999. Look out for the Abbot's Chambers, which were home to the notoriously corrupt Abbot of Bubbling Well Road. Before the Communist Party outlawed religion in 1949, he kept seven mistresses and a White Russian bodyguard.

◖ LANE 1025
南京西路 1025 弄
Nanjing Xilu, near Maoming Beilu
METRO: West Nanjing Road (Line 2)

Escape the crowds of West Nanjing Road and get a taste of *lilong* (traditional Shanghai residential alley) life down Lane 1025. Taking up a whole block between West Nanjing Road and Weihai Road to the south, Lane 1025 contains row upon row of gorgeous red-brick buildings. Three stories high, they are mainly residential, but many of the yards contain cafés, art galleries, and independent boutiques. Unlike the historic *shikumen* (stone arch gate) housing compounds that have mostly been destroyed, Shanghai's *lilong* continue to thrive, and make up much of the city's low-rise housing stock. Once you get inside the Lane complex, it's easy to forget that you're actually at the center of one of the world's biggest cities.

WUJIANG ROAD
吴江路
btwn. Maoming Beilu and Shimen Erlu
METRO: West Nanjing Road (Line 2)

Until recently, the eastern strip of Wujiang Road was one of Shanghai's most vibrant and popular food streets. The arrival of bulldozers in early 2010 spelled the end of an era, as the street stalls, barbecues, and snack shops were sacrificed to the city's pre-Expo cleanup. The western portion of Wujiang Road has become the polar opposite, with Western cafés and stores flanking the pedestrian walkway between South Maoming Road and Shimen 2nd Road. Wujiang Road is a great place to witness Shanghai's urban youth in action; join in by grabbing a latte and perusing one of the Western-branded shops. Many of the cafés and restaurants have outdoor terraces which are great for people-watching.

Old French Concession
Map 10

CITÉ BOURGOGNE
步高里

Corner of Shaanxi Lu and Jianguo Xilu

METRO: Jiashan Road (Line 9)

This lovely red-brick housing complex dates from 1930 and was originally home to 78 families. Now it contains around 450 households, but retains its old-style charm. The vast majority of Shanghai's Concession-era residential districts have been torn down in the name of progress, or turned into chic lifestyle hubs like Xintiandi. Cité Bourgogne is one of few to have survived and is a living, working lane complex with a thriving community of locals. As long as you respect people's living space, you are welcome to stroll down the lanes and alleys, observing and imagining Shanghai life as it once was back in colonial days.

JIASHAN MARKET ECO COMPLEX
嘉善老市

37, Nong 550 Shaanxi Nanlu, near Shaoxing Lu, www.jiashanmarket.com

METRO: Jiashan Road (Line 9)

Fronting the current movement for all things eco-friendly, Jiashan Market is a smaller-scale green version of nearby Tianzifang. A collection of abandoned factories was leased from the municipal government by Brearly Architects and Urbanists and converted into a mixed-usage complex featuring sustainable materials and processes. Offices and residential space take up the top floors, while the ground level is home to a small but diverse selection of eateries, like Korean Annion Kitchen, Malaysian Sambal, organic Melange Oasis, and Japanese Meshi. Regular eco design fairs are held in the central courtyard. The short walk down the lane towards the complex from Shaanxi Road offers a window into local life.

SITE OF THE FIRST NATIONAL CONGRESS OF THE CHINESE COMMUNIST PARTY
第一届中国共产党全国代表大会遗址

76-78 Xingye Lu, near Huangpi Nanlu, 21/5382-2171

HOURS: Daily 9 A.M.–5 P.M. (last ticket issued at 4 P.M.)

COST: Free, ¥10 audio guide

METRO: South Huangpi Road (Line 1)

The location for one of the most defining moments in Chinese history was the Bo Wen Girls' School, close to what is now Xintiandi. On July 23–31, 1921, a group of Marxists, socialists, and communists came together to lay the foundations for the Chinese Communist Party. Among the delegates at this secret meeting was Mao Zedong, a young revolutionary from Hunan Province who would eventually become the first chairman of the new People's Republic. The Shanghai government designated the school as a place of public interest in 1952, and it was converted into a museum in 1999. Life-size models of the 13 delegates sit around a table in a reenactment of the events of July 1921. The large lobby contains a collection of photographs, artifacts, and documents. With nearly two million visitors per year, this is one of Shanghai's best-loved historic attractions and a good place to get an overview of modern Chinese history.

◖ TIANZIFANG
田子芳

Nong 210 Taikang Lu, near Sinan Lu

METRO: Dapu Bridge (Line 9)

If Xintiandi is too commercialized for your tastes, you'll probably prefer Tianzifang (also known as Taikang Road). A warren of alleys tucked away between two main streets, Tianzifang can be hard to find and even harder to find your way out of. Flanked with small galleries, boutiques, jewelry shops, and cafés, this little district started life as a series of residential *longtang* (lanes) beside a candy factory. When the factory was converted into an art gallery in 1998, creative businesses and artists began to set up in the lanes. Popular among the city's hipsters, photographers, and artists (both local and foreign), Tianzifang is also becoming a tourist favorite. Aim to get here before

© SUSIE GORDON

Xintiandi

lunchtime to avoid the crowds. There are numerous cafés and restaurants to choose from, most of which have outdoor seating or roof terraces. Top choices are Bell Bar, Kommune, Lapis Thai, and Origin Café. In the evening, the fairy lights strung between the buildings add to the atmosphere.

XINTIANDI
新天地
Nong 123 Xingye Lu, near Madang Lu
METRO: Xintiandi (Line 10)

Shanghai's "new heaven and earth" is very much a staple on the tourist trail, but it's worth wading through the umbrella-led throngs to experience some classic architecture and diverse dining options. Xintiandi is made up of two blocks of converted *shikumen* (stone arch gate) terraces south of Middle Huaihai Road, with a central boulevard cutting through it from top to bottom. Familiar names, like Starbucks and Coffee Bean and Tea Leaf, sit alongside upscale Asian brands, like TMSK and Shanghai Tang, and expat haunts, like Paulaner Brauhaus and KABB; even the street vendors' wares are a cut above what you'll find in the bazaars. While Xintiandi's North Block is quaint and atmospheric, the South Block is more contemporary, with a glass-fronted mall and cinema complex at the lower end. The Shikumen Open House Museum (North Block, 21/3307-0337, daily 10 A.M.–11 P.M., ¥20) is worth a look if you're interested in the style of architecture that once dominated Shanghai's residential districts before the developers moved in. Xintiandi gets especially crowded on weekends, so aim to visit early in the morning before the hordes descend. The café terraces are great for a spot of people-watching.

IT STARTED WITH XINTIANDI: SHANGHAI'S MODERN LIFESTYLE HUBS

The modern city of Shanghai can often seem like a daunting, somewhat faceless metropolis, but dotted between the elevated highways and busy thoroughfares is a collection of smaller, village-style hubs, often with a creative or lifestyle-oriented vibe. The trend began with Xintiandi in the northeast of the Old French Concession, which has become one of the city's most visited attractions. Xintiandi (meaning "new heaven and earth") stands on the site of a former *shikumen* (stone arch gate) district near Huaihai Road that was cleared for redevelopment in the late 1990s. Two blocks of traditional stone-gate housing blocks were left in tact and purchased by Shui On Land. Benjamin T. Wood and Nikken Sekkei designed a contemporary entertainment district replete with boutiques, terrace cafés, and restaurants, transforming the neighborhood into a magnet for Shanghai's wealthy.

The rise of Tianzifang in the lanes behind nearby Taikang Road has been more organic. A compound of former factories was turned over to the Shanghai Economic Committee in 2000, which established art galleries and shops there. The residential lanes behind the compound were slowly taken over by independent shops, bars, and cafés. More recently, Jiashan Market eco-hub has sprung up in a lane off Shaanxi Road and the ambitious Sinan Mansions project has turned 49 concession-era villas into a high-end complex of entertainment venues and a luxury hotel. North Jing'an District has followed suit with the construction of 800Show in an old factory on Changde Road.

While these lifestyle hubs can be partially thanked for preserving otherwise doomed buildings, the gentrification comes at a price. Over 3,500 families were displaced to built Xintiandi and residents of the Taikang Road lanes are less than happy that their once-quiet neighborhood has been taken over by tourists and visitors who chat and clink glasses late into the night. The Sinan Mansions development took over historic buildings, meaning that the former residents can no longer access part of their heritage. It's a double-edged sword: make the city over completely and destroy everything old, or preserve parts of it by transforming it into commercially viable hubs. The jury's still out.

Old City
Map 11

CHENXIANGGE NUNNERY
沉香阁
26 Chenxiangge Lu, off Jiujiaochang Lu
HOURS: Daily 7 A.M.–4 P.M.
COST: ¥5
METRO: Yu Garden (Line 10)

This beautiful convent near the Yu Garden is home to a group of *bhiksuni* (female Buddhist disciples). The nunnery's name means "fragrant eaglewood" and refers to the material used to make the statue of Guanyin, bodhisattva of mercy. The statue's aroma fills the convent, especially when it rains. As well as the Guanyin Tower, the nunnery has a Hall of the Heavenly Kings and a memorial to a high priestess named Yingci. Look out for the floral wall decorations and gilded Buddha statues. The Chenxiangge Nunnery is a rare corner of tranquility in an otherwise busy and commercially focused part of town. The current building dates from 1989 after the original was almost totally destroyed during the Cultural Revolution. The nunnery was initially built at the request of Pan Yunduan (the Ming official behind the Yu Garden) in 1600 as a memorial for his mother.

◀ CITY GOD TEMPLE
城隍庙
247 Fangbang Zhonglu, near Anren Lu, 21/6386-8649
HOURS: Daily 8:30 A.M.–4 P.M.

COST: ¥5
METRO: Yu Garden (Line 10)

On March 28 each year, the City God Temple comes alive as people gather to venerate the three venerable figures who are worshiped here. The trio is made up of Huo Guang (a Han dynasty chancellor who died in 68 B.C.), Qin Yubo (a civil servant from the early 1300s), and Chen Huacheng, who defended Shanghai during the Opium Wars. The worship of city gods is a tenet of old folk religion, but the temple is now run by Daoists. The building that stands today is a Ming Dynasty structure that was renovated in 2004. Its grand corniced roofs, decorated woodwork, and elaborate statues are a treat for the eyes.

CONFUCIUS TEMPLE

文庙
215 Wenmiao Lu, near Zhonghua Lu, 21/6407-3593
HOURS: Daily 9 A.M.–5 P.M. (last ticket issued 4:30 P.M.)
COST: ¥10
METRO: Yu Garden (Line 10)

Sage and philosopher Kongfuzi (Confucius) shaped the modern Chinese mind and left a legacy of thought that still weighs heavily on the nation's psyche. His life and work are celebrated at this Old City temple. Despite the existence of a Confucius Temple (Wen Miao) in Shanghai since 1267, the only original part of the building that stands today is the three-story Kuixing Ge pagoda. The main temple was built in 1855 and underwent extensive renovation in 1999 for the 2,550th anniversary of Confucius' birth. Inside the temple are statues of Confucius with his disciples, Mencius and Yanhui, as well as a drum and bells (Kongfuzi's favorite instruments), a collection of unusual rocks, and—somewhat bizarrely—a teapot museum.

COOL DOCKS

老码头
505 Zhongshan Nanlu, near Fuxing Donglu
HOURS: Vary
METRO: Xiaonanmen (Line 9)

Shanghai is home to several lifestyle hubs like Xintiandi and Tianzifang. The Cool Docks is South Bund's answer to this phenomenon. It was built in the former Shanghai Oil Plant close to Pu Pier, the city's first wharf. As the area develops, it will eventually fit seamlessly into the South Bund stretch, but for the moment it remains something of an outpost. Cool Docks consists of a main square with a fountain, around which are clustered restaurants and bars. Renovated *shikumen* (stone arch gate) lanes lead to a series of shops and yet more dining venues. Highlights include Kebabs on the Grille, Caffein Intelligentsia, and Stiller's.

DAJING PAVILION

大境阁
269 Dajing Lu, near Renmin Lu, 21/6326-6171
HOURS: Daily 9 A.M.–4 P.M.
COST: ¥5
METRO: Yu Garden (Line 10)

The only surviving portion of Shanghai's old city wall can be viewed at the Dajing Pavilion. The wall was built in 1553 during the Ming Dynasty to guard the city from Japanese pirates. Its 4.8-kilometer (3 mi.) span ringed the Old City on what is now Renmin Road and Zhonghua Road. Ten gates and 30 watchtowers were spaced out along its length. Most of the wall was torn down in 1912, but a 50-meter (164 ft.) stretch remains. The Dajing Pavilion was built on one of the watchtowers and is a pretty, red, three-story building containing a small museum.

PEACH GARDEN MOSQUE

小桃园清真寺
52 Xiaotaoyuan Lu, near Henan Nanlu
HOURS: Interior not open to visitors
METRO: Yu Garden (Line 10)

Unlike the Fuyou Mosque nearby, visitors are not permitted to enter the Peach Garden Mosque. However, it is worth admiring it from the outside thanks to its somewhat incongruous architectural style. The mosque's minaret and the four globes on its roof are a surprising sight in a traditionally Chinese area. The mosque dates from 1917 and is the city's most frequented Islamic site. Designated male only, it is used not by the Turkic Uighur minority, but by Hui Chinese Muslims. Female

Muslims worship at the women's mosque down the street. A vibrant public market takes place outside the Peach Garden Mosque on Fridays.

WHITE CLOUD TEMPLE
百元官

239 Dajing Lu, near Daqinglian Lu, 21/6326-6153

HOURS: Daily 8 A.M.–4:30 P.M.

COST: ¥10

METRO: Yu Garden (Line 10)

Typically for Shanghai, the White Cloud Temple that stands today is actually an exact replica of the original 1882 building. It was torn down in 2004 to make way for housing, but the authorities decided to rebuild it from scratch rather than reassemble it in a new location. However, the modern replica is an attractive replacement. It is the headquarters of the Shanghai Daoist Mission and houses a collection of canonical texts that are sacred to the monks of the Quanzhen sect. There has been a temple on the site since A.D. 126 during the Eastern Han period; the temple was originally for the ancestor worship that was Daoism's forerunner. Look out for the seven copper statues from the Ming Dynasty.

YU GARDEN
豫园

218 Anren Lu, near Fuyou Lu, 21/6328-2465

HOURS: Daily 8:30 A.M.–5:30 P.M.

COST: ¥40

METRO: Yu Garden (Line 10)

Yu Garden (known as Yuyuan in Mandarin) is Shanghai's number one tourist spot. In a city more obsessed with the new than the old, it forms the centerpiece of the historic part of

© SUSIE GORDON

Yu Garden

town. The Yu Garden complex includes the City God Temple and a shopping bazaar, along with the garden itself. The five-acre garden was built in 1577 by a Ming governor named Pan Yunduan for his aging parents. It fell into disrepair after their death, before being bought by rich merchants in 1760. It was ruined again during the Opium Wars and lay derelict until the 1960s when it was renovated and opened as an historic attraction. The garden follows the Suzhou style and features a rockery, several halls and pavilions, goldfish ponds, and a teahouse accessed by a zig-zag bridge.

Pudong

Map 11

JIN MAO TOWER
金茂大厦

88 Shiji Dadao, near Dongtai Lu, 21/5047-5101

HOURS: Daily 8 A.M.–10 P.M.

COST: ¥88

METRO: Lujiazui (Line 2)

The Jin Mao Tower has the look of a pagoda, with its jutting eaves and octagonal floor plan. The latticework that sheaths the building has attracted several free-climbers over the years, keen to scale its 88 floors from the outside. The tower contains office space for Fortune 500 companies and houses the Grand Hyatt hotel. It also has the world's longest laundry

© SUSIE GORDON

Jin Mao Tower

chute. A super-fast elevator takes visitors up 340 meters (3,660 ft.) to the Skywalk observatory in just 45 seconds. Like the Petronas Towers in Kuala Lumpur, the Jin Mao was designed on the principle of the figure 8, important in Eastern numerology. It was designed by Skidmore, Owings, and Merrill in Chicago and cost US$530 million to complete.

◀ ORIENTAL PEARL TOWER
东方明珠塔
1 Shiji Dadao, near Lujiazui Huan Lu, 21/5879-1888
HOURS: Daily 9 A.M.-9:30 P.M.
COST: ¥100
METRO: Lujiazui (Line 2)
In the eyes of some Shanghai residents, the Oriental Pearl is a pink monstrosity. Others find it futuristically attractive. One thing's for sure: It's impossible to miss. At 468 meters (5,040 ft.) tall, the Pearl was Shanghai's first skyscraper back in 1995. Local legend holds that its design was inspired by a Tang Dynasty poem about pearls falling onto a jade plate, but architect Jiang Huancheng denies

it. Each of the main pink spheres contains an observation deck, and the best views are to be had from the Space Module in the highest pod. The sightseeing level at 263 meters (2,830 ft.) has a stomach-churning glass floor, and there's a hotel between the bottom two spheres.

RIVERSIDE PROMENADE
滨江大道
Binjiang Dadao
HOURS: Daily 6:30 A.M.-midnight
METRO: Lujiazui (Line 2)
Binjiang Da Dao (Riverside Promenade) runs along the Pudong waterfront facing the Bund across the Huangpu River. It's the place to go to watch early morning tai chi sessions just after sunrise or to admire the old custom houses and bank headquarters on the other side of the river. The promenade extends from the Donchang Ferry Port to Taidong Road and passes the Super Brand Mall and Shangri-La on its way. Along its length are cafés and restaurants like Paulaner Brauhaus, Haagen-Dazs, and Starbucks. It's a popular venue for wedding photos, so look out for elaborately costumed brides (and grooms).

◀ SHANGHAI NATURAL WILD INSECT KINGDOM
大自然野生昆虫馆
1 Fenghe Lu, near Binjiang Dadao, 21/5840-5921, www.shinsect.com
HOURS: Daily 9 A.M.-5 P.M.
COST: ¥40
METRO: Lujiazui (Line 2)
As soon as you glimpse the giant Disney and Warner characters that welcome guests into the Wild Insect Kingdom, you know you're in for an interesting couple of hours. More of a menagerie than an insect museum, this place has turtles, butterflies, goats, rabbits, and even owls. The insect part is dispensed with pretty early on, after a foray through an oddly antiquated "jungle" greenhouse flanked with sorry-looking lizards and spiders in tanks. The real fun starts once you get into the museum proper. There's a mock up of a rainforest, a petting zoo with hamsters and guinea pigs (and a rogue

HAUNTED SHANGHAI: URBAN LEGENDS AND SCARY TALES

Anyone who believes in ghosts will know that they tend to "appear" in areas of change, turmoil, and terror. Shanghai's history is jam-packed with change and a fair bit of turmoil and terror on top, so it's no surprise that the city is home to several legendary specters.

ANGRY ANIMALS

When the Qiu mansion on Weihai Road was relocated several blocks down the street (seriously) to make room for a new shopping mall, workers on the site reported strange happenings at night. Many were admitted to the hospital with severe bite marks, but no animals were ever seen. The mansion was home to one of the Qiu brothers, who came into money when they found a stash of paint that had been abandoned by a German merchant. They used their newfound wealth to build a pair of extravagant villas (the second was destroyed) and fill the gardens with a menagerie of crocodiles, peacocks, and cats. The brothers disappeared one day and were never seen again.

THE DRAGON'S REVENGE

If you're traveling on the Yan'an Elevated Highway through the city, look for the elaborately decorated pillar at the junction of Chengdu Road. It is covered in nine golden dragons, designed to placate a disgruntled dragon spirit who apparently lives below it. During construction, a feng shui master was brought in to work out why the workers could only drill down so far. He revealed the presence of the dragon and advised that the pillar be built to appease it.

WATCH YOUR STEP

Be careful if you venture close to the lake inside Jing'an Park. The legend goes that water spirits lurk, waiting to pull unwitting victims into their lair. The park was built on the site of an old foreign cemetery. Exhumation disturbed the ghosts of the dead, who are now believed to walk around at night.

DANCING QUEEN

The Paramount Ballroom on the corner of Wanhangdu Road and Yuyuan Road near Jing'an Temple is said to be haunted by the ghost of a former dancing girl who was shot by a Japanese soldier whom she refused to dance with.

THE HAUNTED HOTEL

The burned-out hotel on the corner of West Nanjing Road and Yongyuan Road is said to contain the ghost of a young waitress. On the day of the fire in the 1980s, she was locked in a cupboard as punishment for spilling tea on a guest. When the fire broke out, no one remembered to let her out.

GODDESS OF RETAIL

When the Plaza 66 shopping mall was being constructed on West Nanjing Road, workers had trouble digging the foundation. When the trusty feng shui master was called, he revealed an angry female spirit lurking below. The master suggested that the mall's tower be built in the shape of an incense burner to make eternal offerings to the spirit and keep her quiet. It seems to have worked so far.

---

goat or two), and a whole room devoted to gorgeous neon Lepidoptera. It's not your average museum, and that's what makes it so much fun.

SHANGHAI OCEAN AQUARIUM

上海海洋水族馆

1388 Lujiazui Huan Lu, 21/5877-9988, www.sh-soa.com/en

HOURS: Daily 9 A.M.–6 P.M.

COST: ¥135 adults, ¥70 seniors over 70, ¥90 children under 1.4 meters (4 ft. 7 in.), free for children under 0.8 meters (2 ft. 7.5 in.)

METRO: Lujiazui (Line 2)

If you're traveling with children, or just fancy something a bit different on a rainy day, spend a morning or afternoon at the Shanghai Ocean Aquarium. It opened in 2002 beside the Oriental Pearl Tower and currently has 28 exhibits over nine themed zones. You'll travel through the continents from the Amazon down to Australia via Africa and Southeast Asia, exploring the depths of the ocean and the shallow mangrove swamps. Among the 10,000-odd aquatic creatures on display is the rare Chinese alligator, along with 450 other species. The aquarium's glass observation tunnel is the biggest in the world and attracts over a million visitors each year.

SHANGHAI WORLD FINANCIAL CENTER

上海环球金融中心

100 Shiji Dadao, near Dongtai Lu, 21/5878-0101
HOURS: Daily 8 A.M.-10 P.M.
COST: ¥100-150

METRO: Lujiazui (Line 2)

The tallest of Shanghai's trio of mega-skyscrapers, the Shanghai World Financial Center (SWFC) is the one that's known as the Bottle Opener thanks to its distinctive lacuna. The hole was originally designed to be a circle, but the mayor of Shanghai nixed the blueprints, fearing that the tower would look like a giant Japanese flag. The SWFC measures 492 meters (5,300 ft.) tall and has 101 floors, with the world's highest observation deck on the 100th floor. The Skywalk takes you out across the top of the "hole," offering vertiginous views of the city below. The tower was opened on August 8, 2008, 10 years later than planned due to the Asian Financial Crisis.

Greater Shanghai — Map 12

DUOLUN LU CULTURAL STREET

多伦文化名人街

Duolun Lu, near Sichuan Beilu
HOURS: Shop and museum hours vary
METRO: Dongbaoxing Road (Line 3)

The politics of 20th century China go hand in hand with its literary history, and Duolun Road is a great place to witness the links. The 550-meter-long (0.3 mi.) pedestrian street off North Sichuan Road is accessed by a grand stone arch and is lined with statues of literary heroes like Ling Ding, Mao Dun, and Guo Moruo—members of the League of Left Wing Writers who were instrumental in the May 4 movement. Duolun Lu now contains traditional street stalls selling propaganda cartoon books, jade trinkets, and Mao memorabilia. There are also some decent museums, including one dedicated to Chairman Mao lapel pins (No. 183), a modern art gallery (No. 27), a Chinese-style protestant church dating from 1928, and the quaint Old Film Café (No. 123).

◖ FERGUSON LANE COMPLEX

武康亭

376 Wukang Lu, near Hunan Lu
METRO: Shanghai Library (Line 10)

Located in one of the most picturesque parts of

the Old French Concession, Ferguson Lane is the perfect starting point for a walk around the district. Start off with a caffeine kick at The Coffee Tree and a stroll around the Leo Gallery

© SUSIE GORDON

Ferguson Lane Complex

before heading out to explore Wukang Road and beyond. Alternatively, conclude your afternoon here with dinner at cozy French bistro Franck or the Marseille-style pizza restaurant a couple of doors down. There's also a beauty salon, flower shop, and wine cellar to browse. The imposing white villa at the back of the courtyard was the home of a Chinese diplomat until it was converted in 2005.

JADE BUDDHA TEMPLE

玉佛寺

170 Anyuan Lu, near Jiangning Lu, 21/6266-3668

HOURS: Daily 8 A.M.-4:30 P.M.

COST: ¥20 (extra ¥10 to see the seated Buddha)

METRO: Changshou Road (Line 7)

The Jade Buddha Temple sits northeast of the more renowned Jing'an Temple, in Shanghai's northern suburbs. It contains a treasure trove of statues and Buddhist paraphernalia, including the famous jade Buddha from which it takes its name. The temple building is a contrast to the high-rise apartment towers that surround it, and the street on the temple's southern side is lined with shops selling Buddhist devotional goods. Inside the temple itself is the Chamber of the Four Heavenly Kings and the Great Hall, which contains statues of the 18 arhats and three gold Buddhas (Gautama, Amitabha, and Bhaisajyaguru). On the 2nd floor is the Jade Buddha Chamber, which contains the seated Buddha made of white jade, that was brought back from Burma by the Abbot of Putuoshan and presented to the Qing government. The temple was built in 1882 to house the statue, as well as a meter-long reclining Buddha, also in white jade. The temple is a working monastery and you will more than likely see monks eating at the vegetarian restaurants nearby.

LONGHUA TEMPLE

龙华寺

2853 Longhua Lu, near Longhua Park, 21/6456-6085

HOURS: Daily 7 A.M.-4:30 P.M.

COST: ¥10

METRO: Longcao Road (Line 3)

If you've seen the Spielberg movie *Empire of the Sun,* you may well recognize the pagoda of the Longhua Temple. The temple is dedicated to the Maitreya and dates from the pre-imperial Three Kingdoms Period (A.D. 220–280). It was commissioned by King Sun Quan to house the jewels that apparently sprang from the Buddha's ashes. Longhua is a center of Chan Buddhism and is the largest and most active temple in Shanghai. Most of the buildings on-site today are reconstructions of the Song Dynasty (A.D. 960–1279) temple. The most interesting and impressive parts are the 500 gold statues of the arhat devotees, the seven floor pagoda, and the bronze bell that is rung 108 times every New Year's Eve.

◖ 1933

涝场坊

29 Shajing Lu, near Haining Lu, 21/6501-1933, www.1933-shanghai.com

HOURS: Daily 8:30 A.M.-10 P.M.

COST: Free

METRO: Hailun Road (Line 4, Line 10)

Just half an hour on foot or five minutes by taxi from the Bund is one of Shanghai's most intriguing buildings. Now redeveloped into a lifestyle venue full of cafés, restaurants, and boutiques, the 1933 complex started life as Asia's biggest slaughterhouse, designed by British architect C. H. Stableford. Built in Bauhaus style from pale concrete, the structure consists of a circular central hub joined to a square outer wall by a series of open-air bridges. It's like walking around an M. C. Escher drawing. Spend some time wandering along the walkways originally designed for directing cattle and browse contemporary craft boutiques. There's a small but decent selection of restaurants, including the ever-popular and reasonably priced Noodle Bull. 1933 is relatively quiet even on weekends, so it's great for escaping the Bund crush. Tip: Many taxi drivers don't know Shajing Lu, so ask them to take you to the Jiulong Binguan, which is right next door to 1933.

OHEL MOISHE SYNAGOGUE AND JEWISH REFUGEE MUSEUM

犹太难民在上海博物馆

62 Changyang Lu, near Zhoushan Lu, 21/6541-5008

HOURS: Daily 9 A.M.–4 P.M.

COST: ¥50

METRO: Dalian Road (Line 4)

A visit to Shanghai's old Jewish ghetto provides a good overview of the history of the Jews in the city. The area known as Tilanqiao in Hongkou, north of the Bund, was home to thousands of European Jews who fled persecution in Europe during the 1930s. These Ashkenazi Jews formed the second wave of the diaspora. Shanghai's older Sephardi community dates from 1848 when Jews from Iraq and Mumbai settled and started businesses. Illustrious families like the Sassoons and Hardoons made their mark on the city, constructing buildings like the Cathay Mansions, Sassoon House, and the grand Ohel Rachel synagogue on Shaanxi Road. The Ashkenazi refugees were poor in comparison, living several families to a room in the lanes and alleys of Tilanqiao. They constructed the Ohel Moishe synagogue in 1917, which was removed in 2008 to form the Jewish Refugee Museum. It contains displays about the history of the Jews in Shanghai and a mock-up of how the synagogue looked when it was an active place of worship.

◖ SHANGHAI CLIMB

卢浦大桥–攀登上海

909 Luban Lu, near Longhua Donglu, 800/620-0888, www.lupubridge.com

HOURS: Daily 8:30 A.M.–5:30 P.M.

COST: ¥80

METRO: Lupu Bridge (Line 13)

While Shanghai's most popular views are to be had from the Bund and the Lujiazui skyscrapers, a different perspective can be gained from the top of the Lupu Bridge. The Shanghai Climb takes you 367 steps and 110 meters (1,180 ft.) up over the Huangpu River, onto the peak of the world's second largest arch bridge

(the largest being in Chongqing). A ticket will get you escorted from street level to the start of the bridge in an elevator, and then guided up the steps to the viewing platform at the top. It's not as steep as it looks, and the views from the top are well worth the legwork. The Lupu Bridge connects Luwan District to Pudong and was completed in 2003. Rumor has it that the mayor of Shanghai tweaked the designs to make it larger than necessary, guaranteeing that it broke the world record.

XUJIAHUI CATHEDRAL

圣依纳爵主教堂

158 Puxi Lu, near Nandan Lu, 21/6438-2595

HOURS: Chinese Mass Sun. 6 A.M., 7:30 A.M., 10 A.M.; English Mass noon; Mass Mon.–Fri. 7 A.M.; Sat. vigil and First Fri. Observance 6 A.M.; non-service visiting time: Sat. 1–4:30 P.M.

METRO: Xujiahui (Line 1, Line 9)

Also known as St. Ignatius' Cathedral, this Gothic Romanesque basilica with its twin spires contrasts sharply with the modern apartment blocks and shopping malls that surround it. Built in 1905–1910 by French Jesuits on a design by British architect William Doyle, the cathedral is featured in the opening scenes of Steven Spielberg's *Empire of the Sun*. The spires, ceiling, and stained-glass windows were destroyed by the Red Guards at the start of the Cultural Revolution in 1966, and the cathedral was a state-run grain warehouse until 1978. The spires were restored in 1980 and collaboration between an American Jesuit priest and a Beijing artist saw the replacement of the stained-glass windows in 2009. Regular masses and services run throughout the week, with a capacity of nearly 3,000 worshippers. Visitors are welcome, but make sure you cover your shoulders, as the door guards are quite strict about modest clothing.

RESTAURANTS

Over the past 10 years, Shanghai has become a truly international city when it comes to dining. It's no exaggeration to claim that every imaginable cuisine is represented here, from obscure regional hot pots eaten on plastic seats to gourmet molecular gastronomy overlooking the Bund.

Since migrants make up such a large percentage of Shanghai's population, it's no surprise that regional Chinese food is so prevalent. In recent years, regional food has expanded from home-style neighborhood restaurants to higher-end establishments; places like Sichuan Citizen cater to diners who have more money to spend, but still want authentic flavors.

The city's swelling number of expatriates has inspired a boom in Western restaurants.

The trend is led by a handful of overseas restaurateurs like Australians Craig Willis, executive chef of the Wagas café chain and manager of the eponymous Mr. Willis, and David Laris, among whose many projects is a popular wine bar, the Fat Olive. Other leading lights are Peruvian brothers Eduardo and Marco Vargas and Chinese-American Kelley Lee who runs the Boxing Cat Breweries.

The Bund has always been blessed with excellent restaurants, all benefiting from the highly marketable skyline view. These range from the relatively affordable to the downright exorbitant. The Old French Concession is also a top spot for dining, with countless restaurants and bistros nestled among the trees and villas. The Sinan Mansions complex is a

© LOST HEAVEN

HIGHLIGHTS

LOOK FOR  TO FIND RECOMMENDED RESTAURANTS.

Best Views While You Eat: Look out over the Huangpu River and the skyscrapers as you dine on contemporary international fare at **M on the Bund** (page 186).

Best Local Flavor: Wander over to **Yang's Fried Dumplings** and mingle with locals, where lines for the tasty buns regularly snake out of the door (page 187).

Most Healthy: Enjoy one of the delicious sandwiches and salads brimming with imaginative ingredients at **Wagas** (page 190).

Spiciest Food: Brace yourself for the burn with some fiery Hunan food at **Hunan Xiangcun Fengwei,** a haven for chili lovers (page 192).

Best Regional Chinese Food: The chili-rich dishes of Chengdu are showcased at **Sichuan Citizen,** a restaurant that mixes regional fare with retro, colonial-era decor (page 193).

Best Beer Selection: Southern **Barbarian** in the Old French Concession features one of the longest beer lists in town and flavorful Yunnanese dishes (page 193).

Most Bohemian: Climb the rickety wooden staircase at **The Cottage** and sip vodka-spiked coffee as you overlook the pretty garden (page 194).

Best for People-Watching: The terrace of Mexican taco joint **Cantina Agave** is ideally placed to observe the mix of locals and expats who congregate in the Old French Concession (page 196).

Best-Known Celebrity Chef: Gordon Ramsay's protégé Jason Atherton helms the kitchen at **Table No. 1** inside the boutique Waterhouse Hotel (page 198).

M on the Bund

© M ON THE BUND

series of converted colonial-era houses containing popular, mid-range restaurants and bars. Heading away from the main tourist areas, you're more likely to find one-off, hole-in-the-wall restaurants and snack vendors. There are plenty of Western fast food chains, too. One thing's for sure: In Shanghai, you won't go hungry.

The Bund

Map 7

RESTAURANTS

REGIONAL CHINESE
LOST HEAVEN $$

17 Yan'an Donglu, near Sichuan Nanlu, 21/6330-0967

HOURS: Daily noon-2 P.M., 5:30-10:30 P.M.; bar: daily 6 P.M.-2 A.M.

METRO: East Nanjing Road (Line 2, Line 10)

Fall in love with one of China's more unusual regional cuisines at this date-worthy South Bund gem. Lost Heaven is part of a group that operates several similar restaurants and bars around town, and this venue is arguably the best of the bunch. Inside, the atmosphere is tribal chic, with plenty of dark wood, candlelight, and ethnic wall hangings. The recent addition of a wide roof terrace flanked with bamboo provides a good option for evening drinks when the weather is warm. Foodwise, expect Yunnanese specialties like Dai-style chicken with Tibetan, Thai, and Burmese influences. It's the food of the Mountain Mekong region and it's incredibly versatile.

CAFÉS
NEW HEIGHTS $$

7/F, 3 on the Bund, 17 Guangdong Lu, near Zhongshan Dongyilu, 21/6321-0909

HOURS: Daily 10 A.M.-2 A.M.

METRO: East Nanjing Road (Line 2, Line 10)

Shanghai has a long-standing love affair with the weekend brunch, of which New Heights is one of the most popular venues. Contributing to its fame is a terrace with that all-important view of both the Bund and the skyline. Sit outside on the wooden deck for a sweeping vista of both banks of the Huangpu River or head indoors to chill on the leather banquettes under

a mirrored ceiling. The menu is split into three sections, wittily entitled Things that Walk, Things that Swim, and Things that Fly, and is Western café food done classily, with smoothies and sandwiches that are a cut above.

FRENCH
MR & MRS BUND $$$

6/F, 18 Zhongshan Dongyilu, near Nanjing Donglu, 21/6323-9898, www.mmbund.com

HOURS: Lunch Mon.-Fri. 11:30 A.M.-2 P.M., dinner Tues.-Sat. 6:30 P.M.-4 A.M., Sun.-Mon. 6:30-10:30 P.M.

METRO: East Nanjing Road (Line 2, Line 10)

Helmed by French chef Paul Pairet, Mr & Mrs Bund embodies the concept of late-night fine dining. Its classy but casual atmosphere has made it a firm favorite and top-notch French fare plus 32 wines by the glass keep the city's diners happy until well after midnight. If you're in Shanghai on business, this is a good spot to have lunch, with special set menus Monday–Friday. Chef Paul Pairet puts his international experience to good use. Having worked previously in Paris, Jakarta, Sydney, Hong Kong, and Istanbul, he has plenty of influences and a self-proclaimed motto of "culinary egalitarianism."

GERMAN
DAI'S KITCHEN $$

110 Yan'an Donglu, near Sichuan Lu, 21/6323-2397

HOURS: Mon.-Fri. 5:30-10:30 P.M., Sat.-Sun. 11:00 A.M.-10:30 P.M.

METRO: East Nanjing Road (Line 2, Line 10)

This one is tricky to find, but once you've located it down an alley near the Star Hotel, you'll step into a little corner of Munich in the middle of Shanghai. Chinese chef Dai trained in Germany and brings his expertise home in a seasonal menu of sausages, meat grills, sauerkraut, and other Teutonic favorites. His salads are particularly good and there's an unusually thorough menu of imported German beers. Decor-wise, it's more fine dining than bier keller, with white tablecloths, silver service, and baroque-style ornaments. Shanghai has several other German themed venues, but Dai's kitchen is definitely the most sophisticated.

INTERNATIONAL
THE CUPOLA $$$
7/F, 3 on the Bund, 3 Zhongshan Dongyilu, near Guangdong Lu, 21/6321-0909
HOURS: Daily 11:30 A.M.-10:30 P.M.
METRO: East Nanjing Road (Line 2, Line 10)

Three on the Bund's private dining space is the most exclusive venue in town and is so special that you won't have to share it with anyone. Book a table for lunch or dinner and you get a room all to yourself inside the dome at the top of the Three on the Bund building. When it comes to choosing your food, you can customize the experience even further by choosing from the menus of the restaurants inside Three on the Bund: Take your pick from Whampoa Club's Chinese food, New Heights's Western cuisine, or the French fare from Jean Georges and Nougatine. When you arrive, a butler will meet you at street level and take you up to The Cupola.

M ON THE BUND $$$
7/F, 5 on the Bund, 20 Guangdong Lu, near Zhongshan Dongyilu, 21/6350-9988
HOURS: Lunch Mon.-Fri. 11:30 A.M.-2:30 P.M., Sat.-Sun. 11:30 A.M.-3 P.M., afternoon tea Sun. 3:30-5:30 P.M., dinner daily 6:15-10:30 P.M.
METRO: East Nanjing Road (Line 2, Line 10)

This is one of the longest established restaurants in Shanghai, a longevity that is rare in such a fickle city. M on the Bund mixes beautiful, subtly colorful interior design with a menu of quality international food. The restaurant takes up the 7th floor of the former Nissin Shipping building and has appeared in the Miele Guide to the top 20 restaurants in Asia. Make sure you book in advance to secure a table, especially on weekends. Request to be seated close to the window, as the view out over

---

HAIRY CRABS AND DRUNKEN CHICKEN

Unlike fiery Sichuan and tasty Cantonese, the local cuisine of Shanghai hasn't exactly made a splash overseas. Few people outside of China have ever tried it, and even within the mainland, it isn't the most popular style. But the locals are proud of their food, despite its reputation for being too sweet and gloopy. Shanghainese food is a mixture of the cuisines from neighboring Jiangsu and Zhejiang provinces. Thanks to proximity with the ocean and river network, fish features widely on menus, especially the crucian carp.

Sugar plays a part in local Shanghai dishes, both as a dip and as a marinade, as does alcohol. The famous "drunken" chicken and fish dishes involve soaking meat in spirits, which gives it a distinctive alcoholic tang. One of Shanghai's most famous delicacies is the hairy crab. Available September-November, these crabs come from nearby Yangcheng Lake and are prized for the females' tasty roe. In autumn, the fish markets and shops fill up with purple mitten crabs, which turn orange when cooked.

Shanghainese food really comes into its own at breakfast time, with hearty egg pancakes, meat-filled *baozi* buns, rice balls, and *youtiao* dough sticks. Along with soymilk, these treats make up the "Four Heavenly Kings" of breakfast food. For lunch, Shanghai *mian* – a stir-fry of simple noodles, bean sprouts, pork, and cabbage – is popular. The famous *xiaolongbao* soup dumpling is smaller than the fried pot stickers and steamed *jiaozi* native to other cities; the dumplings contain minced pork or crab bathing in a tasty broth inside a thin skin.

the Bund to the Huangpu River and skyline beyond is one of the restaurant's major draws. The Glamour Bar downstairs is operated by the same management and is equally attractive.

JAPANESE
SUN WITH AQUA ⓢⓢ

2/F, 6 Zhongshan Dongyilu, near Guangdong Lu, 21/6339-2779

HOURS: Daily 11:30 A.M.-2:30 P.M., 6-11 P.M.

METRO: East Nanjing Road (Line 2, Line 10)

This Japanese restaurant goes whole hog on the fish theme, with a huge shark-filled aquarium as the centerpiece. The decor is all pale wood, tatami, and clean lines, while the menu is packed with Tokyo classics like sushi, sashimi, tempura, and teppanyaki, with sake aplenty to wash it down. The fish is carefully sourced and imported regularly, ensuring freshness and quality. SUN is pricier than the city's street-side sushi joints, but worth it for the location and quality. If you want to see the aquarium without committing to a meal, go for a drink instead of eating.

RESTAURANTS

People's Square　　　　　　　Map 8

REGIONAL CHINESE
GAN GUO JU ⓢ

3/F, 198 Nanjing Xilu, near Huanghe Lu, 21/6327-9707

HOURS: Daily 11 A.M.-2 P.M., 5-10 P.M.

METRO: People's Square (Line 1, Line 2, Line 8), exit 9

South China's Guizhou cuisine is one of the eight great traditional styles of Chinese food, but is little known outside of the country. However, its spicy and sour flavors are well represented at Gan Guo Ju. The restaurant's name means dry pot, referring to the method of cooking that typifies many Guizhou dishes. If you're a fan of Sichuan and Hunan food, you'll probably enjoy this style; it's similarly piquant, but has an added kick of sourness. Dishes tend to be dry cooked either in pots or griddles, with earthy herbs and vegetables, and are best enjoyed with nips of fiery Guizhou *moutai* spirit (if you can stomach it). Wooden chairs and white tablecloths give a casual but sophisticated feel, setting Gan Guo Ju above the average regional restaurant.

WANG BAO HE ⓢ

603 Fuzhou Lu, near Zhejiang Lu, 21/6322-3673

HOURS: Daily 11 A.M.-1 P.M., 5-8:30 P.M.

METRO: People's Square (Line 1, Line 2, Line 8), exit 15

A specialty of the Shanghai region is the hairy crab. The whole city goes crazy for crusta-ceans when they come into season in the fall. The best specimens come from Yangcheng Lake near the city of Suzhou, but other sorts are shipped in to satisfy demand. Wang Bao He is the oldest crab restaurant in Shanghai, claiming a pedigree dating back to 1744. Don't worry if you're not in tow n during hairy crab season; the imported crabs are tasty too. Wang Bao He serves one of the best crabmeat and tofu dishes in town, as well as crab soups, dumplings, and most other permutations. The restaurant is smart and clean, with dark wood furniture and white tablecloths. At peak times, expect a *renao* (hot and noisy) atmosphere.

ⓒ YANG'S FRIED DUMPLINGS ⓢ

97 Huanghe Lu, near Fengyang Lu, 21/5375-1793

HOURS: Daily 6:30 A.M.-8 P.M.

METRO: People's Square (Line 1, Line 2, Line 8), exit 9

Try some Shanghainese favorites at this Huanghe Road staple. Yang's Fried Dumplings has several branches across town, but this is one of the most popular and arguably the best. *Xiaolongbao* (soup dumplings) and *shengjian-bao* (pan-fried pork buns) dominate the menu, served in 50-gram portions called *liang*. One *liang* equates to around four dumplings. Pork buns are one of the most popular breakfast foods in Shanghai and are sometimes called *shengjian mantou*. They are cooked in huge flat pans by industrious, white-clad cooks and are sprinkled with chopped onions and sesame seeds. Peak times see the queues snaking out of the door at Yang's, so get there well before midday if you don't want to wait. Most people

LOCAL FLAVOR: SHANGHAI'S HUANGHE ROAD

Shanghai is blessed with several excellent food streets and Huanghe Road is one of the most colorful and diverse. Unlike Beijing's Donghuamen Market in Wangfujing (famous for its weird and wonderful skewers), Huanghe Road is not a snack street, but a collection of restaurants. It has one of the highest concentration of Chinese restaurants in Shanghai and is a great place to try local cuisine. Huanghe means "yellow river" in Mandarin. The street has been a haven for hungry foodies since restaurants began to open here in 1995. Huanghe Road is flanked with neon-lit restaurants on both sides and vendors who peddle their wares at street level.

The street is easy to find. Turn onto the street beside the Park Hotel off East Nanjing Road (the one spanned by a huge sign emblazoned with the oddly-worded caption "Lie Fallow Street") and head down until you see a restaurant or dumpling shop that you like the look of.

A good choice for Shanghainese food is **Lai Tian Hua** (159 Huanghe Rd., 21/6327-3204, daily 10:30 A.M.-10 P.M.), a six-floor behemoth serving Shanghainese and Cantonese food. For a more upscale experience, try **Shanghai Min** (214 Huanghe Rd., 21/3208-9777, www. xiaonanguo.com.cn, daily 10:30 A.M.-4 A.M., ¥200-250). Formerly called Xiaonanguo, the chain serves some of the city's highest quality local fare like crab and "drunken" chicken. Shanghainese and more Western-influenced Chinese food is served at **Tai Sheng Yuan** (50 Huanghe Rd., 21/6375-0022, daily 10:30 A.M.-4 A.M., ¥100-200).

Possibly the best dumplings in Shanghai are to be found at **Yang's Fried Dumplings,** but another good spot for dumplings is **Jia Jia Tangbao** (90 Huanghe Rd., 21/6327-6878, daily 6:30 A.M.-early evening, ¥10). The humble shop is famous around town for *shengjianbao* (pan-fried pork dumplings) as well as for the Shanghainese *xiaolongbao* soup dumplings. Be prepared for a long wait if you get there between 11 A.M. and midday. Many types of dumplings sell out quickly and the store closes when the day's stock has been exhausted.

take their dumplings away to eat on the go or at their desks, but there is limited seating on plastic stools if you want to eat in.

CAFÉS
ELEMENT FRESH 💲💲

6/F, Silver Court Bldg., 228 Xizang Nanlu, near Shouning Lu, 21/6334-3598, www.elementfresh.com
HOURS: Daily 7 A.M.-10 P.M.
METRO: South Huangpi Road (Line 1)

As tasty as Chinese food is, sometimes you need a break from all that spice and salt. Element Fresh is the perfect antidote with its menu of healthy, additive-free salads, warm and cold sandwiches, appetizers, and pastas. This branch is bright and spacious inside and has an outdoor seating area. Salads include classics like Cobb, Caesar, and Niçoise along with rotating seasonal specials and more imaginative creations with an Asian influence. Choose from a drink menu of healthy juices and smoothies, coffee, and tea. There's a selection of entrées and wines for dinner, but Element Fresh flourishes as a lunch venue. It's a good spot for a quick business lunch if you're having meetings during the day, as service is fast and efficient.

FRENCH
CAFÉ DU METRO 💲

Unit G2, Huasheng Metro Shopping Mall, 19-169 Nanjing Xilu
HOURS: Mon.-Fri. 9 A.M.-10:30 P.M., Sat.-Sun. 11 A.M.-10:30 P.M.
METRO: People's Square (Line 1, Line 2, Line 8), exit 10

The snack stands and dumpling joints in the labyrinthine market under People's Square aren't what you would call gourmet, but among them is a small stroke of genius in the form of Café du Metro. Hidden away near exit 10 of People's Square Metro station, it's owned and managed by a charismatic French guy. Don't be put off by the location or misled by its unassuming glass front and blue sign. This place offers some of the tastiest and best-value French food in this part of town with a multitude of classics like chocolate crepes, salads, omelets, and pasta. Set meals include an entrée, salad, coffee, and dessert. Despite its position inside a somewhat inferior shopping mall, it manages to sustain a surprisingly homey and convivial atmosphere.

INTERNATIONAL
KATHLEEN'S 5 $$

5/F, 325 Nanjing Xilu, near Huangpi Beilu, 21/6327-2221, www.kathleens5.com

HOURS: Daily 11 A.M.–midnight
METRO: People's Square (Line 1, Line 2, Line 8), exit 10

Located inside a grand building that was the clubhouse during People's Square's days as Shanghai's racetrack, before gambling was outlawed, Kathleen's 5 is run by serial restaurateur Kathleen Lau. It's a popular choice for pre-theater meals overlooking People's Park and serves a range of European food like pasta, steak, and salad for brunch, lunch, and afternoon tea. Ask for a table on the patio or the glass-enclosed terrace depending on the weather. A daily happy hour 5:30–7:30 P.M. features half-price

drinks. As the restaurant's name suggests, it is Kathleen Lau's fifth project. Its predecessors include the popular brunch spot KABB in Xintiandi. Kathleen is an ardent supporter of gay rights and her restaurants often host LGBT events.

MEDITERRANEAN
ALLURE $$$

Le Royal Meridien, 789 Nanjing Donglu, near X̶ Zhonglu, 21/3318-9999

HOURS: Daily 11:30 A.M.–2:30 P.M., 6–10:30 P̶
METRO: People's Square (Line 1, Line 2, ̶

Hotel restaurants can often lack̶
Allure at Le Royal Meridien ̶
ception. The head chef is M̶
who trained under 3-Mic̶
ter George Blanc. Wendl̶
consist of southern Fren̶
dishes, like sautéed s̶
truffle steak. Allure̶
ing with a modern am̶
wine list. Floor to ceiling̶
onto a garden terrace and a gla̶
connects the levels. The set lun̶
try if you're in the area and need a ̶
street noodles.

Jing'an Map 9

REGIONAL CHINESE
LEGEND TASTE $

1025 Kangding Lu, near Yanping Lu, 21/5228-9961
HOURS: Daily 11 A.M.–2 P.M., 5–10 P.M.
METRO: Changping Road (Line 7)

Unlike its spicier, brasher cousins from Guangdong and Sichuan, Yunnanese food hasn't acquired overseas fame. However, it's one of China's tastiest regional cuisines and one that you should definitely try. Yunnan province's proximity to Laos and Myanmar has a big influence on the flavors and textures of its food and the area's diverse ethnic makeup also adds to the mix. Legend Taste is one of the most popular mid-range Yunnan restaurants in Shanghai and really comes into its own during the warmer months, thanks to the wide terrace

it shares with the other venues on the strip. Inside the mood is atmospheric with hand-woven tapestries on the wall. Feast on Nixi village buckwheat cakes, Dai-style marinated pork, and shredded potatoes, or try Xishuangbanna-style curry and rustic mashed potatoes with pickles and chili.

ASIAN FUSION
JING'AN $$$

2/F, The PuLi Hotel and Spa, 1 Changde Lu, near Yan'an Xilu, 21/2216-6988
HOURS: Daily noon–2 P.M., 7–10:30 P.M.
METRO: Jing'an Temple (Line 2, Line 7)

Flex your wallet and give your senses a treat at this high-end downtown restaurant inside the PuLi Hotel near Jing'an Temple. Its motto is

"resolutely epicurean" and executive chef Dane Clouston crafts seasonal menus of fusion fare fit for an emperor. Jing'an combines luxury contemporary decor with gourmet food, which means attractive surroundings—Zen-like minimalist fixtures, slate walls, and low-hanging lamps—and an imaginative selection of steaks, seafood, and pasta with an Asian twist. Jing'an holds the accolade of serving Shanghai's most luxurious burger, which comes topped with foie gras and truffles and is served with artfully arranged square-cut fries.

CAFÉS
🄲 WAGAS $

265 Jiaozhou Lu, near Xinzha Lu, 21/6272-0353
HOURS: Daily 7 A.M.-11 P.M.
METRO: Jing'an Temple (Line 2, Line 7)

If you're all noodled out and in need of a smoothie or a sandwich, head to Wagas. This non-smoking Western café chain has nearly 20 branches across town and is well liked for its fast Wi-Fi, Illy coffee, and locally sourced, healthy food options. Wagas's bread and cake products come from the Baker & Spice bakery farther downtown and are baked fresh every day. The letters of the café's name apparently stand for "we are good at sandwiches" and the salads are great, too. Daily specials include imaginative salads, soups, and sandwiches. The signature Wagas salad is a nutritious mix of fresh leaves, roasted pumpkin and beetroot cubes, runner beans, and cashews topped with a tangy dressing. Lunchtime can get busy, so head there early morning or late afternoon to be sure of getting a table.

FRENCH
NOVA $$

418 Dagu Lu, near Shimen Yilu, 21/6340-1889
HOURS: Sun.-Thurs. noon-midnight, Fri.-Sat. noon-2 A.M.
METRO: West Nanjing Road (Line 2)

Popular on weekends with the residents of the luxury apartments behind it, this French bistro has one of the best outdoor terraces in the area. Inside, it's classic Gallic decor, with brass fittings, wooden floors, and retro ads on the walls. Go for lunch and some afternoon sun and pick from two set menus for two or three courses or have an à la carte dinner accompanied by one of 30 types of wine. NOVA is a café as well as a restaurant, serving quality coffee, desserts, and snacks. A humorous cartoon on the stairs advertises the dating credentials of the perennially single French manager.

INDIAN
MASALA ART $$

397 Dagu Lu, near Chengdu Beilu, 21/6327-3571
HOURS: Daily 11:30 A.M.-2 P.M., 5:30-10:30 P.M.
METRO: West Nanjing Road (Line 2)

Before the 2010 Expo rolled into town, Dagu Road was best known for its multitude of rip-off DVD shops. Now, the stretch of road between Chengdu Bei Road and Shimen 1st Road is better known as a dining strip. Among its options is Masala Art, an elegant North Indian restaurant that serves a mixture of tandoori meats and curries. Its classy wood-paneled interior and smart, be-suited wait staff make for an upmarket yet reasonably priced experience. The dining area at the back tends to be quieter, but the front section is more aesthetically pleasing. A couple of doors down is sister restaurant Masala Desi, which serves Southern and British Indian cuisine in a more casual environment. Be prepared for beggars on this stretch of the street.

MALAYSIAN
MY NYONYA GALLERY $$

417 Dagu Lu, near Shimen Yilu, 21/6327-0800
HOURS: Daily 10 A.M.-10 P.M.
METRO: West Nanjing Road (Line 2)

With a menu of *rendang, laksa,* rice dishes, and curries, My Nyonya Gallery is one of Shanghai's longest running Malaysian restaurants. Once you get used to the quirky decor (including a bizarre stuffed gorilla on a bicycle outside and randomly strewn fairy lights), the split-level eatery is a great place to have lunch or dinner. Sit upstairs for a quieter experience or down in the main dining area for a more convivial atmosphere. Taste a range of flavors with a set menu or go à la carte if you're familiar with Malaysian food. Classics like *nasi goreng sayur lodeh* are a strong choice. Nyonya is a moniker for Straits Chinese people who migrated to Malaysia in the 15th and 16th centuries, so the food has a definite mainland influence.

MEDITERRANEAN
HAYA'S ❶

415 Dagu Lu, near Shimen Yilu, 21/6295-9511
HOURS: Daily 11 A.M.–10 P.M.
METRO: West Nanjing Road (Line 2)

Also located on the Dagu Road strip is Haya's, a Mediterranean bakery and restaurant specializing in southern European, Middle Eastern, and Israeli cuisine. Enjoy a range of appetizers like pita with hummus and baba ghanouj before choosing from a range of kebabs and entrées. The wraps are particularly good, especially the Balkanize, which features feta and roasted vegetables. Wash it all down with a pitcher of hand-squeezed lemonade. If you fancy taking something home for later, don't forget to check out the bakery. Haya's has a vibrant café atmosphere with colorful walls and paintings and wooden tables and chairs.

MEXICAN
TEOTIHUACAN ❷❸

580 Yuyuan Lu, near Wulumuqi Lu, 21/6226-3098
HOURS: Daily 10 A.M.–midnight
METRO: Jing'an Temple (Line 2, Line 7)

Located on an unassuming street west of Jing'an Temple, this neighborhood Mexican joint is quieter than the more popular downtown options. In addition to all the Mexican favorites you'd expect (burritos, quesadillas, nachos, and tacos), it has a surprisingly thorough menu of rare tequilas. Whether you prefer your tequila straight up or mixed into a frozen margarita, make sure you give it a try. Teotihuacan's decor is reassuringly kitschy, with bright blue walls and Aztec wall hangings. The restaurant's name refers to the home of the gods in ancient Mexican mythology, but lots of

Shanghailanders simply call it "that Mexican on Yuyuan Road."

NEW ZEALAND CUISINE
LITTLE HUIA ❷❸

403 Dagu Lu, 21/5375-0600
HOURS: Daily 9 A.M.–11 P.M.
METRO: West Nanjing Road (Line 2)

Of Dagu Road's many restaurants and bars, this is one of the most interesting. If you've never eaten New Zealand food before, a trip to Little Huia will save you the airfare. It's a cozy, wood-floored venue with a mezzanine level overlooking the main space. New Zealand is known for its excellent wine and lamb and both are well represented on the menu. Little Huia is a great spot at any time of the day, be it for a hearty breakfast, weekend brunch, coffee, or a main meal. As well as lamb dishes, the menu includes fish and chips, green-lipped mussels, baked fish, and meat pies. Tasty desserts like brownies and pavlovas top off the meal.

THAI
CHIANG MAI THAI CUISINE ❷❸

1019 Kangding Lu, near Yanping Lu, 21/5228-1588
HOURS: Daily 10:30 A.M.–2 P.M., 4:30–11 P.M.
METRO: Changping Road (Line 7)

With its orange walls, portraits of the Thai royal family, low lighting, and gold Buddha statues dotted about, Chiang Mai is everything you'd expect from a mid-range Thai restaurant. It has an unpretentious feel and the menu is filled with favorites like red and green curries, papaya salad, satay, and pad thai. If you feel like branching out, try some of the northern specialties, like pork sausage or seafood stir-fry. There's complimentary sweet tea to sip while you wait for your food and a wooden deck out front for the warmer months. Chiang Mai's head chef has nearly 20 years of experience under his belt, so authentic flavors are guaranteed. It's the go-to choice for many of Shanghai's Thai residents and that's always a good sign.

RESTAURANTS

Old French Concession
Map 10

RESTAURANTS

REGIONAL CHINESE
CHARMANT ⑤⑤

1414 Huaihai Zhonglu, near Fuxing Xilu, 21/6431-8107

HOURS: Daily 10 A.M.–4 A.M.

METRO: Changshu Road (Line 1, Line 7)

With its warm atmosphere, tasty Taiwanese fare, and assortment of interesting desserts, Charmant holds a special place in the heart of many Shanghailanders. It's lively without being chaotic and the food is reasonably priced and reliable. Take one of the window booths if they're free and choose from a long menu of noodles, hot dishes, and Taiwanese specialties like omelets and hot pots. Charmant's thick, creamy hot chocolate regularly makes it on to Top 10 lists in Shanghai magazines and the shaved ice desserts are a feast for the eyes as well as the taste buds. Wash it all down with a classic bubble tea. Even better, Charmant is open until 4 o'clock in the morning. The restaurant has a lived-in, cozy feel with brocade chairs and pale brick arches separating the dining space into loose sections.

HOT POT KING ⑤⑤

1/F, 1416 Huaihai Zhonglu, near Fuxing Xilu, 21/6473-6380

HOURS: Daily 11 A.M.–4 A.M.

METRO: Changshu Road (Line 1, Line 7)

A favorite among both locals and expats, this joint is a step up from streetside hot pot eateries and has the advantage of staying open until the wee hours. Bright, warm, and buzzing, Hot Pot King is a fantastic place to experience this classic Chinese culinary tradition. Great for big groups but equally good for couples, the meal revolves around a communal pot into which you drop meat slices, vegetables, tofu, eggs, and whatever else you fancy from the wide menu (be sure to ask for the English version if you don't read Chinese characters). The pot is divided into two parts, one half spicy and one half mild. A generous sauce bar lets you create your own condiments. To mop up the broth, curry bread in various flavors can be ordered from the special "bread waiter."

ⓒ HUNAN XIANGCUN FENGWEI ⑤

168 Wulumuqi Lu, near Anfu Lu, 21/6437-0952

HOURS: Daily 11 A.M.–2:30 P.M., 5:30 P.M.–midnight

METRO: Changshu Road (Line 1, Line 7)

This brightly lit, two-story spice haven has something of a cult following among those in the know. It may not look like much from the outside, but once you start flicking through the menu, you realize that it's a chili-lover's dream. The traditional cuisine of Hunan Province is based around the chili pepper, meaning that most of the dishes at this restaurant come with a kick. The somewhat perplexing English translations of the dishes are more confusing than explanatory (the best being "sub-soviet cooks in a covered vessel the cucumber" and "sheet iron unwearied effort however beef"), but the accompanying photos ensure that you end up with something palatable. The best picks are the pork ribs with Hunan spices, sizzling beef, and smoked pork with pickled beans. Service is fast and there's no guarantee that appetizers and entrées will come in any particular order. Make sure you remind the wait staff about rice, as it's often customary to serve it last.

NOODLE BULL ⑤

A Mansion, 291 Fumin Lu, near Changle Lu, 21/6170-1299

HOURS: Daily 11 A.M.–midnight

METRO: South Shaanxi Road (Line 1, Line 10)

Noodle Bull raises the bar for cheap noodles with a sleek, narrow restaurant space, hearty bowls of beef broth, and free Wi-Fi. Located on the popular Fumin-Changle crossroads, Noodle Bull is popular with the workday lunch crowd and weekend brunch seekers. But, it rarely gets as busy as the other restaurants on this stretch. A small menu features generous soup noodle bowls and rice dishes, as well as a selection of side orders. The bare concrete walls, black furniture, and exposed ceiling pipes create an urban vibe. Even better are the low prices: A meal for two shouldn't cost more than ¥100.

◖ SICHUAN CITIZEN ◍◍

30 Donghu Lu, near Huaihai Zhonglu, 21/5404-1235

HOURS: Daily 11 A.M.-10:30 P.M.

METRO: South Shaanxi Road (Line 1, Line 10)

With its slowly wafting ceiling fans, 1930s pin-up portraits, red velvet couches, and bamboo wall details, Sichuan Citizen mixes Old Shanghai glamour with the fiery spices of central China. Start with a cocktail in the lounge area before heading into the main restaurant with its many booths and private rooms. The photo menu is a tome containing Sichuanese favorites like *ma po doufu* (numbing spicy tofu), *gong bao ji ding* (kung pao chicken), *dan dan* noodles, and palate-burning hot pots. If there's only so much spice you can take, tell the servers *"bu la."* Conversely, since Sichuan Citizen is popular with expats and foreign visitors, the dishes tend to be less spicy than they would be in Chengdu, so ask for *"la"* if you want an authentic flavor. Sichuan Citizen is a spinoff from the popular Citizen Café on Jinxian Road.

◖ SOUTHERN BARBARIAN ◍◍

2/F, Ju'Roshine Life Arts Space, 169 Jinxian Lu, near Maoming Nanlu, 21/5157-5510

HOURS: Daily 10 A.M.-10 P.M.

METRO: South Shaanxi Road (Line 1, Line 10)

Yunnanese food doesn't have the international fame of Cantonese or Beijing cuisine, but it is well worth a try. The region's diverse ethnic groups add a variety of flavors to the communal pot, as does its proximity to Thailand, Laos, and Myanmar. For a cross section taste of Yunnan food, go for the fried goat cheese, shredded potato pancake, barbecue skewers, and pork with sauerkraut. There's a surprisingly diverse beer list, ranging from Trappist brews to fruit varieties. The restaurant has several dining spaces and features unpretentious black tables and slate floors. It can be tricky to find: Head through Ju'Roshine Life Arts Space to the very back, past an antique store and a nail salon.

AMERICAN
BISTRO BURGER ◍◍

A Mansion, 291 Fumin Lu, near Changle Lu, 21/6170-1315

HOURS: Daily noon-11 P.M.

METRO: South Shaanxi Road (Line 1, Line 10)

This upscale burger bar is furnished with dark wood, booth seating, and high stools. On the menu is a long list of patties from your classic hamburger (best ordered medium-cooked) to tuna, chicken, and Cuban ham. You can add extras to create your own designer burger and pair it with twister, waffle, or regular fries. The drinks list features a couple of "spiked" milkshakes and cocktails and the combo deals are great value. If you're still hungry after you've eaten your burger, try one of the American-style desserts. With big portions and excellent-quality meat, Bistro Burger is a great option when you fancy a change from local food.

MADISON ◍◍

3/F, 18 Dongping Lu, 21/6437-0136

HOURS: Daily 6-10 P.M.

METRO: Changshu Road (Line 1, Line 7)

This casual but high-end American restaurant benefits from having Austin Hu as its executive chef. Hu learned his trade at the Gramercy Tavern in New York and brings his skills to Shanghai's dining scene. He is well known around town thanks to the food column he writes for *City Weekend* magazine and he's a great fan of "locavorism": He favors locally produced ingredients and his seasonal menus are full of fruit and vegetables that are in bloom at that time. Madison is a good place for a sophisticated meal in a laidback atmosphere. Wooden floors, warm lighting, and white tablecloths create a cozy environment to enjoy good food and wine.

CAFÉS AND BISTROS
AMOKKA ◍◍

201 Anfu Lu, 21/5404-0998

HOURS: Daily 7 A.M.-2 A.M.

METRO: Changshu Road (Line 1, Line 7)

A café downstairs and a casual bistro on the 1st floor, Amokka has won awards for its atmosphere and Wi-Fi services. You'll often find the ground floor tables occupied by laptop users sipping cappuccinos during the day. The decor looks like a trendy apartment owned by a designer, with exposed beams, patterned furnishings, and shaped plastic chairs. The food menu includes salads, soups, curries, burgers, and sandwiches. The pizzas come from La Strada downstairs, so if you've been there and liked it, you can recreate the experience in a different setting. As the evening wears on, Amokka morphs into a lounge bar.

BAKER & SPICE $

197 Anfu Lu, near Wulumuqi Lu, 21/5404-2733
HOURS: Daily 7 A.M.–8:30 P.M.
METRO: Changshu Road (Line 1, Line 7)

Before Baker & Spice came on the scene, Shanghai's options for decent bread and confectionary products were scant. Now, thanks to this popular bakery and patisserie, the city is well served by quality granary loaves, chocolate éclairs, and crusty baguettes. There are now three branches and this one on Anfu Road is the original. It's located on the bottom floor of the modern conversion that also houses Mr. Willis bistro and Mi Thai. Either find a seat at the long, rough-hewn wooden table or opt for takeout and eat your muffin, cake, or sandwich on the go. Top picks are the carrot and zucchini cake, chocolate muffins, and sandwiches on seed bread. Baker & Spice supplies the Wagas café chain, so you may see their merchandise elsewhere in town. If your hotel breakfast isn't doing it for you, stock up on some healthy granola while you're here.

CITIZEN CAFÉ $$

222 Jinxian Lu, near Shaanxi Nanlu, 21/6258-1620, www.citizenshanghai.com
HOURS: Daily 11 A.M.–12:30 A.M.
METRO: South Shaanxi Road (Line 1, Line 10)

Jinxian Road is one of the smallest in the area, dwarfed by nearby giants like Maoming and Shaanxi Roads, but it has a surprisingly high concentration of cafés, shops, and creative office spaces. Shanghai's original bohemian café, Citizen, is at number 222. The free Wi-Fi, great coffee, and good food have won it several awards. If you get there early enough on a summer day, grab a table on the terrace. The decor is less shabby-chic and more Viennese than most independent cafés in town, with smart framed pictures, white paneled walls, and velvet furniture. Every day, a special martini deal is on offer 4 P.M.–midnight featuring a variety of flavors at a cheap cost. The weekend brunch is a popular draw, but the best Citizen moments are to be had on quiet weekday afternoons.

◖ THE COTTAGE $

25A Taojiang Lu, near Hengshan Lu, 21/6466-0753
HOURS: Daily 11 A.M.–11 P.M.
METRO: Hengshan Road (Line 1)

This charismatic little café is located in what used to be an annex of the German Consul's mansion. The narrow terraced house has three floors connected by a rickety staircase and the walls are decorated in graffiti (there are marker pens available for you to add to it). The owner, Old Mike, lends his name to the signature vodka-spiked coffee. Individual cigarettes can be rolled with the flavored tobacco collection on the 1st floor (although smoking is only allowed downstairs and on the covered balcony). Most of the kitschy ornaments on display are for sale and there's free Wi-Fi throughout. Soft drinks come in recycled jars.

MR. WILLIS $$

3/F, 195 Anfu Lu, near Wulumuqi Lu, 21/5404-0200, www.mrwillis.com.cn
HOURS: Lunch Mon.-Fri. 11 A.M.-2 P.M., dinner daily 5-11 P.M., brunch Sat.-Sun. noon-4 P.M.
METRO: Changshu Road (Line 1, Line 7)

Australian chef Craig Willis has made his mark on Shanghai as head chef for the popular Wagas café chain. His solo endeavor on Anfu Road is an upscale but casual bistro serving hearty comfort food in a relaxed, apartment-style location. Wooden floors and spot-lit tables lead to a wall of windows looking out onto the treetops. Looking in, the open kitchen lets you watch the chefs cook your meal. The simple menu offers Western staples like roast beef and chicken, along with sides of rosemary flecked potatoes and vegetables. Ingredients are locally sourced and often organic. Reservations are recommended, especially on weekends.

25a Taojiang Road
桃江路25号甲

© SUSIE GORDON

Shanghai's The Cottage

VIENNA CAFÉ §

25 Shaoxing Lu, near Ruijin Lu, 21/6445-2131, www.
viennashanghai.com

HOURS: Daily 8 A.M.–8 P.M.

METRO: Dapu Bridge (Line 9)

Well-known around town for its regular Thursday night film screenings, Vienna Café is an asset to one of the Old French Concession's prettiest streets. The decor is smarter and less bohemian than other cafés in the area, with wood-paneled walls, sophisticated striped wallpaper, and Tiffany-style light fixtures. Vienna Café is less of a laptop haven and more of an afternoon tea venue and attracts a slightly older, more sophisticated clientele. The menu runs a little pricier, too, with coffee drinks starting around ¥30. The vibe is definitely Austrian and the food menu includes homemade confections like Sachertorte, banana bread, and carrot cake. Go there for breakfast and choose from three plates: Viennese, international, and healthy. Head to the back to soak up the sunlight that streams through the conservatory windows.

FRENCH
LA CRÊPERIE §

1 Taojiang Lu, 21/5465-9055

HOURS: Daily 10:30 A.M.–11:30 P.M.

METRO: Hengshan Road (Line 1)

The owner of this French crêperie is from Brittany, which guarantees that the crêpes are completely authentic. The restaurant is decked out cheerily with Breton accents, cream walls, and wooden floors and the exterior looks like a beach hut complete with a lighthouse. The menu covers both sweet and savory crêpes and galettes from simple ham and cheese, butter, or chocolate spread to more elaborate concoctions. Get Brittany oysters on the weekend and wash down your crêpe with tasty cider. It's buy-one-get-one-free on crêpes 4–8 P.M. La Crêperie is at the heart of a popular expat area and gets very busy on weekends.

FRENCH FUSION
DAKOTA §§

38 Donghu Lu, 21/5404-8906, www.dakotabistro.com

HOURS: Mon.-Fri. 11 A.M.–1 A.M., Sat. 10 A.M.–1 A.M., Sun. 10 A.M.–10 P.M.

METRO: South Shaanxi Road (Line 1, Line 10)

Dakota looks onto vibrant Donghu Road with a terrace set back from the street. Commandeer a table and watch life go by as you dine on New York bistro fare with a French twist. The menu runs from American fare like burgers and steaks to French gourmet offerings such as foie gras and steak tartare. The menu is modest in choice but big on flavor and quality, with imported oyster specials, seasonal dishes, and a happy hour on drinks 5–8 P.M. Monday–Saturday. The decor is dark wood and brass fittings, placing it somewhere between a Greenwich Village brasserie and a Brittany oyster parlor.

ITALIAN
LA STRADA §§

95 Anfu Lu, 21/5404-0100

HOURS: Daily 11 A.M.–11 P.M.

METRO: Changshu Road (Line 1, Line 7)

This part of Anfu Road is filled with Western restaurants and cafés, dominated by Craig

RESTAURANTS

Willis' empire at number 95. In addition to Mr. Willis and Baker & Spice, there's La Strada, a cozy, modern pizzeria that overlooks the leafy street with floor-to-ceiling windows. With only a handful of tables, La Strada is compact but airy, with a stone pizza oven cooking the pies and infusing the air with the smell of Italian herbs. The pizzas are thin-crust and laden with top-quality ingredients. From the 13 varieties there are regulars like Quattro Stagione and Margarita as well as more unusual options such as the potato pizza. A couple of pasta dishes, salads, and some appetizers complete the menu.

JAPANESE
HAIKU BY HATSUNE 💲💲

28B Taojiang Lu, near Hengshan Lu, 21/6445-0021
HOURS: Sun.-Thurs. 11:30 A.M.-2 P.M., 5:30-10 P.M.; Fri.-Sat. 11:30 A.M.-2 P.M., 5:30-11 P.M.
METRO: Changshu Road (Line 1, Line 7)

If you like your sushi with a twist, Haiku by Hatsune comes highly recommended. Tucked away just off the Hengshan Road bar stretch, this Beijing-based sushi restaurant mixes minimalist urban decor with super-fresh fish and innovative creations. The legendary Moto-roll-ah maki is particularly good (so much so that several Japanese joints across town have copied it) and the tempura is just the right side of light. Adventurous eaters will be rewarded with plenty of interesting sushi choices along with the classics. If you call to reserve (which is recommended), ask for a table on the top floor so you can look out over the pine trees in the enclosed courtyard. The washroom signs are may be confusing: "No Women" is the men's room and "No Men" is the women's room.

MEXICAN
🄲 CANTINA AGAVE 💲💲

A Mansion, 291 Fumin Lu, near Changle Lu, 21/6170-1310
HOURS: Daily 11 A.M.-11 P.M.
METRO: South Shaanxi Road (Line 1, Line 10)

Tiny on the inside with a large terrace overlooking a little park and the art deco apartment blocks on Fumin and Donghu Roads, Cantina

Agave is a mainstay when it comes to Mexican restaurants in Shanghai and is an expat favorite. With a tequila list to make your eyes water and a menu packed with enchiladas, burritos, tacos, and more, it's a popular choice all year round thanks to its outdoor heaters. Summer attracts the (mainly expatriate) crowds to sip frozen margaritas on the terrace, the perfect spot for some people-watching. A very reasonable weekday lunch special offers several menu selections at a reduced price.

SOUTH AMERICAN
CHICHA 💲💲

Sinan Mansions, Block 33, 47 Fuxing Xilu, 21/6418-0760
HOURS: Sun.-Thurs. noon-1 A.M., Fri.-Sat. noon-2 A.M.
METRO: Xintiandi (Line 10)

Peruvian powerhouse Eduardo Vargas is a person you'll hear a lot about if you get to know Shanghai's restaurant scene. Chicha is one of his most recent (and already most popular) endeavors and is a cornerstone of the Sinan Mansions development. With a patio on the main square and a romantic, subtly decorated interior (the only nods to Peru are classy Inca-patterned wall decorations and the odd ornament), Chicha is a top choice for dates. On the drinks list are Latin spirits like cachaça and pisco, and food comes as a generous set menu of multiple courses based on seasonal ingredients.

SPANISH
EL PATIO 💲💲

110 Fenyang Lu, 21/6437-5839, www.elpatio.com.cn
HOURS: Daily 11:30 A.M.-3 P.M., 6-11:30 P.M.
METRO: South Shaanxi Road (Line 1, Line 10)

This popular Spanish restaurant is just as well known for its multiple patios as for its food. Located inside a beautiful mansion on Fenyang Road in the leafy depths of the Old French Concession, El Patio has several dining areas, a patio downstairs, and terraces upstairs. With all the patio seating, the restaurant really comes into its own spring–fall.

The chef hails from Barcelona and creates classic tapas like *patas bravas,* paella, and Spanish omelets to be accompanied by fine wine. The interior is smartly decorated, with all the details that are typical of a Concession-era villa: wooden floors, high ceilings, long windows looking over the treetops. A popular weekend brunch runs midday–5:30 P.M. Saturday–Sunday.

TAPAS
EL WILLY $$

20 Donghu Lu, near Huaihai Zhonglu, 21/5404-5757
HOURS: Mon.-Sat. 11 A.M.-3 P.M., 6-11 P.M.
METRO: South Shaanxi Road (Line 1, Line 10)

Chef Guillermo "Willy" Trullas frequently tops citywide polls for best chef and his eponymous tapas restaurant is perennially popular. His signature "juicy" paella is more soup-like than traditional Spanish rice and his modern twist on Iberian favorites makes for some unique flavors. The extensive (mainly Spanish and South American) wine list has something for every taste and budget. Attention to detail, from the carefully chosen crockery to the quirky menu art, sets El Willy apart from the masses. The interior is stylishly decorated with red and orange ceiling drapes, red velvet chairs, and warm lighting. El Willy's outdoor terrace comes alive during the warmer months.

OSTERIA $$

226 Jinxian Lu, 21/6256-8998, www.osteriaspirit.com
HOURS: Mon.-Sat. 11 A.M.-11 P.M., Sun. 11 A.M.-10:30 P.M.
METRO: South Shaanxi Road (Line 1, Line 10)

Owned by prolific Peruvian restaurateur Eduardo Vargas, Osteria is located on artsy Jinxian Road between several popular cafés. The restaurant is Vargas's foray into European tapas, with oysters, antipasti, and a prix fixe menu that offers one main entrée and unlimited small dishes. Wooden floors and wall panels give a warm, intimate feel and there's a cozy terrace out back. Saturday and Sunday brunch consists of two courses served 11:30 A.M.–4 P.M. Osteria is open all day and makes a good stop for a coffee if the nearby cafés are full. Charismatic host Rudy Guo and sommelier Zoltan Szabo lead the team.

RESTAURANTS

Old City · Map 11

REGIONAL CHINESE
LÜ BO LANG $$

115 Yuyuan Lu, near Fuyou Lu, inside Yu Garden Bazaar, 21/6328-0602
HOURS: Daily 11 A.M.-2 P.M., 5-11 P.M.
METRO: Yu Garden (Line 10)

This attractively decorated restaurant has hosted the likes of Bill and Hilary Clinton in its time, along with England's Queen Elizabeth II. It is located inside a pretty, free-standing Ming pavilion in the Yu Garden compound and offers views of the famous zig-zag bridge over the little lake. Lü Bo Lang serves *benbang* (local) food, which includes steamed crab from Yangcheng Lake, river fish, eel, dim sum, and tofu dishes. Unfortunately, they still have shark fin soup on the menu, despite nationwide campaigns for a ban. For high-end Shanghainese dining it's still a great choice and a good place to try good quality yellow wine and *moutai* spirit. The decor is pleasingly traditional, with lanterns, calligraphy scrolls, and intricately carved screens in dark wood.

NANXIANG MANTOU $

85 Yuyuan Lu, near Jiuqu Bridge, 21/6355-4206
HOURS: Daily 7:30 A.M.-9 P.M.
METRO: Yu Garden (Line 10)

For a taste of Shanghainese *xiao chi* (snacks), head inside the Yu Garden complex and join the queue at Nanxiang Mantou, which sells *xiaolongbao* soup dumplings and *mantou* buns. *Xiaolongbao* are named after the steamer baskets they cook in. Traditionally, they are filled with minced pork or crab and pinched at the top to hold in the soup. They are smooth and translucent, unlike the fluffier *mantou* buns that are more like bread rolls stuffed with meat. If you're willing to brave the lines that gather during peak times, inside you'll see stacks of huge round wooden steamers that are used to cook the dumplings, with white-clad chefs bustling around. The restaurant itself is simply decorated with carved wood window frames; a giant *xiaolongbao* welcomes guests on the ground floor.

INDIAN
KEBABS ON THE GRILLE $

Cool Docks, Main Square, 505 Zhongshan Nanlu, near Fuxing Donglu,

HOURS: Daily 11 A.M.–10:30 P.M.

METRO: Xiaonanmen (Line 9)

Its name may sound like a doner kebab stall, but this restaurant is a solid choice for Indian food. Kebabs on the Grille is a spacious, welcoming venue in the corner of the Cool Docks' main square. Its title refers to the skewers that are cooked at a special grill on each table. As well as the eponymous kebabs, the restaurant serves up a great selection of Subcontinental favorites like rogan josh, chicken tikka, and tandoori items. Warm weather brings diners out onto the patio to admire the fountain. The Indian wait staff is friendly and professional.

INTERNATIONAL
STILLER'S $$$

6/F, Bldg. 13, Cool Docks, 505 Zhongshan Nanlu, near Fuxing Donglu, 21/6152-6501

HOURS: Daily 6–10:30 P.M.

METRO: Xiaonanmen (Line 9)

German master chef Stefan Stiller is the name behind this fine dining venue in the Cool Docks. It takes up the 6th floor and 7th floor terrace of a large converted warehouse and offers amazing views over the river to Lujiazui. Each season, Stiller and his team of chefs design a fresh menu of local-inspired German and other European food. The "Lazy Sunday Brunch" is a big draw, as is the comprehensive wine list. Decor is minimalist, but warm. In addition to the restaurant, Stiller runs a cooking school on the 5th floor and a ground floor deli that's open for lunch.

◖ TABLE NO. 1 $$$

1/F, The Waterhouse Hotel, 1-3 Maojiayuan Lu, near Zhongshan Nanlu, 21/6080-2918

HOURS: Daily 11 A.M.–2:30 P.M., 5–10 P.M.

METRO: Xiaonanmen (Line 9)

Chef Jason Atherton's illustrious career at Gordon Ramsay's London restaurant, The Maze Grill, led him to The Waterhouse Hotel to spearhead the Table No. 1 concept. After it opened in 2010, it quickly became a destination restaurant, admired for its simple, minimalist decor and well-crafted dishes. Choose from a modern European menu split into snack plates, meat, fish, vegetables, and dessert. The restaurant looks out onto the street and the hotel courtyard. You can dine in luxury and style without clocking up a shocking tab.

Pudong
Map 11

REGIONAL CHINESE
DIN TAI FUNG $$

Unit 317, 3/F, Shanghai World Financial Center, Shiji Dadao, near Dongtai Lu, 21/6877-6886

HOURS: Daily 10 A.M.–10 P.M.

METRO: Lujiazui (Line 2)

This award-winning Taiwanese chain started out in the 1980s and slowly took Asia by storm. Shanghai has several branches and this one is the most tranquil. While the Xintiandi store gets crazy busy even on weeknights, you're much more likely to get a table at the SWFC branch. Din Tai Fung's dumplings are a cut above the average street stall when it comes to quality of ingredients. If you're wary of dodgy meat but still want to try *jiaozi* and *xiaolongbao,* this is the place to do it. Of course, the prices are way higher than the street stalls, but you're paying for the decor and service too, both of which are top notch: The interior design is understated but comfortable and wait staff are attentive and polite.

FRENCH
JADE ON 36 $$$

36/F, Tower 2, Pudong Shangri-La Hotel, 33 Fucheng

Lu, near Lujiazui Xilu, 21/6882-3636
HOURS: Daily 6:30-10 P.M.
METRO: Lujiazui (Line 2)

Jade on 36 is the restaurant of the Pudong Shangri-La. It offers contemporary French fine dining paired with a great view and some incredible interior design. The pink- and green-hued interior with its marble floor was created by New York designer Adam Tihany. French chef Paul Pairet helmed the kitchen when Jade first opened, but handed it over to German Fabrice Giraud in 2008. Giraud's menu changes seasonally, but features staples like pan-fried black cod and tenderloin of beef. Sunday brunch runs 11:30 A.M.–3 P.M.; the Jade on 36 bar is open until 2 A.M. on weekends and 1 A.M. during the week.

GERMAN
PAULANER BRAUHAUS 💲💲

2967 Binjiang Dadao, 21/6555-3935
HOURS: Sun.-Thurs. 11A.M.-1A.M., Fri.-Sat. 11A.M.-2A.M.
METRO: Lujiazui (Line 2)

The city's German expats flock to Paulaner for good, authentic food and beer, and that has to be a good sign. The Bavarian brewhouse's branch on Lujiazui's Riverside Promenade is a popular spot, especially thanks to its river-facing terrace. On the beer menu is Paulaner's home-brewed beer, made from a recipe dating back to 1634 and brewed for 28 days. As for delicious, stodgy, starchy German food, Paulaner gets it just right. There's sauerkraut aplenty to accompany pork knuckle, sausages, schnitzel, and more. The Paulaner chain came to China in 2003 and operates branches in the Old French Concession and Xintiandi.

ITALIAN
THE KITCHEN SALVATORE CUOMO 💲💲

2967 Lujiazui Xilu, near Fenghe Lu, 21/5054-1265
HOURS: Daily 11A.M.-2:30P.M., 6-10P.M.
METRO: Lujiazui (Line 2)

Very possibly Shanghai's best high-end Italian restaurant, The Kitchen Salvatore Cuomo offers a small but comprehensive pizza menu along with pastas, salads, seafood, and meat dishes. The restaurant overlooks the river at Pudong Point near the Oriental Pearl Tower, so you get a view over to the Garden Bridge and Hongkou instead of the more common Bund vista. Outside is a slim terrace, while inside the interior decor is clean and calm. Italian-Japanese chef Salvatore Cuomo has his finger in several proverbial pies around town, including Issimo at the JIA Hotel downtown and a pizza place in the Shanghai World Financial Center.

STEAKHOUSE
MORTON'S THE STEAKHOUSE 💲💲

4/F, ifc Mall, 8 Shiji Dadao, near Lujiazui Huan Lu, 21/6075-8888, www.mortons.com/shanghai
HOURS: Sun.-Thurs. 11:30A.M.-10P.M., Fri.-Sat. 11:30A.M.-11P.M.
METRO: Lujiazui (Line 2)

Freshly imported from the United States, Morton's is a dream come true for Shanghai's steak lovers. Unlike many Western brands that open in China and tweak their menu to suit local tastes, Morton's has refused to alter its food. What you get is pure, unadulterated steak with traditional Western side dishes like jacket potatoes, crab cakes, and salads. This branch of Morton's is the biggest in the world when it comes to floor space and it is absolutely immense. The decor is all white tablecloths, smart black chairs, and brass fittings. An attractive weekday happy hour (5–7 P.M.) sees specially priced martinis paired with complimentary filet mignon sandwiches.

RESTAURANTS

Greater Shanghai Map 12

CAFÉS
BISTROW 💲💲

151-153A, Grand Gateway Mall, 1 Hongqiao Lu, near Huashan Lu, 21/6448-2852

HOURS: Daily 7:30 A.M.–10 P.M.

METRO: Xujiahui (Line 1, Line 9)

The Wagas chain may dominate Shanghai's Western café scene, but Bistrow is its more sophisticated cousin. The motto is the same: fresh, tasty ingredients with no preservatives or MSG. Located in the Grand Gateway Mall on street level, Bistrow has a great terrace that's shaded from the sun by big umbrellas. The interior is all wood, dark furniture and globe lights. On the menu you'll find a seasonal selection of hearty but sophisticated Western dishes and a good selection of wine. If you've been shopping all afternoon at the electronics market, Bistrow is a great dinner stop. They also do a good cake and coffee pick-me-up.

JAPANESE
TORIYASU 💲💲

890 Changning Lu, near Huichuan Lu (entrance on Huichuan Lu), 21/5241-1677

HOURS: Daily 11 A.M.–3 P.M., 6 P.M.–2 A.M.

METRO: Zhongshan Park (Line 1, Line 3, Line 4)

For yakitori, Toriyasu is the best you'll find in Shanghai—that's if you can find it. Look for a bamboo-slatted frontage and half-size door on the small road that runs beside the blue-hued Renaissance Hotel near Zhongshan Park. It's open until the wee hours and is always packed with diners keen for cold Japanese beer and piping hot chicken skewers. Chicken is the main attraction at Toriyasu and it comes in every imaginable form: liver, heart, thigh, cartilage, and so on. You can also get ramen, soba, and soup, as well as cuttlefish skewers. Wash it all down with Kirin, Sapporo, sake, or *shochu* while you soak up the buzz.

PIZZA
PIZZA STREET 💲

Shop 36, 818 Changshou Lu, near Wuning Lu, 21/6233-5969, www.pizza-street.com

HOURS: Daily 4–11 P.M.

METRO: Changshou Road (Line 7)

It's less glitzy than most of the pizzerias downtown, but Pizza Street is the go-to for Shanghai residents who know good pies. Located in an unassuming lane off Changshou Road just east of Wuning Road (a huge main highway that leads from downtown into the northern suburbs), Pizza Street does most of its trade through delivery, but has a couple of tables outside. Popular with the expatriates who live in the apartment blocks nearby, it's a pillar of the local community thanks to friendly Australian owner Joel and his Chinese wife. They use top-quality dough and marinate ingredients in oils and spices overnight for flavor. All pizzas include the classic toppings.

VEGETARIAN
WU GUAN TANG 💲

349 Xinhua Lu, near Dingxi Lu, 21/6281-3695

HOURS: Daily 11 A.M.–10 P.M.

METRO: Jiaotong University (Line 10)

Shanghai is a city very much geared towards meat and it's not easy being a vegetarian. Restaurants will cater towards veggies if pressed, but you have to go somewhere like Wu Guan Tang for a real non-meat feast. Located on pretty Xinhua Road (where author J. G. Ballard used to live), it's a favorite among Shanghai's meat-avoiding contingent and is widely held to be the best vegetarian restaurant in the city. Top picks are the stuffed bell pepper, dim sum, and tofu laid out like a flower. All dishes are free of MSG and preservatives, so it's healthy too. With its concrete front, it isn't much to look at from the outside, but it's clean and well-kept inside.

NIGHTLIFE

Whether you're happiest in a wine bar, love dancing until dawn, or enjoy listening to live jams over a cocktail, you'll find something to suit your tastes in Shanghai's varied nightlife scene. As Shanghai has grown over the past couple of decades, nightlife hubs have come and gone. Maoming Road in the Old French Concession was once a thrumming bar street, but the action moved to Tongren Road to make way for development. Now Tongren Road has been cleared for a new retail complex and many of the bars have been relocated to a bizarre, underground Vegas-style compound called Datong Mill on Julu Road.

Often, visitors to Shanghai don't venture beyond the swanky hotel bars that overlook the city (and charge big money for the privilege), but there are some excellent, convivial, and innovative bars that don't cost a fortune. It's possible to drink for free if you're female in Shanghai, thanks to the proliferation of Ladies' Nights at many clubs and bars. It's also possible for both genders to get tipsy for cheap at "open bar" events, where the cost of a ticket entitles you to unlimited drinks all night.

The drinking and clubbing habits of local Shanghainese people tend to be different from the resident Western community. While KTV (karaoke) and dice games form the backbone of Chinese entertainment, expats tend to prefer cocktail lounges, terraces, and sports bars. That isn't to say that the twain never meet; weekends at the big clubs see a good mix of locals and foreigners and the scenes are gradually converging.

© SUSIE GORDON

HIGHLIGHTS

LOOK FOR ❨ TO FIND RECOMMENDED NIGHTLIFE.

❨ **Best Live Music:** You can head-bang to local rock music with Shanghai's indie kids at the small, dark, and smoky **Yuyintang** (page 204).

❨ **Best Location:** Tucked inside People's Park and surrounded by a lily pond, cocktail bar **Barbarossa** is an oasis of calm (page 204).

❨ **Best People-Watching:** Check out the crowds of swanky party-goers at Shanghai's legendary **Bar Rouge** (page 204).

❨ **Most Low-Key:** Japanese cocktail bar **Constellation 3** is a relaxed alternative to the thumping downtown clubs (page 206).

❨ **Most Glamorous:** Glamour Bar is glamorous in name and nature; it's a sophisticated yet artsy bar that attracts Shanghai's most beautiful people (page 207).

❨ **Best Theme:** Rhumerie Bounty is a pirate lover's dream, with its seafaring relics decorating the walls, barrel stools, and home-brewed rums that come in individual bottles (page 209).

❨ **Longest Parties:** Located inside an old bomb hideout, down-and-dirty **The Shelter** offers an alternative to the downtown clubs with its all-night parties (page 210).

❨ **Best Place to Club like a Local:** G Plus, frequented by wealthy Shanghailanders, is a buzzing frenzy of strobe lights, LED screens, whiskey-with-green-teas, and dancing (page 212).

❨ **Best Glass of Wine:** Head to **Dr. Wine** for a stellar glass of wine and French snacks in a cozy yet elegant atmosphere (page 215).

© ANTONIO OQUIAS/123RF.COM

Shanghai thrives after dark, with bars like The Shelter hosting all-night parties.

Live Music

BEEDEES

433 Dagu Lu, near Shimen Yilu, 21/6327-3160
HOURS: Daily 6 P.M.-2 A.M.
COST: No cover charge
METRO: West Nanjing Road (Line 2)
Map 9

This expat-friendly bar hosts regular live music nights as well as open-mic improvisation sessions on Tuesdays and Thursdays. It is long and narrow in dimension with a couple of couches and a well-worn feel and gets packed on busy nights. Bands here mainly play American rock music; local English-speaking comedians regularly take the stage, usually on Wednesday nights. On nights when there's no live music, Beedees morphs into a quiet neighborhood bar with a great selection of beers, spirits, and mixers, where the stereo plays popular artists ranging from Billie Holiday to Led Zeppelin. It's a good place for a post-dinner drink if you've eaten at one of the many restaurants on Dagu Road. If you haven't eaten yet, there's a decent selection of pies.

HOUSE OF BLUES & JAZZ

60 Fuzhou Lu, near Sichuan Lu, 21/6323-2779, www.houseofbluesandjazz.com
HOURS: Daily 4 P.M.-late
COST: No cover charge
METRO: East Nanjing Road (Line 2, Line 10)
Map 7

Now in its fourth location, the House of Blues & Jazz is a stalwart on the city's live music scene. Since it opened in 1995 (a veritable lifetime in Shanghai's capricious nightlife industry) it has hosted jazz acts from all over the world. An extended happy hour runs every day 4–8 P.M. Sunday is open mic night, with a rotating selection of local musicians taking to the stage. The decor is all dark wood panels and velvet furniture, adding to the low-down, smoky vibe. Head over for Mellow Monday at the start of the week and have a bite to eat at the on-site restaurant called the Dining Room, then drink Guinness on tap while you listen to some jazz.

JZ CLUB

46 Fuxing Xilu, near Yongfu Lu, 21/6431-0269, www.jzclub.cn
HOURS: Daily 8 P.M.-2 A.M.
COST: Usually free, but there are covers for special acts
METRO: Shanghai Library (Line 10)
Map 10

The JZ jazz club has been around since 2004 and has a sister branch in the nearby city of Hangzhou. Home to the JZ Allstars and JZ Latino Band, it is a smoky, two-floor haunt with draped velvet curtains and a hidden roof terrace. Sit upstairs for an aerial view of the stage from the gallery (be aware that you will sometimes be asked to pay a deposit on a table) or grab a stool by the bar to enjoy the live acts. There's a Western snack and food menu and a great list of cocktails, spirits, wine, and beer. JZ has a great atmosphere and is refreshingly unpretentious.

MAO LIVEHOUSE

3/F, 308 Chongqing Nanlu, near Jianguo Zhonglu, 21/5258-9999
HOURS: Open only for events
COST: Cover charge depends on the band
METRO: Madang Road (Line 9, Line 13)
Map 10

MAO Livehouse started life in the western Shanghai suburbs in 2010 and is the sister of the Beijing location with which it shares a name. Spring 2011 saw a move to the Old French Concession with a better sound system and larger space. The venue attracts a mix of local rock and punk talent, as well as bands from across China and farther afield. Police crackdowns on rowdiness or banned material mean that acts are sometimes cancelled at the last minute, but if you manage to see a show, you'll get a glimpse into the city's burgeoning rock scene at one of its most interesting nightlife locations. As well as the main hall, there is a smaller bar called Xiao MAO (translation: "small MAO"—a pun on the Mandarin word for kitten).

NIGHTLIFE

YUYINTANG

851 Kaixuan Lu, near Wuyi Lu, 21/5237-8662
HOURS: Tues.-Sun. 9 P.M.-late
COST: No cover charge
METRO: West Yan'an Road (Line 3, Line 4)
Map 12

Shanghai might not yet rival Beijing when it comes to live music, but Yuyintang does a good job of trying. It's a dark, compact, and somewhat dingy venue just south of Zhongshan Park and it plays host to all the best local and visiting indie bands. Notable acts appearing regularly on the roster include a Mongolian throat-singing group called Hanggai and local bands Boys Climbing Ropes and Duck Fight Goose. If the smoke and beer fumes get to be too much, there's a park out back for some fresh air. Yuyintang attracts a different crowd to the glitzier downtown bars: less blingy, more bohemian.

Bars

ATANU

1 Zhongshan Dongyilu, near Yan'an Lu, 21/3313-0871
HOURS: Daily noon-2 A.M.
METRO: East Nanjing Road (Line 2, Line 10)
Map 7

That strange, thin white tower at the bottom end of the Bund contains a very decent little bar called Atanu. Often overlooked in favor of the glitzier Bund-side bars, it is worth a look for its terrace and cocktails that are priced slightly cheaper than average. Chill out and admire the view outside on black wicker lounge chairs or chat with the friendly manager inside. Atanu lies within the Gutzlaff Signal Tower, which dates from 1907. A lighthouse was originally placed here by the French Jesuits to guide ships up the Huangpu and was named after a 17th-century German missionary.

BARBAROSSA

231 Nanjing Xilu, near Huangpi Nanlu, inside People's Park, 21/6318-0220
HOURS: Daily 11 A.M.-2 A.M.
METRO: People's Square (Line 1, Line 2, Line 8), exit 10
Map 8

Watch the sun set over People's Park at this gorgeous lakeside cocktail bar—one of the best-located nightlife spots in downtown Shanghai. Nestled inside a lily grove in an eastern corner of the park, Barbarossa looks like a Bedouin tent floating on the water and features a crenellated terrace looking out onto the lake. Low stools and comfortable velvet divan couches make up the seating and the walls are decorated with mosaics and mirrors that reflect the low, warm lighting. A popular ladies' night runs on Wednesdays, when women can drink free cocktails while listening to house music. On a warm evening, there's no better place to enjoy the night air and watch People's Square come alive beyond the treetops. If you're in need of a meal, check out the North African fusion restaurant downstairs.

BAR ROUGE

7/F, 18 Zhongshan Dongyilu, near Nanjing Donglu, 21/6339-1199
HOURS: Sun.-Wed. 6 P.M.-3 A.M., Thurs.-Sat. 6 P.M.-late
COST: ¥100, more for special events
METRO: East Nanjing Road (Line 2, Line 10)
Map 7

The centerpiece of the Bund nightlife scene is Bar Rouge. Ask any Shanghailander to name that must-go venue and chances are they'll pick this one. A legend among the city's bars, it has everything a Bund location should have: swanky decor, overpriced cocktails, a wide outdoor patio with a terrace, crowds of interesting club-goers, and a matchless view of the glittering skyline. Red velvet drapes adorn the interior and a big island bar sits in the center of the main room. International DJs frequent the decks, but on regular nights you'll be listening to jazz and funk. On weekends, the party goes on until the sun comes up.

BIG BAMBOO

20 Hongmei Lu Entertainment St., Nong 3383

Hongmei Lu, near Yan'an Lu
HOURS: Daily 11 A.M.-late
METRO: Hongqiao Road (Line 3, Line 4, Line 10)
`Map 12`

The mighty Big Bamboo is a small chain of sports bars and this location on the Hongmei Road Entertainment Street places it on the radar of the Western expatriate communities of Hongqiao and Gubei. Built inside a large two-story villa, it's a sprawling bar with two terraces, plenty of seating space, and several pool tables. Big screens show live sports matches, while servers deliver pints of beer and American snacks. The generous food menu covers Mexican fare, burgers, hot dogs, chicken wings, potato skins, and more. Big Bamboo gets packed on sunny weekends, but is usually less busy during the week.

BOXING CAT BREWERY

82 Fuxing Lu, near Yongfu Lu, 21/6431-2091
HOURS: Mon.-Thurs. 5 P.M.-2 A.M., Fri. 3 P.M.-2 A.M., Sat.-Sun. 11 A.M.-2 A.M.
METRO: Shanghai Library (Line 10)
`Map 10`

A leading light on Shanghai's ever-widening microbrewing scene, Boxing Cat serves up a rotating selection of homemade beers and ales. The original branch is out in Minhang. The late owner, Gary Heyne, decided to spread the love into the Old French Concession with this villa location. Now there's a third Boxing Cat in the Sinan Mansions development. The Fuxing Road bar has a small terrace for warm weather and plenty of cozy seating indoors for when it's chilly outside. Choose from six house brews (often with off-beat names) and order from a menu of classic American fare like pulled pork sandwiches and sliders. The interior decor is all warm wood and brick.

THE BULLDOG

1 Wulumuqi Nanlu, near Dongping Lu, 21/6466-7878, www.bulldog-shanghai.com
HOURS: Daily 11 A.M.-2 A.M.
METRO: Hengshan Road (Line 1)
`Map 10`

Despite dropping the "British" from its

HOP TO IT: SHANGHAI'S BURGEONING BEER SCENE

Until recently, if you wanted a beer in Shanghai, you were limited to a bottle of watery Tsingtao or a can of weak Budweiser from the local convenience store. However, the last couple of years have seen a boom in brewing and Shanghai's beer scene is finally something to be proud of. Multi-branch Paulaner Brauhaus was the first on the scene with its microbrewery on Fenyang Road in the Old French Concession. Later came the Boxing Cat Brewery, which was opened by a pair of American beer enthusiasts in early 2008 and now has three branches around the city. With microbrewing facilities on site, Boxing Cat serves authentic beer accompanied by Cal-Tex food. The Shanghai Brewery on Hongmei Pedestrian Street also brews its own beer, as does The BREW at the Kerry Parkside hotel in Pudong.

The two Kaiba beer bars have some of the most varied imported beers in Shanghai, including Belgian Trappist brews like Chimay. Another decent selection can be found at the Southern Barbarian Yunnanese restaurant. The growth of the beer industry in Shanghai has spawned several magazines such as *Hops* and *Drink*, which are available for free in many bars.

name several years ago, The Bulldog retains its English pub atmosphere. The dark wood walls are adorned with posters and framed pictures of British entertainers, and Guinness is served on tap. The bright yellow exterior and gaudy toucan effigy are a stark contrast to the U.S. Consulate on the other side of the road. The Bulldog is spread across three floors and has pool tables and a DJ booth. Regular trivia quizzes and meal-deal nights are complemented by a permanent two-for-one offer on all drinks. Depending on which night of the week you visit, there will be a special food deal, from two-for-one main courses to buy-one-get-one-free on burgers or pastas.

THE CAMEL

1 Yueyang Lu, near Dongping Lu, 21/6437-9446, www.camelsportsbar.com
HOURS: Mon.-Fri. 11 A.M.-2 A.M., Sat.-Sun. 10 A.M.-2 A.M.
METRO: Changshu Road (Line 1, Line 7)
Map 10

Shanghai's newest sports bar benefits from a prime location behind the Hengshan Road bar strip—a corner of town with a high concentration of entertainment venues. The Camel is run by Australian management and regularly screens Aussie Rules football as well as soccer, cricket, and American football. It's a large, airy space with wood floors and a decidedly non-divey atmosphere. Happy Hour runs daily 4–8 P.M. with 25 percent off all drinks. There's a decent Western food menu and a huge selection of bottled and draft beers. The Camel is a cut above the rowdier, neighborhood sports bars in town, but the atmosphere is still rugged.

CAPTAIN'S BAR

6/F, 37 Fuzhou Lu, near Sichuan Lu, 21/6323-7869
HOURS: Daily 11 A.M.-2 A.M.
METRO: East Nanjing Road (Line 2, Line 10)
Map 7

Most bars on the Bund demand a fee commensurate with the view they offer, but if you want to gaze out over the colonial rooftops to the modern skyline beyond, get ye to Captain's—the bar on top of the galleon-themed hostel of the same name. To fit with the nautical bent, the bar is styled as a ship. Sit in the outdoor "helm" on wooden benches or stay in the "galley" if it's too cold outside; the low wicker chairs by the window are a great place to enjoy the view. The drink list covers the usual suspects: beer, wine, average cocktails, and soft drinks. There's an acceptable range of bar snacks, too.

CLOUD 9

87/F, Jin Mao Tower, 88 Shiji Dadao, near Dongtai Lu, 21/5049-1234

HOURS: Mon.-Thurs. 5 P.M.-1 A.M., Fri. 5 P.M.-2 A.M., Sat. 11 A.M.-2 A.M., Sun. 11 A.M.-1 A.M.
COST: ¥120 minimum
METRO: Lujiazui (Line 2)
Map 11

The Grand Hyatt's Cloud 9 bar is a chic space nestled inside the crown of the lofty Jin Mao Tower on the 87th floor. It's considered one of the world's greatest gathering places by *Newsweek* and is the original "view bar" in Shanghai. There's a minimum cost to spend of ¥120 to keep things (kind of) exclusive, but the atmosphere is more casual than stuffy. Ask for a west-facing table for that iconic view of the glittering lights below, or sit facing southeast to admire the Shanghai World Financial Center next door. The drinks menu spans champagnes, sparkling wines, spirits, cocktails, and beers and is not surprisingly pricey. Cloud 9 attracts a variety of clientele, from curious tourists to businesspeople impressing clients and couples on dates.

◖ CONSTELLATION 3

251 Huangpi Beilu, near Jiangyin Lu, 21/5375-2712
HOURS: Daily 7 P.M.-2 A.M.
METRO: People's Square (Line 1, Line 2, Line 8), exit 11
Map 8

This is the third bar in the Constellation trio. While its brothers in the Old French Concession focus on whiskey and Japanese spirits, the menu at this one is centered around bourbon. The decor is plush 1930s, with retro furnishings, old leather couches, and a bar running down one side. On the floor are tiles imported from Marseilles and out of the window you'll see the futuristic Shanghai Grand Theatre. Constellation's 70-plus bourbons are arranged by distillery and come served over a tennis ball–sized sphere of ice in an old fashioned glass. Enjoy the bourbon straight up or choose from a modest cocktail list.

COTTON'S

132 Anting Lu, near Jianguo Xilu, 21/6433-7995, www.cottons-shanghai.com
HOURS: Sun.-Thurs. 11 A.M.-2 A.M., Fri.-Sat. 11 A.M.-4 A.M.
METRO: Hengshan Road (Line 1)
Map 10

Hunan native Cotton Ding is a famous face on Shanghai's nightlife scene. She's the brains behind Cotton's villa bars, the first of which is on quiet Anting Road, not far from the Hengshan Road bar strip. Hidden among lush greenery, this beautiful converted villa features red velvet seating, whitewashed walls, and open fires in winter. The warmer months see the terrace fill up on weekends. But it's a good option for a quiet lunch or drink midweek. Cotton went on to open a second venue in a sprawling villa on Xinhua Road farther west and a Hunan restaurant in a lane house just off Fuxing Road.

CROCUS

528 Kangding Lu, near Xikang Lu, 138/1611-2688
HOURS: Tues.-Sun. 10 A.M.-2 A.M.
METRO: Changping Road (Line 7)
Map 9

A pair of friendly Filipino brothers run the bar at this local spot, which is part of the 528 Kangding complex. It's in a residential area, so most of the clientele tends to come from the nearby expat-centric apartment blocks across the street. Drink prices are cheaper than downtown and the atmosphere is cordial. When it's warm outside, the staff set up a couple of tables on the lane along with a barbecue grill and the crowd often mixes with the customers from the nearby tapas bar and beer keller. Snacks and meals include pizza, pasta, and sandwiches—a relic of Crocus's predecessor, Exit Bar.

C'S

685 Dingxi Lu, near Yan'an Xilu, 21/6294-0547
HOURS: Daily 7:30 P.M.-late
METRO: West Yan'an Road (Line 3, Line 4)
Map 12

Head down the stairs in the lobby of this office building in Changning District and you'll find yourself in a parallel universe of sticky floors, graffitied walls, blindingly cheap drinks, and rough-and-tumble music. C's is a warren of dark rooms, sweaty corridors, and the sort of restrooms you'd rather forget, but it's a legend in Shanghai's nightlife scene. As unpretentious as it gets, it is popular with students, English teachers, and anyone else for whom low prices

trump fancy decor. DJs play from time to time, but mostly it's messy parties, plain and simple.

DADA

115 Xingfu Lu, near Fahuazhen Lu, 150/0018-2212
HOURS: Daily 8 P.M.-late
METRO: Jiaotong University (Line 10)
Map 12

A couple of doors down from the live music venue Anar is Dada, located down an alley beside a restaurant specializing in snake meat. Dada has a decent-size dance floor as well as a raised seating area and some floor-level tables. It attracts a young, indie crowd of local students and hipsters. The walls are adorned with stenciled graffiti and the artwork on the event flyers and posters is often eye-catchingly original. Drinks are on the cheap side. Prior to the closure of LOgO bar in 2010, this little enclave was the go-to for underground nightlife. Anar and Dada are doing their best to keep the dream alive.

FLAIR

58/F, Ritz-Carlton Hotel, 8 Shiji Dadao, near Lujiazui Huan Lu, 21/2020-1778
HOURS: Daily 5:30 P.M.-2 A.M.
METRO: Lujiazui (Line 2)
Map 11

Located atop the Ritz-Carlton in the ifc complex, Flair is Shanghai's newest destination bar. Its terrace brings you up close and personal with the candy-pink spheres of the Oriental Pearl Tower, with a backdrop of the Bund and Hongkou suburbs stretching out behind. Flair is the highest outdoor bar, but you'll be looking at a costly down payment for a table outside. If you're not looking to spend a lot, don't worry: The interior is pretty special too, with leather armchairs and striped sofas, wood floors, and a fireplace for winter. The wine list is thorough and there's a good selection of beers, spirits, and cocktails. A weekday happy hour runs 5:30–7:30 P.M. with two-for-one drinks. There's a ¥350 minimum here, so be prepared to have more than one drink.

GLAMOUR BAR

6/F, 5 on the Bund, 20 Guangdong Lu, near Zhongshan

Dongyilu, 21/6350-9988, www.m-theglamourbar.com
HOURS: Daily 5 P.M.-late
METRO: East Nanjing Road (Line 2, Line 10)
Map 7

One floor down from M on the Bund restaurant is Glamour Bar, a kitschy yet elegant cocktail lounge with thoughtfully mismatched furniture and Moroccan-style colored crystal glasses. You'll pay top brass for a cocktail, but it's worth it for the atmosphere alone. And, the view from the antique-framed windows is second to none. Even the toilets are immaculately designed. This bar cares about style and it shows in the details: The bar's lips logo crops up on the matchboxes. Glamour is Shanghai's most literary bar, too; it hosts regular book events, including the annual Shanghai International Literary Festival in March.

I LOVE SHANGHAI

2/F, 1788 Xinzha Lu, near Jiaozhou Lu, 21/5288-6899
HOURS: Daily 5 P.M.-2 A.M.
METRO: Changping Road (Line 7)
Map 9

If you want an unpretentious, uber-casual drinking experience that is the polar opposite of the pricey Bund-side bars, try I Love Shanghai. You may very well walk in on a beer pong contest or trivia night in full flow, but if not, there's a pool table and arcade games to keep you busy while you drink. The frat house vibe is fueled by American fast food and snacks. If you're in the mood for a bigger meal, there's a pizzeria and a Singaporean diner downstairs. I Love Shanghai is a legend, especially among the TEFL crowd and it gets relatively busy even on weeknights.

JOY BAR

345 South Wuning Lu, near Yuyao Lu, 21/6230-2015
HOURS: Daily 10 A.M.-midnight
METRO: Changping Road (Line 7)
Map 12

This friendly neighborhood bar is popular with the expats who live in the surrounding apartment blocks and is a good alternative to the busier downtown cafés and bars.

Joy is Holland-themed, serving croquettes and Dutch fries along with general Western and Chinese fare. A daily happy hour runs until 9 P.M., when it's buy-one-get-one-free on everything except wine. The interior is cozy in winter, but the terrace is what makes this bar truly great. There's Wi-Fi, too, so it's great for catching up on email. The staff is friendly and amenable and will keep the bar open late if the vibe is good.

KAIBA

528 Kangding Lu, near Xikang Lu, 21/6288-9676
HOURS: Sun.-Thurs. 4 P.M.-midnight, Fri.-Sat.
4 P.M.-2 A.M.
METRO: Changping Road (Line 7)
Map 9

This Belgian beer bar proved so popular that the management opened a second branch in Changning District. The original is located in the 528 Kangding complex, along with a couple of other quality drinking and dining options. Fittingly, Kaiba looks like a Trappist monastery inside—exposed brick walls, arched windows, and rustic wooden tables and chairs. For anyone tired of watery local Tsingtao, this place is a welcome retreat. Choose from a heady menu of Belgian imports, including five Trappist brews. There are discounts during happy hour, weekdays 4–9 P.M. and weekends 2–7 P.M. Warmer weather brings customers out onto the courtyard that's shared with the Shed next door.

LOLA

Surpass Court, Bldg. 4, 570 Yongjia Lu, near Yueyang
Lu, 138/1692-7970
HOURS: Daily 5 P.M.-late
METRO: Hengshan Road (Line 1)
Map 10

The relatively new Surpass Court development brings together an eclectic selection of bars, cafés, and restaurants. One of the most popular nightlife venues to have opened up there is Lola, which combines a tapas joint with a lounge, a roof terrace bar, and a nightclub. The playlist rarely diverges from European house and disco thanks to the Spanish management.

The drinks list includes a number of interesting variations of the classic Bloody Mary. It's the ideal place for a quiet drink on a weeknight or a more energetic party on a Saturday evening.

MOKKOS

1245 Wuding Xilu, near Wanhangdu Lu, 21/6212-1114
HOURS: Daily 7 P.M.-2 A.M.
METRO: Jiangsu Road (Line 2)
Map 12

If you didn't know Mokkos was there, you'd never find it. Located down a narrow lane on an otherwise ordinary suburban street northwest of Jing'an Temple, this little Japanese drinking den is a true hidden gem. Seating is limited to the bar and a handful of tables. The drink menu focuses on *shochu*. Take it neat over balled ice or go for a fruit-flavored *chuhai* blend. There's also *otsurui*, which is distilled only once. Mokkos' owner hails from Kumamoto in Kyushu and knows a thing or two about Japanese spirits. The Tibetan waitress is known for bursting into song, so you may be treated to an impromptu performance while you sip your rice brew.

NAPA WINE BAR & KITCHEN

57 Jiangyin Lu, near Huangpi Lu, 21/6318-0057
HOURS: Daily 6 P.M.-midnight
METRO: People's Square (Line 1, Line 2, Line 8), exit 11
Map 8

You'll find this classy wine bar hidden away from the noise and bright lights of People's Square. It's a welcome rest from the thrum of downtown Shanghai. The pale, Tudor-style brick building sits inside a tree-flanked space with a terrace and seats 40 people inside. It's a little more austere than the casual wine bars of the Old French Concession and the drinks list is considerably longer at over 700 bottles. Many come from the eponymous Napa Valley in California, but other winemaking regions are represented, too, both the well-known and the more obscure. Temperature controlled storage keeps the wine in top condition.

THE PARK TAVERN

840 Hengshan Lu, near Tianping Lu, 21/5465-9312
HOURS: Mon.-Thurs. 11 A.M.-2 A.M., Fri.-Sat. 11 A.M.-late
METRO: Xujiahui (Line 1, Line 9)
Map 12

This four-level villa with a gorgeous terrace has satellite feeds on each floor, meaning that they'll almost certainly be screening the match you want to see. Although it's a sports bar by design, the tavern has none of the rowdiness of its earthier cousins and is classy enough for a glass of wine on the terrace as well as a pint of beer at the bar. The Park Tavern's outdoor patio is well frequented when the weather is nice April–November, but the comfortable interior keeps the customers coming through the winter, too. The food menu features a good range of quality Western bar fare.

THE RABBIT HOLE

408 Shaanxi Beilu, 21/3230-2778,
www.therabbitholeshanghai.com
HOURS: Sun. and Tues.-Thurs. 6 P.M.-1 A.M., Fri.-Sat. 6 P.M.-late
METRO: Jing'an Temple (Line 2, Line 7)
Map 9

The Rabbit Hole is managed by a charismatic Serbian man named Sergio who has helmed several popular Shanghai bars in recent years. His latest project is inspired by Alice in Wonderland and is non-gimmicky enough to have attracted a loyal following since it opened in 2011. The multi-floor venue is part bar, part club, and part restaurant. It's an intriguing venue with some attractive quirks. The food menu runs from three-course meals to bar food, with rabbit stew, pizzas, salads, and Papa Sergio's apple pie for dessert along with sweet crepes. Resident and visiting DJs play house music and techno until the early hours. Happy hour runs on weekdays 6–8 P.M.

◖ RHUMERIE BOUNTY

550 Wuding Lu, near Xikang Lu, 21/2661-9368
HOURS: Mon.-Thurs. 11 A.M.-1 A.M., Fri.-Sat. 11 A.M.-late, Sun. 4 P.M.-1 A.M.
METRO: Changping Road (Line 7)
Map 9

NIGHTLIFE

Themed bars can often veer into tacky territory, but the French-run Rhumerie Bounty has managed to avoid cliché. Known around town as "the pirate bar," it has garnered popularity thanks to its galleon-style interior and selection of homemade rums. Pull up a barrel stool and choose from a blackboard of hand-macerated flavored brews, including ginger, pineapple, and cinnamon, depending on what's in season. Flavored bottles come with a bowl of crushed ice and miniature glasses. Rum cynics can choose from a small but plentiful menu of beers, soft drinks, and fruit smoothies. The interior is completely clad in wood panels, with seafaring relics like fishing nets, bottles, and pirate hats knocking around for effect. If you can't get a table, try the second branch at 47 Yongfu Lu in the Old French Concession.

SALON DE NING

The Peninsula Hotel, B/F, 32 Zhongshan Donglu (enter on Beijing Donglu), 21/2327-6731, www.salondening.com

HOURS: Tues.-Sat. 8 P.M.-1 A.M.

METRO: East Nanjing Road (Line 2, Line 10)

Map 7

This lounge at the Peninsula Hotel is a world away from most soulless hotel bars. Salon de Ning looks like the boudoir of an eccentric colonial woman, decorated lavishly with quirky, mismatched furniture and elaborate chandeliers. Particularly attractive is the gorgeous, wave-like chandelier that fills a whole ceiling. The Peninsulas in New York, Hong Kong, and Manila also have Salons de Ning. This is one of the chain's most interesting bar venues. The drinks list is an impressive rundown of the usual suspects but plays second fiddle to the incredible interior design. Have one too many cocktails and the "upside down" room will make your head spin.

◖ THE SHELTER

B/F, 5 Yongfu Lu, near Fuxing Xilu, 21/6437-0400

HOURS: Wed.-Sun. 9 A.M.-late

COST: cover varies

METRO: Shanghai Library (Line 10)

Map 10

drinks at The Shelter

Long heralded as the ultimate underground club in Shanghai, The Shelter is literally underground. The former bomb hideout is accessed via a long, winding tunnel and consists of a main room plus several arched chambers with couches and tables. Things rarely get started before midnight and parties tend to go on until dawn. The music ranges from reggae, drum and bass, dubstep and funk to electro and more. The cover charge varies depending on who's playing. If you want to get a feel for Shanghai's indie crowd (both local and expat), Shelter provides a good cross-section.

THE SPOT

331 Tongren Lu, near Beijing Lu, 21/6247-3579

HOURS: Sun.-Thurs. 11 A.M.-2 A.M., Fri.-Sat. 11 A.M.-3 A.M.

METRO: Jing'an Temple (Line 2, Line 7)

Map 9

The Spot is one of Shanghai's biggest sports bars, with plenty of screens showing popular games. There's also a pool table, foosball, and darts. A giant menu of international dishes ranges from German and Italian to Thai and Greek—it's one of the most comprehensive menus in town. Go on a Sunday and enjoy an

© SUSIE GORDON

all-you-can-eat special. There's a terrace out front with curved red chairs and a somewhat incongruous Buddha statue. Inside, the seating is a mix of barstools, wooden benches, and sofas draped in white. Unsurprisingly, The Spot gets busy on big game nights.

VUE BAR

32-33/F, Hyatt on the Bund, 199 Huangpu Lu, near Wuchang Lu, 21/6393-1234, ext. 6348

HOURS: Sun.-Thurs. 6 P.M.-1 A.M., Fri.-Sat. 6 P.M.-2 A.M.

COST: ¥100 on weekends

METRO: Tiantong Road (Line 10)

Map 7

This bar is VUE by name, view by nature. Perched on top of the Hyatt on the Bund's west tower, its terrace (complete with a whirlpool tub for those moments when the bubbles in your champagne just aren't enough) looks out onto Shanghai's highlights from a less-vaunted angle. You get the skyline on your left and the Bund on your right, for a change, and you'll even glimpse the towers around People's Square in the distance, if the air is clear enough. VUE has a restaurant, too, and the theme throughout is casual luxury. The cover charge on weekends includes a drink.

WINDOWS SCOREBOARD

11/F, 527 Huaihai Zhonglu, near Chengdu Lu, 21/5383-7757

HOURS: Daily 5 P.M.-late

METRO: South Shaanxi Road (Line 1, Line 10),

Map 10

If you prefer your sports bars rough and ready, try Windows Scoreboard. It's the Old French Concession's branch of a franchise that has venues dotted around town, all of which are popular for cheap drinks, easygoing crowds, and late-night parties. Windows Scoreboard is the sportiest among the branches, offering pool tables, foosball, darts, beer pong tournaments, and more. That's if you can tear your eyes away from the fantastic 11th floor view. This branch

is the least sleazy of all the Windows bars, but you're still likely to bump into the odd colorful character.

YY'S

125 Nanchang Lu, near Maoming Lu, 21/6466-4098

HOURS: Daily 2 P.M.-4 A.M.

METRO: South Shaanxi Road (Line 1, Line 10)

Map 10

Despite its 10-year pedigree, YY's (Yin Yang) remains relatively unknown outside of local circles. Posters of Chairman Mao adorn the dark, wood-paneled walls and a piano is available for anyone with a (revolutionary) tune to play. There's a bohemian vibe about the place that's complemented by a glass of whiskey and a pack of Double Happiness cigarettes. Take a dog-eared copy of Mao's Red Book for extra kudos. The small food menu is surprisingly robust; the wonton soup and fried rice are good, cheap meals. YY stays open late into the night, but the tone remains relatively sedate. With room only to sit down, it preserves its coffeehouse feel.

ZAPATA'S

5 Hengshan Lu, near Dongping Lu, 21/6433-4104, www.zapatas-shanghai.com

HOURS: Daily 5 P.M.-late

METRO: Hengshan Road (Line 1),

Map 10

A legend in its own lifetime, Zapata's has just the right amount of cheesy, kitschy appeal. The Mexican-themed bar stretches across two stories of a garishly painted villa and shares a big terrace with the more sedate Sasha's next door. Indoors, it's R&B and Top 40 on the sound system as revelers dance on the bar. When the terrace is officially open in spring and summer, Mexican snacks and hot dogs are available from the cabana barbecue. Zapata's was one of the first bars in Shanghai to run the now-ubiquitous Ladies' Night, which is still held on Mondays and Wednesdays.

NIGHTLIFE

Dance Clubs

◖ G PLUS

5/F, Xintiandi South Block, Nong 123 Xingye Lu, near Madang Lu, 21/5386-8088, www.clubgplus.com
HOURS: Daily 9 P.M.-late
COST: No cover charge
METRO: Xintiandi (Line 10)
Map 10

Try clubbing Chinese style at this Xintiandi super-club. Strobe lights, smoke machines, blaring commercial hip-hop, and LED screens provide the backdrop for plenty of posturing, as wealthy locals strut their stuff and flaunt their designer gear. G Plus is located inside a shopping mall, which could explain all that designer clothing. A table with whiskey and green tea mixers (sounds like an odd combination, but it's actually quite tasty) will set you back a couple of thousand yuan, so I recommend observing from the sidelines or dance floor for a cheaper night. Frequent drink deals include the ¥100 open bar. Well-known DJs incur a cover charge.

M1NT

24/F, 318 Fuzhou Lu, near Shandong Lu, 21/6391-2811
HOURS: Cocktails daily 6 P.M.-late; club Wed.-Sat. 10 P.M.-late
COST: No cover charge
METRO: East Nanjing Road (Line 2, Line 10)
Map 7

The rich and the beautiful congregate at M1NT, Shanghai's first (and only) shareholder bar. The concept is similar to a members only club, but you don't have to be a shareholder to get in. M1NT has branches in Cannes and Hong Kong and tends to attract the moneyed crowd, as you would expect. It contains a restaurant, bar, cocktail lounge, and nightclub, as well as an eye-popping 17-meter (56 ft.) tank containing a shiver of reef-tip sharks. The decor is sleek, lacquer black and Old Shanghai red, but the atmosphere is most definitely modern. On the decks, DJs spin mainly house music, with some R&B thrown in for good measure.

NOT ME

21 Dongping Lu, near Hengshan Lu, 21/6433-0760, www.not-me.com
HOURS: Mon.-Sat. 6 P.M.-late
COST: No cover charge
METRO: Changshu Road (Line 1, Line 7)
Map 10

Another understated antidote to the blingier downtown clubs, Not Me is known for its reasonably priced drinks and quirky interior. A lone beacon of (relative) innocence on a street of neon-lit escort bars, Not Me's decor is a futuristic meld of pod-shaped booths, alien-like fixtures, and beaded curtains. Famous-around-town DJs play most nights of the week to a largely French crowd. The music is mainly indie-electro and the party goes on until late on weekends. Rent an old-school locker to store your stuff while you dance or snag the foosball table if you're not the dancing sort.

OBAMA

2088 Yan'an Xilu, near Xianxia Lu, 21/6082-5511
HOURS: Daily 9:30 P.M.-3 A.M.
COST: No cover charge
METRO: West Yan'an Road (Line 3, Line 4)
Map 12

Dance clubs in Shanghai don't get any bigger than Obama. This cavernous (and oddly named) behemoth covers a massive 4,000 square meters (43,000 sq. ft.) of Hongqiao real estate and is the largest nightlife venue in the city. Management claims that it was built for the 2010 World Expo, but the connection is tenuous. Las Vegas design specialists Cagley and Tanner were drafted in to deck out the interior with LED panels, chandeliers, balconies, and a huge dance floor complete with poles and podiums. Although it is primarily a dance club, the venue includes KTV (karaoke) rooms, bars, and lounge spaces that flank the domed middle space. Drink deals keep the customers pouring in, but whether or not they ever fill Obama's vast halls is another matter. It's great for people-watching and sampling that Shanghai staple, whiskey and green tea, while you dance to hip hop and R&B.

Gay and Lesbian

D2

Cool Docks, 505 Zhongshan Nanlu, near Fuxing Donglu, 21/6152-6543
HOURS: Wed.-Sat. 8:30 P.M.-late
COST: No cover charge
METRO: Xiaonanmen (Line 9)
Map 11

For an action-packed night of clubbing LGBT style, make D2 your first (or final) stop. It's based in the Cool Docks and attracts a crowd of mainly good-looking, muscle-clad young guys. The club is split into three innovatively named zones: Cruzy (a mezzanine for watching the action on the dance floor below), Crazy (the main dancing area with all the associated trappings), and Lazy (a chilled lounge area with beds and a smaller dance floor). Electro and house rule the sound system. Things rarely kick off until around 11 P.M. and weekend parties go on until the wee hours.

EDDY'S BAR

1877 Huaihai Zhonglu, near Tianping Lu, 21/6282-0521, www.eddys-bar.com
HOURS: Mon.-Thurs. 8 P.M.-2 A.M., Fri.-Sun. 8 P.M.-3 A.M.
COST: No cover charge
METRO: Jiaotong University (Line 10)
Map 12

Eddy's is a good place to start your night or have a quiet drink after dinner. The vibe of this Asian-themed neighborhood bar is relaxed, with warm red lighting, minimalist but cozy Zen decor, and a decent array of drinks. The eponymous owner and manager makes an appearance most nights and likes to chat to both newcomers and old timers. Eddy's caters to Shanghai's older gay crowd, but also attracts a younger clientele who come for an aperitif before heading over to the Shanghai Studio for a more hedonistic night.

FOCUS CLUB

1/F, Harbour Ring Plaza, 730 Yan'an Donglu, near Xizang Zhonglu, 152/1685-7806
HOURS: Daily 9 P.M.-1 A.M.
COST: No cover charge
METRO: People's Square (Line 1, Line 2, Line 8), exit 1
Map 8

This glass-fronted venue at the foot of an office building is a regular café during the day, then morphs into a lesbian bar when night falls. Established and run by a Chinese lady who spent time in Germany, Focus is—as its name suggests—a focal point for Shanghai's *lala* community. It tends to be quiet during the week, but comes alive on Fridays (for Singles' Night) and Saturdays. The interior is smart, with boxy red seating, draped curtains, and low lighting. Special themed parties and karaoke nights happen from time to time and sometimes require an entry fee. The music tends towards Chinese pop, with Western pop and R&B creeping in.

SHANGHAI STUDIO

Bldg. 4, 1950 Huaihai Zhonglu, near Wukang Lu, 21/6283-1043, www.shanghai-studio.com
HOURS: Daily 8 P.M.-2 A.M.
METRO: Jiaotong University (Line 10)
Map 10

One of Shanghai's most popular LGBT venues, the Shanghai Studio is an art gallery and lingerie boutique as well as a bar. A warren of surreal, neon-lit corridors leads to several connecting rooms with bars and dancing areas. Open-bar drink deals help to set the mood. The vibe is either lounge-y or club-y depending on which night of the week you go. The crowd tends to weigh more towards guys, but the city's *lala* (lesbian) population is better represented on weekends. However, Thursday evening's ¥100 open bar brings the crowds in even before the weekend rush.

NIGHTLIFE

Lounges and Karaoke

CONSTELLATION 2

33 Yongjia Lu, near Maoming Nanlu, 21/5465-5993

HOURS: Daily 7 p.m.–2 a.m.

COST: No cover charge

METRO: South Shaanxi Road (Line 1, Line 10)

Map 10

The second in the starry-named triumvirate of Japanese cocktail bars, Constellation 2 is the biggest of the three and is richly decorated with brass fixtures and sumptuous armchairs. A sweeping spiral staircase connects the two stories. The bar runs the length of the back wall on the ground floor. The signature Moscow Mule is served in a wide-brimmed bronze jug. Consetellation 2 has an entirely different look and feel than the branch at 86 Xinle Road, which is stark in comparison, but still worth a look. The third incarnation is at 251 North Huangpi Road near People's Square.

EL CÓCTEL

2/F, 47 Yongfu Lu, near Fuxing Xilu, 21/6433-6511

HOURS: Daily 5 P.M.–3 A.M.

COST: No cover charge

METRO: Shanghai Library (Line 10)

Map 10

Guillermo "Willy" Trullas Moreno of El Willy tapas restaurant has widened his portfolio with this Japanese-style cocktail bar in the 47 Yongfu development. The venue has a lounge-y feel, with vintage furniture and orange-toned dividing walls made of patterned glass. The strict no-standing policy means that it never gets crowded. However, it also means that you may have to wait for a table. Cocktail prices are standard for Shanghai. It's worth it for the quality of the ingredients; the Spanish-style sandwiches are highly recommended.

THE FAT OLIVE

6/F, Silver Court Bldg., 228 Xizang Nanlu, entrance on Shouning Lu, 21/6334-3288

HOURS: Daily 9:30 A.M.–late

COST: No cover charge

METRO: South Huangpi Road (Line 1)

Map 8

Greek Australian chef David Laris has an ever-growing collection of restaurants and bars all around town. The Fat Olive is one of the most popular thanks to its wide terrace dotted with white couches, solid menu of mezze bites, and wine list of Old and New World varieties, served by the glass or the bottle. On a balmy evening, this is the ideal place to unwind with a drink. On weekdays 4–8 P.M. you'll get two for the price of one. The view of the skyline over the low roofs of the Old City is an interesting one, with the Lujiazui skyscrapers forming the backdrop. There is limited seating inside, with barstools and high tables. The bar is inside an office building and the entrance can be tricky to find—it's not on South Xizang Road as you'd expect from the address, but around the corner, on smaller Shouning Road.

HAOLEDI

6/F, 479 Nanjing Xilu, near People's Square, 21/5351-0808

HOURS: Daily 10 A.M.–6 A.M.

COST: No cover charge

METRO: People's Square (Line 1, Line 2, Line 8), exit 7

Map 7

Karaoke is taken extremely seriously in China and is conducted in private rooms instead of the rowdy bars more common in the West. Haoledi is a good place to try it Chinese-style, with waitress service and a huge selection of Mandopop and Western tunes to warble into the mic. The deal is that you rent a room for however many hours you want to stay and pay for drinks and snacks on top of that. As well as being a popular form of innocent entertainment, KTV (karaoke) has a darker side on the edges of prostitution, but Haoledi likes to keep things clean.

100 CENTURY AVENUE

93/F, Park Hyatt Hotel, Shanghai World Financial

Center, 100 Shiji Dadao, near Dongtai Lu, 21/3855-1428
HOURS: Mon.-Sat. 8 P.M.-late
COST: No cover charge
METRO: Lujiazui (Line 2)
Map 11

100 Century Avenue is the tallest bar in the world and offers plenty of drink options to prove that it isn't just about the view. The wine list is one of the longest in town and the whiskey selection is equally impressive (there's a whole room dedicated to it). The bar is split into two sections: The Music Room hosts regular live jazz and blues acts, including semi-celebrity Carlton J. Smith, while the lounge is reminiscent of Shanghai in the 1930s. Above the bar is a pink-hued sculpture, by contemporary artist Liu Jianhua, called "Daily Objects," which fittingly depicts everyday items.

VELVET LOUNGE
91 Julu Lu, near Changshu Lu, 21/5403-2976
HOURS: Sun.-Thurs. 6 P.M.-3 A.M., Fri.-Sat. 6 P.M.-5 A.M.
COST: No cover charge
METRO: Jing'an Temple (Line 2, Line 7)
Map 10

Yet another Old French Concession villa has been made over into a trendy lounge bar, but Velvet has the unique selling point of a wood-fired pizza oven. Its thin-crust pies are frequently featured on the "best in town" lists in the lifestyle magazines. As for the lounge itself, Velvet fills the gap between a full-size nightclub and a small bar. There are two bars plus several interconnected rooms for dancing, lounging, and mingling. The clientele tends to consist of the young and the beautiful that can't quite afford Bund prices.

Wine Bars

◖ DR. WINE
177 Fumin Lu, near Julu Lu, 21/5403-5717
HOURS: Daily 5 P.M.-2 A.M.
METRO: Jing'an Temple (Line 2, Line 7)
Map 10

A couple of streets away from Enoterra, this two-floor wine bar's cozy atmosphere comes from its bare red-brick interior walls and wood floors. The beams and fittings were salvaged from historic buildings. A sophisticated temperature control system means that each bottle is chilled (or warmed) to perfection. Prices per bottle range from the sublime to the ridiculous, but the lower end of the spectrum is reasonable. Downstairs you can either sit around the bar or on the low sofas, while the second level has tables and chairs. Complement your wine with a cheese plate, charcuterie board, or toasted sandwich from the snack menu.

ENOTERRA
53-57 Anfu Lu, near Wulumuqi Lu, 21/5404-0050, www.enoteca.com.cn
HOURS: Daily 10 A.M.-2 A.M.
METRO: Changshu Road (Line 1, Line 7)
Map 10

Formerly known as Enoteca, this is Shanghai's longest established wine bar and still a firm favorite among the city's oenophiles. Direct imports mean that prices start at under ¥100 per bottle. The menu is laid out according to color and "emotion." The food menu features French snack food like *croques monsieur* and baguette sandwiches. The tables and barstools tend to fill up quickly on weekends, but they accept reservations. Bottles and deli items are available for takeout from the room on the right. Enoterra has additional branches in Xintiandi and Lujiazui.

NIGHTLIFE

ARTS AND LEISURE

While the Shanghainese are known more for their fondness for food and browsing shops than for their love of culture, there's actually plenty to do and see that doesn't involve eating or shopping. An array of great museums, fantastic concert venues, and lovely parks are scattered throughout the city.

China's cultural heritage was decimated by the Cultural Revolution of the late 1960s and 1970s. In order to create what he believed would be a brand new state, free from the shackles of the past, Chairman Mao decreed that all old literature, art, drama, and opera be purged and replaced with pro-Socialist, anti-Rightist propaganda. Although many works were hidden and saved, much was lost.

The art scene came back with a vengeance in the late 1980s and early 1990s and is now flourishing. The M50 factory complex on Moganshan Road is now a series of galleries, while the Old French Concession is dotted with exhibition spaces. For music, state-built concert halls stand alongside independently run livehouses.

Although Shanghai looks very much like an urban sprawl, the municipality is broken up by frequent green spaces. From the wilderness of Gongqing Forest Park to the neat, French-style Fuxing Park, there's plenty of opportunity to get a break from the traffic and endless pavement. There are also some excellent museums ranging from the sublime (the well-stocked Shanghai Museum) to the slightly ridiculous (the Tobacco Museum).

HIGHLIGHTS

LOOK FOR ◖ TO FIND RECOMMENDED ARTS AND ACTIVITIES.

◖ **Hidden Gem:** Admire one man's 5,000-piece collection of Mao-era public artwork at the **Propaganda Poster Art Center** (page 219).

◖ **Best Museum Display:** See the city in miniature at the **Urban Planning Exhibition Hall** (page 220).

◖ **Smallest Art Gallery:** Small in size but big in scope, **FQ Projects** displays some great modern Chinese art (page 221).

◖ **Best Contemporary Art:** Witness Shanghai's ever-growing modern art scene at the warehouses of **M50** on Moganshan Road (page 222).

◖ **Most Dramatic:** Catch an English-language play at the **Ke Center for the Contemporary Arts,** a performance facility that's home to the Shanghai Repertory Theater company (page 222).

◖ **Best Music:** The stunning white **Shanghai Concert Hall** inside People's Square hosts regular performances from local and international orchestras, opera companies, and soloists (page 223).

◖ **Best Event for Bookworms:** Held every March, the **Shanghai International Literary Festival** gathers authors from across the globe for talks and Q&A sessions (page 226).

◖ **Best Wilderness Experience:** The largest green space within city limits, **Gongqing Forest Park** has pine forests, lakes, and horses, as well as a theme park (page 228).

◖ **Best Two-Wheeled Adventure:** Take a nighttime bike ride around Shanghai with **BOHDI Adventures** and explore the city in a whole new way (page 230).

◖ **Unique View of the City:** See Shanghai from the saddle or sidecar of a WWII-era motorbike with **Shanghai Sideways** tours (page 231).

Urban Planning Exhibition Hall

The Arts

MUSEUMS

CHINA TOBACCO MUSEUM

728 Changyang Lu, near Tongbei Lu, 21/6535-9966
HOURS: Mon., Thurs., Sat. 9 A.M.-4 P.M.
COST: ¥10
METRO: Dalian Road (Line 4)
Map 12

Offbeat and oddly compelling, the Tobacco Museum tells the story of the leaf that has 350 million Chinese people in its grip. China's cigarette industry is worth around ¥250 billion per year and is big business. This museum is located opposite the Shanghai Cigarette Factory and sits inside a gray, somewhat ungainly, box-like piece of modern architecture. With 150,000 exhibits across seven display halls (one of which, thankfully, is entitled "Harm of Smoking"), the museum pays homage to all things tobacco related. It includes displays of famous smokers, paraphernalia belonging to nicotine-addicted luminaries like Deng Xiaoping and Chairman Mao, and—of course—a smoking room where you can indulge in a puff if so inspired.

MOCA SHANGHAI

231 Nanjing Xilu, near Huangpi Beilu, 21/6327-1282, www.mocashanghai.org
HOURS: Daily 10 A.M.-6 P.M., Wed. open until 10 P.M.
COST: ¥20
METRO: People's Square (Line 1, Line 2, Line 8), exit 10
Map 8

The glass building that houses Shanghai's Museum of Contemporary Art is a reworking of the People's Park greenhouse. It is operated by the Samuel Kung foundation and was the city's first nonprofit independent contemporary gallery when it opened. The ground floor and first level have a total of 1,800 square meters (19,400 sq. ft.) of exhibition space. Big names in the art world have had shows here and frequent retrospectives are held for luminaries of

MOCA Shanghai

© SUSIE GORDON

ARTS AND LEISURE

the fashion and creative world, like Coco Chanel and Salvatore Ferragamo. In addition to exhibitions, MOCA runs seminars and talks throughout the year. The gallery's exterior is a welcome contrast to the greenery of the surrounding park.

◖ PROPAGANDA POSTER ART CENTER

B/F, Bldg. B, 868 Huashan Lu, near Fuxing Xilu,
21/6211-1845, www.shanghaipropagandaart.com
HOURS: Daily 10 A.M.–5 P.M.
COST: ¥20
METRO: Shanghai Library (Line 10)
Map 10

Art lover and historian Yang Pei Ming has spent the past 15 years collecting anti-Capitalist, pro-Cuba, Maoist, and Communist propaganda posters. He displays his favorite pieces from his 5,000-strong collection in the basement of a residential complex on Huashan Road. For anyone interested in how art shaped China's contemporary history, this collection is a must. The highly stylized illustrations in bold colors bear witness to an era when art was bestowed with an unusual power to persuade and convince. If you like what you see and want to take home a souvenir, have a browse in the gift shop for posters and knick-knacks.

ROCKBUND ART MUSEUM

20 Huqiu Lu, near Beijing Donglu, 21/3310-9985,
www.rockbundartmuseum.org
HOURS: Tues.–Sun. 10 A.M.–6 P.M.
COST: ¥15 adults, ¥10 students and seniors
METRO: East Nanjing Road (Line 2, Line 10)
Map 7

The Rockbund Art Museum is a relatively new fixture, but one that has made waves in the city's artistic circles. Part of the Rockefeller Group, it aims to foster the "promotion and exchange" of contemporary art, with a focus on China. It occupies the grand old building formerly used by the Royal Asiatic Society Building on Tiger Hill Road at the top end of the Bund. British architect David Chipperfield reworked the structure in 2007 but retained much of the original building. As well as mounting large-scale art displays, Rockbund hosts regular lectures and seminars to spread the word about fine art in Asia.

SHANGHAI MUNICIPAL HISTORY MUSEUM

Oriental Pearl Tower, 1 Shiji Dadao, 21/5879-3003
HOURS: Daily 9 A.M.–9 P.M.
COST: ¥35
METRO: Lujiazui (Line 2)
Map 11

Delve into Shanghai's murky past at this often-overlooked museum beneath the Oriental Pearl Tower. Simply bypass the long lines waiting for the elevators and head through to the museum entrance. Inside you'll find a potted history of Shanghai up until the Communists came to power in 1949, ending its sinful heyday of vice and villainy. Dioramas depict the Bund, Nanjing Road, and the French Concession during colonial times, while a selection of trolley cars from 1908 make an impressive display. Audio guides are available, but the displays are so well labeled that you won't need them.

SHANGHAI MUSEUM

201 Renmin Dadao, near Huangpi Beilu, 21/6372-3500,
www.shanghaimuseum.net
HOURS: Daily 9 A.M.–5 P.M. (last ticket issued at 4 P.M.)
COST: ¥20 special exhibitions
METRO: People's Square (Line 1, Line 2, Line 8), exit 9
Map 8

Located inside the brick building in People's Park that looks like an ancient Chinese *ding* cooking pot, Shanghai Museum is a wealth of cultural and historical information about the city. It moved to its current location in 1996, having grown too large for the old clubhouse building that is now the Shanghai Art Museum. Browsing your way through all 120,000 relics would take a while, so focus your energies on the bronzes, Ming and Qing furniture, coins, and jade halls for an overview of Chinese history. To make sure you see the best parts, book yourself onto a personal guided tour through www.newmantours.com.

SHANGHAI NATURAL HISTORY MUSEUM

260 Yan'an Donglu, near Henan Zhonglu,
21/6321-3548
HOURS: Tues.–Sun. 9 A.M.–5 P.M.

ARTS AND LEISURE

(last ticket issued at 3:30 P.M.)

COST: ¥5 adults, ¥2.5 students

METRO: People's Square (Line 1, Line 2, Line 8), exit 1
Map 7

Get up close to a 140-million-year-old dinosaur skeleton from Sichuan province and admire display cases of stuffed animals. The Natural History Museum opened in 1956 in the old British Cotton Exchange and seems to have changed very little since. The museum's gorgeous mosaic floors and stained glass windows bear witness to its heritage, but the rest of the building is somewhat run down. The construction of the Yan'an elevated highway just inches from its facade has not helped matters. However, there is plenty to see, with nearly a quarter of a million specimens of flora and fauna. Look out for indigenous Chinese animals, like the prehistoric Yellow River mammoth, the giant panda, and the Yangtze alligator. Quirky and quaint, the museum is a fun and affordable way to pass an hour.

SHANGHAI SCIENCE AND TECHNOLOGY MUSEUM

2000 Shiji Dadao, J-06 Yataishenghui Nanjie, 21/6863-2000

HOURS: Tues.-Sun. 9 A.M.-5:15 P.M.
(last ticket issued at 4:15 P.M.)

COST: ¥60 adults, ¥40 students, ¥20 children

METRO: Science and Technology Museum (Line 2)
Map 11

Most people use the Science and Technology Museum Metro station just to get to the visa office or the underground market, but the museum itself is a fun way to pass a couple of hours in Pudong. It opened in 2001 in a huge futuristic building that was designed especially for it. Fronted by a giant lake, it covers nearly 100,000 square meters (1.1 million sq. ft.). There are 14 permanent displays on a variety of interesting topics, including "World of Robots," "Spectrum of Live," "Information Era," and "Children's Science Land." Look out for the display about Chinese scientists and explorers. The museum also contains an IMAX cinema and a greenhouse.

◖ URBAN PLANNING EXHIBITION HALL

100 Renmin Dadao, near Xizang Lu, 21/6318-4477, www.supec.org

HOURS: Mon.-Thurs. 9 A.M.-5 P.M. (last ticket issued at 4 P.M.), Fri.-Sun. 9 A.M.-6 P.M. (last ticket issued at 5 P.M.)

COST: ¥30

METRO: People's Square (Line 1, Line 2, Line 8), exit 20
Map 8

One of Shanghai's most interesting museums, the Urban Planning Exhibition Hall occupies the futuristic white building on the eastern edge of People's Square. In the lobby is a giant sculpture featuring the best of Shanghai's architecture (oddly not to scale) surrounded by a flock of golden seagulls, but the highlight is upstairs: a huge 3D floor model of the city, complete with viewing decks and walkways. There's also an excellent rundown of each municipal district, cupboards full of pullout photographs of the old city, and a ship simulator that lets you navigate a boat into Shanghai's harbor. The ominously named Grand Hall of the Master Plan contains information on how the city will grow in the years ahead.

ART DISTRICTS AND GALLERIES

ELISABETH DE BRABANT ART CENTER

299 Fuxing Xilu, near Huashan Lu, 21/6466-7428, www.elisabethdebrabant.com

HOURS: Tues.-Fri. 10 A.M.-7 P.M., Sat. 1:30 A.M.-6:30 P.M., Mon. by appointment only

METRO: Shanghai Library (Line 10)
Map 12

New Yorker Elisabeth de Brabant opened this art center in 2009 to build upon her long held passion for Asian art. Set across four stories of a beautiful 1933 house on West Fuxing Road, the center contains two galleries, a café, and offices. Its aim is to promote connections between Eastern and Western artists and presents regular symposiums and lectures on this theme. Focusing on contemporary art, the gallery hosts exhibitions by artists like Hung Liu and Li Lei and sculptors such as Jinjiang Bo and Beili Liu. De Brabant lives nearby and is an important figure in Shanghai's contemporary art scene. Before she opened the art center, she housed her art collection in her own home.

■ FQ PROJECTS

No. 76, Nong 927 Huaihai Zhonglu, near Maoming
Nanlu, 21/6466-2940, www.fqprojects.com
HOURS: Wed.-Sun. 10 A.M.-6 P.M., Thurs. open until 10 P.M.
METRO: South Shaanxi Road (Line 1, Line 10)
Map 10

Shanghai's smallest gallery lies a short way down the famously artsy Huaihai Fang lane off busy Middle Huaihai Road. Measuring 34 by 38 meters (370 by 410 ft.), it's more intimate than the cavernous warehouse galleries of M50 on Moganshan Road or the airy villa conversions of the leafier parts of town. FQ has just enough space for a selection of small-scale artwork by young contemporary artists covering sculpture, painting, installation, video, and photography. The emphasis is on artists who break away from the mainstream and attempt something new. Exhibitions rotate every month or so and the 12-square-meter (130 sq. ft.) courtyard is used for shows in summer.

IFA GALLERY

621 Changde Lu, 21/6256-0835, www.ifa-gallery.com
HOURS: Tues.-Sun. 10 A.M.-7 P.M.
METRO: Changping Road (Line 7)
Map 9

One of the most interesting galleries outside of the M50 complex, ifa gathers work by Asian contemporary artists in a beautiful old villa dating from 1923 in Jing'an District. The house was owned by a British customs official during colonial times and was taken over by ifa in 2008. Prior to that, the gallery was set up in M50 in 2006, then moved to its current location two years later. Curator Zane Mellupe turns the focus on Chinese artists, promoting recent graduates from the prestigious art academies in Beijing and Hangzhou. Inside, the gallery is just as attractive as the exterior, with white walls, wooden floors, and high ceilings.

JAMES COHAN GALLERY

Nong 1, Bldg. 1, 170 Yueyang Lu, 21/5466-0825, www.
jamescohan.com
HOURS: Tues.-Sat. 10 A.M.-7 P.M., Mon.
by appointment only

METRO: Zhaojiabang Road (Line 7, Line 9)
Map 10

This Shanghai exhibition space is an extension of the famous James Cohan Gallery in New York City. Located on the ground floor of a stunning 1930s garden villa in the prettiest part of the Old French Concession, the gallery opened in 2008 and hosts shows by international artists. It's a beautiful location for great art and its white walls and window bays form the perfect backdrop for paintings and sculptures. Look up and you'll notice that many of the ceilings are decorated with intricate patterns. As well as art exhibitions, the James Cohan Gallery holds lectures, talks, and concerts.

KUNST.LICHT

210 Wulumuqi Lu, near Nanjing Xilu, 21/6249-0737,
www.kunstlicht.sh
HOURS: Daily 11 A.M.-7 P.M.
METRO: Jing'an Temple (Line 2, Line 7)
Map 9

This small gallery based in a street-facing lane house is devoted to contemporary fine art photography and is a platform for up-and-coming photographers from all over the world. White walls, high ceilings, and bright, airy rooms show off the artwork to good effect and a frequently rotating exhibition schedule keeps things fresh. If you decide to buy a print, staff will advise you on framing options and conservation. The gallery operates an online talent-spotting scheme called nextkunst.licht through which photographers can submit work for consideration by the curators. Several promising young artists have been spotted through the scheme so far.

LEO GALLERY

376 Wukang Lu, near Hunan Lu, 21/5465-8785,
www.leogallery.com.cn
HOURS: Tues.-Sun. 11 A.M.-7 P.M.
METRO: Shanghai Library (Line 10)
Map 12

This bright, airy gallery in a red-brick house inside the Ferguson Lane complex attempts to integrate art into daily life and promotes contemporary artists who are at the peak of their career. Displays include small sculptures, paintings, and drawings by artists who hail mainly from Asia, but Europeans and Americans are featured from time to time. Leo Gallery has recently expanded across the lane into an annex, meaning more space for great art. It's still small enough to retain an intimate atmosphere, but it now offers fresh wall space for bigger exhibitions. Its location places it at the heart of a creative enclave that also includes office space, cafés, and restaurants.

M50

50 Moganshan Lu, near Changhua Lu, 21/6359-3923, www.m50.com.cn
HOURS: Daily, gallery opening hours vary
METRO: Changshou Road (Line 7)
Map 12

The epicenter of Shanghai's contemporary art scene is a complex of renovated warehouses beside the Suzhou Creek in the north of the city. Engulfed in residential blocks, the area is unlovely on the whole, but worth a trip to see M50. Shanghai's modern art scene kicked off in the late 1980s when local artists met to discuss the politics of their work. A community grew up in the old Chunming Slub Mill and Xinhe Spinning Mill, which now form the main part of M50. Today, the complex is home to some excellent galleries, the most notable of which are island6 (home of the electronic art collective Liu Dao), Vanguard, Eastlink, Twocities, and the ShanghART Warehouse. Pick up some coffee table tomes at Can's Book and refresh with a coffee at the café near the complex entrance.

SHANGHAI GALLERY OF ART

3/F, Three on the Bund, 17 Guangdong Lu, near Zhongshan Dongyilu, 21/6321-5757, www.shanghaigalleryofart.com
HOURS: Daily 10 A.M.-9 P.M.
METRO: East Nanjing Road (Line 2, Line 10)
Map 7

The Shanghai Gallery of Art's extensive exhibition space (1,200 meters to be exact) exists thanks to the groundbreaking structural engineering that went into the construction of the building that houses it. The Union Building on the Bund was built in the Free Renaissance style in 1916 and was the first steel-framed edifice in Shanghai. That meant that interior walls weren't necessary, producing the expansive floor space seen today in the gallery. The building was reworked in 2004 by architect Michael Graves and opened as Three on the Bund. The Shanghai Gallery of Art prides itself on displaying museum-worthy art with a Chinese focus.

ACROBATICS
SHANGHAI CIRCUS WORLD

2266 Gonghexin Lu, near Guangzhong Lu, 21/5665-3646
HOURS: Box office daily 9 A.M.-7:30 P.M.; performances Fri.-Sat. 7:30-9 P.M.
COST: ¥80-100
METRO: Shanghai Circus World (Line 1)
Map 12

Shanghai's acrobats are famous around the country and Circus World is the best place to see them do their thing. The ERA troupe is China's answer to Cirque du Soleil. They perform here twice weekly and change their show on a seasonal basis. Their motto is "Miss it, miss Shanghai," and it is certainly a spectacle. Shanghai Circus World also hosts the annual Magic Festival in November. The building was completed in 1999 and covers over 22,000 square meters (236,800 sq. ft.). With room for 1,638 spectators beneath its futuristic Epcot-like dome, it is one of the city's largest performance spaces.

MUSIC, THEATER, AND OPERA
KE CENTER FOR THE CONTEMPORARY ARTS

613-B Kaixuan Lu, near Wuyi Lu, 21/6131-3080, www.kecenter.org.cn
HOURS: Daily 10 A.M.-10 P.M.
METRO: West Yan'an Road (Line 3, Line 4)
Map 12

This multi-purpose venue is best known as a theater. It's the home of the Shanghai

Repertory Theater troupe, one of the city's foremost drama groups. Their seasonal schedule includes regular performances of Shakespeare and contemporary plays. The building started life as the Daming Rubber Factory in the 1960s and now houses a gallery, bookshop, and terrace café as well as performance space. The complex covers 1,200 square meters (12,900 sq. ft.) over three floors. It can be difficult to locate from Kaixuan Road, so look out for the stylized character under the overhead Metro line. Head down the lane and the complex will be on the left.

MAJESTIC THEATRE

66 Jiangning Lu, near Nanjing Xilu, 21/6217-4409
HOURS: Box office daily 10 A.M.–9 P.M.
METRO: West Nanjing Road (Line 2)
`Map 9`

This attractive art deco theater was built in 1941 and seats over 1,000 people for traditional Chinese opera, classical dramas, and Western musicals. Its Chinese name means "flawless jade" and it is one of the best-preserved art

deco buildings in Shanghai. The crystal chandelier in the lobby and the gorgeous curved staircases make it well worth a look, even if you don't stop to see a show. If there's a Chinese opera playing when you visit, get a ticket if you can. It's a world away from the Western style and the costumes are stunning. The style most often performed in Shanghai is *kunqu*, which is different from the more famous Peking variety.

◖ SHANGHAI CONCERT HALL

523 Yan'an Lu, near Jinling Lu, 21/6386-2836, www.shanghaiconcerthall.org
HOURS: Box office daily 9 A.M.–7:30 P.M.
METRO: People's Square (Line 1, Line 2, Line 8), exit 1
`Map 8`

It's hard to imagine just by looking at it, but the entirety of this European-style theater relocated 66 meters (700 ft.) to the southeast between 2002 and 2004 to make way for the Yan'an elevated highway. The hall started life as the Nanking Theatre in 1930, designed by Chinese architect Fan Wenjiao. It became the Beijing Cinema after the creation of the

© SUSIE GORDON

Shanghai Grand Theatre

PRC in 1949 and was given its current name 10 years later. Today it sits in its own special "music park" inside the boundaries of People's Park. Thanks to its excellent acoustics, it attracts classical, popular, and chamber performers from all over the world.

SHANGHAI DRAMATIC ARTS CENTER

288 Anfu Lu, near Wukang Lu, 21/6473-0123, www.china-drama.com

HOURS: Daily 9 A.M.–8 P.M. (box office)

METRO: Shanghai Library (Line 10)

Map 10

Home to some of Shanghai's best English and Chinese productions, the Dramatic Arts Center lies in close proximity to the Shanghai Theater Academy, where some of China's finest acting talent is nurtured. The theater is the result of a collaboration between the People's Art Theater and the Youth Drama Troupe, which were the city's major troupes post-1949. The two joined forces in 1995 to create the Shanghai Dramatic Arts Center, housed inside an imposing building on Anfu Road. The 15,000-square-meter (161,000 sq. ft.) performance space puts on over 20 operas, Shakespeare plays, and drama recitals every year. Check their website for current event listings.

SHANGHAI GRAND THEATRE

300 Renmin Dadao, near Huangpi Beilu, 21/6386-8686, www.shgtheatre.com

HOURS: Box office daily 9 A.M.–7 P.M.

METRO: People's Square (Line 1, Line 2, Line 8), exit 11

Map 8

This glass-fronted white giant inside People's Park was designed by French architect Jean-Marie Charpentier. The building is a modern take on the upturned eaves of traditional Chinese architecture. It consists of 10 stories behind a glass atrium and has three performance spaces. The main stage sits 1,800, while the drama theater and studio are designed for smaller shows. The sound and lighting facilities are world class. A regular roster of international operas, ballets, concerts, and recitals brings the stage to life. Even if you don't have time to see a show, it's worth having a look around the lobby or having a drink at the on-site café.

SHANGHAI HELUTING CONCERT HALL

20 Fenyang Lu, near Yueyang Lu, 21/5258-3600

HOURS: Box office open daily 9 A.M.–5 P.M.

METRO: Changshu Road (Line 1, Line 7)

Map 10

This beautiful classical venue holds regular chamber recitals and symphonic concerts and is affiliated with the Shanghai Conservatory of Music. With its modest red brick frontage, Heluting doesn't look like a concert hall from the outside, but inside it's everything you'd expect from a fine performance venue: plush velvet seats, gilded ornaments, and a reverential air. It's perfect if you want to see a concert but don't fancy one of the larger venues. This part of town is particularly picturesque too, with piano and violin shops flanking the quiet, tree-lined streets.

SHANGHAI ORIENTAL ART CENTER

425 Dingxiang Lu, near Yingchun Lu, 21/6854-1234, www.en.shoac.com

HOURS: Daily 9 A.M.–9 P.M.

METRO: Science and Technology Museum (Line 2)

Map 11

This beautiful modern building looks like a butterfly orchid from above and each "petal" contains a different performance space. A focal point of culture in Pudong, the Oriental Art Center was designed by French architect Paul Andreu. The space includes halls for opera, concerts, exhibitions, and general performances, along with a grand entrance. The whole complex covers 40,000 square meters (430,000 sq. ft.) and cost ¥1 billion to complete. Since it opened in the summer of 2005, the Oriental Art Center has hosted world-renowned orchestras, like the Berlin Philharmonic, as well as traditional Chinese opera and the popular brunch concert series. The Café du Soleil on the 2nd floor is open before and during performances.

PERFORMANCE VENUES

MERCEDES-BENZ ARENA

1200 Shibo Dadao, 400/1816-688, www.mbarena.com

HOURS: Open for performances

COST: ¥100-1,000

METRO: Yaohua Road (Line 7)

Map 12

This huge, futuristic venue started life as the World Expo Cultural Center and was the epicenter of the 2010 Expo opening and closing ceremonies. When Expo finished in October 2010, it was turned over to a Chinese-American joint venture and transformed into a performance venue that sits 18,000 spectators for concerts and events. It's an imposing sight, glowing white on the riverbank like an enormous flattened pearl, and plays host to big concerts by international acts like Usher. After-parties and smaller gigs take place at the on-site Mixing Room. Along with the China Pavilion, Shanghai Exhibition Center, and the Shanghai Theme Pavilion, the arena was built to survive as a legacy of the 2010 Expo.

CINEMA
FILM ART CENTER
160 Xinhua Lu, near Panyu Lu, 21/6280-4088, www.filmcenter.com.cn
HOURS: Daily 9 A.M.–10 P.M.
COST: ¥90
METRO: Jiaotong University (Line 10)
Map 12

Along with the Crowne Plaza Hotel next door, the Film Art Center dominates this residential area in the western part of the Old French Concession. Its contemporary, curved white facade sits at the crossing of Xinhua and Panyu Roads, close to the former residence of J. G. Ballard, author of the book *Empire of the Sun*. The Film Art Center plays host to the annual Shanghai Film Festival each summer, which attracts big names like Jackie Chan, Wong Kar-Wai, and Tsui Hark. Mondays and Tuesdays see a half price deal on all cinema tickets. With a Starbucks, Iceason gelateria, and imported goods shop, it's more than just a cinema.

GRAND CINEMA
216 Nanjing Xilu, near Xizang Lu, 21/6327-4260, www.shdgm.com
HOURS: Daily 9 A.M.–10:30 P.M.
COST: Tickets ¥80–90, half price Tues.–Wed
METRO: People's Square (Line 1, Line 2, Line 8), exit 7
Map 8

One of the many notable buildings around People's Square, the Grand Cinema is an art deco delight with a striped exterior and eye-catching tower. It was designed in 1928 by architectural luminary László Hudec and got off to a rocky start in the early 1930s. Salvation came in the form of a joint venture between Cantonese businessman Lu Geng and a British national, who reopened it and revived its fortunes with a more attractive billing. The cinema underwent extensive renovation in 2008 to create the current 1,000-seat hall and five separate screens. There's a whole floor dedicated to the building's history, full of archive photos and footage, as well as billboard posters and flyers. A café and terrace provide pre- and post-movie sustenance.

XINGUANG FILM ART CENTER
586 Ningbo Lu, near Guangxi Lu, 21/6351-5866
HOURS: Box office daily 1–7:30 P.M.
COST: ¥50–100
METRO: People's Square (Line 1, Line 2, Line 8), exit 7
Map 8

This cozy, European-style cinema is redolent with old-style charm. The theater features a 1930s-style corner entrance and beautiful patterned brick detail on the facade. It played host to Charlie Chaplin during Shanghai's Golden Age and was the first movie house to screen a Chinese film with sound. It was restored to its past glory in 1995 and now hosts movie events like the Short Film Festival as well as regular film screenings of Chinese movies and Western blockbusters. Its compact viewing rooms seat just 380 guests.

ARTS AND LEISURE

Festivals and Events

WINTER
CHINESE NEW YEAR

Spring Festival (or, as it's known to Westerners, Chinese New Year) sees Shanghai empty out dramatically, as the huge migrant worker population heads back home to celebrate the year's main holiday. The traffic is refreshingly light, the streets are less chaotic, and the city feels a bit like a ghost town. Many smaller businesses remain closed for the week of festivities, so you may find that your experience is less fulfilling if you visit around this time. However, the people who do stick around make sure that the New Year is welcomed with a bang—literally. Fireworks illuminate the sky until dawn on New Year's Eve and people flock to light "first incense" at the Buddhist temples. People exchange red *hongbao* envelopes stuffed with money and don newly bought outfits. The final day of the holiday week is Lantern Festival, when locals gather at the City God Temple in the Old City to watch illuminated lanterns and venerate the Buddha. The Bund comes alive with vendors and visitors, many wearing ox horns, tiger ears, or whichever animal has risen in the zodiac with the New Year. Traveling on the rail and domestic air network around this time is an absolute nightmare, so make sure you avoid it whenever possible.

SPRING
JUE FESTIVAL

www.juefestival.com

China's most influential artists and musicians get together to host this annual springtime arts festival in Shanghai and Beijing. Run by the Split Works creative collective, JUE has been running since 2009, and is a popular fixture on Shanghai's cultural calendar. During the festival, events take place at venues all over the city, from gigs and jam sessions at live music haunts Yuyintang and MAO, to art battles and poetry slams at the Rockbund Art Museum. If you're going to be in Shanghai (or Beijing) mid-March–early April, check the website for events.

◖ SHANGHAI INTERNATIONAL LITERARY FESTIVAL

Glamour Bar, M on the Bund, 6/F, 5 on the Bund, 20 Guangdong Lu, near Zhongshan Dongyilu, 21/6350-9988, www.m-theglamourbar.com/literary-festival.html

COST: ¥65 per event
METRO: East Nanjing Road (Line 2, Line 10)
Map 7

China's largest and most important English-language literary event takes place every March at the Glamour Bar. It was established

WRITE ON: SHANGHAI'S LITERARY SCENE

As well as spawning modern Chinese writing talent like blogger Han Han, rebel Mian Mian, and Wei Hui (whose 2000 novel *Shanghai Baby* was made into a movie starring Bai Ling), Shanghai has a thriving English-language writing scene. Glamour Bar on the Bund is the city's most literary venue, hosting the Shanghai International Literary Festival every March. The month-long event attracts big-name authors like Louis de Ber-niéres and Thomas Keneally as well as local writers and historians. Glamour Bar also runs regular writers' workshops and reading groups.

Bursting onto the literary scene in late 2009 was HAL Publishing. Run by a coterie of mainly Swedish, British, and Canadian expatriates, the group published a collection of short stories in December 2010. Available at Garden Books, the anthology includes China-centric work in English by local and foreign writers. Shanghai Repertory Theater formed around the same time and stages work by new playwrights as well as the classics.

in 2003 by Michelle Garnaut (owner of M on the Bund and Capital M in Beijing) and Jenny Laing Peach and gathers fiction and non-fiction writers from around the world to present hour-long author talks and Q&A sessions over several weekends. Each year features around 90 authors across 65 sessions. Previous events included big names like Louis de Bernières, Thomas Keneally, Gore Vidal, and Amy Tan. The schedule also includes literary lunches and round table debates. Tickets for each event are sold separately on the website. They usually cost ¥65 apiece and include a drink.

SUMMER
SHANGHAI FILM FESTIVAL

160 Xinhua Lu, near Panyu Lu, www.siff.com
METRO: Jiaotong University (Line 10)
Map 10

The annual Shanghai Film festival falls in June each year and was established in 1993 to promote the Chinese film industry and laud its denizens. The festival includes the Golden Goblet award and Asian New Talent prize. It runs a series of international screenings at the Shanghai Film Art Center in the west of the Old French Concession.

FALL
JAZZ FESTIVAL

www.jzfestival.com

Organized and run by the JZ jazz club, this annual festival happens in October at various indoor and outdoor venues like Shanghai Centre Theatre and Century Park. It attracts world-renowned jazz musicians to the city and is a great, laidback event for music fans who don't like the rough and tumble of rock or pop festivals.

NATIONAL DAY

The city comes alive on October 1 each year to commemorate the day when Chairman Mao spoke at the Forbidden City in Beijing, auguring a new era for China and founding the People's Republic. To celebrate this momentous event properly, Chinese workers are given a week off, which is known as Golden Week. People who stay in town tend to flock to the attractions, so the Bund, Yu Garden, and parks can be extremely busy. Few official events happen in Shanghai; there is little point in purposely scheduling your trip to coincide with Golden Week. In fact, it may be more sensible to avoid it, especially if you will be travelling to other Chinese cities.

Recreation

PARKS
CENTURY PARK

1001 Jinxiu Lu, near Minsheng Lu, 21/3876-0588
HOURS: Daily 7 A.M.–6 P.M.
COST: ¥10
METRO: Century Park (Line 2)
Map 11

This huge green space extends for 140 hectares (346 acres) across Pudong and is the largest downtown park in the city. Its lakes, lawns, and pathways are popular with bike riders, kite flyers, and city dwellers in need of some fresh air. The park was designed by a British landscaping company, but the style of the gardens is Japanese and Chinese. It was constructed to act as a "green lung," providing extra oxygen to the city's air, thanks to its many trees. Wilderness areas sit side by side with seven scenic spots, like ponds and pavilions, with the huge central lake as a focal point. Rent tandem bikes to explore the farthest extremities or bring your sneakers and jog around the six-kilometer (3.7 mi) perimeter. The park is easily reachable by the metro station of the same name.

FUXING PARK

105 Yandang Lu, near Fuxing Lu, 21/5386-1069
HOURS: Daily 24 hours
COST: Free
METRO: Xintiandi (Line 10)
Map 10

In 1909, pretty Fuxing Park was landscaped in Parisian style. The plot of land was previously known as Gujiazhai before being taken over

ARTS AND LEISURE

Gongqing Forest Park

by the French. Its manicured lawns, boulevards, fountains, and carousel give a distinctly European feel, along with a somewhat incongruous statue of Communist theorists Marx and Engels. Fuxing Park is one of Shanghai's more tranquil green spaces, with paths to stroll along and areas where elderly people practice tai chi and ballroom dancing. The park is also home to a handful of bling-y nightclubs, including Guandi, which is owned by Taiwanese actor David Wu, and a karaoke venue. The clubs attract the young and the moneyed who want to show off their designer spoils, so avoid the park at night if that's not your scene.

☪ GONGQING FOREST PARK

2000 Jungong Lu, near Yinhang Lu, 21/6574-0586, www.shgqsl.com
HOURS: Daily 6 A.M.–5 P.M.
COST: ¥15
METRO: Shiguang Road (Line 8)
Map 12

Gongqing Forest Park is a true wilderness in the Yangpu District of northern Shanghai,

complete with roaming horses, sprawling lakes, and relative calm. It covers 131 hectares (324 acres) and includes a fun fair, barbeque pits, arboretums, a zip-wire over the lake, and even wooden chalets where guests can spend the night. Gongqing is as close to the countryside as you can get within the city limits, but a stroll up to the "scenic lookout point" reminds you that you're in an industrial metropolis. Instead of rolling hills and blue skies, the vista is a dockyard with container ships and tankers cruising by on the river. Getting to the park is something of a trek (the nearest Metro is a short taxi ride from the entrance), but it makes a great day trip or afternoon jaunt.

JING'AN PARK

189 Huashan Lu, near Yan'an Lu, 21/6248-3238
HOURS: Daily dawn–late
COST: Free
METRO: West Nanjing Road (Line 2)
Map 9

Tucked between West Nanjing Road and the roaring elevated highway, Jing'an Park sits

© SUSIE GORDON

Jing'an Park

opposite the temple, on the grounds of the old Bubbling Well Road Cemetery. It was converted into a public recreation ground in 1955 and Shanghai legend has it that ghosts roam after dark. Whether you believe in spooks or not, the park is a nice antidote to the urban overload of this district. Inside the park, a Balinese restaurant sits beside a lake, and waterfalls trickle over grottos and caves. A couple of Western cafés flank the West Nanjing Road entrance. The bizarrely named Email Fashion Plaza leads to the Metro.

XUJIAHUI PARK

889 Zhaojiabang Lu, near Tianping Lu, 21/5448-3887
HOURS: Daily 24 hours
COST: Free
METRO: Xujiahui (Line 1, Line 9)
Map 12

Laid out on the site of an old brick factory, Xujiahui Park is a surprisingly lush expanse of public space in the middle of a busy residential and commercial district. Apartment blocks rise up around its perimeters and a handful of buildings break up the greenery within. Look out for the sky bridge, which lights up at night (but looks oddly out of place during the day); an unusual tree sculpture; and a pond frequented by black swans. The attractive red brick villa sitting close to Hengshan Road is an upscale Spanish restaurant from three-Michelin-starred chef Martin Berasategui.

ZHONGSHAN PARK

780 Changning Lu, near Huichuan Lu, 21/6211-7994
HOURS: Daily 6:30 A.M.-8:30 P.M.
COST: Free
METRO: Zhongshan Park (Line 2, Line 3, Line 4)
Map 12

Named in honor of China's founding father, Dr. Sun Yat-Sen, Zhongshan Park is a green haven of lawns, paths, pavilions, and lakes in Changning District west of Jing'an. The park started as the private garden of a British property developer named Fogg and was developed as Jessfield Park by the municipal government in 1914. It gained its current name in 1944. Zhongshan Park sits between shopping malls in the shadow of the

ARTS AND LEISURE

PARK LIFE: TAI CHI, BALLROOM DANCING, AND "KEEP OFF THE GRASS"

Since the majority of urban Shanghainese live in high-rise apartment blocks, outdoor space is limited to local parks. As a result, inner-city green spaces are rather more boisterous than the tranquil parks of other countries. However, certain bizarre rules seem to defeat the purpose. Most parks prohibit ball games and very few allow visitors to sit on the grass. People still manage to have plenty of fun, with elderly citizens practicing tai chi in the morning and ballroom dancing in the evening and children running about with bubble blowers and kites. Traditional stone bridges, pavilions, and scenic spots are generously interspersed with cafés and gift shops, creating a bizarre but appealing atmosphere. The farther out of the city center you go, the larger and wilder the parks become. Gongqing Forest Park is a veritable wilderness of pine forests and wooden chalets.

neon blue–trimmed Renaissance Hotel and is an ideal spot to escape the thrill of downtown. Don't expect too much tranquility though: Shanghai parks are renowned for being some of the noisiest places in the city.

GO-KARTS
STAMPEDE KARTING

Basement C, Bailian Shopping Center, 1288 Zhenguang Lu, near Meichuan Lu, 10/6139-5095, www.stampedekarting.com
HOURS: Daily 11 A.M.-2 A.M.
COST: ¥85 for seven minutes
METRO: Beixingjing (Line 2)
Map 12

Let out your frustrations with the Shanghai traffic at Stampede Karting, the city's premier go-karting rink located just north of the main city. At 5,000 square meters (53,800 sq. ft.), it's

the biggest go-kart track in Asia. A race doesn't come cheap, but it's worth it for the quality of the equipment and the Bose sound system blaring tunes. The bar area is quite glamorous, with booths and banquettes overlooking the track. Bar food includes imaginatively named bites like "Pit Lane Squid Balls," Taiwanese chicken nuggets, and an array of Western fast food done well. Stampede Karting was dreamt up in 2008 by wealthy go-kart enthusiasts and came into fruition in 2010.

GYMS
ONEWELLNESS

2/F, Bldg. C, 98 Yanping Lu, 21/6267-1550, www.onewellness.com.cn
HOURS: Daily 6 A.M.-11 P.M.
COST: Day pass ¥100
METRO: Jing'an Temple (Line 2, Line 7)
Map 9

Designed as a showcase for the equipment produced by Technogym (which has an office in the same complex), OneWellness is popular with the many expatriates who live in this part of Jing'an District. It's cleaner and better managed than many Shanghai gyms and employs trainers from China and abroad to teach Pilates, yoga, weight, and aerobics classes. The gym is divided into two floors, with the changing rooms, studio, juice bar, and terrace on the 1st and the machines and weights on the mezzanine above. High, wood-beamed ceilings create an airy atmosphere. Full-time membership doesn't come cheap, but day and short-term passes are available.

HIKING AND BIKING
◖ BOHDI ADVENTURES

Room 2308, Bldg. 2, 2918 Zhongshan Beilu, near Caoyang Lu, 21/5266-9013, www.bohdi.com.cn
HOURS: Daily 9 A.M.-7 P.M.
COST: ¥500 day trip, ¥1,300 overnight trip
METRO: Caoyang Road (Line 3, Line 4)
Map 12

Escape the city with a BOHDI Adventures trip. Dedicate a whole day to cycling in the bamboo-groves of Moganshan near Hangzhou or spend an afternoon exploring a water town on foot or by bike. If you want to get out of town overnight, sign up for a two-day visit to a nearby mountain or lake. With over a decade of experience, BOHDI is well-placed to provide safe, fun, and interesting trips. You don't even need to leave Shanghai; they also run nighttime bike rides and walks. All biking equipment is provided, so all you need to do is show up. Also included in your trip fee are transportation, outdoor insurance, water, and food.

SPECTATOR SPORTS
SHANGHAI SHENHUA FOOTBALL CLUB

Hongkou Football Stadium, 444 Dongjiangwan Lu, 21/5812-8877, www.shenhuafc.com.cn

COST: ¥40

METRO: Hongkou Football Stadium (Line 3, Line 8)

Map 12

A proud member of the Chinese Super League, Shanghai Shenhua soccer club is based at Hongkou Stadium in the north of town. When the guys aren't playing, the venue is given over to concerts and events, but during soccer season it comes alive with cheering fans. Shenhua used to be called Shanghai Football Club. It only turned professional in 1993. The team was bought in 2007 by businessman Zhu Jun, who is a part-owner, along with Shanghai Media and Entertainment Group and several other investors. The team's rival, Shanghai United, is also owned by Zhu Jun, but there seems to be no conflict of interest. There are several foreign players on the team, though Shenhua is predominantly Chinese. Call ahead or check the local English press for details of games when you're in town.

GUIDED TOURS
◖ SHANGHAI SIDEWAYS

Meeting points at various places around town, 138/1761-6975, www.shanghaisideways.com

COST: ¥5

Touring the Old French Concession from the sidecar of a vintage, WWII-era motorbike is one of the most fun and unique ways of getting to know the area. The Shanghai Sideways team is made up of expert bikers with an encyclopedic knowledge of the city, who will help you design your trip beforehand. Tours run for one, two, or four hours and take in a mixture of famous sites and secret corners. If you're interested in other parts of town, Shanghai Sideways can also take you up to the old boundaries of the International Settlements in the north part of the city and across the river to Lujiazui.

SHOPS

With a treasure trove of boutiques, craft shops, mammoth malls, and everything in between, Shanghai won't disappoint when it comes to shopping. As you'd expect from a city that is China's financial nerve center, there's plenty of money flying around, evidenced by the Lamborghini showrooms, Gucci stores, and Cartier boutiques. Take a walk down West Nanjing Road and it won't be long before you hit a luxury mall. However, there's more to Shanghai's retail offerings than bling alone. Mid-range Western names like H&M and Gap are well represented, as well as many domestic Chinese brands. The Old French Concession is home to some lovely independent boutiques selling clothing, shoes, and housewares; Xinle Road and Changle Road are particularly good for clothing.

The "fake market" phenomenon is one that you'll either embrace or choose to shun completely, depending on your stance on intellectual property. If you're keen to take home a replica Mulberry satchel or Louis Vuitton wallet, you'll definitely find one. Often, vendors keep their best quality goods behind a false screen, so make it clear that you want the best and you'll be ushered into their secret stockroom. Most vendors speak limited English, but most transactions are bashed out with a calculator and vehement gestures.

Shanghai's main fabric market is great for having clothes tailored, but the process takes a good week from measurements to completion. If you're in Shanghai for more than a week, go to the market on your first day so that there's time to pick up your clothing before you leave. If it's gifts and souvenirs you're after, try the Dongtai Road Antiques Market or the huge bazaar at the Yu Garden.

© SUZHOU COBBLERS

HIGHLIGHTS

LOOK FOR ❰ TO FIND RECOMMENDED SHOPS.

❰ **Most Fashionable:** Snap up some one-off local designs as you wander down picturesque **Changle Road and Xinle Road** (page 234).

❰ **Best Knickknacks:** Get your fill of kitschy Communist statues, retro housewares, and traditional Chinese souvenirs at **Dongtai Road Antiques Market** (page 234).

❰ **Best Haggling:** Hone your bargaining skills and nab some knock-off designer gear at **Fenshine Plaza** (page 235).

❰ **Best Mall:** The **Super Brand Mall,** in a prime Pudong District location, has floor upon floor of mid-range designer brands, along with a large selection of restaurants to choose from (page 237).

❰ **Best Nostalgia:** Browse books of photography (compiled by the owners) charting Shanghai's past over a coffee at the **Old China Hand Reading Room** (page 240).

❰ **Best Sneakers:** Get your hands (and feet) on a pair of classic Feiyue or Huili sneakers at **Culture Matters** (page 241).

❰ **Most Eco-Friendly Fashion:** Improve your wardrobe and do the environment a favor by shopping at **NuoMi,** a boutique that focuses on producing garments with sustainable products like bamboo and soy (page 242).

❰ **Best Electronics:** Stock up on the latest and greatest tech gadgets at the **Pacific Digital Plaza** (page 245).

❰ **Most Classy Kitsch: Madame Mao's Dowry** sells high-quality retro ornaments, gifts, and clothing (page 245).

❰ **Best Tea:** Stock up on high-quality Chinese and European teas at **Song Fang Maison de Thé**; be sure to get some caddies and tins in the boutique's signature robin's-egg blue (page 246).

Song Fang Maison de Thé

Shopping Districts

⬛ CHANGLE ROAD AND XINLE ROAD

Changle Lu (btwn. Fumin Lu and Shaanxi Lu) and Xinle Lu (btwn. Fumin Lu and Xiangyang Lu)
HOURS: Varies by shop
METRO: Changshu Road (Line 2, 7)
Map 10

Changle and Xinle Roads are leafy, photogenic streets. They run parallel from east to west across the Old French Concession and are known for their plethora of clothing and accessory shops. Xinle Road is the shorter of the two, so start at the junction of North Xiangyang Road and head west. You'll pass a variety of local clothes shops; the choices get better the farther west you go. The Source (No. 158) is a hipster haven and NuoMi (No. 196) is great for eco-conscious womenswear. Get onto Changle Road via Fumin Road and head east. The portion that stretches as far as South Shaanxi Road has plenty of great shops (including a bunch of maternity-wear boutiques close to the children's hospital)

but it starts to get a bit "Watch? Bag? DVD?" thereafter.

WEST NANJING ROAD

Nanjing Xilu, btwn. Tongren Lu and Chengdu Beilu
HOURS: Varies by shop
METRO: West Nanjing Road (Line 2)
Map 9

The stretch of West Nanjing Road that lies between Tongren Road to the west and North Chengdu Road to the east is lined with shops of every imaginable sort. The western end is populated by high-rise malls like Plaza 66, Citic Square, and the Westgate Center, while the area around the Metro station is home to international brands and stores like Gap, Nike, UNIQLO, and Marks & Spencer. At street level you'll find jewelers, Chinese-brand clothing stores, confectionery shops, and opticians. Stop for a bite to eat on pedestrian Wujiang Road just behind West Nanjing Road or have a coffee on a terrace and watch the shoppers pass by.

Department Stores, Malls, and Markets

ASIA PACIFIC XINYANG PLAZA

Inside Science and Technology Museum Metro Station
HOURS: Daily 9 A.M.-late
METRO: Science and Technology Museum (Line 2)
Map 11

Cousin to Puxi's Fenshine Plaza, this sprawling mall is conveniently located inside the Shanghai Science and Technology Museum's metro station. The southern half is a fabric market where you can buy suits, skirts, shirts, and pretty much anything else made to order. The northern half is a haven of knockoff bags, watches, and sunglasses. Vendors can be extremely pushy, so be prepared to stand your ground. Be sure to offer 10–30 percent of their original asking price and be prepared to haggle. Fakes range from totally convincing to laughably bad, but there are also some decent original gift items, like silk dressing

gowns, jade statues, and decorated chopsticks, to be found.

⬛ DONGTAI ROAD ANTIQUES MARKET

Xizang Lu, near Liuhe Lu
HOURS: Daily 9 A.M.-6 P.M.
METRO: Laoximen (Line 10)
Map 11

Get your Mao memorabilia and propaganda posters at the Dongtai Road Antiques Market. While most of the items on display have a history no longer than a couple of years (decades at the very most), there are some great, quirky items to be had if you have the time to browse. The market is laid out across an axis of four narrow pedestrian streets that meet in the middle. Some specialize in old alarm clocks, some in beat-up suitcases, and some in carved wood. Others sell vintage photographs, ceramic statues of Mao, and every permutation of jade and wooden statuary. There's also Yunnan-style fabric, fans, and typical Chinese souvenirs. Be prepared to bargain.

◖ FENSHINE PLAZA
580 Nanjing Xilu, near Chengdu Beilu
HOURS: Daily 10 A.M.-10 P.M.
METRO: West Nanjing Road (Line 2)
Map 9

Whatever your stance on *shanzhai* (fake goods), you'll find them in abundance here. Look away now if the thought of faux Vuitton and ersatz Gucci makes you cringe. Intellectual property laws go out the window at Fenshine. However, if you're on the hunt for some *shanzhai* designer goods, be prepared to haggle hard. Don't accept a vendor's first price: Offer 10 percent of the price and see what they say. If the vendor doesn't budge, offer a third of the original price. Beware: Stall holders here are known to be relentless. Hold your ground and don't be intimidated, and that knock-off Mulberry Alexa will be yours. There's also plenty of gift-worthy chinoiserie, like silk dressing gowns, chopsticks, jade figurines, and other assorted knick-knacks.

GRAND GATEWAY
1 Hongqiao Lu, near Huashan Lu, 21/6407-0111
HOURS: Daily 10 A.M.-10 P.M.
METRO: Xujiahui (Line 1, Line 9)
Map 12

Nestled between Xujiahui's 52-story landmark twin towers, the Grand Gateway mall spans six floors. With international brands, a multitude of restaurants, and a multiplex cinema, it's a retail haven in the center of Shanghai's commercial hub. Easily accessible by the metro and a short taxi ride from People's Square, it is one of the city's most popular malls. The Grand Gateway complex was completed in 2005 after a long hiatus caused by the Asian Financial Crisis. The twin towers are the 9th tallest buildings in Shanghai and 71st tallest in the world. Being the only tall buildings in the area, they are particularly striking.

IFC MALL
8 Shiji Dadao, near Lujiazui Huan Lu, 21/2020-7000
HOURS: Daily 10 A.M.-10 P.M.
METRO: Lujiazui (Line 2)
Map 11

Pudong's newest shopping mall is a deluxe addition to the area's already booming retail

---

FAKING IT

There's pretty much nothing that can't (and won't) be faked in China. From DVDs and designer bags right through to smartphones and even foodstuffs (fake peas, anyone?), nothing escapes being cloned. All Westerners will at some stage be accosted with shouts of "Watch? Bag? DVD?" while walking down Nanjing, Huaihai, or Shaanxi Roads and those who follow the vendors down narrow alleys will be led into warehouses filled with knockoff Rolex, Gucci, Prada, and Chanel. The two main fake markets on West Nanjing Road and in the Science and Tech Museum metro station are huge emporia dedicated to designer rip-offs. Of course, copyright infringement is illegal, but the police turn a blind eye. Token crackdowns occur once in a while, but things get back to normal almost immediately. For the sake of appearances, most of the city's fake DVD shops were converted into legitimate stores by the addition of false walls. Only genuine items are on display in the shop front, but merchants are permitted to pass through a secret door to access the true stock behind it.

Many visitors see the fake markets as a source of funky gifts or a chance to grab the latest Chanel purse without paying top dollar. However, as harmless as the industry sounds, serious issues bubble under the surface. The fake industry fuels a whole network of organized crime across Asia and the rest of the world and the infringement of intellectual property laws is damaging for legitimate companies.

landscape. It sits at the bottom of the new International Finance Center, below the twin towers that make up part of Shanghai's modern skyline. The six-floor, glass-fronted ifc Mall holds luxury Western brands, like Bottega Veneta and Charlotte Ronson, as well as a wide variety of food offerings, including Haiku by Hatsune sushi, Donut King, Morton's The Steakhouse, and ISOLA Italian. It is also home to Shanghai's flagship Apple store. In the basement is a sprawling organic supermarket and Western-style delicatessen. The ifc complex was designed by Cesar Pelli and contains Grade A office space and a Ritz-Carlton hotel.

INPOINT MALL
169 Wujiang Lu
HOURS: Daily 10 A.M.–10 P.M.
METRO: West Nanjing Road (Line 2)
Map 9

Many Shanghainese lament the loss of Wujiang Road's former status as a bustling food street full of local restaurants and snack vendors. Running parallel to West Nanjing Road, the street's eastern half is now dominated by the InPoint Mall, while the western part is still undergoing redevelopment. Despite the destruction of the food street, Wujiang Road's current incarnation has a festive atmosphere as a pedestrian stretch filled with cafés and open-air restaurants. Some of these are part of InPoint, such as Costa, Coffee Bean, Krispy Kreme, and Carls Jr. Inside the mall are four levels of mainly local shops and a food court.

PARKSON
918 Huaihai Zhonglu, 21/6415-8818,
www.parkson.com.cn
HOURS: Daily 10 A.M.–10 P.M.
METRO: South Shaanxi Road (Line 1, Line 10)
Map 10

Parkson is the department store of choice for middle-class Shanghainese. It has clothes, accessories, electronics, and beauty products under one roof, as well as restaurants and cafés. The Parkson empire began in Beijing in 1994 to cater to the ever-growing mid-range earners with money to spend. It now has stores in 30 cities across China, with three branches in Shanghai. Even if you're not looking to buy anything, it's interesting to walk around and compare it to department stores back home. Aside from the Chinese characters on the signs and the local designer boutiques, it isn't that different.

PLAZA 66
1266 Nanjing Xilu, near Shaanxi Beilu, 21/6279-0910
HOURS: Daily 10 A.M.–10 P.M.
METRO: West Nanjing Road (Line 2)
Map 9

Located inside the tallest building this side of the river, Plaza 66 gathers international luxury designers like Prada and Gucci along with mid-range brands like Miss Sixty and French Connection. The exterior square is used for seasonal displays, while the interior is bright, marble-clad, and super-shiny—everything you'd expect from a high-end Shanghai mall. The basement and 5th floor have some good dining choices, including the upmarket TMSK Peony and spicy Sichuanese chain Pin Chuan. Plaza 66 is right next door to several other big malls, so if you don't find what you're looking for, there are plenty more choices nearby.

RAFFLES CITY
268 Xizang Zhonglu, near Fuzhou Lu, 21/6340-3600
HOURS: Daily 10 A.M.–10 P.M.
METRO: People's Square (Line 1, Line 2, Line 8), exit 15
Map 8

The Raffles City complex opened in 2003 and is comprised of an office tower and an eight-floor shopping mall, as well as an exit of the People's Square metro station. There is an array of international mid-range fashion and lifestyle brands available here. Standalone stalls sell more interesting goods like jewelry, kitsch gifts, and accessories. In the basement you'll find Western snack food like Subway, Cold Stone Creamery, Papa John's, and Carl's Jr. and there's a Starbucks on street level if you can't live without a caramel macchiato. More substantial dining options are dotted across the floors.

SOUTH BUND FABRIC MARKET
399 Lujiabang Lu, near Zhongshan Nanlu,

21/6377-7288
HOURS: 9 A.M.-6:30 P.M.
METRO: Nanpu Bridge (Line 9)
`Map 11`

If you have more than a week in Shanghai and fancy some tailor-made threads, head to the South Bund Fabric Market as soon as you arrive and your goods will be ready by the time you leave. The market has stalls catering to every imaginable garment, from dresses and skirts to denim jeans. As for choosing a specific stall, it's often the luck of the draw. Most will have examples of their work on mannequins outside, which is a good indicator of their style and quality. All vendors will be happy to copy items from photographs or from existing garments.

◖ SUPER BRAND MALL

168 Lujiazui Xilu, near Lujiazui Huan Lu, 21/6887-7888
HOURS: Daily 10 A.M.-10 P.M.
METRO: Lujiazui (Line 10)
`Map 11`

Built in 2004, Super Brand is one of Shanghai's longest established shopping malls. Covering 13 floors inside a striking domed building crouching among the skyscrapers, it received China's Golden Mall award in 2006. At busy times, around 300,000 visitors pass through its doors each day. Inside you'll find a lattice of escalators leading up through the atrium to the various floors. Brands like Sephora, UNIQLO, H&M, Zara, and Benetton dominate the floor space. Food and drink options include Coffee Bean and Tea Leaf, Starbucks, and several decent restaurants like Element Fresh (healthy Western salads and sandwiches) and South Beauty (spicy Sichuan fare).

TIANZIFANG

Nong 210 Taikang Lu, near Sinan Lu, www.taikanglu.com
METRO: Dapu Bridge (Line 9)
`Map 10`

Tianzifang's lanes are full of one-off boutiques, art studios, and gift shops, making it the ideal one-stop location for gift buying. You'll get better bargains at the Yu Garden bazaar, but Tianzifang has higher quality goods. Most shops are fixed price, which is an advantage if you can't get your head around haggling. Top

shopping spots are Shokay (Lane 210, No. 9) for ethically-produced Tibetan yak knitwear, ChuQiBuYi (Lane 248, No. 51) for fabric teddy bears handmade near Hangzhou, and Roger & Guy (Lane 210, No. 3) for contemporary home accessories with a Chinese twist. If you need refreshment, try Bell Café (Lane 248, No. 11).

XINTIANDI STYLE

245 Madang Lu, Xintiandi, 21/5382-0666, www.xintiandistyle.com
HOURS: Daily 10 A.M.-10 P.M.
METRO: Xintiandi (Line 10)
`Map 10`

This extension of the Xintiandi lifestyle hub is a welcome addition to an area that is a magnet for money. It is one of the newest malls in Shanghai and benefits from its position close to the retail heaven of Huaihai Road to the north. Xintiandi has always attracted Shanghai's richest and Xintiandi Style doesn't disappoint when it comes to high-end shops. However, there are plenty of mid-range names represented, such as Nine West and Steve Madden, and lots of local designers. The mall connects to the South Block of Xintiandi and covers four floors, two in the basement and two above ground. Food and beverage outlets include Costa Coffee, Coffee Bean, and Dairy Queen.

YU GARDEN BAZAAR

Anjie Lu, near Fuyou Lu
HOURS: Daily 9 A.M.-5:30 P.M.
METRO: Yu Garden (Line 10)
`Map 11`

The shops that make up about half of the Yu Garden complex range from tacky toy stalls to gold and jade boutiques. It's a tourist trap to be sure, but worth a look for typical Chinese souvenirs like decorated chopsticks, fans, and embroidered silk. The bazaar and garden get absolutely rammed at holiday periods and are best avoided. Outside of the main complex is a street of low-rise stalls selling similar goods. Also in the Fangbang Road vicinity is the Yu Cheng Fashion Garden and Dragon Gate Mall, both of which contain modern brands and stores like Marks & Spencer.

Bath, Beauty, and Massage

APSARA

457 Shaanxi Beilu, 21/6258-5580, www.apsara.com.cn
HOURS: Daily 11 A.M.-midnight
METRO: West Nanjing Road (Line 2)
Map 9

Treat yourself to some pampering at the luxurious (but reasonably priced) Apsara in Jing'an. Just north of busy West Nanjing Road on a quiet stretch of North Shaanxi Road, Apsara is a Cambodian-style spa using imported products. It is named after the legendary Cambodian dancing goddesses who are depicted on the walls of the Angkor Wat temples. The spa is a tranquil retreat from the noisy city. You'll feel your stress go down a couple of notches as soon as you step inside. Staff are polite and well trained and the treatment rooms are warm, dimly lit havens, subtly decorated in Southeast Asian style. Choose from head, foot, and body massages; body scrubs; facials; waxing; and slimming treatments.

DRAGONFLY SPA

84 Nanchang Lu, near Yandang Lu, 21/5386-0060, www.dragonfly.net.cn
HOURS: Daily 10 A.M.-midnight
METRO: South Shaanxi Road (Line 1, Line 10)
Map 10

The Dragonfly chain is a cut above your average street-side massage parlor and you know exactly what you're going to get: clean, warm massage rooms with soft lighting, trickling Zen water features, and professional staff. You'll pay a bit more for the privilege, but it's worth it if you're not familiar with massage etiquette. This branch offers the full gamut of foot and body massages, as well as facials, waxing, and manicure and pedicure treatments. Dragonfly has stores across China from Qingdao to Hong Kong, with nine in Shanghai alone. A relaxing foot or back massage is a perfect end to a busy day of sightseeing.

FRANCK PROVOST

Shop 2, 164 Anfu Lu, 21/3356-3188,

NAVIGATING SHANGHAI'S MASSAGE CULTURE

Shanghai didn't get its reputation as a city of sin for nothing. The seedier side of the city is especially visible in the side-street "massage parlors" with their glowing pink lights. If you're a guy who is looking for an innocent body or foot massage, you should avoid these places unless you want to be propositioned for other services.

Shanghai has many blind massage parlors, which offer a legitimate source of work for sightless people. These are always above board, as are the branded chains like Dragonfly, Jiu Hao, and Apsara. Most of the 5-star hotels have spas and massage rooms, but are significantly more expensive than street-side parlors. If you're not sure whether your parlor of choice is dodgy and don't fancy being pestered to buy "extras," go with a partner or female friend and request to stay together for your massage.

www.franckprovost.com.cm
HOURS: Daily 10 A.M.-10 P.M.
METRO: Changshu Road (Line 1, Line 7)
Map 10

Parisian salon Franck Provost has been voted number one in Europe and number two in the whole world and has a presence in 25 countries across the globe. Franck has four salons in Shanghai; the Anfu Road branch is the newest. Stylists are rigorously trained in the ways of Western hairstyles, so you can feel confident entrusting your locks to their capable hands. Jazz music plays and the smart white-and-black interior creates a trendy vibe. Stylists use products from L'Oréal and Kérastase and many can speak English and French. Franck Provost has a pedigree of 30 years in Paris, and international fans include Penélope Cruz, Naomi Campbell, and Diane Krueger.

GLAMOUR NAILS

208 Nanyang Lu, 21/6279-0170
HOURS: Daily 11 A.M.-11 P.M.
METRO: Jing'an Temple (Line 2, Line 7)
Map 9

Manicures and pedicures are amazingly cheap in China compared to overseas. Glamour Nails is one of Shanghai's many independent parlors. The dinky salon contains two throne-like massage chairs for pedicures and a long table where four people can get their nails done at the same time. Choose from two whole walls of nail polish from O.P.I., Essie, and Chanel and browse English and American magazines while you're being primped. If you fancy something a little wilder than the regular colors, go for a glittery overlay or jewel decorations. Depending on how extravagant you go, a mani/pedi should set you back no more than ¥200. Staff speak limited English, but the manager is fluent. Every customer gets a free drink from the menu, which runs from beer to soda and herbal tea. There's a display cabinet full of glittery jewelry and phone accessories and a DVD shop in the back.

GOLDEN RESORT

678 Shaanxi Beilu, near Wuding Lu, 21/6217-8628
HOURS: Daily noon-2 A.M.
METRO: Changping Road (Line 7)
Map 9

Cheaper than the multi-chain downtown massage parlors, Golden Resort is surprisingly luxurious once you navigate the rather nondescript storefront entrance. Go down the stairs into the cavernous but tranquil basement, where candles flicker and the smell of incense abounds. You'll swap your shoes for straw sandals and sip complimentary tea before your treatment. Choose from Chinese or Balinese oil massage techniques on your feet, body, or head and zone out while the masseurs work their magic. If you're here with a friend or a partner, you can request a double room. Afterward you'll be given a tropical fruit plate while staff retrieve your shoes.

SHANGHAI TATTOO

Maoming Nanlu, near Yan'an Lu, 135/8594-4558,
www.shanghaitattoo.com
HOURS: Daily 11 A.M.-10 P.M.
METRO: Xiaonanmen (Line 9)
Map 10

More than just a tattoo parlor, Shanghai Tattoo is central to the city's inking community, from tattoo fans to artists and designers. Run by charismatic tattooists Ting Ting and Dylan (both speak English), it is one of the only reputable and reliable parlors in town. If you fancy getting inked to commemorate your visit to Shanghai, this is the place to do it. Electro music plays while the artists work, scoring tribal designs, Chinese calligraphy, portraits, and cover-ups onto willing bodies. It's not always necessary to make an appointment, but calling ahead is a good idea, especially so the artists can have some prior warning to prepare the design of your dreams. All needles are single-use only and equipment is thoroughly sterilized between clients. Shanghai Tattoo also sells a huge array of body jewelry.

SKIN CITY 5.5

476 Dagu Lu, 21/6340-1235, www.skincity55.com
HOURS: Daily 10 A.M.-10 P.M.
METRO: West Nanjing Road (Line 2)
Map 9

Run by a super-friendly woman named Connie who has a passion for spas, Skin City 5.5 is located on foreigner-friendly Dagu Road near People's Square. It's modern and funky inside, with photography by American artist Trey Ratcliff on the walls. You can choose what type of music is played in your treatment room before you go in and pick from a menu of massages, facials, scrubs, and microdermabrasion. Skin City uses products by German brand Babor and has six treatment rooms, two VIP suites, and several steam rooms. Massage therapists don't tend to speak English, but the manager and receptionist do, so you should have no problem communicating.

SUGAR & SPICE

193 Jiaozhou Lu, 21/5213-5777
HOURS: Daily 11 A.M.-midnight

SHOPS

METRO: Jing'an Temple (Line 2, Line 7)
Map 9

Head to the cozy Sugar & Spice massage parlor for guaranteed cleanliness and good service. Although the masseuses don't speak much English, the bilingual treatment menu is all you need. The half-hour head, neck, and shoulder massage is particularly good. You can choose one area for the masseuse to concentrate on. The parlor is named after its two female managers and has a relaxing, Zen-like atmosphere with Southeast Asian accents. In terms of price, Sugar & Spice sits between the expensive hotel spas and the lower-end street parlors. If you like a particular masseuse and want to visit again, ask for her staff number and request her again when you go back.

Books

CHATERHOUSE
Shop 104, Shanghai Center, 1376 Nanjing Xilu, near Xikang Lu, 21/6279-7633
HOURS: Daily 9 A.M.–9 P.M.
METRO: Jing'an Temple (Line 2, Line 7)
Map 9

Chaterhouse is originally a Hong Kong brand. This little store is popular among the expatriates who live in the Shanghai Center's attached apartments. It stocks a good selection of books by mainly English and American authors, as well as notebooks and gifts. Because most of the books are imported, prices tend to be steeper than what you'd pay back home, but it's fine for emergency reading material and local interest titles that you might not find anywhere else. Fiction is near the front of the shop, along with staff picks. Head to the back for Western magazines and children's books.

GARDEN BOOKS
325 Changle Lu, near Shaanxi Nanlu, 21/5404-8728, www.gardenbooks.cn
HOURS: Daily 10 A.M.–10 P.M.
METRO: South Shaanxi Road (Line 1, Line 10)
Map 10

Garden Books combines a bookshop, café, and a gelateria. The bookshop has a wide selection of literature in English, French, and Spanish, as well as Mandarin study guides, notebooks, and travel titles. The China interest section is one of the most comprehensive in town. Garden has a reputation for hosting regular author events with well-known writers; many of the locally published books you see will be signed copies. Prices for imported books are worked out by current exchange rates. Head up to the 2nd floor to peruse Chinese art prints or dive into your new book over a coffee and ice cream.

◖ OLD CHINA HAND READING ROOM
27 Shaoxing Lu, near Shaanxi Nanlu, 21/6473-2526, www.han-yuan.com/shudian/main-haibao.htm
HOURS: Daily 10 A.M.–midnight
METRO: Jiashan Road (Line 9)
Map 10

Run by local photographer Deke Erh and Shanghai historian Tess Johnston, this small café is replete with antiques and books. A big, curved bookshelf takes pride of place in the tastefully decorated room. Together, Erh and Johnston have put together an invaluable body of work to document and preserve Shanghai's history in the face of development and destruction, he with his camera and she with her words. Erh's special focus is Shanghai's art deco architecture; the city has the highest concentration of art deco buildings anywhere in the world. A small selection of snacks and drinks are available.

SHANGHAI BOOK TRADERS
390 Fuzhou Lu, near Fujian Lu, 21/2320-4994
HOURS: Daily 9:30 A.M.–7 P.M.
METRO: East Nanjing Road (Line 2, Line 10)
Map 8

Fuzhou Road is the place to go in Shanghai when you're looking for art supplies, stationery, engraving services, and books. The stretch between Yunnan Road and Henan Road is lined with stores carrying everything from human-size calligraphy brushes to imported magazines. Shanghai Book Traders has the best stock of

English language books in town and the prices tend to be around the same as what you'd pay back home. If your trip inspires you to learn some Mandarin, this is a good place to pick up some learning materials. When you enter the store, turn right for English fiction and left for language books. Upstairs you'll find more fiction, plus foreign magazines. Also for sale are electronic dictionaries, bargain Western classics, and music CDs.

Clothing and Shoes

◖ CULTURE MATTERS
63 Jing'an Villa, Nong 1025 Nanjing Xilu, near Maoming Beilu, 21/5213-0889
HOURS: Daily noon–9 P.M.
METRO: West Nanjing Road (Line 2)
Map 9

This shop lies off the beaten track down picturesque Lane 1025 and stocks every imaginable permutation of China's answer to Converse, the mighty Huili (Warrior) shoe. Created in the 1970s, Huili was the nation's first homegrown sneaker and is still popular among hipsters and kung fu practitioners alike. For an extra cost, Culture Matters will customize a pair for you. Or, you can pick from the ready-decorated pairs. The shop also sells original Shanghainese Feiyue sneakers with their distinctive red and blue logo. Culture Matters isn't the only place to buy Feiyue and Huili shoes, but it definitely has the best selection and most creative renderings.

DUTCH ITEMS SHANGHAI
Block K, Rm. 111 and Basement, Ferguson Lane Complex, 376 Wukang Lu, 21/6126-7661, www.disshanghai.com
HOURS: Sun.-Fri. 10 A.M.-6 P.M., Sat. 10 A.M.-7 P.M.
METRO: Shanghai Library (Line 10)
Map 12

Fashion in the Netherlands is simple, functional, and built to last. This two-shop clothing boutique in the Ferguson Lane complex on Wukang Road showcases the designs of Dutch Jolie van Beek. She brought her concept to Shanghai in 2006 and proved instantly popular among women in their 30s and older. Her block color garments with their clean lines and quality fabrics appeal to more sophisticated dressers and the European sizes cater to Shanghai's expat

THAT'S CONVENIENT: SHANGHAI'S CORNER STORES

In a 24-hour city like Shanghai, you don't have to worry if you forgot to buy milk or need a beer fix at 4 A.M. There's a convenience store on literally every street. Open around the clock, these handy shops sell essentials like soft and hard drinks, phone cards, cigarettes, candy, chips, basic toiletries, magazines, fruit, and eggs. The main chains are Lawson's, Kedi, and All Days, with Seven Elevens springing up in ever-greater regularity. Middle-aged Shanghainese women, who get grumpier as the night wears on, generally staff these much-loved shops. Many convenience stores have a distinctive aroma thanks to the snack skewers that sit stewing on the counter. For a couple of kuai you can pick up a paper cup full of oddly shaped reconstituted meat and fish chunks. They are hugely popular with the after-school crowd and are actually quite tasty, but the smell might put you off.

population. As well as van Beek's own designs, Dutch Items stocks garments from Netherlands designers, like eco-label The Barn, and has farther branches in Pudong and Hongqiao.

KAILEENI
2/F, Bldg. 3, Nong 179 Chongqing Nanlu, 21/6386-3417, www.kaileeni.com
HOURS: By appointment only

Mayumi Sato boutique on Anfu Road

METRO: South Huangpi Road (Line 1)

Map 10

Chinese-American apparel designer Cairn Wu Reppun was born and brought up in Los Angeles and is the creative director of a fashion boutique called William the Beekeeper at 84 Fenyang Road. She started Kaileeni—her own personal fashion line—in 2007 after leaving a career in economics and moving to Shanghai. Inspired by the urban environment, her line consists of ready-to-wear menswear and womenswear and accessories in mainly neutral tones. Reppun constructs many of her garments out of vintage fabric, and adds quirky touches and androgynous elements. Her full range is only viewable by appointment, but William the Beekeeper stocks some pieces.

MAYUMI SATO

196 Anfu Lu, near Wulumuqi Lu, 21/5303-3903, www.mayumisato.com
HOURS: Daily noon–9 P.M.
METRO: Changshu Road (Line 1, Line 7)

Map 10

This cute boutique with its red polka dot awning is a great place to find unique, individual pieces. Featured frequently in Asian fashion magazines, Japanese designer Mayumi Sato creates fun, casual wear with a twist. Sato uses 100 percent natural silk, cashmere, and cotton to craft her brightly patterned pieces, as well as vintage kimono fabric. Since her first collection back in 2006, she has used all her fabric scraps to make pom-poms. These are often her most popular items and she uses them to decorate accessories like belts and hats. She updates her designs each season and only ever makes a handful of each garment.

NUOMI

96 Xinle Lu, near Donghu Lu, 21/5403-4199
HOURS: Daily 11 A.M.–10 P.M.
METRO: South Shaanxi Road (Line 1, Line 10)

Map 10

This small, white-fronted boutique sells unique, eco-conscious womenswear made from materials like soy, cotton, and bamboo. NuoMi's style is sophisticated-casual, rather

Shanghai Tang

than hippy-dippy, and prices reflect the quality. It's great for items like plain T-shirts, neutral-colored cardigans, and quirky skirts. The brand has grown to five branches since 2006 and is managed by Filipina fashion designer Bonita Lim who was honored as "most stylish woman" at the 2009 Asian Tatler Ball. NuoMi means sticky rice in Mandarin, which is a reference to Bonita's grassroots charitable work with developing countries.

SHANGHAI TANG

Xintiandi North Block, Nong 181 Taicang Lu, 21/6384-1601, www.shanghaitang.com
HOURS: Daily 10:30 A.M.–11 P.M.
METRO: South Huangpi Road (Line 1)
Map 10

Take home some designer clothes with traditional Chinese influences at the Xintiandi branch of this Hong Kong fashion chain. Shanghai Tang was established in 1994 and is famous for its beautiful, high-quality clothes and accessories for men and women. Designed for modern times while paying homage to

Chinese heritage, its garments have a distinctive appearance. Traditional fabrics and materials like jade, silk, and cashmere are used to craft scarves, jewelry, and clothing, and a personal tailoring service is available for made-to-order items. There are 40 Shanghai Tang boutiques across the world, of which 3 are in Shanghai.

SHIRTFLAG

240 Taikang Lu, 136/8175-1804, www.shirtflag.com
HOURS: Daily 10:30 A.M.–8 P.M.
METRO: Dapu Bridge (Line 9)
Map 10

If you've been to Beijing and bought a T-shirt from Plastered, add to your collection at ShirtFlag, a fashion brand established in 2003 that sells tongue-in-cheek shirts with propaganda-style logos and motifs. With a second branch in Moganshan Road's M50 art district, ShirtFlag appeals to hipsters, rebels, and creative souls who like to make a statement. If you like the simple but eye-catching (and politically charged) images from Communist propaganda art, you'll love ShirtFlag's designs. East and West are blended ironically, with socialist workers holding up a Gameboy, a Chinese maiden with McDonald's on her mind, and other irreverent images. As well as T-shirts, the store sells hoodies, bags, badges, and other giftworthy items.

SUZHOU COBBLERS

Rm. 101, 17 Fuzhou Lu, near Zhongshan Dongyilu, 21/6321-7087, www.suzhou-cobblers.com
HOURS: Daily 10 A.M.–6:30 P.M.
METRO: East Nanjing Road (Line 2, Line 10)
Map 7

For the sort of silk slippers you won't find at the markets, pay a visit to Suzhou Cobblers. Even if you don't end up buying a pair, you won't forget the sight of all that beautiful fabric and intricate embroidery. The store is owned and run by Huang Mengqi, who likes to be known as Denise. Back in 1998 she realized that there were no traditional shoemakers left who still made silk slippers, so she decided to open a cobbler shop. She changes her designs frequently, giving them cute names like Mandarin Duck, Plum Flower, and—less cute—Propaganda. All slippers have leather soles and come in slip-on or arch-back styles. If you regret not buying a pair when you get home, the good news is that they ship worldwide through their website.

THE VILLA

1 Taojiang Lu, 21/6466-9322, www.shopthevilla.com
HOURS: Tues.-Sun. 11 A.M.-9 P.M.
METRO: Changshu Road (Line 1, Line 7)
Map 10

Featured in *Elle China,* The Villa became an instant hit with Shanghai's fashion addicts as soon as it opened. The multi-label womenswear boutique gathers pieces from local and Western designers in a beautiful 315-meter (1,033 ft.) space on one of the Old French Concession's leafiest streets. Gorgeous interior decor is the perfect backdrop to garments by the likes of Hervé Leger, Proenza Schouler, Jason Wu, and Marchesa. Each piece is carefully selected by The Villa's owner and manager, Sara Villareal, who likes to stock up-and-coming designers

as well as established names. She's usually on hand to offer style advice and a cup of coffee while you browse.

YOUNIK

2/F, Bund 18, 18 Zhongshan Dongyilu, near Nanjing Donglu, 21/6323-8688
HOURS: Daily 10 A.M.-10 P.M.
METRO: East Nanjing Road (Line 2, Line 10)
Map 7

Opened in 2004 to showcase the work of established Asian designers and newcomers to the trade, YOUNIK occupies prime retail space inside the Bund 18 complex. Floor to ceiling storefront windows display the sartorial delights inside, which include pieces by designers like Uma Wang, Chen Ping, and Jane Zhu. Whether you know their names or not, their clothes are worth a look. You're guaranteed to go home with something unique, as the shop's name promises. As well as selling off-the-rack creations, YOUNIK matches designers with clients in a special program called "Fabrics," in which the designers produce one-off, made-to-order garments for their clients.

Electronics

APPLE STORE

Unit 27, LG2/F, ifc Mall, 8 Shiji Dadao, near Lujiazui Huan Lu, 21/6084-6800
HOURS: Daily 10 A.M.-10 P.M.
METRO: Lujiazui (Line 2)
Map 11

Apple goods are cheaper in China than in many countries and a trip to Shanghai's flagship store in the ifc Mall is a good opportunity to stock up. This Apple store opened to great fanfare in summer 2010. Its entrance is an unusual glass column emblazoned with the company's unmistakable logo, into which guests descend via a staircase. The shop is a temple to all things Apple, stocking the full gamut of products from Nanos and mini MacBook Airs to Apple TVs and desktop computers. The interior is as cool and calm as you'd expect, complete with a Genius Bar, VIP room, and knowledgeable staff.

BU YE CHENG

118 Tianmu Xilu, near Meiyuan Lu
HOURS: Daily 9 A.M.-10 P.M.
METRO: Shanghai Railway Station (Line 1, Line 3, Line 4)
Map 12

Its name means "city that never sleeps" in Mandarin, and Bu Yu Cheng is certainly lively. Shanghai's premier cell phone market hums with life into the late hours, as customers browse the latest models, haggle over prices, and bid for the phone number that contains the most 8s. Bu Yu Cheng sits opposite the Shanghai Railway Station plaza and is impossible to miss thanks to its gold front. Inside are several floors of vendors, each with their wares laid out in glass counters. All the major brands are represented, along with plenty of domestic labels. Some are real and some are fake, so it's a question of trusting your gut or believing the vendor. If you don't want to risk it, there are plenty of phone accessories to browse. Buying a Chinese SIM card and a cheap cell phone to use while you're in Shanghai can work out to be a lot more affordable than roaming on your cell from home.

LOMOGRAPHY

126 Jinxian Lu, near Maoming Lu, 21/6256-1054
HOURS: Daily noon–10 P.M.
METRO: South Shaanxi Road (Line 1, Line 10)
`Map 10`

This five-story shop on Shanghai's funkiest street is a shrine to the analogue art of lomography, an Austrian photography movement inspired by the cameras of the LOMO optical company, distinctive for its characteristic images featuring blur, color saturation, and fish-eye perspective. The shop stocks cameras, film, accessories, and even T-shirts and there's a media lounge on the 2nd floor where you can browse albums of snapshots by local lomo legends. Whether you're an expert on lomo techniques or can't tell a Diana from a Holga, it's interesting to browse the shelves of books and apparatus.

OSCAR'S CLUB

562 Fengyang Lu, near Chengdu Beilu, 21/6217-9229
HOURS: Daily 10 A.M.–11 P.M.
METRO: West Nanjing Road (Line 2)
`Map 9`

Before the great Expo clean-up of early 2010, Shanghai was home to a plethora of knock-off DVD shops. When the police targeted these vast emporia, many of the managers employed sneaky tactics to stay in business, such as creating fake doors and walls to hide the merchandise within. Some ended up closing down altogether, but Oscar's lived to fight another day. The fake doors and walls appear periodically, so you might have to negotiate something of a rabbit warren to get to the good stuff. Alternatively, you may just be able to stroll straight in from the street. Whatever the situation, you'll find plenty of choice. Depending on whether your conscience extends to intellectual property rights, this could be a good or a bad thing!

(PACIFIC DIGITAL PLAZA

1117 Zhaojiabang Lu, near Caoxi Beilu, 21/5490-5900
HOURS: Daily 10 A.M.–8 P.M.
METRO: Xujiahui (Line 1, 9)
`Map 12`

This three-story electronics emporium sells every imaginable device, cable, screen, and screw, across a warren of stalls and vendors. All the major international brands are represented, along with some that look familiar but are clever fakes. Use your intuition when it comes to weeding out the dodgier deals and be sure to haggle on prices. If you go for repairs, don't agree to leave your device at the shop; unscrupulous vendors may switch all the internal parts for fakes before handing it back. If you don't find what you're looking for, there's always Metro City down the road at 1111, which has a Starbucks, Haagen-Dazs, and several restaurants.

Gifts and Souvenirs

(MADAME MAO'S DOWRY

207 Fumin Lu, near Julu Lu, 21/5403-3551,
www.madamemaosdowry.com
HOURS: Daily 10 A.M.–7 P.M.
METRO: Changshu Road (Line 1, Line 7)
`Map 10`

For kitschy and retro Chinese gifts, try this quiet, airy boutique on Fumin Road. Replica propaganda postcards, revolutionary memorabilia, metal Mao-era mugs emblazoned with slogans, and even Communist-style clothing line the shelves. The prices are higher than you'll find at the markets, but the relaxed shopping experience and great quality make it worth paying a bit extra. The shop's exterior is painted a pretty, duck-egg blue color. It sits on the same stretch as various tea stores, pottery boutiques, and split level cafés. Farther down the street is a popular cluster of bars and restaurants.

mrkt

MRKT

741 Julu Lu, near Fumin Lu, 21/5403-0691,
www.mrktstore.com
HOURS: Daily noon–10 P.M.
METRO: Jing'an Temple (Line 2, Line 7)
Map 10

Replicate the Shanghai urban look with a laptop bag or iPad sleeve from mrkt, the city's favorite design-led lifestyle store. Putting the fun into functional, mrkt creates seasonal collections of the sort of thing you never knew you needed until you see it. Most of the products are made from recycled felt and come in bright primary and pastel colors. From desk organizers and keyboard mats to coasters and hair accessories, mrkt covers every angle for the modern creative type. Two architects from Harvard who wanted to produce something "extraordinary" out of recyclable materials launched the brand in 2007. Mrkt is deeply involved in Shanghai's arts community and gives generously to local charities.

☕ SONG FANG MAISON DE THÉ

227 Yongjia Lu, near Shaanxi Nanlu, 021/6433-8283,
www.songfangtea.com
HOURS: Daily noon–10 P.M.
METRO: South Shaanxi Road (Line 1, Line 10)
Map 10

This attractive three-story shop and teahouse is owned and managed by a French tea enthusiast named Florence Samson, who also happens to be a Harvard Business School graduate. She opened the store in 2007 inside a converted 1930s lane house. Choose from over 70 varieties of Chinese and European teas, as well as a selection of covetable caddies and cups decorated with Song Fang's signature powder-blue and pink logo. China is synonymous with tea, so if you want to go home with a special tea-related souvenir or gift, this is the place to find it. Samson sources her tea in the provinces of Yunnan and Fujian and blends her brews with almonds and lavender.

Jewelry and Accessories

FLYING SCISSORS HANDBAGS

341-1 Zizhong Lu, 21/6473-9916, www.flyingscissors.cn
HOURS: Mon.-Fri. 10 A.M.-8 P.M., Sat. 1-8 P.M.
METRO: Xintiandi (Line 10)
`Map 10`

Handbag designer Tali Wu was born in Paraguay to Chinese parents and brought his passion to Shanghai in 2008, after graduating from the California College of Arts in San Francisco in 2004. Tali ran with a rock-and-roll crew when he was younger and it was an encounter with the members of Beijing band Brain Failure that inspired the name of his handbag boutique. He described one of their shows as sounding like "flying scissors," and thus his brand was born. His line includes clutches, hobos, and man bags in an edgy, urban style made from Italian leather. He also produces accessories like bracelets and cuffs.

IF-U

139-1 Changle Lu, 21/6384-1978, www.if-u.cn
HOURS: Daily 11 A.M.-10 P.M.
METRO: South Huangpi Road (Line 1)
`Map 10`

If you've had your fill of the clothing shops on Changle Road, try If-U for some unique accessories instead. For gifts with a difference, it's a great choice. The boutique sells porcelain jewelry handmade by artists from the China Academy of Fine Art. Among its most popular items is a range of simple red, white, and blue accessories, but there are plenty of more elaborate designs for more adventurous tastes. Rings representing the animals of the Chinese zodiac make great souvenirs and gifts. The shop itself is white inside, with minimalist shelves arranged on the walls in curves and lines.

MR BILLY'S HANDMADE SHOES

1238 Changle Lu, 130/6167-0957, www.billyshoes.com
HOURS: Daily 10 A.M.-9 P.M.
METRO: Jing'an Temple (Line 2, Line 7)
`Map 10`

Veteran Shanghai shoemaker Billy Wang counts Chinese celebrities like Jackie Chan and director Stanley Tong among his satisfied customers. Westerners living in or visiting Shanghai often find it hard to get shoes big enough, since Chinese feet tend to be smaller on average. One way of solving this quandary is having shoes made to measure. If you're in town for a couple of weeks, drop by Billy's shop and ask him how long it would take to make a pair of whichever shoes you fancy (he does boots, brogues, heels, flats, loafers—pretty much any permutation for both genders). Tell him you're on a tight timeline and he will try his best to get your shoes done on time.

NO CONCEPT BUT GOOD SENSE

327 Changle Lu, 21/5403-3983, www.noconcept.com.tw
HOURS: Daily 11 A.M.-8 P.M.
METRO: South Shaanxi Road (Line 1, Line 10)
`Map 10`

For a pair of shoes with a difference, try No Concept But Good Sense. It's a great name for a lovely little store. Every pair of shoes is individually crafted from soft sheepskin, then lined with pigskin and hand-stitched with cute flowers, shapes, and designs. Plainer varieties are available for the less adventurous and there are slip-on, flat, and heeled varieties in black, silver, and cream. Shoes don't come cheap and more-elaborate pairs will cost much more. No Concept is originally a Japanese brand. It was brought to Shanghai by Connie Emery who fell in love with the shoes and wanted to bring them to a wider audience.

HOTELS

Thanks to the 2010 World Expo, Shanghai's hotel options have mushroomed over the last couple of years. As well as the regular metropolitan array of Hyatts, Hiltons, and Ritzes, there are plenty of boutique hotels and interesting one-offs like the historic Park Hotel on People's Square and the newly opened luxury Waldorf Astoria on the Bund. For folks on a budget, there's a wide array of great hostels that are often just as good as mid-range hotels when it comes to services and cleanliness.

CHOOSING A HOTEL

The diversity and number of Shanghai's hotels is huge. Thanks to the very size of the city, the area you choose to stay in will have an impact on how you experience the city. Staying in or around People's Square will place you at an advantage for visiting the downtown area. You'll be close to Nanjing Road, the Bund, and the Old City, and the Old French Concession is just a short metro or taxi ride away. This part of town is relentlessly busy though, so if you're looking for a more tranquil trip, think about staying in the Old French Concession instead. Hotels farther out of town are a good option, too; the fast, efficient metro network makes it easy to get around.

A standard room in a Shanghai hotel will have either a single king- or two queen-sized beds, a private bathroom, television, safe, and refreshments. The bigger hotels provide parking facilities, and breakfast is usually included in your room rate. These things are worth double-checking when you book, however, if any are particularly important to you.

Shanghai's hostels should not be overlooked

HIGHLIGHTS

LOOK FOR ☾ TO FIND RECOMMENDED HOTELS.

☾ **Best Value:** The **Captain Hostel** is a fantastic choice for travelers on a budget, thanks to its prime location on the Bund; get your money's worth simply by visiting the hostel's rooftop bar and taking in the stunning views of the city (page 250).

☾ **Best Taste of Old Shanghai:** The grand old **Fairmont Peace Hotel** on the Bund was once the Cathay Hotel, host to celebrities like Charlie Chaplin. Check out the original lobby with its art deco dome and yellow marble floors, and get transported back in time (page 250).

☾ **Most Charmingly Quirky:** The Norweigan-Gothic **Hengshan Moller Villa Hotel,** complete with turrets and a lush garden, was originally built by a British businessman as a fairytale castle for his daughter (page 253).

☾ **Best Location:** The artsy **JIA Shanghai** sits just off West Nanjing Road's busy shopping district and is a short walk away from People's Square and Jing'an Temple (page 253).

☾ **Most Surprisingly Peaceful:** **Le Tour Traveler's Rest** hostel is close to Shanghai's main sights, but still quiet, thanks to its location down a hidden lane in Jing'an (page 254).

☾ **Greenest Hotel:** Sleep easy at the boutique **URBN Hotel** in Jing'an, China's first carbon-neutral hotel (page 254).

☾ **Best Urban Luxury:** Near the Cool Docks, the **Waterhouse** boutique hotel is a renovated factory with a handful of minimalist rooms that feature simple yet luxurious furnishings. The vibe here is decidedly hip and boho (page 256).

☾ **Best 5-Star Experience:** The **Kerry Hotel Pudong** offers a respite from the bustle of downtown Shanghai with elegantly furnished rooms and on-site entertainment that includes a microbrewery (page 257).

☾ **Best Boutique:** The super-hip and visually stunning **M Suites** on Suzhou Creek provides a good alternative to the busier downtown hotels (page 257).

☾ **Most Friendly:** Situated just north of downtown, the **Shanghai City Central Youth Hostel** has a super-helpful staff and the most welcoming common room and bar in town (page 258).

HOTELS

© URBN HOTEL

URBN Hotel

if you want to cut down on expenses. All hostels listed in this chapter are on par with 3-star hotels or above, and provide a friendly atmosphere that is sometimes missing from bigger establishments. If you opt for a dormitory, be prepared for simplicity; you will almost certainly be provided with a towel, but room facilities will be minimal. In a private hostel room you'll most likely get simple refreshments and toiletries.

PRICE KEY

- $ Under ¥100 per night
- $$ ¥100-500 per night
- $$$ ¥500-1,500 per night
- $$$$ Over ¥1,500 per night

The Bund

Map 7

ASTOR HOUSE PUJIANG $$

15 Huangpu Lu, near Dongdaming Lu, 21/6324-6388, www.astorhousehotel.com
METRO: Tiantong Road (Line 10)

Formerly one of the most famous hotels in the world, the Astor House is a surprisingly affordable choice if you go for a standard room. It was the first Western hotel in Shanghai, opening in 1846 under the aegis of tycoon Peter Felix Richards. His name lives on in the Richards Restaurant and Bar. Shanghai's first telephone call was made from the Astor in 1901. The hotel lit the city's first electric lamps back in 1882. The modern hotel has all the furnishings and accoutrements you would expect and is well placed to explore the often overlooked Hongkou district. Guest rooms are decorated simply with a touch of luxury. The ballroom has some attractive throwbacks to its colonial heyday, like scalloped balconies and chandeliers. From the outside, the hotel is an imposing, curved corner building that looks particularly good when it's lit up at night.

🄲 CAPTAIN HOSTEL $

37 Fuzhou Lu, near Sichuan Lu, 21/6323-5053, www. captainhostel.com
METRO: East Nanjing Road (Line 2, Line 10)

A great budget option, this youth hostel has a prime location and an excellent rooftop bar where you can soak up the skyline view without shelling out too many red hundreds. The hostel's naval theme is more than just a gimmick; it's a tightly run ship—clean and well

kept, with friendly staff. The lobby downstairs is home to the hostel's information desk and café and is where guests gather for breakfast. The food doesn't claim to set the culinary world alight, but it's more than decent for the price. Captain Hostel is one of the bigger downtown hostels, but it's also one of the most popular, so book ahead if you can.

🄲 FAIRMONT PEACE HOTEL $$$$

20 Nanjing Donglu, near Zhongshan Dongyilu, 21/6321-6888, www.fairmont.com/peacehotel
METRO: East Nanjing Road (Line 2, Line 10)

In its first incarnation as the Cathay Hotel, this legendary lodging hosted the celebrities and luminaries of Shanghai's heyday. Charlie Chaplin stayed here and Noel Coward wrote his play *Blithe Spirit* in one of its suites. Victor Sassoon's Bund-side project was renamed the Peace Hotel in 1956. Its green copper pyramid roof has been a part of Shanghai's fabric ever since. The building fell into disrepair during the early days of the People's Republic, but was renovated and reopened in 2010 as one of the largest, grandest hotels in Shanghai. Sassoon's original lobby with its art deco dome and shining yellow marble floors is worth a look even if you don't spend the night and the Jasmine tearoom offers a glimpse of Golden Age glory.

SHANGHAI MINGTOWN ETOUR HOSTEL $

55 Jiangyin Lu, near Chongqing Beilu, 21/6327-7766
METRO: People's Square (Line 1, Line 2, Line 8), exit 1

HOTELS

© WALDORF ASTORIA

Waldorf Astoria

One of the cheapest options in this part of town is the Mingtown Etour Hostel. Tucked away from the throng of People's Square, it is located inside an old townhouse with a shady courtyard. It's right beside the JM Marriott Tomorrow Square, which is one of the most recognizable buildings in Shanghai thanks to its pencil-nib point. Mingtown Etour has 20 standard rooms and over 100 dorm beds. The communal area is particularly attractive, with a two-floor glass fronted café and common room looking onto the garden.

WALDORF ASTORIA $$$$

Heritage Bldg.: 2 Zhongshan Dongyilu, near Guangdong Rd.; New Tower: 88 Sichuan Lu, near Guangdong Lu, 21/6322-9988, www.waldorfastorishanghai.com

METRO: East Nanjing Road (Line 2, Line 10)

A paean to Shanghai's legendary boom years of the early 20th century, the Waldorf Astoria harks back to the glory days of merchants, entrepreneurs, and gentlemen's clubs. Indeed, the hotel's heritage section started life as the Shanghai Club and its Long Bar was famous around the world. The Waldorf Astoria is spread across the historical Bund-facing building and a modern tower behind, making it one of the most spacious hotels in Shanghai. The two parts are connected by Peacock Alley (the same concept is featured in New York's Waldorf)—a long corridor containing an elegant coffee lounge. During restoration, designers and architects studied archive photos to make sure no detail was missed. The Long Bar is open for business again and the good news is that you don't have to be a local celebrity to sit near the window any more. There's an upscale American restaurant called Pelham's on-site, along with a tearoom. Room rates range from the pricey to the extortionate.

People's Square

Map 8

HOTELS

LANGHAM
YANGTZE BOUTIQUE 🅢🅢🅢🅢

740 Hankou Lu, near Yunnan Lu, 21/6080-0800, www.
yangtzeboutique.langhamhotels.com

METRO: People's Square (Line 1, Line 2, Line 8), exit 14

In the midst of the low-rise neighborhood behind People's Square is the striking, white art deco corner building that contains the 5-star Langham Yangtze Boutique Hotel. If money is no object, this is a worthy choice for a mix of modern facilities and Old Shanghai atmosphere. The Langham is well located for both the Bund and People's Square and the Metro is only a block away. Most of the 96 rooms have a balcony and measure more than 40 square meters (430 sq. ft.). Dining options include Italian, Japanese, and Chinese fine dining at Ciao, Mado Izakaya, and T'ang Court, respectively. For drinks there's the Palm Court tearoom and The Bar.

LE ROYAL MERIDIEN 🅢🅢🅢

789 Nanjing Donglu, near Xizang Zhonglu,
21/3318-9999, www.starwoodhotels.com

METRO: People's Square (Line 1, Line 2, Line 8), exit 19

The striking tower that houses Le Royal Meridien is razor slim at its peak and topped with two antenna. Inside are 761 rooms spread across 66 stories, all with floor-to-ceiling windows and smart, neutral furnishings. Le Royal Meridien is ideally located for downtown Shanghai's major sites; it faces People's Park and East Nanjing Road runs alongside it down to the Bund. The rest of town is easily reached by the Metro, which has a stop directly outside the hotel. There's a swimming pool and spa, as well as six restaurants and bars spanning Italian, Chinese, and French cuisines.

PACIFIC HOTEL 🅢🅢🅢

108 Nanjing Xilu, near Xinchang Lu, 21/6327-6226,
pacific.jinjianghotels.com/en_index.asp

METRO: People's Square (Line 1, Line 2, Line 8), exit 10

Perennial avoiders of chain hotels will love the Pacific. Its neoclassical facade was originally the headquarters of the Hua'an Life Insurance

Shanghai's historic Park Hotel

© SUSIE GORDON

Company and was designed by American architect Eliot Hazzard in 1926. It opened as a hotel in 1940. Its grand exterior made it popular with visiting dignitaries. As with many historic buildings in Shanghai, this one was given over to the government when the Communists rose to power in 1949, but it was restored to its former glory in 1958. Today its marble lobby and well-equipped rooms are an affordable luxury. The 182 guest rooms are split into Standard, Business, and Superior.

PARK HOTEL $$$

170 Nanjing Xilu, near Fengyang Lu, 21/6327-5225, www.park.jinjianghotels.com

METRO: People's Square (Line 1, Line 2, Line 8), exit 9

Looking for a slice of history without the eye-watering price tag? The famous Park Hotel is a good choice. Designed by Lázsló Hudec, the building was the tallest in Asia until 1954. Back in the day, it overlooked the British horse-racing track that is now People's Park and hosted a bevy of eminent guests like Henry Kissinger. It was stripped of its opulence in the 1950s under the new Communist government

and has never quite regained its illustrious reputation, despite a full overhaul by the Jinjiang hotel group. However, its 252 rooms are perfectly adequate and the location is top-notch. The lobby café is overpriced and strangely austere, so go elsewhere for a caffeine fix.

RADISSON NEW WORLD $$$

88 Nanjing Xilu, near Fengyang Lu, 21/6359-9999, www.radisson.com

METRO: People's Square (Line 1, Line 2, Line 8), exit 9

The skyscraper that houses the 5-star Radisson New World is pretty hard to miss thanks to the alien spaceship that adorns its peak. This space pod actually contains the hotel's revolving Sky Dome bar and restaurant. Located right on People's Square, the Radisson is super-convenient for transportation and sightseeing. There are lots of options for eating and drinking nearby if you don't fancy the on-site offerings. Each of the 520 rooms is equipped with all the modern hotel conveniences you'd expect of a 5-star, plus you get access to a range of facilities including pools and a fitness center.

Jing'an   Map 9

◖ HENGSHAN MOLLER VILLA HOTEL $$$

30 Shaanxi Nanlu, near Yan'an Lu, 21/6247-8881, www.mollervilla.com

METRO: Jing'an Temple (Line 2, Line 7)

This eye-catching building provides one of those frequent "double take" moments that characterize Shanghai's architecture. Constructed in 1936 in Norwegian-Gothic style, the Moller Villa was a gift from a wealthy British tycoon to his young daughter, whose dream was to live in a fairytale castle. These days, the pretty turrets and gingerbread-colored walls are home to the Hengshan Moller Villa Hotel, opened in 2001. One of Shanghai's first boutique hotels, it blazed a trail for what is now a flourishing scene. Its 3-star ranking belies its 5-star standards and services; each of its 43 rooms is tastefully decorated and furnished

with all of the modern conveniences you'd expect. Two restaurants and a garden with a lush lawn complete the experience.

◖ JIA SHANGHAI $$$

931 Nanjing Xilu, near Taixing Lu, 21/6217-9000, www.jiashanghai.com

METRO: West Nanjing Road (Line 2)

This 55-room boutique hotel benefits from an excellent downtown location and a luxury atmosphere that has a surprisingly reasonable price tag. Its name means "home" in Mandarin and it occupies a quirky 1920s corner building in the heart of the commercial district. One-off art installations dot the hallways and public areas. Each room is fitted with its own kitchen. If you don't feel like cooking, there's a great Italian restaurant, Issimo, on the 2nd floor, set up by celebrity chef Salvatore Cuomo. JIA is located within walking distance of People's Square and Jing'an Temple and is just a couple of Metro stops away from The Bund and the Old French Concession. If you like to be in the center of things, this is the hotel for you.

🎇 LE TOUR TRAVELER'S REST 🟢
Nong 319 Jiaozhou Lu, near Wuding Lu, 21/6267-1912, www.letourshanghai.com
METRO: Changping Road (Line 7)

A great budget option, this hostel is hidden away down a lane between Jiaozhou and Yanping Roads. Tucked away as it is, its appearance is deceptive—it's actually one of the largest downtown hostels with several floors of dorms and guest rooms. It has everything you'd expect from a hostel and more, such as bike rentals, free Internet, a TV lounge, and a reading room. There's also a great rooftop terrace and café that attracts non-guests when the weather is fine. Since Expo, hostel prices in Shanghai have tended to rival hotel rates, but Le Tour is an afforable exception. Le Tour can be tricky to find at first: It's on the stretch of Jiaozhou Road between Wuding and Xinzha; the lane is marked with a hostel sign.

PULI HOTEL AND SPA 🟢🟢🟢🟢
1 Changde Lu, near Yan'an Lu, 21/3203-9999, www.thepuli.com
METRO: Jing'an Temple (Line 2, Line 7)

If money is no object, try the PuLi Hotel and Spa. It occupies one of the towers in the cluster opposite Jing'an Temple and has been named among the 50 best hotels in the world by two independent publications. Aiming for a resort feel in the middle of the city, it mixes minimalist decor with luxurious fittings and fixtures for a non-typical 5-star feel. Each of the 193 rooms is equipped with a 32-inch LCD television and Bose sound system, as well as great views of the city below. On-site drinking and dining options are the 32-meter (105 ft.) Long Bar and the fine-dining Jing'an Restaurant. It's definitely one for the high rollers: The Jing'an Suite costs upwards of ¥25,000 per night.

KEEP IT CHEAP: HOSTEL LIFE

If you're traveling to China on a budget, it goes without saying that youth hostels are by far your best bet for accommodations. With dorm beds costing just a few dollars a night, it's definitely the most cost effective option. However, even if you have a bit more money to spend, you shouldn't rule out the idea of staying in a hostel instead of a hotel. Single or twin rooms in many hostels rival the equivalent in a hotel for cleanliness and comfort. A lot have en suite bathrooms and televisions and, while the decor may not be as plush as a Marriott or a Hilton, you get great value for your money. Another advantage of staying in a hostel is the social life. If you are traveling alone or planning to move on to a different city, the people you meet in the hostel common room will most probably be in the same boat. Hostel staff members are usually very friendly and helpful and will book tours and onward travel tickets for you.

🎇 URBN HOTEL 🟢🟢🟢
183 Jiaozhou Lu, near Beijing Xilu, 21/5153-4600, www.urbnhotels.com
METRO: Jing'an Temple (Line 2, Line 7)

China's first carbon-neutral hotel is located within walking distance of busy West Nanjing Road, making it the ideal accommodation choice for eco-conscious visitors who want to be in the thick of things. URBN's rates are at the upper end of reasonable, but it's worth it to know that your carbon footprint has been curtailed. The minimalist but comfortable decor includes neutral-colored furniture and slate detailing on the floor and walls. Shanghai celebrity chef David Laris helms the hotel's restaurant, which uses organic ingredients and materials throughout, from the food to the servers' aprons. With just 26 rooms, URBN is a welcome change from the homogeneous brand-name hotels that clog the downtown area.

Old French Concession

Map 10

JING'AN HOTEL 💲💲

379 Huashan Lu, near Changshu Lu, 21/6248-0088,
http://shanghai.jinjianghotels.com

METRO: Jing'an Temple (Line 2, Line 7)

Another well-located, mid-range option, this white-fronted garden hotel lies below Jing'an Temple at the northerly edge of the Old French Concession. Its 126 rooms (18 of which are suites) are spread across 10 floors of a Spanish-style villa dating from the 1920s. Many of the superior guest rooms have stained glass windows. There's a Spanish restaurant and a lobby bar, along with amenities like a gym, 24-hour room service, money exchange, and a florist. The building was originally called Haig Court and was used by the government after the founding of the People's Republic in 1949.

MANSION HOTEL 💲💲💲

82 Xinle Lu, near Xiangyang Beilu, 21/5403-9888,
www.chinamansionhotel.com

METRO: South Shaanxi Road (Line 1, Line 10)

Formerly the clubhouse of notorious Shanghai gangster Du "Big Ears" Yuesheng in the 1930s, this 5-star hotel sets the standard for luxury in the Old French Concession. As Shanghai's first boutique hotel, Mansion features only 30 rooms, but ticks all the boxes when it comes to historic hotel chic: stunning five-story colonial villa designed by Lafayette, panoramic views over the trees from the rooftop restaurant, faultless service, and beautifully decorated rooms fitted with every imaginable convenience. The pricing scheme is commensurate with the level of luxury, so expect to pay top brass for even a standard room. But if you've got the budget, it's well worth it.

PUDI BOUTIQUE HOTEL 💲💲💲

99 Yandang Lu, near Nanchang Lu, 21/5158-5888,
www.boutiquehotel.cc

METRO: Xintiandi (Line 10)

Located on the relatively tranquil Yandang Road pedestrian street just off the busy Huaihai thoroughfare, Pudi Boutique Hotel has 52 rooms furnished in contemporary style, with the luxury of butler service and aromatherapy toiletries in every en suite bathroom. Pudi has the advantage of a prime location close to Xintiandi, Middle Huaihai Road, and Fuxing Park, as well as luxury services and an original feel that you won't find in the international chain hotels. The building is an attractive art deco original with a refitted interior from French designer Pierre Maciag and is filled with contemporary artwork from upcoming Chinese talent. Reservations are required, so make sure you book in advance.

QUINTET BED AND BREAKFAST 💲💲

808 Changle Lu, near Changshu Lu, 21/6249-9088,
www.quintet-shanghai.com

METRO: Changshu Road (Line 1, Line 7)

If you want the boutique hotel experience without the steep price tag, try Quintet Bed and Breakfast. Its location places you right in the heart of the Old French Concession and each of its six rooms features a unique style and layout that is redolent of Shanghai's colonial heyday. Staff can arrange airport pickups as well as Chinese cooking classes, yoga lessons, and workouts at a nearby gym (at an extra cost). Breakfast selections are a step up from most B&B offerings, with cold and cooked options in Continental and English styles. Quintet is something of a hidden gem, but it's a good idea to book ahead to be sure of getting a room.

HOTEL INDIGO $$$

58 Zhongshan Donglu, Pier 16, 21/3702-9999,
www.shanghai.hotelindigo.com
METRO: Xiaonanmen (Line 9)

This high-end boutique hotel on the South Bund opened in December 2010 and has already cemented its reputation as one of the best regarded hotels in Shanghai. Part of the Pier 16 (Shiliupu) development, the hotel offers some of the best views in the city, looking out over the Bund, the Old City, and the new Lujiazui skyline. It has 184 rooms, including 23 suites, and each is decorated individually in a mix of contemporary and typically Chinese styles. There are quirky pieces of furniture, interesting ornaments, and tasteful murals throughout. Dining options are the CHAR Bar and Grill and the QUAY all-day café. Don't miss the beautiful swimming pool with its red mosaic tiles on the 7th floor.

OLD WEST GATE HOSTEL $

115 Penglai Lu, near Henan Nanlu, 21/6366-5798
METRO: Yu Garden (Line 10)

Right in the center of the Old City, this welcoming hostel mixes old-style charm with modern amenities for a quality budget experience. Rooms at the Old West Gate are simple, clean, and comfortable, while the communal areas provide a great space to relax and chat with other travelers. After a day of sightseeing, relax on red armchairs and patterned sofas, play some pool, or check your email using the free Wi-Fi. There's also an outdoor seating area. The Old West Gate is ideally located for touring the Old City and is within easy reach of Xintiandi, Huaihai Road, People's Square, and the Bund.

RENAISSANCE SHANGHAI YUYUAN $$$

159 Henan Nanlu, near Guangdong Lu, 21/2321-8888,
www.marriott.com
METRO: East Nanjing Road (Line 2, Line 10)

This 5-star hotel is geared towards business travelers, but it's a firm choice even if you're in Shanghai on vacation. Located within walking distance of the Bund, the Old City, and People's Square, it occupies space in one of the city's most interesting districts. High-rise apartment buildings vie for space among lowrise lane communities and briefcase-carrying businesspeople share the pavement with local noodle makers and butchers. The Renaissance Shanghai Yuyuan contains 340 rooms plus a presidential suite, along with several "Yu"-themed entertainment venues like Yu Garden Café, Yu Bar, and Yu Terrace. The services, amenities, and plush furnishings are everything you'd expect from a 5-star hotel.

◖ WATERHOUSE $$$

1-3 Maojiayuan Lu, near Zhongshan Nanlu,
21/6080-2988, www.waterhouseshanghai.com
METRO: Xiaonanmen (Line 9)

Boutique hotels are all the rage in Shanghai and the Waterhouse near the Cool Docks is one of the newest and most innovative. The focus is on minimalist comfort; each of the 19 guest rooms is individually decorated with artsy modern furniture and simple but luxurious furnishings by Japanese and Danish designers. The Table No.1 restaurant put the Waterhouse firmly on the map thanks to its celebrity chef Jason Atherton—a protégé of Gordon Ramsay. The hotel was designed by Neri and Hu around an old corner building in old dockland territory. The exterior is concrete and wood, while the interior features an open courtyard onto which many of the guest rooms look out. The Waterhouse has a hip, urban boho vibe, and is well located for the Bund and the Old City.

Pudong

Map 11

GRAND HYATT 💲💲💲💲

53-87/F, Jin Mao Tower, 88 Shiji Dadao, near Dongtai
Lu, 21/5049-1234, shanghai.grand.hyatt.com

METRO: Lujiazui (Line 2)

One of the highest hotels in the world, the
Grand Hyatt takes up the 53rd to 87th floors
of the Jin Mao Tower. The rooms are laid out
around a central atrium that makes for a vertiginous view from any of the lobbies. Each room
measures a minimum of 40 square meters (430
sq. ft.) and contains an LCD television, marble
bathroom, art deco–style interior design, and
a panoramic view of the city. The hotel's food
and beverage venues are destinations in themselves, like the Cloud 9 Bar, Kobachi Japanese
restaurant, and the 24-hour Grand Café buffet. The Grand Hyatt is a luxurious choice and
you'll pay top dollar for it.

PUDONG SHANGRI-LA 💲💲💲💲

33 Fucheng Lu, near Yincheng Nanlu, 21/6882-8888,
ext. 21, www.shangri-la.com/en/property/shanghai/
pudongshangrila

METRO: Lujiazui (Line 2)

The Pudong Shangri-La purports to have the
biggest rooms in town, as well as the largest
ballrooms. The hotel is split into the Grand
Tower and the River Wing and is located right
on the Lujiazui riverfront. This means that
great views are guaranteed and downtown
Puxi (the area west of the Huangpu River that
contains People's Square, Jing'an Temple, and
the Old French Concession) is only a couple of
metro stops away. Lodging in this part of town
puts you right at the heart of the modern financial district, with plenty of retail, tourist, and
dining options in the vicinity. The Shangri-La
has 577 guest rooms plus the famous Jade on
36 restaurant and bar. Each room is decorated
sumptuously in neutral tones.

SHANGHAI HIDDEN GARDEN HOSTEL 💲

840A, Nong 834 Pudong Dadao, near Fushan Lu,
21/5831-2370

METRO: Pudong Avenue (Line 4)

This quiet hostel feels like a world away from
the busy Lujiazui financial zone down the
road. It's a great choice if you'd rather be on
the east side of the river and within easy reach
of Century Park and the Pudong CBD. The
Hidden Garden has a pleasant outdoor yard
area with a moon gate, along with a cozy
glass-walled common room filled with wicker
lounge chairs and red sofas. There are bikes
available for hire and DVDs to borrow and the
atmosphere is casual and friendly.

HOTELS

Greater Shanghai

Map 12

🏨 KERRY HOTEL PUDONG 💲💲💲💲

Kerry Parkside, 1388 Huamu Lu, 21/6169-8888,
www.shangri-la.com/en/property/shanghai/
kerryhotelpudong

METRO: Huamu Road (Line 7)

Located near the Maglev railway, Century Park,
the SNIEC exhibition facility, and the future
Shanghai Disney Resort (set to open in 2015),
the Kerry Hotel Pudong is a Shangri-La property. It is part of the Kerry Parkside complex
that also contains office space, serviced residences, a gym, spa, and shopping mall. The
31-story hotel occupies one of the two towers
and contains beautifully furnished rooms as
well as ample meeting space and ballroom facilities. The on-site dining concept is called The
MEET, The COOK, and The BREW and is an
interconnected steakhouse, marketplace-style
restaurant, and microbrewery. Kerry Pudong
is widely used by delegations attending exhibitions at SNIEC, but is laidback enough to be a
good choice for leisure visitors who want to be
away from the downtown bustle.

🏨 M SUITES 💲💲

88 Yincheng Lu, near Jiangning Lu, 21/5155-8399

METRO: Zhongtan Road (Line 3, Line 4)

M Suites is a hip boutique hotel on the banks of the Suzhou Creek at the Pier One development close to M50 and Mengqing Park. Formerly the Union Brewery, the building has an arresting white frontage capped with a boxy tower looking out over the creek. Inside, the decor is equally attractive, decked out mainly in white. Each of the 24 rooms is an exercise in contemporary design and the trendy Mimosa Supperclub and Monsoon terrace bar comprise the drink and dining options. While it's located a little farther out of town than other hotels, M Suites' stunning appearance and great facilities more than make up for the extra mileage. In any case, a taxi into town takes around 15 minutes, so you won't be too far from the action.

PULLMAN SHANGHAI SKYWAY $$$

15 Dapu Lu, near Zhaojiabang Lu, 21/3318-9988, www.pullmanshanghaiskyway.com
METRO: Dapu Bridge (Line 9)

The Pullman is a solid mid-range option in this part of town. It's close enough to Xujiahui and Huaihai Road to benefit from the downtown buzz and is a landmark thanks to its unusual blue-hued latticed crest that sits atop the 52nd floor. Despite being located in a built-up area, the Pullman sits in a beautifully landscaped garden with a lake. A white marble lobby leads to 645 well-appointed rooms; there's also a gym, swimming pool, and spa on-site. The Pullman is a good business option too, with 17 meeting rooms and six dining and drinking locations to entertain colleagues.

RENAISSANCE ZHONGSHAN $$

1018 Changning Lu, 21/6155-8888, www.renaissancezhongshanpark.com
METRO: Zhongshan Park (Line 2, Line 3, Line 4)

The building that houses the Renaissance Zhongshan is one of the most striking on Shanghai's skyline. Sixty floors high, it glows neon blue, lighting up the sky above Zhongshan Park in Changning District, three metro stops west of Jing'an Temple. With 672 guest rooms, it's a big hotel and is conveniently located near Hongqiao Airport in the western suburbs. The building sits atop a shopping mall called Cloud Nine, with several other retail centers nearby. It's one of the busiest spots outside of downtown and is conveniently placed for three metro lines. Food and beverage spots include Zpark Coffee, Zpark Bar, the Azur European Restaurant and Wine Bar, and the Celadon Tea Lounge and Thai restaurant.

◖ SHANGHAI CITY CENTRAL YOUTH HOSTEL $

50, Nong 300 Wuning Lu, near Zhongshan Beilu, 21/5290-5577, www.hostelshanghai.cn
METRO: Caoyang Road (Line 3, Line 4)

Central by name, but slightly less so by nature, this youth hostel is one of the most spacious and comfortable in town. It's located about 15 minutes by taxi from People's Square and is a 5-minute walk from a well-connected Metro station. The gaudy blue and yellow building sits among high-rise apartment blocks and is well signposted from the street. It contains two big blocks of private rooms and dorms with a big common room and bar in between. The hostel's motto is "Champagne lifestyle, lemonade budget," so the emphasis is on creating a comfortable environment without the heavy price tag. Buffet breakfast is included in all room fees. The hostel arranges trips to nearby water towns and offers bikes to rent.

© SUSIE GORDON

Shanghai City Central Youth Hostel

EXCURSIONS FROM SHANGHAI

Shanghai is blessed with a variety of attractions in relatively close proximity. If you fancy a day (or a couple of nights) outside of the city, there's plenty to do. An hour from Shanghai by bullet train, the beautiful lakeside city of Hangzhou has inspired poets and musicians along the ages thanks to its willow-strewn vistas, forest-clad hills, and ancient pagodas. The modern city to the east of the lake has little in the way of attractions; the majority of scenic spots are clustered around West Lake, while Qihefang Street contains some tasty street-food and traditional old-style shops and stalls.

The lower Yangtze region is dotted with a series of pretty water towns (known as the Venices of the East) thanks to a proliferation of canals, rivers, and waterways. Many have now fallen foul to their own popularity, morphing into crowded tourist traps. However, Zhujiajiao in Shanghai's Qingpu district has not yet been over-run by tour groups and Tongli on the outskirts of Suzhou is still a relatively peaceful spot if you avoid weekends and national holidays. Shanghai's Sex Culture Museum relocated to Tongli in 2004, boosting its popularity with tourists in need of some (admittedly mild) titillation. The city of Suzhou lies just half an hour from Shanghai by train and is home to some of the most beautiful traditional gardens in China. Nine of them are UNESCO World Heritage Sites with peaceful oases of rock gardens, ponds, and pavilions.

All four of the towns included here can be seen comfortably in a day, but Hangzhou and Suzhou lend themselves well to staying overnight. Having said that, if you fall in love with Zhujiajiao and Tongli, there are some quaint guesthouses and hostels available to spend the night.

© SUSIE GORDON

HIGHLIGHTS

LOOK FOR [to FIND RECOMMENDED SIGHTS, ACTIVITIES, DINING, AND LODGING.

[**Most Scenic:** There's plenty to see around Hangzhou's **West Lake** – explore the lake via boat or take a stroll and admire the willows lining the shore (page 262).

[**Best Lifestyle Complex: Xihu Tiandi** in Hangzhou offers a variety of shops, restaurants, and cafés in a prime location on West Lake (page 264).

[**Best Historic Sight:** Suzhou's **Pan Gate** offers insight into the history of the city, as well as a chance to feed koi and visit a pagoda (page 272).

[**Best Classical Garden:** The traditional gardens of Suzhou are well worth the 30-minute train ride from Shanghai; the finest is the **Humble Administrator's Garden,** with its lotus ponds and rockeries (page 273).

[**Best Museum:** Tongli's **Sex Culture Museum** provides the lowdown on matters of a reproductive nature with a selection of eye-opening statues and exhibits (page 278).

© SUSIE GORDON

Hangzhou's West Lake at sunset

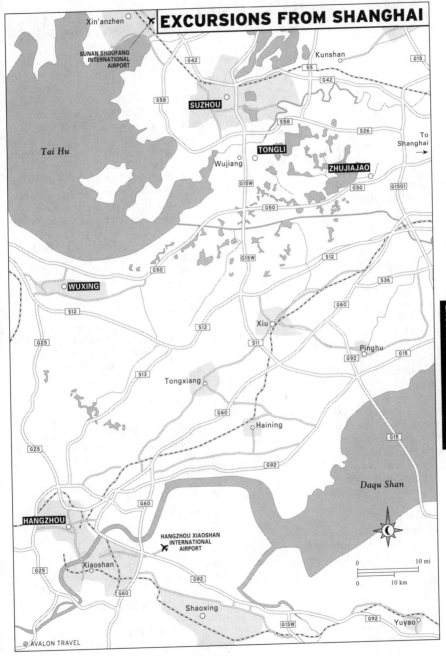

© AVALON TRAVEL

Hangzhou 杭州

The city of Hangzhou is the capital of Zhejiang Province in the east of China, 180 kilometers (112 mi) southwest of Shanghai. Nicknamed "Paradise on Earth," it is known for the scenic beauty of West Lake, around which many of the city's attractions are located. The modern city is a vibrant metropolis with nearly nine million inhabitants and is one of the richest regions of China. The central business district and surrounding suburbs are situated on the north and eastern shores of the lake, leaving an unimpeded view of the rolling hills on three sides.

Hangzhou was the capital of China during the Southern Song Dynasty that began in 1123. Called Lin'an in those days, it remained the center of power until the Mongols invaded and set up the Yuan Dynasty in 1276. Since the start of the 10th century, Hangzhou had been a center for art and culture in the south of China, along with Nanjing and Chengdu. The city was officially established during the Qin Dynasty as Qiantang County and named Hangzhou in A.D. 589 (meaning river-ferry district). The city wall was built in A.D. 591 and steady economic growth made it one of the Seven Ancient Capitals of China. Its prosperity began with the completion of the Grand Canal in A.D. 609; Hangzhou was the southern terminus, receiving goods sent down from Beijing. There has been settlement in the area since the Neolithic age. There is evidence of a people called the Liangzhu who lived around 5,000 years ago. Their jade carvings are some of the oldest to be discovered.

SIGHTS
◖ West Lake

Much of your time in Hangzhou will be spent around West Lake (Nanshan Rd.). Aside from a couple of nightlife and leisure districts on the north and east shores, most of the city's important sites are located around the lake. Xi Hu, as it is known in Mandarin, covers 5.6 square kilometers (2.1 sq. mi) to the west of downtown Hangzhou. It has a circumference

of 15 kilometers (9.3 mi) and three causeways, constructed from silt dredged from the lakebed, cross it. Ten thousand years ago, West Lake was a lagoon, but silt deposits blocked the Qiantang River that led to the sea, causing a vast body of water to form. Nowadays, the causeways and shores are lined with willow trees, creating the sort of scenery that looks great even when it's raining.

West Lake is split into five distinct sections, the largest being Outer West Lake. Solitary Hill (Gushan) sits between the Outer Lake and North Inner Lake and the causeways (Sudi, Baidi, and Yanggong Di). For ¥45, you receive three tickets to use for boat trips to the evocatively named Fairy Islet, Three Pools Mirroring the Moon, and the Mid-lake Pavilion. A full trip takes around three hours. There are piers at Yue Fei Temple, north of Su Di; Huagang, south of Su Di; opposite the Tomb of King Qian on Nanshan Road in front of the Academy of Art; and at Lakeside Park, near Hubin Road. If you don't fancy a boat trip, a walk around the lakeshore offers equally attractive and photogenic views.

Six Harmonies Pagoda

The ancient Six Harmonies Pagoda (Liuhe Ta, Yuelun Hill, daily 6 A.M.–6:30 P.M., ¥20, plus ¥10 to climb pagoda) peeks out from the surrounding pine forest on Yuelun Hill in the south of Hangzhou and is one of the city's most iconic sites. Overlooking the Qiantang River that flows into West Lake, the view from the top of the pagoda is photo-friendly to say the least. Occupying a special position in Chinese history, the Six Harmonies Pagoda was built in A.D. 970 during the Northern Song Dynasty. It was destroyed in a battle in 1121 and renovated in the Middle Ages, when extra decorations and eaves were added. A Buddhist artifact, the harmonies that give the pagoda its name are the precepts of heaven and earth, plus north, east, south, and west. A spiral staircase links the seven floors of the pagoda. Each of the

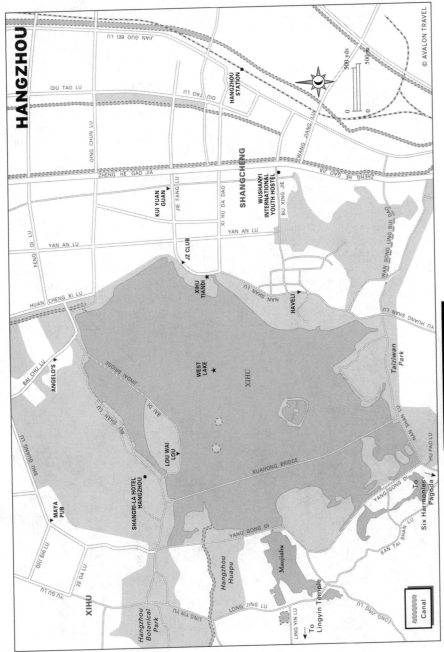

EXCURSIONS FROM SHANGHAI

ceilings is carved with intricate bird and flower designs. An exhibition hall on-site offers insight into pagoda architecture.

Lingyin Temple

One of China's most important ancient Buddhist temples, Lingyin Temple (Lingyin Si, 1 Fayun Alley, Lingyin Rd., daily 7 A.M.–6:15 P.M., ¥30, ¥45 to enter Feilai Feng) is a place of active worship for members of the Chan sect. Tucked between two forest-covered hills just west of the lake, it was built in the Jin Dynasty of the 4th century A.D. when an Indian monk visited the area. He proclaimed West Lake to be the "home of the Immortals" and established a temple here. A flourishing of Buddhism in the 10th century swelled Lingyin Temple's size and population; it had 1,300 rooms when the Cultural Revolution began in the late 1960s. Unfortunately, the Red Guards did their worst and many of the chambers and halls were destroyed. The temple seen today is the result of a renovation project in the 1970s. Highlights of the temple include the double-eaved Hall of the Heavenly Kings with its Laughing Buddha, the Grand Hall of the Great Sage that contains a gilded Sakyamuni, the Sutra Library, and the Feilai Feng grottoes.

◖ Xihu Tiandi

Far less glitzy than Shanghai's Xintiandi, Hangzhou's Xihu Tiandi (147 Nanshan Rd., Mon.–Fri. 9 A.M.–2 P.M.) is a pleasant complex of cafés, restaurants, and shops jutting out into the lake from Nanshan Road. It sits close to the scenic spot known as Orioles Singing in the Willows and was built in 2003 by Shui On Group—the company behind Xintiandi. The area is based around Yong Jin Lou, a heritage site from the Zhenghe era of Northern Song Dynasty (960–1127). It used to be a place where court officials celebrated the passing of exams and receiving of awards. These days, you can patronize Western cafés and Chinese restaurants inside beautiful white buildings with upturned, blue-tiled eaves. Xihu Tiandi is a good spot to start your explorations of West Lake; whether you head north or south,

bridge on Hangzhou's West Lake

you'll come across sites of interest almost immediately.

RESTAURANTS

Try authentic Zhejiang cuisine at **Lou Wai Lou** (30 Gushan Rd., Solitary Island, West Lake, 571/8796-9023, www.louwailou.com.cm, daily 10:30 A.M.–2:30 P.M., 4:30–8:30 P.M.), such as Dongpo pork and beggar's chicken. It will taste extra-special thanks to the gorgeous lake views from the windows. Lou Wai Lou was established in 1843, making it one of Hangzhou's oldest surviving restaurants. It is constructed so that it looks (and feels) as if it's floating on the lake. In fact, there is a boat on-site to take guests out onto the water after their meal. With a series of private rooms and a sumptuously decorated main dining area, it offers luxury and great food at a surprisingly reasonable price. Of course, you'll pay more here than at a street-side restaurant downtown, but you're paying for the view as much as for the food. Signature Zhejiang specialties include Sister Song's fish soup, freshwater carp with vinegar sauce, and shrimp with green tea. Lou Wai Lou gets busy, so reservations are recommended.

A Subcontinental feast awaits at **Haveli** (77 Nanshan Rd., 571/8707-9677, daily 11 A.M.–2 P.M., 5 P.M.–2 A.M.), widely claimed to be Hangzhou's best Indian restaurant. It looks kind of wacky from the outside, with elaborate purple drapes and some eye-catching neon signage, but inside it's authentic all the way. Dark carved wood adds an exotic atmosphere and the smell of cooking curry hits you as you walk in. There's indoor and outdoor seating available, so ask for a seat on the terrace if you want an unimpeded view of the lake. An English-language menu lays out the options, with curry classics, naan bread, lassis, and the like. Belly dancers take to the stage most evenings at 7:30 P.M., so plan your visit either to correspond or to avoid, depending on your preference. Smoking is forbidden until after 9 P.M.

See a different side of Hangzhou at **Angelo's** (No. 6, Lane 2, Baoshi Hill, Baochu Rd.,

© SUSIE GORDON

a pavilion on the north shore of West Lake

571/8521-2100, www.angelos-restaurant. com, daily 11 A.M.–2 P.M., 5:30–11 P.M.), a self-styled "slice of Italy" at the northeast corner of the lake (you can't miss the bright orange sign). Long term expatriates congregate here for a taste of the West, from Philly cheese steak to Caesar salad, pizza, pasta, and snacks. It's a medium-size modern Italian bistro with the sophistication of New York and is popular with the foreign crowd, especially on weekends. Check out the inventive pizza menu and try the Beijing duck variety if you dare. There are also conventional toppings like Margarita and Quattro Stagione, as well as beef and truffle, and curry chicken if you want to go off piste. The drink list is among the best in Hangzhou, with wines by the bottle for well under ¥500. Though the kitchen closes at 11 P.M., Angelo's is open until 2 A.M.

Kui Yuan Guan (154 Jiefang Rd., 571/8702-8626, Mon.–Fri. 9 A.M.–2 P.M.) is famous for its noodles and the legend that inspired the restaurant's popularity. A businessman from neighboring Anhui Province opened Kui Yuan in 1867. When it first opened, business was slow. One day, a nervous-looking student came in who was heading to his imperial examinations. The restaurant owner decided to add three eggs to the student's noodles to symbolize the exams he was about to take. When the student aced his tests, he went back to the humble noodle restaurant with friends who were yet to take their exams. Soon, people were coming from all over the region to taste Kui Yuan's magic lucky noodles. The house specialty is a style of dish called *pian er chuan* that contains noodles in a spicy soup with lean minced pork and bamboo shoots. Another favorite is *xia bao shan mian* (eel and shrimp noodles).

NIGHTLIFE

Hangzhou's branch of the Shanghai-based **JZ Club** (6 Liuying Rd., 517/8702-8298, www.jz-club.cc, daily 6:30 P.M.–2:30 A.M.) is the go-to for live jazz in the city. It's located in an attractive villa by the lake in a stretch of bars and restaurants and is a great place to start (or finish) a night on the town. Covering three floors, the stage is overlooked by balconies on the upper levels. Red velvet drapes and cozy corners give an intimate vibe that's ideal for smokey jazz, although smoking is not permitted on the ground floor. As well as a great wine list and a good collection of single malt whiskies, there's a food menu of quality Western-style meals and snacks.

Make **Maya Bar** (94 Baishaquan, Shuguang Rd., 571/8799-7628, daily noon–2 A.M.) your entry point into the Shuguang bar scene. Situated north of West Lake in a largely residential area, it's the drinking spot of choice for locals and expats alike. Maya appeals to fans of good beer; there's Tiger on tap and Budvar, Guinness, and Old Speckled hen by the bottle. Maya is great both as a café in the afternoon (thanks to a wall of books and magazines) and a bar in the evening. The menu of simple Mexican staples endears it to the Westerners who live nearby. There's a friendly vibe and the place gets busy most evenings and weekends with live music and enthusiastic revelry fueled by jugs of strong cocktails.

HOTELS

The **Shangri-La Hangzhou** (78 Beishan Rd., 571/8797-795, www.shangri-la.com, ¥1,400) mixes luxury with thoughtful design, as you might expect from a Shangri-La property. On the north shore of West Lake overlooking Solitary Island and Xiling Bridge, the Shangri-La Hangzhou has 382 guest rooms across two wings and three villas. The building channels traditional architecture with upturned roof corners and carved wooden verandahs; it's a low-rise so it doesn't look out of place on the lakeside. The lobbies and communal areas are decked out with Chinese artworks, bonsai trees, and marble floors and the subtle but opulent decor continues into the guest rooms. On-site are a health club, business center, lounge, and swimming pool, along with Chinese and Western dining options. Guests can ride bikes in the 40-acre hotel grounds and beyond.

Hangzhou has a handful of excellent hostels, but the **Wushanyi Hostel** (17 Neidatong Ave., 22 Zhongshan Middle Rd., 571/8533-3969, ¥40–160) gets my vote for its peaceful location, great staff, and clean, comfortable rooms. Set back off the main lakeside drag and tucked up on a hill at the foot of Wu Mountain, Wushanyi sits behind a traditional moon gate (a circle cut into a wall). It's just one kilometer (0.6 mi) away from the lake and is within easy walking distance of Qihefang Street and the lakeshore nightlife. You can choose between a bed in a dorm or a private room. There's a common room with a TV, a restaurant that's separated from the main building by a stone path across a lawn, and a convivial breakfast room complete with a cat and dog. Plus, there are the regular hostel amenities like bike rentals, laundry, and free Wi-Fi.

GETTING THERE AND AROUND
By Train

Hangzhou is only an hour away from Shanghai thanks to the fast bullet train that began running in 2011. Trains leave Shanghai's Hongqiao Station every 30 minutes and arrive

45–60 minutes later at Hangzhou South, reaching speeds of 350 kilometers per hour (217 mph). A one-way ticket costs around ¥80 and is available from the station or from ticket booths around Shanghai. Trains arrive at either Hangzhou Railway Station or Hangzhou South. Regular trains to Hangzhou take 1.5–2 hours from Shanghai South Railway Station and Shanghai Railway Station.

By Bus

The bus route between Hangzhou and Shanghai is well developed and the trip takes 2–3 hours. Shuttle buses leave Pudong Airport for Hangzhou Dragon Sport center at 10:30 A.M., noon, 1:30 P.M., 3:30 P.M., 5:30 P.M., and 7 P.M., as well as from various points around town including the Railway Station. A one-way ticket costs around ¥50.

Zhujiajiao 朱家角

The water towns in Zhejiang and Jiangsu provinces are famous for their willow-banked canals, quaint alleys, craft shops, and lantern-strewn lanes. Lesser-known Zhujiajiao is a lot quieter than the most tourist-visited towns and has the added advantage of being just 40 minutes away from downtown Shanghai in the Qingpu district.

Modern Zhujiajiao is home to around 60,000 people, but the enchanting old quarter is considerably more tranquil. With 36 stone bridges spanning the canals and streams, it has earned itself the nickname "Venice of the East," as have all the water towns at some point in their existence. Habitation dates back several thousand years, but Zhujiajiao flourished in the Yuan Dynasty (1271–1368) as a marketplace. It's strategic placement at the confluence of several rivers made it ideal for passing trade. In recent years, Zhujiajiao has become popular with artsy Shanghai residents keen to escape the city; several bohemian cafés, bars, hostels, and galleries have sprung up. The newcomers live down the narrow lanes alongside the locals.

The ancient quarter of Zhujiajiao is set slightly apart from the new town and there is a nominal ¥10 entry fee. However, since there are so many entrance points to the old town, it's difficult to enforce. If you want to fly solo and avoid a guided tour, go for it, but if you want to hire a guide, expect to pay around ¥120 for three hours. Various sets of attraction tickets can be bought that allow entry into a number of sites. Tickets and guides can be acquired at the main entrance to the old quarter.

The great thing about Zhujiajiao is that you can stroll around it in a couple of hours. Another good way of getting around is by hopping onto one of the many gondolas you'll see on the canals. The gondolas seat six people and run along two routes: a short trip for ¥60 per boat that takes you up and down the main canal and a longer tour around town for ¥120. Tickets are sold at the wooden booths next to the main attractions.

Zhujiajiao opens to visitors at 7:45 A.M. and closes at 5:30 P.M., thus the hours of operation for every establishment listed here are, essentially, 7:45 A.M.–5:30 P.M. The bars that are open later won't be of great interest to visitors leaving when the old quarter closes, but if you're staying at one of the hostels overnight, you may be interested. Many of the bars serve as daytime cafés, in any case.

SIGHTS

Stretching for about a kilometer (0.6 mi) through Zhujiajiao's old quarter, **North Street** (Bei Dajie) is flanked with traditional buildings from the Ming (1368–1644) and Qing (1644–1911) Dynasties. Once the town's main thoroughfare, it crosses northeast to southwest from the Fansheng Bridge to the Handicraft Exhibition Hall and the Tongtianhe. The striking five-arched **Fangsheng Bridge** is Zhujiajiao's largest and tallest, stretching for 70 meters (230 ft.). It was built in 1571 and is carved with dragons and lions.

One of Zhujiajiao's most famous landmarks is the **Old Post Office** at the southwest end of Xihu Street near Caohe Street. It dates from the reign of the Qing emperor Tongzhi in 1903 and went through many guises over the years, from a private post office to a customs house.

From Great North Street, cross Tai'an Bridge to get to the **Yuanjin Buddhist Temple** across the Caogang River. Built in 1341 during the reign of the Zhizheng emperor of the Yuan Dynasty, the temple has several colorful statues. Next, head south to the Daoist **City God Temple** with its old gingko tree.

Close to the entrance to the old quarter is Zhujiajiao's most famous attraction: **Kezhi Garden** dates from 1912 and is the result of 15 years of work. The garden's design mixes Chinese and Western sensibilities and is split into two sections: Ke and Zhi. Ke means "to learn," while Zhi means "to plant," implying that knowledge is acquired through diligent work.

Ticket Information

The ticket office (164 Xinfeng Rd.) sells three combinations: Type 1 (9 attractions): ¥80 gets you a river boat ride, plus entry into the Y-Art Gallery, Tong Tian He Chinese Pharmacy, Old Post Office, City God Temple, Shanghai Handicraft Exhibition Hall, Yuanjin Buddhist Temple, Hanlin Stele Museum, Kezhi Garden, and Shanghai Quanhua Art; Type 2 (8 attractions): ¥60 gets you entry into all of the Type 1 attractions, minus the Hanlin Stele Museum; Type 3 (4 attractions): for ¥30 you get entry to Tong Tian He Chinese Pharmacy, Old Post Office, Yuanjin Buddhist Temple, and Kezhi Garden.

RESTAURANTS AND NIGHTLIFE

Since Zhujiajiao is so small, most of the cafés double up as bars and restaurants and the hostels and lodging houses offer food and drink. The intriguingly named **Bum Cafe** (44 Caohe St.) is fun for photo opportunities as well as a cup of coffee and a snack, while **HEIMa Bar** (25 Donghu St.) brings a taste of Iceland to this corner of China. Run by a couple of

Bum Cafe in Zhujiajiao

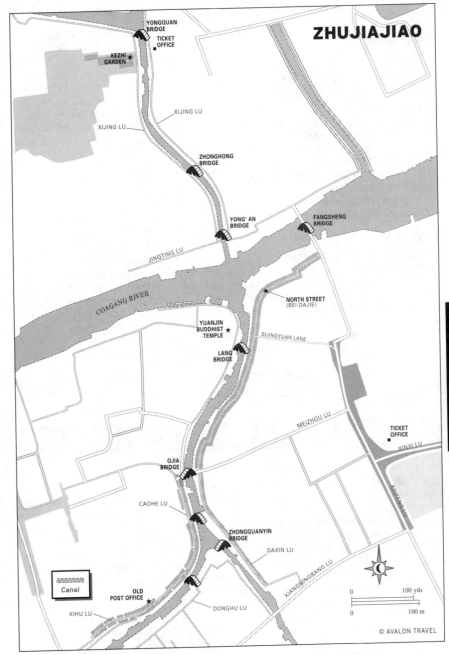

ZHUJIAJIAO

YONGQUAN
BRIDGE
TICKET
OFFICE

KEZHI
GARDEN

XIJING LU

XIJING LU

ZHONGHONG
BRIDGE

YONG' AN
BRIDGE

FANGSHENG
BRIDGE

JINGTING LU

COAGANG RIVER

NORTH STREET
(BEI DAJIE)

YUANJIN
BUDDHIST
TEMPLE

SIJINGYUAN LANE

LANG
BRIDGE

MEIZHOU LU

TICKET
OFFICE

XINXI LU

OJIA
BRIDGE

CAOHE LU

ZHONGGUANYIN
BRIDGE

DAXIN LU

XIANGNINGBANG LU

XINENG LU

Canal

OLD
POST OFFICE

XIHU LU

DONGHU LU

0   100 yds

0   100 m

© AVALON TRAVEL

EXCURSIONS FROM SHANGHAI

Scandinavian expats, the two-floor bar serves bottled beer, cocktails, and shots and is a café during the day.

The best known venue in town is **Zher** (118 Xijing St.). Run by a local punk musician named Frank, Zher (meaning "here" in Mandarin) is small, but the fun spills out onto the willow-decked outdoor area when the weather is fine. Inside, Frank's space is decked out with comfortable armchairs, a film projector, and a foosball table. Drinks, snacks, and full meals are available. **Jazz Age** (58 Caohe St.) is a café owned by a jazz enthusiast named Zhou. As well as making coffee and welcoming guests, Zhou collects jazz CDs and sells knock-off copies for ¥20 each.

HOTELS

If you decide to stay overnight in Zhujiajiao, your best bet for accommodation is one of the bohemian hostels that have sprung up in the past few years. Located inside quaint old buildings, often with canal views, these lodgings are cheap and convivial.

Cao Tang (31 Dongjing St., 152/2136-1365, ¥80–175) offers the option of a dorm bed in one of its beautifully decorated rooms or a double private room with en suite bathroom. The popular on-site bar serves Sinkiang black beer. The **My Way** (29–31 Xihu St., 21/5923-0927,

¥300) is right next to the Old Post Office and has river-view rooms, Wi-Fi access, boho decor, and free breakfast for guests. The international **1, 2, 3 Guesthouse** (123 Xijing St., 134/8262-9203, ¥80–200) located down a lane near the Kezhi Garden offers mixed dorm and twin private en suite accommodations. Other options are **Uma** (No. 4, Lane 103 Xijing St., 21/5924-0487 or 189/1808-2961, ¥30) and an apartment belonging to the manager of **HElma Bar** (23 Donghu St., ¥400).

GETTING THERE AND AROUND

The two best bus options are Tour Bus 4 that leaves from Shanghai Sightseeing Bus Center (Staircase 5, Shanghai Stadium, 666 Tianyaoqiao Rd., 21/6426-5555) daily, every half hour 7:30 A.M.–4:30 P.M. (¥23 one-way) and the ¥9 pink Huzhu Express line that leaves from the junction of Chengdu Road and Dagu Road, running daily every half hour 7:30 A.M.–4:30 P.M. Last buses leave Zhujiajiao to come back to Shanghai around 9 P.M. The bus ride takes about an hour each way.

A one-way trip in a taxi will cost around ¥150. There are usually taxis waiting at the exit to the water village to take visitors back to Shanghai. If not, ask the visitors' center to call one for you.

Suzhou 苏州

Along with Hangzhou, Suzhou is the most famous day-trip destination outside of Shanghai. Lying only half an hour by train out of downtown Shanghai, it's easy to visit in a day. If you want to stay the night there are plenty of excellent hotels and guesthouses. Suzhou's most famous area is the old quarter that covers Pingjiang, Canglang, and Jinchang districts. The modern city has little to differentiate it from any second-tier Chinese metropolis apart from the Suzhou Industrial Park area and Ligongdi, districts on the shore of Jinji Lake that feature Western restaurants and bars.

Located in Jiangsu Province, Suzhou rose to

prosperity thanks to its location on the Grand Canal. There was settlement there 2,000 years ago and the first records date back to the Shang Dynasty (1600–1046 B.C.), making it one of the oldest inhabited areas in the lower Yangtze Delta. In 514 B.C., King Helu of the Wu State made the city its capital. It received its modern name in A.D. 589 during the Sui Dynasty. Thanks to the silk industry that flourished during the Song era (A.D. 960–1279), Suzhou's wealth and position increased; it was home to many important scholars, writers, artists, and ministers. The city's many beautiful gardens bear witness to its standing.

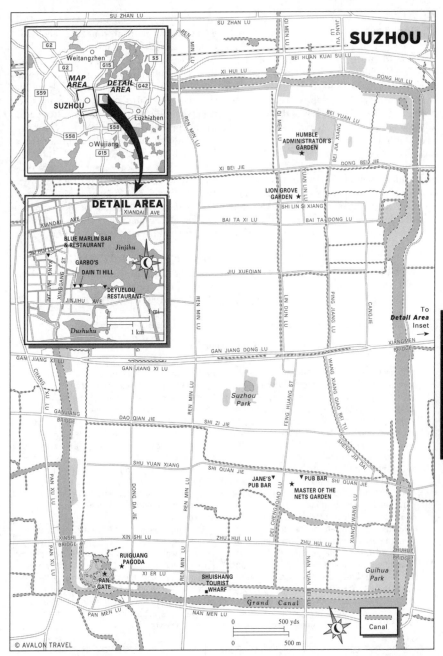

EXCURSIONS FROM SHANGHAI

SIGHTS
◀ Pan Gate

Pan Gate (Pan Men, Dongda St., daily 7:30 A.M.–5:30 P.M., ¥25 for Pan Gate scenic area, free for children under 1.2 meters tall, ¥6 to climb Ruiguang Pagoda) dates back 2,500 years to the Wu Kingdom of the Warring States era (770–476 B.C.). It is both a land gate and a water gate and is five meters (16.4 ft.) high at its tallest point, where it is topped with a double-eaved gatehouse. It was built as the only entry into the city as part of a protective wall built in 514 B.C. A visit to the Pan Gate scenic area gets you entry to a garden where you can feed koi carp, take a boat ride, cross a footbridge, and visit the ancient Ruiguang Pagoda (for an additional fee) that dates from 247 B.C.

Tiger Hill

Tiger Hill (8 Mennei St., Huqiu Hill, 512/6723-2305, daily 7:30 A.M.–6 P.M., ¥60 Apr. 1–Oct. 30, ¥40 Oct. 31–Apr. 15) is named for the mystical white tiger who is said to have sat upon the grave of King Helu of Wu when he died in 496 B.C. It also contains the stone that Helu used to test his swords, complete with a worn groove, and a pool that apparently contains the bodies of the 1,000 men who built his tomb. Less sinister but no less interesting is the Wanjing Villa that contains a bonsai nursery and a leaning pagoda. Yunyan Temple's octagonal pagoda is the oldest in Suzhou and leans several degrees to the northwest. Tiger Hill was also the site where ancient tea expert Lu Yu penned his "Classic of Tea"—the first published book about the art of the brew. The water in the area is particularly good for making tea, according to his treatise.

Master of the Nets Garden

Suzhou's smallest garden, Master of the Nets (Daichengqiao Rd., 11 Kuojiatouxiang, 512/6529-3190, daily 7:30 A.M.–5 P.M., ¥30

THE CONSTANT GARDENERS

The traditional residential gardens of the lower Yangtze region are thought to be the finest in the whole of China. The Chinese Garden (also known as Scholar's Garden) is a unique style of landscaping that has its roots way back in prehistory. The intricately designed rock gardens, pavilions, ponds, and paths that can be seen today are the result of millennia of honing. The first records of Chinese gardens date back to the prehistoric Shang Dynasty and appear in sacred Daoist texts like the *I Ching*. It was during the Jin Dynasty (A.D. 265-420) that ideals of Neolithic shamanism melded with Confucian and Daoist practices to form the origins of the great traditional garden. There are four main styles – that of North China, Central China, the Yangtze Delta, and South China. The variety constructed in the Yangtze Delta are the most enduringly popular and include the famous gardens in Suzhou.

Built inside the private residences of scholars and civil servants, Chinese Gardens were more than just a place to relax. Designed to be a physical manifestation of poetry and landscape paintings, they were also places where the human spirit could connect with nature. Heavy symbolism abounds in the placement of rocks (found exclusively in Tai Lake, in the case of the Yangtze region's gardens) and choice of fauna. For example, bamboo represents strength, peonies stand for wealth, lotus means purity, and chrysanthemums signify splendor. The flowering plum found in many gardens is symbolic of renewal and rebirth.

Five simple elements are found in every garden: wall, hall, pool, hill, and tree. The interplay between water and rock is integral to garden design (so much so that the Mandarin word for landscaping is shanshui meaning "hill and water"), as it represents the opposing principles of yin and yang. It's common to find lucky orange koi carp, goldfish, and Mandarin ducks in garden pools.

Apr. 16–Oct. 30, ¥20 Oct. 31–Apr. 15, evenings ¥80), measures just 5,400 square meters (58,100 sq. ft.), but appears much larger thanks to clever landscaping techniques. It originally belonged to a minister of the Song Dynasty, who commissioned it in 1140. He longed to turn his back on his ministerial duties and lead the life of a simple fisherman, hence the garden's name. It passed through several hands until 1785 when it was acquired by a Qing-era government official who added much to its design. As with most traditional gardens, it is divided into three sections. The main area contains a large pond with walkways and a pavilion. The small inner garden has been replicated at the Pompidou Centre in Paris and the Metropolitan Museum of Art in New York City.

Lion Grove Garden

Attractive Lion Grove Garden (23 Yuanlin Rd., 512/6727-8316, daily 7:30 A.M.–5 P.M., ¥30 Mar. 1–May 31, Sept. 1–Nov. 3, ¥20 June 1–Aug. 31, Dec. 1–Apr. 30) started life as part of a Buddhist temple in 1342. A monk named Tianru ordered his disciples to landscape it in memory of his master, Zhongfeng. After Tianru himself died, the disciples disbanded and the garden fell to ruins. It was bought by a relative of the contemporary architect I. M. Pei who handed it over to the state in 1950 and it has been restored to its former beauty. Twisting paths meander between gnarled rock formations taken from Lake Tai; rockeries are reflected in tranquil pools. Lion Grove Garden was particularly popular with the Qing emperor Qianlong and is one of Suzhou's finest.

◖ Humble Administrator's Garden

The Humble Administrator's Garden (178 Dongbei St., 152/6751-0286, daily 7 A.M.–5:30 P.M., ¥70 Mar. 1–May 31, Sept. 1–Nov. 3, ¥50 June 1–Aug. 31, Dec. 1–Apr. 30) is Suzhou's largest and is widely believed to be the most beautiful in China. It takes its name from the retired imperial governor. It was originally the garden of a Tang dynasty scholar, but

Humble Administrator's Garden

was turned over to the Dahong Temple in the Yuan era. In 1513 it was acquired by a former governor who transformed it into a beautiful landscaped garden with the help of an artist friend. Willing to pass the twilight of his life enjoying simple pleasures instead of the privileges of imperial life, he is the "humble administrator" of the garden's name. The landscaping work was completed in 1526, forming one of the loveliest Ming-era gardens in the country. It covers 52,000 square meters (560,000 sq. ft.) and is a UNESCO World Heritage Site. The garden is split into three main areas, the central of which is mainly water. Around it are pavilions, lotus ponds, rock formations, hills, and the Hall of Distant Fragrance with its long windows.

The Grand Canal

Suzhou owes its prosperity to the Grand Canal (Shuishang Tourist Wharf, Xinshiqiaotu, boat rides daily 9 A.M.–8:30 P.M., ¥35), which starts in Beijing and terminates in nearby Hangzhou. The longest canal in the world was completed during the Sui Dynasty (581–618 B.C.) and stretches for 1,776 kilometers (1,103 mi). The canal was actually begun close to Suzhou, when King Fuchai of Wu decreed that a trade route be created when he conquered the Qi State. As it passes through Suzhou, the Grand Canal is called Jiangnan. Riding a boat along its length is a good way to see Suzhou; boats leave every half hour from the Shuishang Tourist Wharf.

It's possible to travel all the way from Suzhou to Hangzhou on the Grand Canal overnight. A cruiser leaves the wharf at 306 Renmin Road at 5:30 P.M. and arrives at Wulinmen dock in Hangzhou at 6:30 A.M. the next morning. The return boat leaves Hangzhou at 5:30 P.M. and gets to Suzhou at 7 A.M. the following day. Twin or quad berths cost ¥78–208 depending on the type of boat.

RESTAURANTS

Deyuelou (8, 18 & 22 Ligongdi, Suzhou Industrial Park, 512/6265-6999, daily 11 A.M.–2 P.M., 5–9 P.M.) has two locations, but it's the newer branch on Ligongdi that's worth a visit to try some Suzhou specialties. The Deyuelou name dates back 400 years to the reign of the Ming emperor Jiajing and it's something of a byword for great local food. Like the Shanghainese cuisine it inspired, Suzhou food is sweet and light. Thanks to the proliferation of lakes and rivers in Jiangsu province, freshwater fish looms large on menus, often cooked with a sweet marinade. Deyuelou offers regional favorites like steamed mandarin fish and sliced ham with honey. The decor is simple but plush, with calligraphy on the walls. The staff speaks limited English, but there's an English menu.

Firmly at the center of the expatriate scene, **Blue Marlin** (168 Xinghai St., Suzhou Industrial Park, 512/6288-9676, www.bluemarlin.cn, daily 10 A.M.–2 A.M.) provides a change of scenery from Suzhou's ancient sights. The Suzhou Industrial Park has a very different atmosphere from downtown, with wide causeways and views out over Jingji Lake and the technology district nearby. With a 10-year pedigree, Blue Marlin is something of a Suzhou institution among the city's foreign contingent. With a bar serving Erdinger, Tiger, San Miguel, and Carlsberg on draft, and a restaurant offering Asian and Western meals, it's a self-styled "home away from home." A daily half-price happy hour runs 4–7 P.M. to attract the post-work crowd; food is served until 10 P.M.

Campy **Dain Ti Hill** (A12, Phase 2, Ligongdi, Suzhou Industrial Park, 512/6299-8980, daily 11 A.M.–10 P.M.) is something of an enigma thanks to its interesting mix of classic and modern decor. There's plenty of subtle neon, including some elaborate contemporary chandeliers, and the food is a fusion of Japanese, Taiwanese, and Southeast Asian. The dish that almost everyone orders is the potato and pumpkin salad, though the sizzling beef is a good bet, too. The menu has some unusual items like a prawn and vegetable wrap that arrives upright in several segments. There's a non-smoking section as well as areas of low, romantic seating. Dain Ti Hill is easy to spot from the outside thanks to its glowing neon front.

NIGHTLIFE

Part of the thriving Ligongdi nightlife scene on Jinji Lake, **Garbo's** (A16, Ligongdi, 512/6295-3698, daily noon–late) is managed by a Swedish man named Lars. The atmosphere is relaxed. Garbo's serves up pub food like sausages and mash and Swedish meatballs to patrons sipping Stella, Krombacher, and Boddingtons beer on tap. There's also bottled beer and cocktails on the menu. The daily 3–9 P.M. happy hour sees 30 percent off drink prices, making a ¥35 pint even more reasonable. There's nothing fancy or sophisticated about Garbo's, but it's a decent, honest bar with a laidback vibe. Framed photos on the walls and wooden furniture keep things homey.

There are two similarly named pubs on this stretch of Shiquan Street—the **Pub Bar** (463 Shiquan St.) and **Jane's Pub Bar** (621 Shiquan Street, 133/3800-0976, daily 4 P.M.–2 A.M.). The former was one of Suzhou's first Western bars and is quieter and more laidback. The latter is bigger and more sport-focused, with big screens showing matches. Happy hour runs daily 3–8 P.M. with draft beer for ¥20 and Tsingtao for ¥10. There's an upbeat vibe and live music Monday–Saturday. If you find it too rowdy, head down the road to the Pub Bar, which is usually quieter. Either venue is a good place to start a night exploring Shiquan Street's bar scene.

HOTELS

A member of Hostelling International, the Mingtown Suzhou Hostel (28 Pingjiang Rd., 512/6581-6869, ¥50–160) is located in the old part of the city near the Grand Canal. It's about a 10-minute walk from the main gardens and has a friendly atmosphere that has endeared it to legions of backpackers and tourists. By way of facilities, there's the Riverside bar and restaurant, Internet, a reading room, and a travel center, along with a laundry and bikes for rent. The common spaces and rooms are decorated simply with traditional touches; there's a comfortable, well-worn feeling about the place. Rooms and dorms are clean and well kept. Choose a six-bed mixed dorm or a single private room.

The beautiful 4-star **Garden View** (66 Luoguaqiao, Lindun Rd., 400/810-6868, ¥400–1,600) on the canals of the old quarter has 188 guest rooms ranging from standard to deluxe. If you're looking for a traditional atmosphere, this is the place for you. Its white walls, gray tiled roofs, and red lanterns are evocative of old China, while the services are definitely modern. Breakfast is included in the room rate and there are both Chinese and Western restaurants on-site. Choose from a reasonably priced single room, a superior room, or a suite.

The **Sofitel Suzhou** (818 East Hanjing Rd., 512/6801-9888, www.sofitel.com/suzhou, ¥700) is the only 5-star hotel in downtown Suzhou and is located next to the buzzing Guanquan shopping area. The Sofitel name tends to speak for itself and this branch is no exception. With the canal flowing in front and a sweeping staircase in the lobby, the Sofitel is one of the most opulent hotels in Suzhou. However, it is low-rise and subtle enough not to be an eyesore, with nods to traditional architecture in its peaked roofs. Inside are 314 guest rooms, 10 meeting rooms, a health club, and a swimming pool. If you're looking for a night of luxury away from Shanghai, this is a good choice.

GETTING THERE AND AROUND
By Train

The train from Shanghai to Suzhou is fast and efficient. Since many people commute between the cities, there are multiple trains leaving every hour from Shanghai Railway Station starting at 5:45 A.M. Buy your ticket from the hall at the station or from one of the booths around town. Your hotel or hostel will almost certainly be able to help you book a ticket. The journey takes around half an hour and costs about ¥40 each way.

By Bus

Buses run from the stop at 210 Hengfeng

Road (21/5663-0230) in Shanghai. The first bus leaves at 7:20 A.M., with departures roughly every half hour until 6:30 P.M. A one-way ticket is ¥25–29; returns can only be bought in Suzhou. If you book by telephone, a ¥2 charge is added. For an extra ¥12, your ticket can be delivered to your address in Shanghai. Coming back the other way, buses leave Suzhou Bus Station (29 Xihui Rd., 512/753-6566) every half hour 7 A.M.–6:30 P.M. They cost the same as tickets for the outward journey.

Tongli 同里

One of the loveliest water towns in the area, Tongli doesn't suffer from the same volume of crowds as the others. However, the relocation of Shanghai's Sex Culture Museum in 2004 raised its profile and its location just 18 kilometers (11.2 mi) from central Suzhou adds to its charms. It's easily accessible directly from Shanghai too, with a bus leaving the sightseeing center at the Shanghai stadium every morning.

Tongli has a history reaching back over 1,000 years. It was originally called Fushi and prospered thanks to the trade that flowed through the region in the Song Dynasty (960–1279). The modern town is home to around 50,000 people, but the old quarter has preserved its quaint, historic charms. Built over seven islands, five lakes, and 15 rivers, it is famous for its 49 ancient bridges. Tongli old town is open to visitors daily 7:30 A.M.–5:30 P.M.; all attractions are open 8:30 A.M.–5:15 P.M. There is an ¥80 fee to enter, which includes entry to all of the attractions except for the Sex Culture Museum.

SIGHTS
Tongli's Bridges and Halls
Tongli is known primarily for its bridges—49

Garden of Retreat and Reflection

© ROBERT PAUL VAN BEETS/123RF.COM

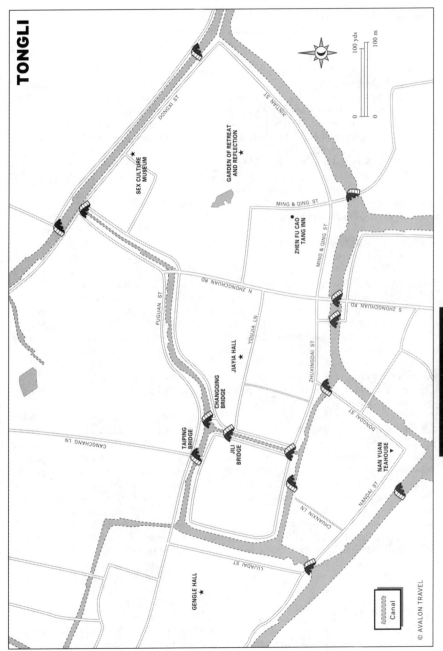

TONGLI

SEX CULTURE MUSEUM ★

GARDEN OF RETREAT AND REFLECTION ★

ZHEN FU CAO TANG INN ●

JIAYA HALL ★

CHANGQING BRIDGE

TAIPING BRIDGE

JILI BRIDGE

GENGLE HALL ★

NAN YUAN TEAHOUSE ▼

DONGXI ST

XINTIAN ST

MING & QING ST

MING & QING ST

N ZHONGCHUAN RD

S ZHONGCHUAN RD

FUGUAN ST

YOUJIA LN

ZHUXINGDAI ST

CANGCHANG LN

DONGDAI ST

CHUANXIN LN

NANDAI ST

LUJIADAI ST

100 yds
100 m

Canal

© AVALON TRAVEL

in total—that span the rivers and canals. Three of the most important are **Taiping** (Peace), **Jili** (Luck), and **Changqing** (Celebration); the legend goes that if you cross all three in succession, you will be blessed with health, prosperity, and a long life.

Tongli's great residential halls are also among its most important sights. **Gengle Hall** is the largest. It was the home of Ming Dynasty aristocrat Zhu Xiang and contains three courtyards, 41 rooms, and a large garden. **Jiayin Hall** is the newest of the halls. Built in 1912 in the Ming style, it was the residence of local scholar Liu Yazi. The third famous hall, **Chongben,** has four courtyards and three doorways, as well as some beautiful wood carvings from classical literature.

Garden of Retreat and Reflection

The Garden of Retreat and Reflection (Tuisi) was built by a retired official called Ren Lanshang in 1887. It covers 700 square meters (7,535 sq. ft.) and includes traditional garden elements like a pavilion, terrace, tower, and porch appearing to "float" on a pond. Your ticket entitles you to a trip over to **Luoxing Islet,** on which you'll find a selection of Buddhist, Daoist, and Confucian buildings. Home to a Buddhist temple since the Yuan Dynasty (1206–1368), the current buildings date from a renovation in the late 1990s.

◖ Sex Culture Museum

Tongli's famous Sex Culture Museum charts 6,000 years of sex and sexuality in China. The museum relocated here from Shanghai's Bund neighborhood in the early 2000s, making Tongli a prime destination for tourists. The museum contains over 3,500 artifacts that are arranged into categories like erotica, sexual health, the marriage system, and sexuality in religion. Of particular intrigue are the museum's collection of chastity belts and jade toys. You'll know you're in the right place when you see the particularly well-endowed statue at the entrance.

RESTAURANTS

Tongli has some great street-side food booths and snack vendors selling local Jiangsu fare like lotus root and grain pancakes. If you can get beyond the smell, try some *chou doufu* (stinky tofu). You'll smell it before you see it, as this delicacy is aptly named. Tofu is marinated in a brine of fermented milk and vegetables before being deep-fried and eaten with chili sauce.

If you want to sit down and eat, try **Nan Yuan Teahouse** (86 Yuxing St.). The two-floor restaurant dates from the Qing Dynasty (1644–1911) and serves family-style food in a rustic, wood-beamed teahouse. Along with a wide variety of tea, Nan Yuan serves dim sum and local dishes on pretty porcelain plates.

HOTELS

The gorgeous 5-star **Tongli Lakeview Hotel** (8 Jiulihu Rd., 203/027-9779, ¥700) on Tongli Lake is a world away from the simple charms of the water village nearby. Opened in 2004 and shaped like a large semicircle, it has 247 guest rooms along with a swimming pool and a beautiful garden. The hotel was designed primarily as a business hotel, but it appeals to leisure travelers, too, thanks to its luxury facilities and high standards. The on-site Japanese restaurant runs a popular buffet and there are Western and Chinese options as well. Guest rooms overlook either the garden or the lake; a sauna, gym, and karaoke facility complete the picture.

Stay inside Tongli's old quarter at the **Zheng Fu Cao Tang Inn** (Mingqing St., 512/632-0576, ¥400–1,300), an attractive 4-star hotel situated behind a traditional moon gate set into a wall. Guest rooms and suites are simply decorated with Chinese-style accents and are categorized as family rooms, "quaint" bedrooms, and "quaint" suites. Some have beautiful, wooden four-poster beds. The hotel is built around a courtyard that contains a pretty rock pool, watched over by a golden Buddha statue. The lounge looks like a traditional pavilion with its wooden ceiling beams and wall panels.

GETTING THERE AND AROUND

A direct bus leaves Shanghai for Tongli every day at 8:30 A.M. and takes around two hours.

It leaves from the Shanghai Sightseeing Bus Center (Staircase 5, Shanghai Stadium, 666 Tianyaoqiao Rd., 21/6426-5555) and same-day return tickets are ¥160, including entrance to Tongli, several halls, and the Garden of Retreat and Reflection (Tuisi). If you want to come back the next day, the ticket is slightly more expensive. The returning bus leaves Tongli to come back to Shanghai at 4 P.M.

Getting to Tongli from Suzhou by bus is relatively easy. Suzhou bus station is just across the bridge in front of the railway station. Ignore the scalpers that will try to sell you taxis and tickets. Head to the ticket booth down the first road on the right when you cross the bridge. A single ticket with entry to Tongli and the main attractions is ¥80. The return fare is ¥10. The bus ride takes just under an hour. Once you arrive, you will again be beset with touts offering to drive you in a taxi or a rickshaw to the old quarter. Once again, ignore them; the old city takes about five minutes on foot and is easy to find. Turn right out of the bus station and take the first right, and you'll see the gate.

BACKGROUND

The Land

GEOGRAPHY

The municipality of Beijing sits at the northern tip of the North China Plain, bordered by Hebei Province and surrounded by mountains to the north, northwest, and west, with desert steppes and agricultural land behind. The Jundu Mountains lie to the northwest in Yangqing and Huairou counties and the Xishan range is located to the west. The Great Wall runs across the northerly reaches of the municipality. The city itself is very flat and is arranged as a series of five concentric ring roads spreading out from the Forbidden City. As of 2010, the Beijing municipality was home to 19.6 million people, which makes it the 26th largest city in China in terms of population and the fourth most-densely populated.

Shanghai municipality spreads across 18 districts and one county and has a population of 23 million. Around 9 million are permanent or long-term migrants. The Huangpu River cuts the city into two distinct areas: Puxi (literally "west of the Huangpu"), which contains the Old City, former foreign concessions, and main commercial areas; and Pudong ("east of the Huangpu"), which is home to the modern skyline, Lujiazui Financial Zone, and the international airport. The Huangpu is the last stretch of the great Yangtze River before it meets the East China Sea. Shanghai is the

© J. LESLIE HOWARD

centerpiece of the Yangtze River delta area on China's eastern coast, about halfway between Beijing and Hong Kong. This area is one of the most prosperous parts of China and a hub of trade and industry.

THE CLIMATE

Beijing has four distinct seasons; its climate is generally dry. Winters are cold and crisp, with temperatures dipping below -4 degrees Celsius (-20 degrees Fahrenheit) in January and early February. Snowfall is common (sadly, the pretty white flakes quickly turn brown with city grime). Spring begins in late March and runs to mid-June, auguring some of the most pleasant months in the calendar, as far as weather is concerned. Beijing summers can be scorching hot, with temperatures reaching 40 degrees Celsius (104 degrees Fahrenheit) in July and August. Beijing gets most of its rainfall in July, with an average precipitation level of 185 millimeters (7 in.). Humidity is generally low, reaching a peak of 77 percent in August. September through November is fall; these months are similarly clement to spring. The air in Beijing is known for being dry-visitors should carry a packet of throat lozenges to counteract a raspy throat.

Farther south on China's east coast, Shanghai has a subtropical monsoon climate. Humidity is constant throughout the year, hovering around 75–82 percent. There are two rainy seasons in Shanghai: The Plum Rains hit for several weeks at the end of June, ushering in the heat of summer and ripening the plums that grow in the Yangtze Delta. After a month of 28-degree-Celsius (82-degree-Fahrenheit) heat in July, another swath of rain falls throughout August. Despite being farther south than Beijing, Shanghai's average temperatures are actually lower, due to the city's proximity to the ocean. Winters can be cold and damp, but temperatures never fall below 5 degrees Celsius (28 degrees Fahrenheit). Snow is rare, but not unheard of. The most pleasant times to visit Shanghai are late March to late June and mid-September to mid-November. If you're there in winter, make sure to pack warm clothes: Shanghai is classed as South China; thus, most buildings are not centrally heated as they are in Beijing.

Environmental Issues

Both Beijing and Shanghai are notorious for poor air quality. Shanghai's air is often so smoggy that the taller buildings disappear behind a hazy shroud of car fumes and industrial emissions. Dust storms from the surrounding deserts make Beijing's air dry and factories around both cities contribute to the pollution. China's rapid industrialization and its current position as a production center have adversely affected air quality, but measures are in effect to turn things around—albeit slowly.

The run-up to the 2008 Olympics saw several drives towards clean air in Beijing. Over US$17 million were spent to improve air quality. Factories were closed for the duration of the Games and a traffic scheme was inaugurated whereby cars with odd- and even-numbered registration plates could enter the city on alternate days. The public transport system was improved with the addition of two subway lines, and fleets of new, more eco-friendly taxis and buses replaced some of the old models.

In Shanghai, the development of Chongming Island and the drive towards renewable energy are positive moves. The municipal government installed 100,000 photovoltaic systems on rooftops in 2005, which create 430 million hours of power per year. This cuts carbon dioxide emissions by 40,000 tons and saves 20,000 tons of coal. This helps towards the central government's goal for 3 percent of China's energy to come from solar power by 2020. Further advances in clean-energy include a large-scale wind farm built by the Shanghai Environment Group and Shanghai Huadian Electric Power Development Company. It generates 50 million kilowatt hours of power to the city, which is definitely a step in the right direction.

History

ANCIENT CHINA

China is immensely proud of its 5,000 years of uninterrupted history and culture. Chinese civilization began during the Neolithic ages in what is now southern Shaanxi and western Henan. The extant sources for early Chinese history are the *Bamboo Annals* and the *Records of the Grand Historian* by Sima Qian. The very earliest period is shrouded in myth and mystery. It starts with the prehistoric Three Sovereigns and Five Emperors period during which China was governed by three kings—the rulers of Heaven, Earth, and Humans—and five demigods. Next came the Xia Dynasty (3000–1500 B.C.) and the rule of the semi-legendary Yellow Emperor (Huangdi) who is said to have invented martial arts.

LAND OF THE EMPERORS

The Xia Empire was overthrown by rebels who began the Shang Dynasty, which lasted 1523–1028 B.C. with 30 emperors. The Shang era saw the development of a writing system using inscriptions on oracle bones. Agriculture also flourished, as did metal casting. The Shang fell to the Zhou, which was the longest dynasty in imperial history (1045–256 B.C.). The Zhou came from Gansu and Shanxi and established their capital at Chang'an (modern Xi'an). This period is known as the starting point of Chinese philosophy, with sages like Confucius, Mencius, and Laozi writing and teaching.

The era was divided into the Eastern Zhou and Western Zhou by the brief Qin Dynasty and was a time of political turmoil with the Warring States and Spring and Autumn Period. Worship shifted from pagan earth religions to heavenly deities and the divine right of emperors was instated. It was during the Qin Dynasty that the first official imperial court was established, replacing old feudal methods of rule. The Terracotta Army was built to commemorate the first Qin emperor and the Great Wall was begun.

The relatively peaceful Han Dynasty (206 B.C.–A.D. 220) followed, auguring a golden age of astronomy, ocean navigation, and papermaking. This era gives its name to China's main ethnic group and is one of the most important dynasties, despite its short length. Peace was disturbed only by small-scale peasant uprisings like the quaintly-named Turban Rebellion and Five Pecks of Rice Rebellion, but the Three Kingdoms era that came next (A.D. 220–280) was not so tranquil. China was divided into the Shu, Wei, and Wu kingdoms and infighting was endemic. Despite the violence, Buddhism and Taoism gained in popularity and painting flourished.

The Jin Dynasty (A.D. 265–420) saw China expand to the west and south and the capital was moved from Xi'an to Nanjing. During the Southern and Northern Dynasties (A.D. 420–589) the army and navy were strengthened and Buddhism arrived from India. The short Sui Dynasty (A.D. 581–618) followed, with the expansion of the Great Wall and the beginning of the Grand Canal that would eventually stretch from Beijing to Hangzhou. One of the most famous and important dynasties was the Tang Dynasty (A.D. 618–907). As well as introducing China and Chinese goods to the rest of the world via the Silk Road, the Xi'an-based Tang court was a powerhouse of poetry and painting. China's population stood at around 50 million and was difficult to control, leading to divisions in the Five Dynasties and Ten States era (A.D. 907–960).

CHINA IN THE MIDDLE AGES

The Song Dynasty (A.D. 960–1279) ushered in China's medieval period. The capital moved to Kaifeng in modern-day Henan Province, but despite unity and power, the Mongol empire was encroaching under Genghis Khan. His grandson, Kublai Khan, invaded China in 1271 and began the Yuan Dynasty that lasted until 1368. During this time, the Mongolian kingdom was the biggest empire in world history. Beijing was the Yuan capital and was known as Dadu. Marco Polo visited China and took back cultural observations that shaped China's reputation in the West.

Zhu Yuanzhang overthrew the Mongols in 1368 and began the Ming Dynasty in Nanjing. It was during this era that great cities grew, classical literature was written, and Chinese art and pottery became more and more sophisticated. Legendary eunuch navigator Zheng He set sail with his giant ships and the Forbidden City was built in Beijing for the emperor's court. This long dynasty ended in 1644 when a weak emperor was overthrown by tribal leaders advancing from Manchuria in the far north.

THE LAST EMPIRE

China's last imperial dynasty, the Qing, was founded by Manchu insurgents who established their capital in Beijing. Chinese territory stretched to Tibet and Xinjiang. Emperors Kangxi, Yongzheng, and Qianlong led the Qing Golden Age of the 18th century. Central power was compromised by the Opium Wars of the mid-1800s and the Taiping Rebellion (1850–1864), when a Christian heretic rose up against the government, claiming to be the brother of Jesus. Corruption during the reign of the Dowager Empress Cixi fostered revolutionary feeling among anti-government luminaries like Sun Yat-sen, who led the Xinhai Revolution in 1911. Two millennia of imperial rule came to an end and China was a republic at last.

TURMOIL IN THE 20TH CENTURY

The first half of the 20th century was a time of political upheaval, civil war, and general unrest. The last emperor, Puyi, abdicated in February 1912 under pressure from the Chinese Revolutionary Alliance. The Han majority had come to resent Manchu rule and the revolutionary movement had widespread support. Sun Yat-sen founded the nationalist Guomindang (KMT) party to rule the new Republic of China. He was succeeded by Chiang Kai-shek in 1925. Chiang led the Northern Expedition in 1926 to unify China

and purge the Communists. The Guomindang hung on to power throughout several decades of war with the Japanese and Western colonization, but finally fell to the Communists under Mao in 1949. Chiang fled to Taiwan with China's gold reserves and around two million followers in December 1949, declaring Taipei the capital of the Republic of China (ROC).

Chairman Mao Zedong officially established the People's Republic of China (PRC) on October 1, 1949. Using Marxist-Leninist ideals, he set up a socialist one-party system and closed China to the rest of the world. During the three decades that followed, unquantifiable suffering went on in the guise of development schemes like the Cultural Revolution (during which anything and anyone bourgeois or anti-Communist was purged or sent to the countryside for re-education) and the Great Leap Forward (which compromised agriculture and caused millions to die of starvation). Mao died in 1976 and was succeeded by Hua Guofeng, who had previously taken over from Zhou Enlai, the first prime minister of the PRC. Hua ousted the Gang of Four (including Mao's wife) and ended the Cultural Revolution, but was overthrown by Deng Xiaoping in 1978. Deng had been purged twice during the Cultural Revolution for espousing non-Maoist ideals and when he came to power he instigated many of the changes that have launched China as a world power.

Deng Xiaoping opened China up to the rest of the world again and instigated economic reforms. From his time in the West during his student years, he realized the advantages of a free market, capitalist economy. Privately-owned enterprises were permitted once again and China's clout began to grow. It is now the second largest economy in the world after the United States and has grown by an average of 10 percent each year for the past three decades. It is the largest exporter and second largest importer in the world and overtook the United States as the biggest manufacturer in 2011. Not bad for a country that started the 20th Century as a medieval-style, un-industrialized imperial state.

RISE OF THE PARIS OF THE EAST

Shanghai's history is relatively short compared to Beijing's. It was a small fishing village until 1074 in the Song Dynasty when it was granted the status of a market town. It became a county in the Yuan Dynasty in 1292 and remained so until it acquired city status in 1927. The construction of a Ming Dynasty city wall in 1554 to quell Japanese pirate attacks and the building of a City God Temple in 1602 raised Shanghai's status. The early years of the Qing Dynasty saw the Kangxi Emperor lift the trade sanctions that had been in place since 1525. Once again, ships were allowed to pass through the city. This established Shanghai as an important point of trade in the Yangtze Delta, with the Huangpu River leading to the sea. In 1732 the Yongzheng Emperor moved Jiangsu Province's customhouse from Songjiang to Shanghai and by the time the first Opium War broke out, the city was important enough to be seized as a treaty port by the British.

THE INTERNATIONAL SETTLEMENTS

The first Opium War between China and Britain raged 1839–42, with the Qing government seeking to quash the illegal trade in opium between British merchants and local gangsters. The first war ended with the government signing over Hong Kong to Britain and opening five treaty ports to foreign trade under the Treaty of Nanjing. These ports were Shanghai, Guangdong, Ningbo, Fuzhou, and Xiamen. The Unequal Treaties, as these deals were rightly known, decreed that British merchants were exempt from paying transit duties. In the treaty ports, foreign concessions were set up to house the rich merchants and their households, while local Chinese became the scorned underclass.

Shanghai's International Settlement was established in 1842 and included the parts of the city north of Bubbling Well Road (the old name for West Nanjing Road) up to the Suzhou Creek. It was originally called the British Concession, but later expanded to include the French and American territories to the north and south. The French Concession became a separate entity in 1862. The Chinese parts of Shanghai came under Japanese occupation after the Battle of Shanghai in 1937. On one of the darkest days of this battle, a Chinese plane dropped a bomb on East Nanjing Road to offload during an air pursuit by the Japanese, but the pilot aimed badly and over a thousand people were killed or injured. The International Settlement was occupied in 1941 and the city remained under Japanese control until 1945.

The International Settlement's most striking legacy comes in the form of the 52 buildings that line the Huangpu waterfront on the Bund. Built in a range of Western styles, like Gothic, art deco and neoclassical, these customhouses, banking headquarters, and grand hotels form one of Shanghai's most iconic vistas. The Old French Concession has a totally different look and feel, with its tree-arched streets, sun-dappled villas, and European-style apartment blocks.

Beijing's foreign concession is known as the Legation Quarter and sits to the east of Tian'anmen Square. It was established after the second Opium War to house the capital's consulates. Most of the diplomatic offices were closed at the start of the second Sino-Japanese War in 1937 and several of the buildings were torn down, including the HSBC building that fell to the wrecker's ball in the 1980s.

SIN CITY

Shanghai has long been a byword for sin and depravity. Sailors press-ganged into joining a crew were said to have been "Shanghaied" and the opium dens, gambling houses, cabarets, and brothels gave the city a well-deserved reputation of vice. Until the Communists took power in 1949, Shanghai was ruled by an underground federation called the Green Gang, led by the colorfully-named "Big Ears" Du Yuesheng and "Pockmarked" Huang Jinrong. The Green Gang was so influential that it helped finance Chiang Kai-shek's Guomindang. Du Yuesheng masterminded the massacre of Communists known as the White Terror in 1927 and was made a general for his efforts. However, Chiang Kai-shek's son jailed most of Du's family and cronies after World War II, in an attempt to clear the Guomindang of any criminal associations. Du refused to join Chiang Kai-shek when the Nationalists fled to Taiwan in 1949.

Shanghai's dance hall boom of the early- to mid-20th century was financed by the city's gangster elite. From his grand residence in the French Concession (now the attractive Donghu Hotel), Du Yuesheng controlled his empire of cabarets and jazz clubs. After the Communist victory in the Civil War and the establishment of the People's Republic, dancing, gambling, and prostitution were outlawed, spelling an official end to Shanghai's tenure as a city of sin.

MAKING OF THE MODERN CITY

When the Communists rose to power, most of the foreign firms operating in Shanghai moved their offices to Hong Kong and foreign investment waned. Many grand old buildings were converted into state offices or factories and the once-colorful metropolis was draped in shades of socialist gray and communist red. The Cultural Revolution of 1966–1976 further chipped away at Shanghai's soul and stringent economic schemes redirected much of the city's wealth to central government and surrounding provinces. Deng Xiaoping's reforms of the late 1970s and early 1980s had little effect on Shanghai's wealth and it wasn't until 1991 that economic development was permitted. Until the mid-1990s, Shanghai was a relatively low-rise city; Lujiazui Financial Zone started to grow with the completion of the Oriental Pearl in 1994 and the Jin Mao tower in 1998. The unfettered economic boom of the early 21st century has made Shanghai into one of the world's most dynamic cities.

Government and Economy

GOVERNMENT
The Emperor

Modern China is ruled by a single-party government under a Maoist Communist regime. Hu Jintao leads the country as Paramount Leader and General Secretary, with a tripartite system made up of the Communist Party of China, the Central People's Government, and the People's Liberation Army. The Communist Party and State Council sit at Zhongnanhai near the Forbidden City; the State Council is elected by the National People's Congress—the PRC's only legislative house. The Chinese constitution was written in 1954 and is now in its fourth incarnation.

The cities of Beijing and Shanghai have their own municipal government to administrate city-level affairs. The old saying goes that "heaven is high and the emperor is far away," implying that the further you get from central government, the less power the government wields. This can be seen today in Shanghai, which seems to work on its own agenda. That

© SUSIE GORDON

Chairman Mao – the Great Helmsman

The Bund in 1963

isn't to say that liberalism is permitted; any inkling of a Tian'anmen-style uprising is quickly quashed, such as the short-lived pro-democracy protests in February 2011, inspired by Tunisia's Jasmine Revolution. The Chinese state-run media is tightly controlled and Western social networks like Facebook and Twitter cannot penetrate the Great Firewall. China's shaky human rights record put off a lot of foreign visitors, but the chances of encountering any unrest are extremely slim.

Socialism

The fact that China looks very much like a capitalist nation is due to Deng Xiaoping's particular brand of socialism. Begun with the economic reforms of the late 1970s, the Chinese brand of socialism differs from Soviet and Western models due to its basis in feudalism and not capitalism. While Western nations that fell to communism had years of capitalism in which to develop economically and socially, socialist China had a lot of catching up to do after Deng's "opening up." Characteristics of

Chinese socialism are developments in the private sector and a free market economy under a single-party system.

The One-Child Policy

One of Chairman Mao's dreams for China was a huge population. Boosted by Communist fervor, he encouraged the people to go forth and multiply. Anyone who discouraged this (like population expert Ma Yanchu) was purged. However, Mao agreed to a national census in 1953, which revealed that China's population had tipped 600 billion. Unsustainable in the long term, both economically and socially, the growth had to be curtailed. Under Deng Xiaoping, the One-Child Policy was passed in 1979. Couples from the Han ethnic majority could have one child only or face crippling fines. Rural couples were allowed a second child if their first was a girl, since boy children were favored for their strength and position within the family.

As far as achieving its aim was concerned, the One-Child Policy was a great success, with 400 million fewer people born 1979–2008.

However, thanks to the preference for male children, China now has 60 million more men than women. Countless millions of girl babies were aborted, killed, and abandoned, leading to a swell in international adoption of Chinese girls. Conditions in China's orphanages horrified the rest of the world when a documentary called *The Dying Rooms* was released in 1995, showing secretly filmed footage of infants left to perish. As a result of the film, orphanage conditions were improved and propaganda was released to assure parents that girls were just as good as boys. The One-Child Policy is still in effect, but single children can have more than one baby if their partner is also an only child.

ECONOMY
Wealth and Poverty

Walk through almost any district of Beijing or Shanghai and China's wealth gap will be plain to see. Beggars rattle their money dishes outside luxury shopping arcades, and ramshackle huts coexist with shiny new apartment blocks and office complexes. The Gini coefficient for measuring wealth inequality places China outside the World Bank's suggested limits. China's Gini is 0.496, on a scale in which 1 is the widest wealth gap and 0 is the smallest (for comparison, Sweden's is 0.23). Figures from China's Director of Statistics reveal that there are 130 billionaires in China and 150 million citizens living below the poverty line. Not only is this unfair, but a skewed Gini coefficient is said to lead to social unrest—a nightmare for China's harmony-obsessed government.

Deng Xiaoping's predictions that "some people will get rich first" through his economic reforms have come true, but prime minister Wen Jiabao is determined to even things out. He plans to allow migrant workers to access healthcare, housing, and education for their children in towns and low-tier cities. Recent tax regulations mean that high-earners will be monitored more closely and a minimum wage of ¥1,000 per month is in operation in Shanghai, Guangdong, and Zhejiang.

People and Culture

DEMOGRAPHY

The vast majority of China's population belongs to the Han racial group, but 8.49 percent come from 55 minority ethnicities. A Chinese citizen's ethnicity is marked on his or her ID card and non-Han people are permitted to have more than one baby under the One-Child Policy. Most Chinese ethnic minorities are found in pockets in the south, north, and west; most of eastern China is populated by the Han majority. The second most common ethnicity after Han is Zhuang, with 16.2 million members, mostly in Guangxi Province. Other populous minorities are the Manchu of Liaoning, the Miao (Hmong) of the southwest, and the Tujia of Hunan Province. The smallest ethnic group is the Lhoba in southeast Tibet, numbering under 3,000 members. A large ethnic mix is found in Yunnan Province, where groups include the Yi, Dai, Bai, and Miao. Many preserve their traditional ways of life, dressing in ethnic costume and using old-fashioned farming methods.

RELIGION

Religion was officially outlawed by the Communist Party, but thousands of years of folk worship, Buddhism, and Daoism were not stamped out completely. In both Beijing and Shanghai you'll see countless temples, as well as the churches, mosques, and synagogues built by migrants over the centuries. The government still keeps a close eye on religious organizations, but practitioners of the main religions are left alone.

Buddhism

One of modern China's most practiced religions, Buddhism arrived from India in the 1st century A.D. on the Silk Road. The Chan (Zen) sect developed during the 5th

PICK A NUMBER

In the West, it's common to avoid and even fear the number 13, while the number 7 is often revered for its supposedly lucky properties. In China, however, things are a little different, as it's the number 4 that's considered unlucky; 8 is considered extremely lucky.

When a new set of license plates or phone numbers is released, there's a mad scramble to grab the ones with the most 8s and 9s, and steer clear of any with multiple 4s. You may remember that the Beijing Olympics started at 8:08 on August (the eighth month) 8, 2008. Shanghai's Jin Mao Tower was built with 88 floors. You'll rarely see a 4th or 14th floor in a building, the same way the 13th floor is often missing in Western buildings. So what's the story behind these superstitions?

It all comes down to the fact that Mandarin has many words that sound like each other. Since it is a tonal language, a lot of meaning is attributed to both context and tones. *Si*, the word for the number 4, has many homonyms, one of which means death. *Yao si*, the word for 14 sounds like the phrase "want to die."

Conversely, *ba*, the word for 8, is a homonym for "accumulating wealth." Other lucky numbers are 9, which sounds like "everlasting," 6, which sounds like "flowing," and 7, a homonym for "rise up." The number 2 is considered auspicious thanks to its character's symmetry, while 3 is a symbol of regeneration, as it sounds like "birth" in some dialects.

century, merging with Confucianism and Daoism during the medieval Song Dynasty. The Mongol leaders of the Yuan empire established Buddhism as the official religion of China and Tibetan lamas were integrated into the court. Chan Buddhism came back with the Ming Dynasty and the Gelukpa school gained popularity during the Qing. Chinese Buddhism pays special attention to Guanyin, the bodhisattva of mercy. Her image can be seen in many Buddhist temples in Beijing and Shanghai.

Daoism

Practicing the tenets of the 3rd century Dao De Jing by Laozi, Daoists lead their lives by the esoteric concepts of "the way" (dao/tao), the relationship between humans and their environment, simplicity (pu), virtue (de), and inaction (wu wei). Daoist practices include ancestor worship, feng shui, and traditional medicine. Many Shanghainese Daoists worship at the White Cloud Temple—the headquarters of the Shanghai Taoist Association. The temple of the same name in Beijing is its twin. Many Daoist temples were used as state factories during the Cultural Revolution, like the City God Temple in Shanghai's old quarter. It was given back to the Daoists in 1994.

Confucianism

Although a philosopher and a sage, the 5th century scholar Confucius has been venerated to almost godlike status over the years since. Confucianism was the state ideology of the Han Dynasty and went on to inform the social structure of modern China. At times vilified under the Communists for feudal leanings, Confucius survives today as a figure of respect. His teachings about respect to one's parents and family values still underpin contemporary society.

Islam

Islam is said to have arrived in China in A.D. 651 with the uncle of the Prophet Mohammed. The Tang Emperor Gaozong built the Huaisheng Mosque in Guangzhou to commemorate this visit; Muslim advisors were a common sight in the courts of the Yuan and Ming Dynasties. Muslims were treated less well under the Manchu Qings, with ritual animal slaughter forbidden and pilgrimages to Mecca banned. Ten of China's ethnic minorities are Muslim, including the Uighurs of Xinjiang and the Hui. There are beautiful places of worship like the Ox Street Mosque in Beijing and around 20 million followers of Islam on China's mainland.

Judaism

The first wave of Jewish settlers arrived in Shanghai in the 1850s, bringing Sephardi and Baghdadi Jews from Iraq and India. They included the wealthy Sassoon and Hardoon families, who made their mark on the city's public face with buildings like the Cathay Mansions, Sassoon House, and the Metropole Hotel. This Jewish community built the Beth El synagogue in 1887, which was replaced by the Ohel Rachel on North Shaanxi Road in 1920. Six other synagogues were built around the city, but only Ohel Rachel and Ohel Moishe in Hongkou survive (the latter is now the Jewish Refugee Museum). The second wave of Jewish migrants came with the onset of World War II, when Russian and Polish Ashkenazi Jews arrived in the early 1930s to escape persecution. While the Sephardi community was made up of wealthy tycoons, bankers, and businessmen, the Azhkenazim worked in lower paid industries like shop keeping.

Shanghai's modern Jewish community numbers several hundred and is growing every year. Rabbi Shalom Greenberg is a leading figure, organizing dinners, social events, and bar-mitzvah training. Beijing's Jewish history is less rich and the city has no synagogues. However, there are several Jewish organizations like Chabad Lubavitch and Kehillat Beijing.

Christianity

A Persian missionary brought Christianity to China in A.D. 635 during the Tang Dynasty, but Christian converts were persecuted under Emperor Wuzong. It wasn't until the arrival of Italian Jesuits at the close of the Ming Dynasty that Christianity had its heyday in China. Matteo Ricci was the most famous of the Italian Jesuits coming to Beijing in the late 16th century. The Qing Dynasty brought Jesuits to Shanghai,

too, and an enclave of the Old French Concession in Xujiahui served as their headquarters. The grand, twin-spired St. Ignatius Cathedral bears witness to their influence. Both Beijing and Shanghai have some lovely churches and cathedrals, many of which are still used for active service in Mandarin and English. There are an estimated 10 million Protestants and 4 million Catholics in China and all are free to worship as long as they register with the authorities.

LANGUAGE
Mandarin

China's official language is Mandarin—the most widely spoken tongue in the world with over 800 million native speakers. Known in China as Putonghua (standard speech), Zhongwen (language of the Middle Kingdom), and Hanyu (language of the Han people), Mandarin gets its English name from the Portuguese word for government official. It is a member of the Sino-Tibetan language group and uses a logographic writing system made up of thousands of symbols called hanzi. A tonal language, Mandarin has fewer sounds than European languages and a relatively simple grammar system. Verbs don't conjugate and meaning is largely context-based. Standard Mandarin is based on the dialect of Beijing and is a lingua franca in a country of mutually unintelligible regional variations. Cantonese is a dialect of Mandarin, as is Hakka and Shanghainese. The Mandarin spoken in Beijing is known for its rhotic "r" sounds, which turn a word like "chuan" (meat skewer) into "chuarrr."

Shanghainese

Although Mandarin is the official language of mainland China, the city of Shanghai has its own dialect. Shanghainese is a sub-branch of the Wu dialect spoken across Zhejiang Province, southern Jiangsu, and areas of Jiangxi, Anhui, and Fujian. Shanghai natives tend to be bilingual in Mandarin and Shanghainese, but the older generation may only speak dialect. Shanghainese has 13

THE YEAR OF THE WHAT?

Unlike the Western zodiac in which the months of the year are split into 12 signs, the Chinese calendar separates signs by years. The Chinese lunar year begins in late January or early February with Spring Festival (known more commonly to Westerners as Chinese New Year). There are many stories and legends behind the 12 animals that make up the Chinese zodiac. One of the best-loved and most interesting is the tale of the Jade Emperor and his helper friend, the rat.

Legend has it that in ancient times, the Jade Emperor decided to create a zodiac. He asked his favorite animal, the rat, to help him gather 12 different animals – one for each year of the lunar cycle. The rat agreed, and set about organizing a race across the river. The first 12 animals to reach the other side would take their place in the zodiac according to the order in which they finished the race.

RAT

The rat hitched a ride across the river on the back of an ox, along with a cat that had heard about the race. As they were about to reach the other side, the rat pushed the cat into the river, and swam ahead to finish first and become the first animal in the zodiac.

Characteristics: People born in the Year of the Rat can be wily, inventive, and resourceful.
Years: 1936, 1948, 1960, 1972, 1984, 1996, 2008, 2020

OX

The strong, steadfast ox was the second creature to cross the river.

Characteristics: People born in the Year of the Ox are dependable, but can be stubborn.
Years: 1937, 1949, 1961, 1973, 1985, 1997, 2009, 2021

TIGER

The powerful tiger leapt effortlessly across the river, and won himself third place.
Characteristics: People born in the Year of the Tiger are self-assured, confident, and can be arrogant.
Years: 1938, 1950, 1962, 1974, 1986, 1998, 2010, 2022

RABBIT

Next was the dragon, but he stopped to make rain for a drought-stricken town. The rabbit overtook him and came into fourth place.
Characteristics: People born in the Year of the Rabbit are sociable and can sometimes be non-confrontational.
Years: 1939, 1951, 1963, 1975, 1987, 1999, 2011, 2023

DRAGON

The mystical dragon was next to arrive on the river bank.
Characteristics: As the only mythological animal in the zodiac, the dragon is seen as a particularly lucky sign. People born in the Year of the Dragon make charismatic leaders and are generous souls.
Years: 1940, 1952, 1964, 1976, 1988, 2000, 2012, 2024

---

million native speakers—the same as Swedish. It comes from the same roots as Mandarin, but is more similar to Japanese in terms of word order. Non-speakers describe its sound as "ji-ji ga-ga" for its fast, guttural sound.

English

There are still plenty of areas in Beijing and Shanghai where English isn't spoken, but the main tourist districts and city centers are replete with English speakers. Picking up a few key Mandarin phrases goes a long way, even if you don't understand the response! Learning English from an early age is becoming the norm for most of Beijing and Shanghai, with language schools popping up across both cities. The abundance of English teaching work attracts Westerners to China, where a decent salary and apartment awaits the intrepid TEFL (Teaching English as a Foreign Language) holder.

SNAKE

Coming up next was the horse, but before he could get to the riverbank, the snake unwound himself from the horse's leg and slithered ahead to the finish.

Characteristics: Those born in the Year of the Snake can be sneaky and sly, but are also creative, resourceful, and persuasive.

Years: 1941, 1953, 1965, 1977, 1989, 2001, 2013, 2025

HORSE

The good-natured horse arrived next, unperturbed by the snake's successful attempt to overtake him.

Characteristics: People born in the Year of the Horse are optimistic and gregarious, and love to be the center of attention.

Years: 1942, 1954, 1966, 1978, 1990, 2002, 2014, 2026

SHEEP

The sheep teamed up with the monkey and rooster to build a raft to cross the river. The sheep jumped off the raft first to finish ahead of his teammates.

Characteristics: People born in the Year of the Sheep are good team players.

Years: 1943, 1955, 1967, 1979, 1991, 2003, 2015, 2027

MONKEY

Next to finish was the jovial monkey.

Characteristics: People born in the Year of the Monkey are quick, fun-loving, and humorous; they love playing pranks.

Years: 1944, 1956, 1968, 1980, 1992, 2004, 2016, 2028

ROOSTER

The rooster was the next animal to make it to the other side of the river.

Characteristics: People born in the Year of the Rooster are clever and love the limelight.

Years: 1945, 1957, 1969, 1981, 1993, 2005, 2017, 2029

DOG

Steady and determined, the dog made his way across the river and into the zodiac.

Characteristics: People born in the Year of the Dog tend to be loyal, selfless, and can be single-minded.

Years: 1946, 1958, 1970, 1982, 1994, 2006, 2018, 2030

PIG

The sleep-loving pig woke up just in time to join the race and claim the final place in the zodiac.

Characteristics: People born in the Year of the Pig are humorous and sociable, but can sometimes be lazy.

Years: 1947, 1959, 1971, 1983, 1995, 2007, 2019, 2031

CAT

The cat never managed to catch up with the rat, and so missed out on being part of the zodiac. However, if someone asks you which sign you are and you don't want to reveal your age, you can say "The Year of the Cat" and smile enigmatically.

URBAN SPACES AND GENTRIFICATION

It is estimated that by the year 2015, 60 percent of mainland Chinese will live in cities. Around 100 Chinese cities will have a population of 1 million or more by 2020. Figures like this highlight the need for town planning and urban development, but China's often heavy-handed approach (i.e., knocking down the old to make way for the new) doesn't always sit well with city dwellers. Two major events thrust China into the world spotlight at the start of the 21st century. The 2008 Beijing Olympics and the 2010 World Expo in Shanghai gave the municipal government ammunition to ride roughshod over old districts. In Beijing, countless *hutong* (alleys) and *siheyuan* (courtyard residences) were destroyed to make the city look more attractive. Some residents, distraught at losing their homes, protested using such extreme measures as self-immolation and suicide. Shanghai's Expo cleanup saw the destruction of *shikumen* (stone gate–style) lanes and traditional hawker streets like Wujiang Road.

However, Shanghai's government has recognized the value of preserving and gentrifying old districts with a view to making money. If a traditional lane or alley can be commoditized, it can stay. One such project is Xintiandi. Spearheaded by American architect Benjamin Wood and bankrolled by Shui On Land, the "New Heaven and Earth" development saw the renovation of an old *shikumen* that had been tagged for demolition. It is now one of the city's most luxurious areas, with fancy restaurants, expensive bars, and designer boutiques, flanking an alley dotted with fountains and statues. A more recent example is the Portman House Jian Ye Li project in the Old French Concession, which has transformed a 1930s *shikumen* into a complex of luxury apartments, villas, and retail space. Since *shikumen* were originally homes for Shanghai's working classes, this particular redevelopment could be seen as tasteless.

Urban developers have missed the mark in Shanghai's One City, Nine Towns scheme. This overly ambitious plan saw the construction of nine new towns to mop up urban overspill in Shanghai's suburbs, each modeled on a European or North American town. These include the German-style Anting and Lingang Harbour City, Italian-inspired Pujiang, and the Thames Town suburb of Songjiang that mimics an English village. The fact that most of these towns lie empty suggests that Shanghai residents aren't willing to live in gimmicky, hurriedly (and badly) constructed conurbations.

Beijing seems more attuned to the problems of redevelopment than Shanghai. The Cultural Heritage Protection Center is a non-profit organization that lobbies against the destruction of old buildings. Founder and president Hu Shunzhong was behind the protests against redeveloping the old *hutong* (alley) neighborhoods around the Drum and Bell Towers—a move he compared to "building hotels in the Forbidden City."

While it's easy to decry this widespread demolition, it shouldn't be forgotten that China is a country in the throes of development. To privileged Western eyes, destruction of old buildings is a tragedy, but many of the structures foreigners admire (such as the art deco villas of Shanghai's Old French Concession) stand as reminders of colonial rule. A fine balance must be struck between honoring history and moving forward.

The Arts

It has taken China's arts scene several decades to get over the effects of the Cultural Revolution, when books, artworks, and creative ideas were destroyed in the name of progress. While Shanghai tends to hide her artistic light under a bushel, projecting a more commercial public image, Beijing's creative scene is flourishing.

ARCHITECTURE

Both Beijing and Shanghai display a dizzying contrast of ancient and modern when it comes to architecture. The distinction is more acute in Beijing, where more Ming and Qing buildings have survived modern urbanization. Modernist structures like the new CCTV tower and Financial Street high-rises jostle for attention among the upturned eaves and blue slate roofs of the Forbidden City. Traditional courtyard residences known as *siheyuan* lie along the *hutong* alleys, fanning out from the grid-like road system around the old Imperial city.

While much of Beijing is low-rise, Shanghai reaches to the clouds with its bristling skyline. Some of Asia's tallest buildings flank the Lujiazui waterfront in Pudong, creating an iconic panorama that comes alive at night. But Shanghai has some old architecture too, mostly found in the Old City. The streets of the Old

French Concession are lined with colonial-era villas in European and art deco styles.

Shanghai's Art Deco

You wouldn't instantly identify Shanghai as the city with the most art deco buildings in the world, but spread among its new developments are hundreds of beautiful historic villas, apartment blocks, cinemas, and theaters. Art deco was popular around the world between 1925 and 1939, combining early 20th century styles like cubism, neoclassicism, modernism, and art nouveau to create a design movement with simple lines, block colors, and—importantly—no political implications or allegiances. The Great Depression stopped the spread of art deco in the West (with the exception of Mafia-controlled Miami Beach), but Shanghai was in the middle of its first boom when the movement arrived. At that time it was the fifth largest city in the world, with around four million inhabitants and was rich in culture and economy thanks to years of colonial power. The cosmopolitan Paris of the East was perfect for art deco and designers moved in to revamp the city. Reacting against the austerity of the Bund and the complexity of traditional Chinese architecture, their buildings were fresh and modern.

At the forefront of the art deco movement in Shanghai was Czech-Hungarian László Hudec. Working between 1918 and 1945, he was responsible for some of the most famous and attractive buildings in the city, such as the Park Hotel on West Nanjing Road, the Grand Theater, and the Normandie Apartments in the French Concession. Another Czech architect, C. H. Gonda, designed cinemas including the Capitol and the Cathay, both of which survive. Sadly this hasn't been the case for many of Shanghai's art deco gems. The inexorable march of progress has seen hundreds of buildings destroyed to make way for modern developments. Shanghainese photographer Deke Erh is trying to raise awareness of the city's art deco heritage through his gallery in the Tianzifang lane complex. His

2007 book, *Shanghai Art Deco,* includes over a thousand photographs as well as text in both Chinese and English about the importance of preserving these buildings. Many buildings have also been saved by the municipal government's realization that visitors are willing to pay for art deco. The recent renovation of the Peace Hotel on the Bund is a testament to this.

MUSIC

Classical Chinese music has its origins in the Zhou Dynasty (1122–256 B.C.) and flourished in the imperial courts of the Qin, Han, and Tang. Traditional instruments include the two-stringed erhu, guqin lute, and zheng zither. Based on a simple modal scale, Chinese music has a distinctive sound. Fast forward to the Republican Era of the early 20th century and Eastern music met Western styles in the New Culture Movement. Symphony orchestras and jazz became popular in the major cities. When the Communists came to power, traditional Chinese folk songs were reworked into revolutionary choral epics, like "The East is Red," and "The Yellow River Cantata."

The era of modern Chinese music began in Shanghai with a fusion of jazz and traditional music known as shidaiqu. The major proponents of this style were the Seven Great Singing Stars, including the tragic diva Zhou Xuan. These all-singing, all-dancing performers appeared on the soundtracks of many Chinese films, making cinema even more popular. Shidaiqu was outlawed by the Communists and continued in Taiwan and Hong Kong, eventually becoming Mandopo and Cantopop.

Mandopop developed in Singapore with the promotion of Mandarin in the early 1980s as one of the island state's official languages. The Supergirl and Superboy reality TV shows pushed Mandopop to new audiences in the early 2000s, spawning young stars with each series. Rock music began in 1986 with the release of "Nothing to My Name" by Beijing musician Cui Jian. The rock scene went underground after the Tian'anmen Square incident. Beijing is still a haven for live music. Shanghai is slowly catching up, with its very own MAO Livehouse to match the original in Beijing.

Opera

One of the most enduring symbols of Chinese music is the Beijing Opera mask. The elaborate costumes, gilded headdresses, and complex roles of traditional opera date back to the 18th century in the Qing Dynasty, when visiting troupes assembled to perform for the Qianlong emperor's birthday. The art form grew in popularity over the years. Different from the lyrical austerity of Western opera, the Chinese variety involves acrobatics, martial arts, and dance. During the Cultural Revolution, the classical repertoire was culled of its feudal pieces and eight revolutionary model operas were performed instead. The original repertoire was continued in Taiwan, where the Republican government preserved it. The traditional opera performed in Shanghai is Kunqu, which is similar to Beijing opera, but takes its melodies from the city of Kunshan.

The stock characters of traditional Chinese opera include the *sheng* (male lead), *dan* (main female role), *jing* (painted face male), and *chou* (clown). Within these roles are variations on age, occupation, and social standing. The opera is performed on a square stage with accompaniment from an orchestra made up of a stringed jinghu, a yueqin lute, and three drums.

Like Western classical music, Chinese opera is suffering a wane in popularity, but efforts to make it more accessible are in place, including a dedicated channel (11) on CCTV.

ART

Traditional Chinese figurative art with its simple brushstrokes, natural subject matter, and clean lines flourished in the Tang Dynasty, with roots in early Buddhist art and paintings of the Jin Dynasty. Tang art took the form of *shanshui* (mountain and water) landscapes, often featuring the karst peaks of southern China. The study of perspective continued into the Song and Yuan Dynasties that followed. Art grew more complex and detailed in the Ming and Qing periods, with the Shanghai

political graffiti in Shanghai

© SUSIE GORDON

School flourishing through the early 20th century. Chinese artistic talent was put to political use during the Republican and Communist periods, with cheerful Shanghainese painted advertisements contrasting with the bold color-blocked propaganda posters of the 1950s. The Cultural Revolution was the death knell for creative output and it wasn't until the late 1980s that any sort of art scene began to flourish again. Beijing's 798 and Shanghai's M50 were the hubs of the reawakening and still form the epicenters of Chinese contemporary art. One of the most famous Chinese contemporary artists is Ai Wei Wei, known around the world for his refusal to tone down his opinions about his homeland. This has gotten him into trouble with the authorities and he is regularly arrested.

LITERATURE

Before the Tang Dynasty, much of what survives as Chinese literature consists of historical annals like the *Records of the Grand Historian* by Sima Qian, *The Art of War* by Sun Zi, and Lao Zi's *Dao De Jing*. Prolific Tang poets like Li Bai and Bai Juyi popularized literature as an art form and a compendium of Tang poems was published during the Qing Dynasty in 1705 to gather the great classical works. The Four Great Classical Novels of Chinese literature are the 14th century *Romance of the Three Kingdoms* by Luo Guanzhong and *Water Margin* by Shi Nai'an, the 16th century fantasy epic *Journey to the West* by Wu Cheng'en, and the 18th century *Dream of the Red Chamber* by writer Cao Xueqin.

Modern Chinese literature dates from the late Qing and early 20th century, particularly from the post-revolutionary New Culture Movement that ran 1917–1923. A new vernacular style was introduced by Hu Shi and Chen Duxui and made famous by the legendary Lu Xun. The left wing writers behind the May 4 movement, including Mao Dun and Guo Moruo, penned works of socialist realism. As with all other art forms, literature suffered under the Cultural Revolution. Countless books were banned and burned and creative output was forced underground.

The 1980s and 1990s saw a commercialization of literature and a move towards blogging. Writers who have achieved fame online include Han Han and Guo Jingming. Writers who stray too far from the party line are silenced, such as Ma Jian, whose 2008 novel *Beijing Coma* took the aftermath of the Tian'anmen Square protests as its subject matter.

PERFORMANCE

Acrobatic shows are enduringly popular in Beijing and Shanghai. The long-running Kaleido troupe performs at Shanghai Circus World and there are several acrobatic houses in the capital. Originating from ancient village harvest festivals, acrobatic performances involve tumbling, balancing, and plate spinning.

CINEMA

Shanghai has been the center of the Chinese film industry since the nation's first motion picture was screened here in 1896. The glamorous screen stars of the 1930s included Jiang Qing, who later married Chairman Mao. Shanghai's burgeoning film scene helped boost Hong Kong's movie industry. Shanghainese Wong Kar-wai's *In The Mood for Love* focuses on a neighborhood of Shanghai folk living in Hong Kong and is one of the best-loved Chinese films ever made. Kungfu stars Jet Li, Jackie Chan, and Bruce Lee spread Chinese cinema across the world.

Post-Cultural Revolution, contemporary Chinese cinema has developed in stages. The 5th Generation was led by 1982 graduates of the Beijing Film Academy, including Zhang Yimou and Chen Kaige. The group disbanded after the Tian'anmen Square incident and a 6th Generation rose up (or down—they operated underground to avoid censorship). Their documentary style is typified by the work of Jia Zhangke and Wang Xiaoshuai (who made the film *Beijing Bicycle*). The current crop of filmmakers calls themselves dGeneration, with "d" standing for digital.

ESSENTIALS

Getting There

BY AIR

Beijing is served by the award-winning Beijing Capital International Airport (PEK, BJS) in the Chaoyang district. Dating from 1958, the airport has undergone several large-scale developments to bring it to international standards and is now one of the region's major transportation hubs. With three terminals (the third being the newest), it is the busiest airport in Asia. All international and domestic flights come into Capital Airport and it is well connected for transportation into the city, thanks to an extension of the subway system.

Shanghai's Pudong International Airport (PVG) opened in 1999 to ease traffic at Shanghai Hongqiao International Airport (SHA). Since Hongqiao Airport is located in the city's western suburbs, expansion was impossible. Hongqiao Airport is still used for domestic and some international flights including to Hong Kong and is only a 20-minute taxi ride from downtown.

Pudong International sits on 40 square kilometers (15 sq. mi) of land by the coast, 30 kilometers (19 mi) from the city center. Like Beijing Capital Airport, it is an important transportation hub and one of the busiest airports in the world. The high-speed Shanghai Maglev train connects Pudong International with the city and Metro line 2 joins it to Hongqiao Airport. Terminal 1 is used mainly for domestic flights, while international carriers operate from Terminal 2.

© SUSIE GORDON

Getting Around

ADDRESS SYSTEM

For visitors who don't read Chinese, getting around in Beijing and Shanghai is fairly straightforward, thanks to the fact that the vast majority of street signs are written in both Chinese and English. In both cities, addresses are often given with the main street plus a cross street, since many roads are extremely long. For example, if a restaurant is at 1468 Middle Huaihai Road, the address will include West Fuxing Road as well, so you have a better idea of where the venue sits on the road.

In both Beijing and Shanghai, long streets are split into "directional" sections: Outer (Wai), Inner (Nei), Middle (Zhong), North (Bei), South (Nan), East (Dong), or West (Xi). It's important to know that these sections are considered to be individual streets with their own numbering systems, so 1 Wulumuqi Road is a different address from 1 South Wulumuqi Road and 1 Middle Wulumuqi Road.

In Shanghai, most streets take the suffix *lu* which means "road." There are a handful of *dadao* (avenues), several *guangchang* (squares) and even fewer *jie* (streets). The lanes and alleys running off from the main roads are called *nong* which means "lane." Streets are named mostly after heads of state (as in Zhongshan Road for Sun Yat-Sen), cities and provinces in China (as in Fuzhou Road and Shandong Road), or virtues and qualities (such as Changle Road; *changle* means "long happiness"). When parts of Shanghai were ruled by foreign powers during the colonial era, many streets were given French and English names, like Route Lafayette (now Middle Fuxing Road). When these foreign powers retreated after World War II, the Chinese government hastily renamed the roads. The streets running from the Bund to People's Square were named after Chinese cities, and the streets that crossed them going north to south were named for Chinese provinces.

In Beijing, many of the main streets around the Forbidden City are named after the old gates that once guarded the capital. They contain the Mandarin word for gate, *men*, so you'll see street names like Andingmen, Fuchengmen, Qianmen, and Di'anmen. Beijing's many *hutong* (alleys) have two main naming systems: the simple "Hutong," and "Tiao," which is a word used to describe a street. Tiao are named in order: 1 Tiao, 2 Tiao, 3 Tiao. Unlike Shanghai, whose street names are Lu (roads), Bejing's thoroughfares are mostly Jie (streets). Larger streets and avenues in Beijing are called Dajie.

AIR

Air travel within China is relatively cheap and easy to organize. Countless domestic airlines connect the main cities, including China Eastern, Shanghai Airlines, and China Southern, and tickets are often the same price as rail travel. The flight from Beijing to Shanghai takes under two hours and off-peak fares can be as low as ¥500. Several flights per day operate between the cities.

TRAIN

China's train network is one of the most comprehensive and efficient in the world. All major cities and many smaller ones are connected and trains are clean and safe. Options range from the cheapest hard seat on short journeys to the lavish luxury soft sleeper on overnight trips. The journey between Beijing and Shanghai recently got a lot shorter thanks to the new high-speed line. For the same price as an air ticket (around ¥600), the train gets you from one city to the other in just under four hours—a journey of 1,318 kilometers (819 mi). The same journey on a regular train takes 10–12 hours and it's a good idea to go soft sleeper if you want some shut-eye. On newer trains, luxury soft sleeper carriages have two beds, a toilet, and a television, while regular soft sleeper class has four bunks. Hard sleepers contain six bunks and are noisy and spartan. If you don't mind sitting instead of lying down, seated class is considerably cheaper.

Train tickets can be bought at the railway station or at designated booths around each city. Your hotel or hostel will help you book them 3–10 days in advance. For shorter journeys it's fine to show up at the railway station and buy a ticket on the day of travel. For the new high-speed line, passengers need to show ID when they book.

It's best to avoid travelling around Chinese New Year in late January or early February, as the network becomes overcrowded with migrant workers making their way home to celebrate with their families. The Golden Week holiday (Oct. 1–7) is also best avoided due to the sheer volume of people travelling.

Useful websites for timetables and routes are www.cnvol.com and www.china-train-ticket.com.

BUS

Bus travel in Beijing and Shanghai is cheap and convenient, but can be confusing if you don't speak or read Chinese. Staff at your hotel or hostel will be able to guide you to the right lines to get to the main sights; journeys are incredibly cheap at ¥1 or ¥2 depending on the route and standard of the bus.

Beijing's bus network has several types of routes. The daytime buses travel 5:30 A.M.–11 P.M., while the night buses (numbers 201–215) operate thereafter. Routes numbered 1–100 run within the third ring road; the outer suburbs are served by lines 300–810. Long distance lines are 900–998. Bus journeys are ¥1 if paid to the bus driver, or ¥0.4 with a transportation smartcard. These are available for ¥20 from subway stations and convenience stores and can be charged with credit.

In Shanghai, over 1,000 bus routes connect all parts of the city. Regular downtown routes are numbered 1–200, while extra rush hour buses are numbered 201–299. Night buses are numbered 301–399 and cross-river services are 401–499. Pudong is served by routes 601–699 and the outer suburban lines are 701–799. Make sure you have coins to pay the driver, as there is often no conductor. For an English guide to Shanghai's bus lines, visit msitting.wubi.org/bus.

SUBWAY

Both cities have excellent, efficient subway systems that are easy to navigate even for visitors not used to China and unfamiliar with the language. Signs are in both English and Chinese and nearly all stations are wheelchair accessible. The Beijing Olympics and Shanghai Expo left a legacy of extra lines and shiny new trains, meaning that subway travel is the easiest and one of the cheapest ways of getting around.

The Beijing subway system is the oldest in China and the second longest after Shanghai's. It began in 1969 and now has 172 stations across 14 lines and 336 kilometers (209 mi) of track. All journeys cost a flat fee of ¥2. At street level, look out for blue signs with a "D" enclosed by a circle, standing for ditie—the Mandarin word for subway. The main lines serving the city center are Line 1 (running east to west under Tian'anmen Square), Line 2 (encircling the city center around the Forbidden City), Line 4 (crossing north to south to the west of the Forbidden City), and Line 5 (north to south in the east of the Forbidden City). A special express line connects Line 10 and Line 2 with Beijing Capital Airport. For interactive subway maps and journey planners, visit www.explorebj.com.

Shanghai's mighty Metro is the longest subway system in the world, with 11 lines covering 400 kilometers (248 mi) of track. By 2020 it will have 20 lines fanning out from the center into the outer suburbs. Currently, Line 2 cuts across the city from east to west, while Line 1 goes north to south. Line 4 encircles the city in a ring. Over five million people ride the subway each day, with figures peaking at rush hour, 7:30–9 A.M. and 5–6:30 P.M. It's best to avoid traveling at these times as the trains and stations become crowded with commuters and you'll end up with barely enough room to move or breathe. Journeys cost ¥3 or ¥4 depending on the length; tickets can be bought from banks of machines in Metro stations. Rechargeable transport cards are available from stations and convenience stores. The Shanghai Metro logo is a red zigzag "s" shape on a white background.

© SUSIE GORDON

signage for the Shanghai Metro

DRIVING

It is difficult for visiting foreigners to drive in China, whether or not they have an international license. The application process can be long winded, and a Chinese residency permit is required. Even if the process were easy, driving in Beijing and Shanghai would still be difficult, thanks to the oft-chaotic traffic. If you'd like to get around without relying on taxis or public transportation, you can hire a car and driver through car rental companies like Avis and Hertz that operate at the airports in Beijing and Shanghai.

TAXIS

Thanks to their cheapness and abundance, taxis are a quick and affordable way of getting around the cities (outside of rush hour, that is). In Beijing, taxis are dark green or blue with a gold stripe. Free cabs have a red light in the front window, which is operated by the driver. There's a ¥10 flag fare, after which the meter goes up ¥1 every kilometer after an initial three kilometers (1.9 mi). After 15 kilometers (9.3 mi), the fare

rises to ¥3 per kilometer. For journeys over three kilometers (1.9 mi) you'll be asked to pay a fuel surcharge of ¥2. Between 11 P.M. and 5 A.M., the flag fare goes up to ¥11, with each kilometer costing ¥2.4 after the initial three kilometers. Most Beijing taxi drivers can speak little to no English but can recognize the Mandarin names of most main attractions. If you're asking to be taken to a street address, try to specify a crossroad too. A taxi from the airport to downtown costs ¥100–200 depending on the time of day.

Shanghai taxis come in a range of colors. The most reputable are light blue (Dazhong) and gold (Qiangsheng), while maroon cars (Fanlanhong) are less well kept. There's a flag fare of ¥12 which lasts for the first three kilometers (1.9 mi), after which it's ¥2.4 for every kilometer and ¥3.6 after 10 kilometers (6.2 mi). Between 11 P.M. and 5 A.M. the flag fare rises to ¥16 followed by ¥3.1 per kilometer. Talks are underway to raise the fares, so they may have gone up by the time you visit. At present, seatbelts are only available in the special Expo people-carrier cabs.

© SUSIE GORDON

bicycles in Beijing

In both cities, be sure to ask for a receipt *(fa piao)* so you can reclaim any lost property.

BIKING

Cycling is one of the best and most interesting ways of getting around Beijing thanks to the flat, wide streets and plethora of bikes and bike shops. Many hotels and most hostels offer bike rental schemes, while cheap models are available from street-side shops for a couple of hundred yuan.

Shanghai has its fair share of cyclists too, but motorbikes and electric scooters tend to be more popular. As in Beijing, there are designated bike lanes, but traffic can be hectic so be sure to wear a helmet and take extra care at junctions. Red lights are often ignored, so keep your wits about you.

Visas and Officialdom

Foreigners who want to visit China must acquire a visa before they leave their home country. You can apply for a tourist visa (L Visa) at the Chinese embassy or consulate in your nearest city. You will usually need to provide at least two passport photographs, a completed application form, and copies of your plane tickets and hotel reservations. Travelers must have at least six months of validity remaining on their passport and at least one blank visa page in their passport in order to obtain an L Visa. Make sure you apply for your visa several weeks to a month before you need to travel to ensure that it's ready on time. Most embassies offer an express service at extra cost.

Once the visa is issued, travelers should be aware that traveling to China with improper documentation will subject them to possible

CONSULATES AND EMBASSIES IN BEIJING AND SHANGHAI

CANADA

- **Canadian Embassy in Beijing:** 19 Dongzhimen Ave., 10/5139-4000 or 613/996-8885 in an emergency, Mon.-Fri. 8 A.M.-noon and 1-4:30 P.M.

- **Canadian Consulate General in Shanghai:** 604 West Tower, Shanghai Centre, 1376 West Nanjing Rd., 21/3279-2800 for general inquiries or 800/140-0125 in an emergency, Mon.-Fri. 9-11:30 A.M.

UNITED KINGDOM

- **British Embassy in Beijing:** 11 Guanghua Rd., Jianguomenwai, 10/8529-6083 for inquiries and assistance, ukinchina.fco.gov.uk/eng, Mon.-Fri. 8:30 A.M.-noon and 1-5 P.M.

- **British Consulate General in Shanghai:** Suite 301, Shanghai Centre, 1376 West Nanjing Rd., 21/3279-2000 for inquiries and assistance, ukinchina.fco.gov.uk/eng, Mon.-Thurs. 8:30 A.M.-5 P.M. and Fri. 8:30 A.M.-3:30 P.M.

UNITED STATES

- **American Embassy in Beijing:** 55 Anjialou Rd., 10/6532-1910 for American Citizen Services or 10/8531-4000 in an emergency, beijing.usembassy-china.org.cn.

- **American Consulate General in Shanghai:** 1469 Middle Huaihai Rd., 21/3217-4650 for American Citizen Services or 21/3217-4650 and press "0" for an operator for after-hours emergencies, shanghai.usembassy-china.org.cn, Mon.-Fri. 8:30-11:30 A.M. and 1:30-3:30 P.M., closed on Wed. afternoon.

---

fines and deportation. An L Visa is valid for 90 or 180 days from the date it's issued (depending on whether you have a Single or Double Entry visa), which means that you must enter China no later than 90 or 180 days after the visa was issued. If you miss this window, your visa will expire and you must apply for another. An L Visa lasts for 30 days from the date that you entered China.

Visitors to China must register with the police within 24 hours of their arrival. (If you're staying in a hotel, though, not to worry: The staff there will register you automatically.) Head to the local police station and present your passport to register.

Extending your L Visa is possible once you're in China, and usually takes about a week. Contact the embassy or consulate of your home country in China to find out how to do it.

Conduct and Customs

SAVING FACE

The concept of "face" is complex and thorny, but basically revolves around mutual respect. Face is given when you offer praise and can be lost when you shout at someone, criticize them, or humiliate them. Face has its origins in Confucian ideals about social harmony, but is often seen by non-Chinese as an excuse to avoid blame or responsibility. The Mandarin for losing face is *shi mianzi* or *diu mianzi,* while giving face is *liu mianzi.*

SOCIAL INTERACTIONS

Most relationships in China revolve around *guanxi* (connections). It's nigh on impossible to make a business deal with a company without first being introduced by an intermediary or mutual friend and most people get their jobs thanks to a network of contacts. Confucius decreed that the most important social relationships were between master and subject, husband and wife, father and child, brother and sister, and friends.

While not so strict with politeness as the Japanese, Chinese people tend to make much of these close relationships and offer respect where due.

When meeting Chinese people, don't call them by their first names unless they expressly tell you to. Having said that, many younger Chinese people who deal with foreigners tend to take English names. These range from the commonplace (Maggie, Lydia, Kevin) to the bizarre (Sunshine, Echo, Milk). Since women do not take their husband's surname when they marry, couples are never referred to as Mr. and Mrs. Zhang, for example. Adding lao (old) to a man's surname, e.g., Lao Li, is a friendly but respectful form of address, while the corresponding xiao (small), e.g., Xiao Wang, is used for younger friends.

Most white-collar workers in China have a business card and you will most probably be offered at least one on your travels. Accept it with both hands, one clutching each corner, and read it carefully before you pocket it. Most have the person's name and details in English on one side and in Chinese on the other.

If you are in the position of giving a gift to a Chinese person, money inside a red envelope (available at street-side stationery stores) is a good bet, as long as there is no number four in the total figure, be it four notes or a multiple of four. Fruit goes down well too, especially baskets or displays. Never offer flowers, as these are associated with funerals.

DINING ETIQUETTE

When eating with Chinese people, the focus is on sharing. Instead of ordering and eating a meal of one's own, common practice is to pile the table with dishes and help yourself to each, putting morsels into your own rice bowl that you raise to your mouth to eat from with chopsticks. If you can't get to grips with the aforementioned, many restaurants will give you a fork or a spoon if you ask. Street-side Chinese restaurants are usually rowdy, convivial places with bright lighting and constant bustle. Attracting the waitstaff's attention is almost impossible unless you shout. In restaurants, cigarettes are smoked with abandon. The one big no-no is to stick your chopsticks vertically into your bowl of rice, as it looks like funeral incense. It's also not polite to take the last piece of food or to put bones in your bowl. Higher-end restaurants in Beijing and Shanghai adhere to Western habits when it comes to etiquette.

Tips for Travelers

TRAVELING WITH CHILDREN

Chinese people love children and Western kids are a source of great fascination. Be prepared to be stopped in the street for photographs or affectionate pinches if you have a toddler or baby. Traveling with children in Beijing and Shanghai can be enjoyable and relatively hassle free as long as you take enough supplies of diapers and favorite snacks with you. Despite several attempts at a smoking ban, cigarettes are still permitted in most local cafés and restaurants, but Western chains are smoke free and many venues have a non-smoking area. Both cities have kid-friendly museums and parks; many attractions offer discounted rates for children.

WOMEN TRAVELERS

Women enjoy equal rights in China thanks to Chairman Mao's proclamation that they "hold up half the sky." Women visitors will find Beijing and Shanghai to be refreshingly devoid of sleazy guys and will rarely feel threatened or afraid when walking the streets at night. Chinese men are generally respectful of foreign women and any looks or remarks you receive will simply be surprise at your height, hair color, or other typically Western features.

SENIOR TRAVELERS

The older generation of travelers will find Beijing and Shanghai to be an overall pleasant experience. Older people are venerated in

China and you will be treated with respect by default. However, it's a good idea to get a medical check-up before you travel, as well as a note from your doctor for any medication you have to carry and updated travel insurance. Take extra medicine and keep it in your hand luggage when you travel. If you have difficulty walking, the subway systems are easily accessible and taxis are cheap and plentiful. Retirees benefit from cheaper airfares and hotel rates outside of peak seasons.

GAY AND LESBIAN TRAVELERS

Although homosexuality isn't fully accepted in China, Shanghai and Beijing both have thriving LGBT scenes. It is extremely rare that gay and lesbian couples will be stared at, hassled, or be made to feel otherwise threatened. Many straight men walk around arm in arm with their male friends and it's a common sight for female friends to hold hands, so the sight of same-sex partnerships is not shocking. However, more intimate shows of affection may raise eyebrows.

Homosexuality is not illegal in China; the issue that arises for some is that gay unions will in most cases not yield grandchildren. Especially with the One-Child Policy, parents rely on a single child to support them in their old age and pass on the family name. Confucian values still loom large, particularly among the older generation and this will take time to subside. Thankfully there is very little hate crime and there is a thriving gay community online.

TRAVELERS WITH DISABILITIES

Even with improvements to infrastructure augured by the 2008 Olympics and 2010 Expo, neither Beijing or Shanghai will win any awards for accessibility. While the subway systems of both cities are wheelchair-accessible, the majority of attractions still don't cater to disabled visitors. Even within the subway stations, it can be a trial to call over a staff member to operate the chair lift. Things are slowly changing though, with both the Forbidden City and the Great Wall at Badaling installing accessibility ramps and lifts.

Beijing has a fleet of 70 special white taxis that are outfitted for wheelchair users. They can be hired out 24 hours a day, seven days a week at no extra cost than the fare, but the number (10/961001) is Chinese only, so you'll need to ask your hotel reception desk to call for you. Vision-impaired travelers are allowed to take their guide on buses free of charge. In Beijing, several tour companies operate trips designed for travelers with disabilities, such as Tour Beijing (www.tour-beijing.com). In Shanghai, the Shanghai Disabled Persons' Federation (SDPF) has been in operation since 1986 and the website (www.shdisabled.gov.cn/clinternet/platformData/infoplat/pub/disabled_132/enshouye_13003/) contains useful information about accessibility.

Health and Safety

HOSPITALS

Public hospitals in Beijing and Shanghai are passable but not as advanced as the West. Major hospitals in both cities have dedicated wards for foreigners where the staff speaks English, but for safety's sake you will probably want to seek out private hospitals in which hygiene and quality of treatment is higher. Beijing's best hospitals are Beijing United Family Hospital (http://unitedfamilyhospitals.com/en/bj) and International

SOS (www.internationalsos.com). In Shanghai, the most trustworthy hospital is Parkway Health (www.parkwayhealth.cn). These hospitals accept Western insurance policies and credit cards (American Express, MasterCard, and Visa).

PHARMACIES

Few pharmacies have English-speaking staff, so if you think you will need to buy medication while you're in China, it's a good idea to research the name in both English and Chinese before you leave and write it down so you can show it to the pharmacist. Cough, cold, flu, and headache medication is available off the shelf, as is the contraceptive pill. Some downtown pharmacies are open 24 hours a day.

EMERGENCY SERVICES

The ambulance and fire services operate only in Chinese, so if you need to call in an emergency, make sure there is someone who can speak Mandarin to explain the situation and location. The number to call for an ambulance is 120; for a fire it's 119. The number for the police is 110 and the English-language service is 8402-0101.

CRIME AND HARASSMENT

By and large, China is a very safe country. The main crime threat comes from pickpockets who home in on "rich" Western tourists to divest them of cameras, wallets, and phones. Keep your possessions close at hand when traveling on the subway and in busy tourist areas. Many of China's pickpockets come from the western Xinjiang Province and work in groups. Both Beijing and Shanghai have large beggar populations; many beggars are known to use children or people with disabilities to appeal to public sentiment. But

however heartbreaking it is to see people being used like this, giving money will only help organized crime gangs to flourish. The sad truth is that many gangs kidnap children and purposefully maim them to use as begging tools. If you want to help, the best thing to do is give food.

Avoiding Scams

Unfortunately, scammers exist in all major cities in China. In Beijing and Shanghai, "students" may approach you and offer to take you to see an art show or drink tea and "practice English." Don't be fooled. They will take you to a gallery or tearoom and leave you with an exorbitant bill. Saying that you have no cash on you won't get you out of it; you'll be frog-marched to an ATM and forced to take money out. Often the scammers will be incredibly friendly and persuasive, but don't fall for their charms.

Another common scam is the Chinese Traditional Medicine ruse. You'll be invited to tour a pharmacy and "diagnosed" with a condition that requires exorbitantly expensive medication to cure. Unfortunately, the police don't tend to do much about scams like this, so if you end up being conned, there's very little chance that you'll see your money again. It's better to be safe than sorry.

Information and Services

CURRENCY

China's currency is the RMB, which stands for Renminbi, meaning "the people's money" in Mandarin. The main denomination of the RMB is the yuan, which is made up of 10 jiao and 100 fen. Few people use the words yuan and jiao, however, preferring the slang *kuai* and *mao* respectively. The yuan comes in 1, 5, 10, 20, 50 and 100 notes, while the coins are 1 jiao, 5 jiao, and 1 yuan. The fen is very rarely seen in big cities.

Counterfeit currency is a huge problem in China, with the ¥100 and ¥50 notes being the most regularly copied. There are many ways to tell a fake, but the easiest is to rub the portrait

of Chairman Mao's jacket. If it is textured, it's real; if it is flat, it's fake.

ATMS

Banks and ATMs are found on almost every street in both Beijing and Shanghai. The main banks are Bank of China, ICBC, HSBC, and Citic; there are many regional banks, too. The bigger banks allow withdrawal on foreign cards. The limit for each withdrawal is usually ¥2,500 (although your own bank may impose a lower limit) and ATMs give out only ¥100 notes. Charges depend on the bank. Often you'll see CDM and CRM beside the ATM—these are for cardholders to make deposits into their bank accounts.

Communications and Media

PHONES

There are payphones dotted around on most streets in the downtown districts of both cities, some with internet capabilities. As for cell phones, if you're going to be making a lot of calls within China, it's a good idea to buy a pre-paid Chinese SIM card to put in your phone. These can be found at branches of China Mobile and Unicom as well as at street booths. You can pick up a cheap cell phone for as little as ¥100. Before you leave your home country, check with your phone supplier about roaming charges if you plan to use your regular SIM.

INTERNET SERVICES

Both Beijing and Shanghai have plenty of Internet bars where you can surf the Internet cheaply, but these are usually smoky dens filled with gaming addicts who spend all day and night there. If you have a laptop or Smartphone, you'll find that most cafés, restaurants, and bars have their own Wi-Fi network that they will let you use for free as long as you buy a drink or a meal. The Internet is heavily censored and even Western social media sites fall behind the Great Firewall. You won't be able to access Facebook, Twitter, and Blogger without a VPN (virtual private network) or a proxy server. Free proxies are available through a quick web search, while VPNs cost a little more but are far more reliable.

MAIL SERVICES

The Chinese postal service can be erratic, with postcards taking up to two months to arrive at their destination. China post offices have dark green facades and are easy to spot.

NEWSPAPERS AND PERIODICALS

The English language news press in China is dominated by state-run *China Daily,* which is propagandist in its leanings. No less partisan are *Global Times*—an English subdivision of the *People's Daily*—and *Shanghai Daily,* which give a government-approved version of national and international news.

Censorship

The media and arts are heavily censored in China, from news reports and websites to books and theater performances. Anything criticizing the Communist Party is banned, along with stories that cast aspersions on leaders past and present or speak badly of China in any way. Controversial topics like Tian'anmen Square, Tibetan independence, the Dalai Lama, and the Falun Gong religious sect are banned outright, with web searches severely doctored. To view any material about these matters you have to use a VPN.

The online community has found a way to bite back at the government without fear of redress. Users of the Wiki-based Baidu Baike website have created 10 mythical creatures that poke fun at the system, including the Grass Mud Horse and River Crab. The Mandarin language has many homonyms: The words for Grass Mud Horse are *cao ni ma,* which sounds like a vulgar curse when said with different tones. The River Crab's name is *he xie,* which sounds the same as "harmony," which is another word for censorship. Often the crab is pictured with a wristwatch—this is because the Mandarin phrase for wearing a watch, *dai biao,* sounds like the Mandarin for Three Represents, a socio-politcal ideology of China's Communist Party. One of the other animals, the French-Croatian Squid or *fa ke you,* needs little explanation. . . .

RADIO AND TELEVISION

Chinese television and radio are strictly controlled by the state, so little is broadcast aside from news, soap operas, and game shows. China Central Television (CCTV) operates under the Propaganda Department of the Communist Party and has 19 channels.

RESOURCES

Glossary

GEOGRAPHY AND DIRECTIONS

bei north
chuzuche taxi
dadao avenue/boulevard
dajie avenue
daxue university
dong east
dongyue eastern peak
gong palace
gongyuan park
guangchang square
gulou drum tower
guo country
he river
hu lake
huochezhan train station
hutong alley, lane
jiang river
jie street
laozhihao legendary establishment
lilong traditional Shanghai residential lane
longtang lane or alley
lu road
men gate
nan south
Peking former English name for Beijing
qiao bridge
shan mountain
shikumen traditional stone-arch gate, found in Shanghai
shui water
si temple
siheyuan courtyard residences
ta pagoda
tian sky, heaven

you right (direction)
zhan station
Zhongguo China
zhonglou bell tower
zuo left (direction)

FOOD AND DRINK

baijiu distilled alcoholic beverage
baozi steamed bun or dumpling
chuan'r meat kebab
dongbei northern Chinese cuisine; literally "east north"
guo ying state-run restaurant
jiaozi slim type of dumpling, equivalent to pot stickers
kaoya duck; usually seen as Beijing *kaoya*
lu rou braised donkey meat
mian noodles
paocai pickled dish, usually cabbage
roujiamo pita bread stuffed with cilantro and pork, lamb, or chicken; known as the Chinese hamburger
san bei ji three-cup chicken, a traditional Taiwanese dish
shaomai dumpling made with thin dough, featuring frilly, pleated edges
shengjianbao pan-fried pork dumplings; served in 4-dumpling portions called *liang*
shengjian mantou alternate name for *shengjianbao*, or pork buns
shi food
suantang yu sour fish soup
xiangbai bohe peppermint salad
xiao chi snacks
xiaolongbao soup dumplings
yang rou chuan'r lamb kebabs

youtiao fried dough sticks; also known as Chinese donuts

zhou congee, or rice porridge

zongzi stuffed rice balls

CONCEPTS

dianying movies; literally "electric shadows"

feng shui type of ancient geomancy of wind and water, whereby the careful placement of objects within their space promotes harmony and balance

gong xi fa cai literally "happiness and prosperity"; a greeting bestowed to others during Spring Festival (also known as Chinese New Year)

guanxi complex network of influence that governs many interpersonal relationships in China, both for business and leisure

lala Mandarin slang term for lesbian

laowai gently derogatory term for a foreigner

liuli glass artwork

niupi brown craft paper

pinyin literally "spell sound"; system of transliterating Chinese sounds into Roman script

Putonghua China's common language, based on the Beijing form of Mandarin; serves as a lingua franca in a nation of many dialects

renmin the people of China

renminbi Chinese currency; abbreviated RMB

shichen ancient method of measuring time

tongzhi slang term for a gay man, originally meaning "comrade"

Uighur ethnic minority living in the Xinjiang Autonomous Region in the west of China

xiu bloom or flourish

yuan monetary denomination of the renminbi

PEOPLE AND EVENTS

Confucius Kongzi, as he is known in China, was a philosopher and scholar of the Spring and Autumn Period. He is worshipped as a deity, and his teachings still shape the Chinese psyche. Morality and family values are among his most famous ideals.

Cultural Revolution (1966-1976) The Great Proletarian Cultural Revolution was a sociopolitical movement designed by Chairman Mao to eradicate all vestiges of Capitalist and bourgeois ideals. The period saw a wholesale purge of literature, art, and religion by the notorious Red Guards in an attempt to promote Maoism.

Deng Xiaoping (1907-1997) Deng led the Communist Party between 1982 and 1987, and was responsible for opening China to the rest of the world, forging ahead with a free market economy by which the country is still ruled.

Great Leap Forward (1958-1961) Mao's plans to move China from an agrarian society to an industrialized and collectivized nation backfired, with 16-46 million deaths from widespread famine. This egregious scheme contributed to Mao's checkered reputation.

Han China's main ethnic group makes up 92 percent of the population, alongside 55 smaller minorities. Most Han fall under the One Child Policy, while members of ethnic minorities are allowed more than one baby. A Chinese person's ethnicity appears on their national ID card.

Hu Jintao (1942-) Paramount leader of China since 2003, Hu represents a new generation of politicians, less ostentatious and more economically progressive than his predecessors.

Huangdi The semi-mythological Yellow Emperor appears in the records of historian Sima Qian. He is heralded with leading the Xia Dynasty and inventing the oracle bone writing system.

Jiang Zemin (1926-) President between 1993 and 2003, Jiang was in power when Hong Kong was handed back to China. He also oversaw great economic growth, and reforms of state-run industry.

Laozi A mysterious figure who penned the Daoist text *Dao De Jing*, philosopher Laozi appears in the historical records of Sima Qian as a contemporary of Confucius.

Mao Zedong (1893-1976) China's Great Helmsman, Chairman Mao led the nation into Communism in 1949 with the foundation of the People's Republic. Much maligned and yet admired (and immortalized on every coin and note), the Hunan native is one of the most enduring political figures in world history.

Qin Shi Huang Responsible for uniting China in 221 B.C. after the Warring States period, the

Qin Emperor set the wheels in motion for two millennia of imperialism.

Sun Yat-sen (1866-1925) A Hawaiian-born Hakka, Sun Yat-sen founded the Nationalist Guomindang army and became president of the new republic in 1912 after the last emperor was overthrown. His Mandarin name was Zhongshan, and he is commemorated with a park and street in almost every Chinese city.

Wu Zetian China's only empress ruled during the Tang era, creating her own dynasty called the Zhou. A symbol of female power, she gave herself the rather lofty moniker "Sacred and Divine Empress Regnant."

Zhou Enlai (1898-1976) Zhou was the first prime minister of the People's Republic of China. He smoothed the way for Nixon's visit in 1972, and was a supporter of Deng Xiaoping in developing the country's economy.

Mandarin Phrasebook

With nearly 850 million speakers, Mandarin is the most widely spoken language in the world. It is part of the Sino-Tibetan language group, and is also known as Putonghua, or "standard speech." It is called Guoyu in Taiwan and Huayu in Singapore, and shouldn't be confused with Cantonese, which is actually a dialect spoken in Guangdong Province and Hong Kong.

WRITTEN MANDARIN

Mandarin has a reputation for being a tricky tongue to master, and it is equally tough when it comes to the written form. There are over 50,000 individual Chinese characters (known as Hanzi). While they might look random to the untrained eye, they actually involve a complex system of radicals and phonetic markers. Most Chinese people know several thousand characters. In mainland China and Singapore, simplified characters have been used since the 1950s; in Hong Kong, Macao, and Taiwan, the traditional complex characters are still employed.

When you see Mandarin written in roman letters, this is called pinyin. The system was devised in the 1950s as a means of transliterating Chinese words into roman script, and designating Mandarin-style names for Western concepts and figures. For instance, U.S. President Barack Obama's pinyin name is Ao-ba-ma, and his predecessor's pinyin name is Bu-shi.

SPOKEN MANDARIN

Compared to other languages, Mandarin has relatively few sounds. There are four tones (flat, rising, dipping, and falling) which aid meaning, but for beginners this can be confusing. The sound *shi* can mean different things, including "lion," "stone," "to be," and the number 10, depending on the tone. Likewise *ma* can mean "mother," "horse," or "curse"; it is also used to signify a question. This can lead to all sorts of confusion and amusement, and forms the basis for many jokes and innuendos. For example, the sentence *"Wo ge ge chang chang chang ge,"* may sound indecipherable, but when said with the correct tones, it means "My brother often sings."

Luckily, Mandarin's grammar system is relatively simple. It follows a subject-verb-object structure; verbs don't change form depending on who is doing them, and most nouns don't change to imply plurality. A simple sentence goes thus:

Wǒ	ài	nǐ.
I	love	you.

Nǐ	ài	wǒ.
You	love	me.

To turn it into a negative, simply add *bù*:

Wǒ	bù	ài	nǐ.
I	don't	love	you.

And to make it into a question, just tack *ma* onto the end:

Nǐ	ài	wǒ	ma?
You	love	me?	

Although it takes many years of study and practice to truly master Mandarin, it's not impossible to pick up some phrases and vocabulary before and during your trip. The people you speak to will be delighted that you have made the effort, even if most will be eager to practice their English in return.

PRONUNCIATION GUIDE

Mandarin pronunciation is relatively easy to grasp, and there are few (if any) exceptions to the rules. In Beijing, many words are pronounced with a rhotic "rrr" on the end.

Consonants

Most Mandarin consonants are pronounced the same way as in English, with the following exceptions:

c like ts, as in "tsar"
q like ch, as in "cheek"
r with the tongue curled back: like zh
x halfway between ss and sh
z like dz, as in "roads"
zh like dj, as in "jam"

Vowels

a like ah, as in "father"
an after y: like en, as in "men"
ai like aye, as in "lie"
ao like ow, as in "cow"
e like eh, as in "err"
ei like ay, as in "way"
i like ee, as in "me"; after c, ch, r, s, sc, z, and zh: like uh, as in "truck"
ian like yen
ie like aa, as in "yeah"
iu like yo, as in "show"
o like oh, as in "for"
ou like oh
u like oo, as in "flute"
ui like ay, as in "way"
uo like oh, as in "whoa"
yu with rounded lips: like ee, as in "keep"
ü like yuh, as in the German ü

BASIC AND COURTEOUS EXPRESSIONS

Hello. *Ni hao.*

How are you? *Ni hao ma?*
I'm very well. *Wo hen hao.*
And you? *Ni ne?*
thanks *xie xie*
good *hao*
not good *bu hao*
You're welcome. *Bu ke qi.*
Goodbye. *Zai jian.*
please *qing*
yes *shi de* or *dui*
no *bu*
sorry *bu hao yisi*
Sorry to bother you... *Mafan ni...*
Wait. *Deng yi xia.* (Shanghai) or *Deng yi hui'r.* (Beijing)
I don't like... *Bu xihuan...*
I don't want... *Bu yao...*
What's your name? *Ni jiao shenme?*
My name is... *Wo jiao...*
How old are you? *Ni duo da le?*
I am...years old. *Wo...sui.*
Do you speak English? *Ni hui shuo Yingwen ma?*
A little bit. *Yi dian dian.*
Your English is really good. *Nide Yingwen shuo de hen hao.*
My Chinese is not good. *Wode Zhongwen shuo de bu hao.*
I don't understand [something spoken]. *Wo ting bu dong.*
I don't understand [something written]. *Wo kan bu dong.*
I don't get it. *Bu ming bai.*
Are you from Shanghai? *Ni shi Shanghairen ma?*
Are you from Beijing? *Ni shi Beijingren ma?*
I am American/Canadian/British. *Wo shi Meiguo/Jianada/Yingguo ren.*
I am Australian/from New Zealand. *Wo shi Aodaliya/Xinxilan ren.*
What do you do for a living? *Ni zuo shenme gongzuo?*
I am a businessperson. *Wo dang shang ren.*
I am a teacher. *Wo dang laoshi.*

TERMS OF ADDRESS

you (formal) *nin*
you (informal) *ni*

you (plural) *nimen*
he, she *ta*
they *tamen*
Mr. *xiansheng*
Mrs. *nushi*
Miss *xiaojie*
husband *zhangfu*
wife *qizi*
boyfriend *nanpengyou*
girlfriend *nupengyou*
father *baba*
mother *mama*
son *erzi*
daughter *nu'er*
child *haizi*
older brother *gege*
younger brother *didi*
older sister *jiejie*
younger sister *meimei*

TRANSPORTATION

Where is...? *...Zai nali?* (Shanghai) or
  Nar...? (Beijing)
How do you get to...? *...Zenme zou?*
I'm lost. *Wo mi lu le.*
north; south *bei; nan*
east; west *xi; dong*
from... to... *cong... dao...*
address *dizhi*
taxi *chuzuche*
bus *qiche*
train *huoche*
bicycle *zixingche*
Take me to... *Qing dai wo qu...*
Is it far? *Yuan bu yuan?*
behind; in front of *zai houmian; zai qianmian*
near *fujin*
on the corner *guaijiao*
opposite *zai*
Where can I buy tickets? *Nali mai piao?*
Is it direct? *Shi zhi da de ma?*
luggage *xingli*
one way; return *dancheng; shuangcheng*

FOOD AND DRINK

breakfast *zaocan*
lunch *wufan*
dinner *wanfan*

snack *xiaochi*
restaurant *canting*
café *kafeiguan*
bar *jiuba*
to eat *chi fan*
to drink *he*
to smoke *chouyan*
delicious *hao chi*
menu *caidan*
the check *maidan*
Bring another... *Zai lai...*
I'll have one of these/those. *Gei wo yi fen zhege/nage.*
I'm allergic to... *Wo dui...guomin*
I'm vegetarian. *Wo chi su.*
I can't eat... *Wo bu neng chi...*
halal *qing zhen*
kosher *you tai*
knife; fork; spoon *daozi; chazi; shaozi*
chopsticks *kuazi*
salt; pepper *yan; hujiao*
vinegar *cu*
soy sauce *jiangyou*
hot sauce *lajiao*
spicy *la*
MSG *weijing*
sugar *tang*
meat *rou*
chicken *jirou*
pork *zhurou*
beef *niurou*
lamb *yangrou*
fish *yu*
shrimp *xia*
crab *pangxie*
egg *jidan*
milk; skim milk *niunai; tuozhi niunai*
soy milk *doujiang*
fruit *shuiguo*
apple *pingguo*
banana *xiangjiao*
lemon *ningmeng*
mango *mangguo*
orange *chengzi*
strawberry *caomei*
pear *lizi*
watermelon *xigua*
vegetables *shucai*

broccoli *xilanhua*
carrot *huluobo*
green bean *sijidou*
tomato *xihongshi*
mushroom *mogu*
tofu *doufu*
salad *shala*
bread *mianbao*
sandwich *sanmingzhi*
hamburger *hanbaobao*
pizza *bisa*
rice *mifan*
fried rice *chaofan*
noodles *mian*
fried noodles *chaomian*
dumpling *jiaozi*
steamed bun *baozi*
soup *tang*
omelet *danbing*
Beijing duck *Beijing kaoya*
dim sum *dian xin*
water *shui*
beer *pijiu*
coffee *kafei*
tea; green tea *cha; lucha*
red wine; white wine *hong putao jiu; bai putao jiu*
juice; orange juice *guozhi; chengzi zhi*
soda; diet soda *kele; jianyi kele*

NUMBERS

one *yi*
two *er* or *liang*
three *san*
four *si*
five *wu*
six *liu*
seven *qi*
eight *ba*
nine *jiu*
10 *shi*
11 *shiyi*
12 *shi'er*
13 *shisan*
14 *shisi*
15 *shiwu*
16 *shiliu*
17 *shiqi*
18 *shiba*
19 *shijiu*
20 *ershi*
30 *sanshi*
40 *sishi*
50 *wushi*
60 *liushi*
70 *qishi*
80 *bashi*
90 *jiushi*
100 *yi bai*
1,000 *yi qian*
10,000 *yi wan*
1,000,000 *yi bai wan*

TIME AND DATE

What time is it? *Xianzai jidian zhong?*
It's 10 o'clock. *Shi dian.*
It's 10:15. *Shi dian shiwu fen.*
It's 10:30. *Shi dian sanshi fen.*
It's 10:45. *Shi dian sishiwu fen.*
What time does it open/close? *Jidian kaimen/guanmen?*
hour *xiaoshi*
minute *fenzhong*
yesterday *zuotian*
today *jintian*
tomorrow *mingtian*
Monday *Xingqiyi*
Tuesday *Xingqi'er*
Wednesday *Xingqisan*
Thursday *Xingqisi*
Friday *Xingqiwu*
Saturday *Xingqiliu*
Sunday *Xingqiri*
weekend *zhoumo*

WEATHER AND SEASONS

the weather *tianqi*
raining *xiayu*
sunny *qinglang*
snowing *xue*
cold *leng*
warm *re*
spring *chuntian*
summer *xiatian*
autumn *qiutian*
winter *dongtian*

ACCOMMODATIONS

hotel *jiudian* or *fandian*
hostel *luguan*
dormitory *duorenfang*
standard room *biaozhun fangjian*
double room *shuangren fangjian*
Do you have any vacancies? *You mei you kong fangjian?*
I have a reservation. *Wo you yuding.*

SHOPPING

I'd like to buy... *Wo xiang mai...*
this; that *zhege; nage*
How much does it cost? *Duo shao qian?*
too expensive *tai gui le*
Make it a little cheaper. *Pianyi yidian.*
Do you take credit cards? *Nimen shou xin yong ma?*

EMERGENCIES

Help! *Jiuming!*
Go away! *Zou kai!*
Thief! *Xiao tou!*
Fire! *Zhao huo la!*
Be careful! *Xiao xin!*
police station *paichusuo*
Get a doctor. *Jiao yisheng lai ba.*
Call an ambulance. *Jiao yi liang jiuhuche ba.*
hospital *yiyuan*
doctor *yisheng*

pharmacy *yaofang*
dentist *yayi*
consulate *lingshiguan*
embassy *dashiguan*
Can you help? *Neng bang wo ma?*
Where is the restroom? *Xishoujian zai nali?*

SHANGHAINESE

In Shanghai, the Shanghainese dialect is the language of the streets, with most born-and-bred city dwellers speaking it as a mother tongue along with Mandarin. Despite efforts by the government to promote Putonghua (standard Mandarin), Shanghainese is still widely heard, especially among the older generation. It is quite distinct from Mandarin, sounding more guttural and snappy. Because it isn't a written language, it can be tricky to learn, but here are a few useful phrases that will earn you some kudos.

Hello. *Nong ho.*
How are you? *Nong ho va?*
Fine, thanks. *Ngu mheho, jaja.*

thanks *jaja*
My name is... *Ngu tsio...*
How much does it cost? *Jidi?*
sorry *tevechi*
Goodbye. *Tze wei.*

Suggested Reading

HISTORY AND GENERAL INFORMATION

Aldrick, M.A. *The Search for a Vanishing Beijing: A Guide to China's Capital Through the Ages.* Hong Kong: Hong Kong University Press, 2008. One of the best histories of Beijing, this book charts the development of the capital through imperial times right up to the modern day.

Chang, Leslie T. *Factory Girls: From Village to City in a Changing China.* New York: Spiegel & Grau, 2009. Charting the lives of several female migrant workers, this account of China's mass migration from the countryside to the cities makes for compelling reading.

DeWoskin, Rachel. *Foreign Babes in Beijing.* New York: W. W. Norton, 2006. Rachel DeWoskin's account of her years as the star of a Chinese soap opera provides some laughs as well as serious social commentary on what life is like for an expatriate living and working in Beijing.

Dong, Stella. *Shanghai: The Rise and Fall of a Decadent City.* New York: Harper Perennial, 2001. This excellent, fast-paced history of Shanghai provides a good overview of the city's existence, from its humble beginnings as a riverside village to the world-changing upheavals of the 20th century.

Fallows, Deborah. *Dreaming in Chinese: Mandarin Lessons in Life, Love, and Language.* New York: Walker & Company, 2010. This light-hearted book is part travelogue, part language study. Linguist Deborah Fallows delves into the quirks of Mandarin, weaving in her own experiences of living in China. Covering history, sociology, and psychology, it's a great introduction to both the language and the country.

Hessler, Peter. *Oracle Bones: A Journey Through Time in China.* New York: Harper Perennial, 2007. China expert Peter Hessler has written a study of the nation through the ages, from the discovery of ancient oracle bones to the mega-cities of modern times.

Short, Philip. *Mao: A Life.* New York: Henry Holt & Co., 2000. There have been many biographies of Mao published, but this stands out thanks to its comprehensive study of the Great Helmsman's life and times as well as some never-before-seen photos.

FICTION

HALiterature. *Party Like It's 1984: Short Stories from the People's Republic of.* Hong Kong: HALiterature, 2010. This anthology of short stories deals with modern issues like sexuality, identity, and politics in China. It is available online and in bookshops in Shanghai and Beijing.

Hui, Wei. *Shanghai Baby.* New York: Washington Square Press, 2002. Wei Hui's controversial (in China) novel about a young Shanghainese waitress named Nikki has been made into a movie starring Bai Ling. The book charts Nikki's exploits as a young party girl in the big city, consorting with married men, bohemians, and artists.

Internet Resources

GENERAL INFORMATION
China Daily
www.chinadaily.com.cn
Like the English-language newspaper it is affiliated with, China Daily presents a censored version of Chinese and international news. It can be useful to browse before and during your trip to keep abreast of current affairs.

EVENT LISTINGS
City Weekend
www.CityWeekend.com.cn
The City Weekend website has separate versions for Beijing and Shanghai (and Guangzhou too), offering the same content as the print magazine with some web-only extras. The event listings are probably the best you'll find.

SmartShanghai
www.smartshanghai.com
Much more than just an events listing website, SmartShanghai is one of the most popular expat- and visitor-oriented websites at the moment. Thanks to the irreverent tone of the main editor (cryptically known as Da Admiral) and his weekly email newsletters, the website has attracted a cult following. With interactive maps, restaurant reviews, travel articles, and city living specials by talented young writers, it's definitely worth checking out.

The Beijinger
www.thebeijinger.com
If you can't find a copy of *The Beijinger* magazine, go online for all the same listings, articles, and reviews. There's also a useful forum where Beijing residents and visitors can chat and exchange tips.

Time Out Beijing
www.timeoutbeijing.com
Just like the print magazine, this website is a comprehensive guide to what's on and what's hot in Beijing, with restaurant and bar reviews, venue information, and blogs.

TRAVEL

Ctrip
www.english.ctrip.com
If you're booking onward flights and hotels within China while you're in Shanghai or Beijing, your best bet is Ctrip. It's an easily navigable site that accepts international credit cards and issues e-tickets or sends tickets to wherever you're staying. They also offer package deals, tours around China, and international flights.

eLong
www.elong.net
Part of Expedia, eLong is similar to Ctrip, offering flights, hotels, and packages both inside China and beyond.

BEST BLOGS

Despite heavy censorship of blogging platforms, plenty of excellent blogs manage to get through the Great Firewall.

China Rhyming
www.chinarhyming.com
Paul French is the author of several excellent books on China and his blog is, in his own words, "a gallimaufry of random China history and research interests." He is particularly interested in conservation, so many blog entries are about buildings that have recently been demolished. He also reviews China-related books and posts photos of Old Shanghai.

chinaSMACK
www.chinasmack.com
A site that gathers news reports, memes, and phenomena from Chinese-language websites and translates them into English, including reader comments from the original sources. It includes a useful and interesting glossary of slang terms and web acronyms.

Shanghaiist
www.shanghaiist.com
Part of the U.S.-based Gothamist network of city-blogs, Shanghaiist reports on news from around the city and beyond, inviting reader comments. The site also features a job board and personals section.

Shanghai Scrap
www.shanghaiscrap.com
Shanghai-based American journalist and writer Adam Minter writes a blog covering politics, government, the environment, and cross-cultural issues. He focuses on China, but includes posts on Asia in general as well.

Index

Restaurants Index

BEIJING

SHANGHAI

Nightlife Index

BEIJING

SHANGHAI

Shops Index

BEIJING

SHANGHAI

Hotels Index

BEIJING

SHANGHAI

Acknowledgments

Firstly, heartfelt thanks go to my editor Leah Gordon, whose support and patience have made the process of writing this book a pleasure. Thanks also to Darren Alessi and Albert Angulo for their help with the non-word-related side.

I would like to dedicate this book to my late grandfather, J. Leslie Howard, whose photographs of China can be seen throughout the book. His travels to Shanghai and Beijing during the 1960s and '70s were a precursor to my own, and his stories and relics inspired my interest in China.

Thanks to Amanda for her probing "Moon questions" to test my knowledge, and to Yuliya for her advice over coffee and red wine. Thanks also go to Zak in Beijing for his expert tips on the nightlife scene, and to my parents for their unwavering support. And, of course, to Vincent—for everything.

www.moon.com

DESTINATIONS | ACTIVITIES | BLOGS | MAPS | BOOKS

MOON.COM is ready to help plan your next trip! Filled with fresh trip ideas and strategies, author interviews, informative travel blogs, a detailed map library, and descriptions of all the Moon guidebooks, Moon.com is all you need to get out and explore the world—or even places in your own backyard. While at Moon.com, sign up for our monthly e-newsletter for updates on new releases, travel tips, and expert advice from our on-the-go Moon authors. As always, when you travel with Moon, expect an experience that is uncommon and truly unique.

KEEP UP WITH MOON ON FACEBOOK AND TWITTER
JOIN THE MOON PHOTO GROUP ON FLICKR

MAP SYMBOLS

▦ Expressway	◖ Highlight	✕ Airfield	⚲ Golf Course
▦ Primary Road	○ City/Town	✈ Airport	ⓟ Parking Area
▦ Secondary Road	◉ State Capital	▲ Mountain	⬟ Archaeological Site
▦ Unpaved Road	◉ National Capital	✛ Unique Natural Feature	⛪ Church
----- Trail	★ Point of Interest		⛽ Gas Station
·········· Ferry	● Accommodation	◔ Waterfall	▨ Glacier
▦ Railroad	▼ Restaurant/Bar	▲ Park	▨ Mangrove
▦ Pedestrian Walkway	■ Other Location	⬛ Trailhead	▨ Reef
▦ Stairs	Δ Campground	⛷ Skiing Area	▨ Swamp

CONVERSION TABLES

°C = (°F - 32) / 1.8
°F = (°C x 1.8) + 32
1 inch = 2.54 centimeters (cm)
1 foot = 0.304 meters (m)
1 yard = 0.914 meters
1 mile = 1.6093 kilometers (km)
1 km = 0.6214 miles
1 fathom = 1.8288 m
1 chain = 20.1168 m
1 furlong = 201.168 m
1 acre = 0.4047 hectares
1 sq km = 100 hectares
1 sq mile = 2.59 square km
1 ounce = 28.35 grams
1 pound = 0.4536 kilograms
1 short ton = 0.90718 metric ton
1 short ton = 2,000 pounds
1 long ton = 1.016 metric tons
1 long ton = 2,240 pounds
1 metric ton = 1,000 kilograms
1 quart = 0.94635 liters
1 US gallon = 3.7854 liters
1 Imperial gallon = 4.5459 liters
1 nautical mile = 1.852 km

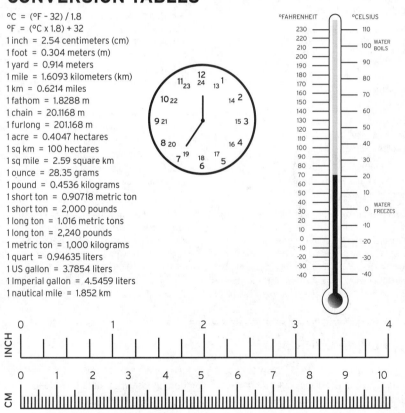

MOON BEIJING & SHANGHAI

Avalon Travel
a member of the Perseus Books Group
1700 Fourth Street
Berkeley, CA 94710, USA
www.moon.com

Editor: Leah Gordon
Series Manager: Erin Raber
Copy Editor: Naomi Adler Dancis
Graphics Coordinator: Darren Alessi
Production Coordinator: Darren Alessi
Cover Designer: Darren Alessi
Map Editor: Albert Angulo
Cartographers: Kaitlin Jaffe, Chris Henrick,
    Heather Sparks, Kat Bennett, Albert Angulo
Proofreader: Danielle Miller

ISBN: 978-1-61238-055-1
ISSN: 1945-2985

Printing History
1st Edition — 2008
2nd Edition — April 2012
5 4 3 2 1

KEEPING CURRENT

If you have a favorite gem you'd like to see included in the next edition, or see anything that needs updating, clarification, or correction, please drop us a line. Send your comments via email to feedback@moon.com, or use the address above.

BEIJING & SHANGHAI

SUSIE GORDON

Contents